ENDPAPER
PANEL 3
Fully temporal
relvars without
intervals—sample
values (Figure 4.3).

S_FROM_TO

S#	FROM	TO
S1	d04	d10
S2	d02	d04
S2	d07	d10
S3	d03	d10
S4	d04	d10
S5	d02	d10

SP_FROM_TO

S#	P#	FROM	TO
S1	P1	d04	d10
S1	P2	d05	d10
S1	P3	d09	d10
S1	P4	d05	d10
S1	P5	d04	d10
S1	P6	d06	d10
S2	P1	d02	d04
S2	P1	d08	d10
S2	P2	d03	d03
S2	P2	d09	d10
S3	P2	d08	d10
S4	P2	d06	d09
S4	P4	d04	d08
S4	P5	d05	d10

D1604687

ENDPAPER
PANEL 4
Fully temporal
relvars with
intervals—sample
values (Figure 5.1).

S_DURING

S#	DURING
S1	[d04:d10]
S2	[d02:d04]
S2	[d07:d10]
S3	[d03:d10]
S4	[d04:d10]
S5	[d02:d10]

SP_DURING

S#	P#	DURING
S1	P1	[d04:d10]
S1	P2	[d05:d10]
S1	P3	[d09:d10]
S1	P4	[d05:d10]
S1	P5	[d04:d10]
S1	P6	[d06:d10]
S2	P1	[d02:d04]
S2	P1	[d08:d10]
S2	P2	[d03:d03]
S2	P2	[d09:d10]
S3	P2	[d08:d10]
S4	P2	[d06:d09]
S4	P4	[d04:d08]
S4	P5	[d05:d10]

TEMPORAL DATA AND THE RELATIONAL MODEL

TEMPORAL DATA AND THE RELATIONAL MODEL

A Detailed Investigation into the Application of Interval and Relation Theory to the Problem of Temporal Database Management

C. J. Date

Hugh Darwen

Nikos A. Lorentzos

MORGAN KAUFMANN PUBLISHERS

AN IMPRINT OF ELSEVIER SCIENCE

AMSTERDAM BOSTON LONDON NEW YORK
OXFORD PARIS SAN DIEGO SAN FRANCISCO
SINGAPORE SYDNEY TOKYO

Acquisitions Editor	Lothlórien Homet
Publishing Services Manager	Edward Wade
Editorial Assistant	Corina Derman
Project Management	Elisabeth Beller
Cover Design	Ross Carron
Cover Image	Lord's Cricket Ground
Cover Image Color Correction	Michael Fantasia
Text Design	Rebecca Evans
Technical Illustration	Dartmouth Publishing, Inc.
Composition	David Van Ness
Copyeditor	Joan Flaherty
Proofreader	Ken DellaPenta
Printer	The Maple-Vail Book Manufacturing Group

The cover illustration is the famous weathervane "Old Father Time" from Lord's Cricket Ground in London.

Designations used by companies to distinguish their products are often claimed as trademarks or registered trademarks. In all instances in which Morgan Kaufmann Publishers is aware of a claim, the product names appear in initial capital or all capital letters. Readers, however, should contact the appropriate companies for more complete information regarding trademarks and registration.

Morgan Kaufmann Publishers
An imprint of Elsevier Science
340 Pine Street, Sixth Floor
San Francisco, CA 94104-3205
www.mkp.com

07 06 05 04 03   5 4 3 2 1

Library of Congress Control Number: 2002110398
ISBN: 1-55860-855-9

This book is printed on acid-free paper.

*We would like to dedicate this book to the innocent victims who died on
September 11th, 2001 and during the weeks and months thereafter*

C. J. DATE, HUGH DARWEN, NIKOS A. LORENTZOS

*Also to the memory of Elydia Davis, my editor
for over 15 years—she is very much missed*

C. J. DATE

*And to the memory of my friend Adrian Larner, who
had such a huge influence on my database thinking*

HUGH DARWEN

And to the memory of my father, Antonios

NIKOS A. LORENTZOS

Time present and time past
Are both perhaps present in time future,
And time future contained in time past.

T. S. Eliot

The database is not the database—the log is the database,
and the database is just an optimized access path
to the most recent version of the log.

B.-M. Schueler

Nothing puzzles me more than time and space;
and yet nothing troubles me less, as I never think about them.

Charles Lamb

Eternity's a terrible thought;
I mean, where's it going to end?

Tom Stoppard

My object all sublime
I shall achieve in time.

W. S. Gilbert

It's about time.

Anon. (just about everybody, actually)

Contents

Part II Laying the Foundations 51

PREFACE

Temporal database systems are database systems that include special support for the time dimension; in other words, they are systems that provide special facilities for storing, querying, and updating historical and/or future data (referred to generically in this book as temporal data). Conventional database management systems (DBMSs)—including *all* of the existing mainstream products—are not temporal in this sense: They provide essentially no special support for temporal data at all, at least at the time of writing. However, this situation is likely to change soon, for the following reasons among others:

- Disk storage is now cheap enough that keeping large volumes of temporal data has become a practical possibility.

- *Data warehouses* are therefore becoming increasingly widespread.

- Users of those warehouses have begun to find themselves faced with temporal database problems, and they have begun to feel the need for solutions to those problems.

- The SQL standards bodies have therefore begun to think about incorporating temporal database features into the SQL standard.

- Likewise, vendors of conventional DBMS products have begun to think about adding temporal database support to those products. (There is a huge market opportunity here.)

Research into temporal databases is not new; technical papers on the subject have been appearing in the literature since the early 1980s, if not earlier. However, much of that research ultimately proved unproductive: It turned out to be excessively complicated, or it led to logical inconsistencies, or it failed to solve certain aspects of the problem, or it was unsatisfactory for some other reason. For such reasons, we have little to say in this book about that early research. More recently, however, a more promising approach has begun to attract attention. One feature that sharply distinguishes that more recent proposal from earlier ones is that *it is firmly rooted in the relational model of data,* which earlier ones mostly were not. As a direct consequence of this fact, there is reason to believe the newer proposal will stand the test of time (as it were!). In this book, therefore, we naturally focus on that more recent approach. Moreover, since the approach in question is directly and primarily due to one of the authors (Lorentzos), the book can be regarded as authoritative.

The book also includes much original material resulting from continuing investigations by all three authors, material that is currently documented nowhere else. Examples include new database design techniques, a new normal form, new relational operators, new update operators, a new approach to the problem of granularity, and support for cyclic point types. Overall, therefore, the book can be seen as, among other things, an abstract blueprint or logical foundation for the design of a temporal DBMS and the language interface to such a DBMS. In other words, it is forward-looking, in the sense that it describes not just how temporal DBMSs might work today, but rather how we think they should and will work in the future.

It follows that the book does necessarily have a somewhat academic flavor. In particular, it is not (in fact, it cannot be!) concerned with commercial products, nor with the SQL language. Nevertheless, it can still be of direct relevance to the commercial IT world as well as the academic world, for the following reasons among others:

- It is an established fact that users are already struggling with temporal problems.

- It is also an established fact that previous attempts to solve those problems have not been entirely successful.

- As a result, users are at a loss to know what kind of support they should be asking the DBMS vendors to provide.

- *This book can help:* It can help users explain to vendors precisely what problems they are struggling with and what kinds of solutions they need to those problems.

One further point: Although this book concentrates on temporal data specifically, many of the concepts are actually of wider applicability. To be more specific, the basic data construct involved is the *interval,* and intervals do not have to be temporal in nature. (On the other hand, certain of the ideas discussed are indeed specifically temporal—for example, the notion often referred to, informally, as "the moving point *now*.")

STRUCTURE OF THE BOOK

The body of the book is divided into three major parts:

    I. Preliminaries

   II. Laying the Foundations

  III. Building on the Foundations

Part I covers certain essential preliminaries. Chapter 1 provides an overview of the relational model, with emphasis on aspects that do not seem to be as widely understood or appreciated as they ought to be. Chapter 2 gives details of a language we call **Tutorial D**, which we use in coding examples throughout the book.

Part II (Chapters 3 through 9) covers basic temporal concepts and principles. It explains some of the problems that temporal data seems to give rise to, with reference to queries and integrity constraints in particular, and describes some important new operators that can help in the formulation of those queries and constraints. NOTE: We should immediately explain that those new operators are all, in the last analysis, just shorthands for certain combinations of operators that can be expressed using the traditional relational algebra. However, the shorthands in question turn out to be *extremely* useful—not only because they simplify the formulation of queries and constraints (which is a laudable goal in itself, of course), but also, and more important, because they serve to raise the level of abstraction (and hence the overall level of discourse) regarding temporal issues in general.

Part III (Chapters 10 through 16) covers more advanced temporal concepts and principles; in effect, it uses the material from Part II to show how those principles can be applied to such matters as temporal database design, temporal database updates, the formulation of temporal database constraints, and a variety of more specialized topics.

In addition to the foregoing, there are three appendixes. Appendix A discusses implementation and optimization issues; Appendix B addresses the possibility of generalizing certain of the operators introduced in the body of the book; and Appendix C gives an annotated and consolidated list of references. NOTE: References to items in that bibliography take the form of numbers in square brackets. For example, the reference "[2]" refers to the second item in the list of references in Appendix C: namely, a paper by James F. Allen entitled "Maintaining Knowledge about Temporal Intervals," published in *Communications of the ACM*, Vol. 16, No. 11, in November 1983.

Please note that, with the possible exception of Part I, the book is definitely not meant for "dipping." Rather, it is meant to be read in sequence as written. In particular, if you skip a chapter (at least after Chapter 2), you are likely to have difficulty with later chapters. While we would be the first to agree that this state of affairs is a little undesirable, the fact is that temporal data does seem to suffer from certain innate complexities, and the book necessarily reflects some of those complexities. Moreover:

- It is only fair to warn you that, beginning with Chapter 10 (the first chapter of Part III), you will probably notice a definite *increase* in complexity.

- At the same time, you should be aware that the full picture only begins to emerge with that same chapter.

Please note too that this is not a closed subject! Several interesting research issues remain. Such issues are touched on and appropriately flagged at pertinent points in the book. Also, portions of the text use certain running examples; those examples are shown in summary form on the endpapers at the front and back of the book, and those endpaper summaries are referenced explicitly at appropriate points in the body of the book.

Last, two remarks regarding our use of terminology:

1. We adhere almost exclusively to the formal relational terms *relation, tuple, attribute* (and so forth), instead of using their SQL counterparts *table, row, column* (and so forth). It is our very firm opinion that those possibly more familiar terms have done the cause of genuine understanding a massive disservice over the years. Besides, the constructs referred to by those SQL terms include deviations from relational theory, such as duplicate rows, left-to-right column ordering, and nulls. We want to avoid giving any impression that we might condone such deviations.

2. We have been forced to introduce our own terms for several concepts—"packed form," "U_ operators," "U_keys," "sixth normal form," and others—because the concepts themselves are new (for the most part). However, we have tried in every case to choose terms that are appropriate and make good intuitive sense, and we have not intentionally used familiar terms in unfamiliar ways. We apologize if our choice of terms causes any unnecessary difficulties.

INTENDED READERSHIP

Who should read this book? Well, in at least one sense the book is definitely not self-contained—it assumes that you are professionally interested in database technology and are reasonably well acquainted with conventional database theory and practice. However, we have tried to define and explain, as carefully as we could, any concepts that might be thought novel; in fact, we have done the same for several concepts that really ought not to be novel at all but do not seem to be as widely understood as they ought to be ("candidate key" might be a case in point). We have also included a set of review questions and exercises at the end of each chapter. (Answers to those questions and exercises can be found online at *www.mkp.com.*) In other words, we have tried to make the book suitable for both reference and tutorial purposes. Our intended audience is thus just about anyone with a serious interest in database technology, including but not limited to the following:

- Database language designers and standardizers

- DBMS product implementers and other vendor personnel

- Data and database administrators

- "Information modelers" and database designers

- Database application designers and implementers

- Computer science professors specializing in database issues

- Database students, both graduate and undergraduate

- People responsible for DBMS product evaluation and acquisition
- Technically aware end users

The only background knowledge required is a general understanding of data management concepts and issues, including in particular a basic familiarity with the relational model.

NOTE: There are currently few college courses, if any, devoted to the topic of temporal data. Because we see a growing demand for proper temporal support, however, we expect such courses to appear in the near future. And we believe this book could serve as the text for such a course. For academic readers in particular, therefore (students as well as teachers), we should make it clear that we have tried to present the foundations of the temporal database field in a way that is clear, precise, correct, and uncluttered by the baggage—not to mention mistakes—that usually, and regrettably, seem to accompany commercial implementations. Thus, we believe the book provides an opportunity to acquire a firm understanding of that crucial foundation material, without being distracted by irrelevancies.

ACKNOWLEDGMENTS

First of all, we are pleased to be able to acknowledge the many friends and colleagues who gave encouragement, participated in discussions and research, offered comments (both written and oral) on various drafts of this book and other publications, or helped in a variety of other ways: Nathan Allan, Ron Fagin, Vi Ma, Patrick Pribyl, Bryn Rhodes, Steve Tarin, and Bob White (and we apologize if we have inadvertently omitted anyone from this list). We would also like to acknowledge the many conference and seminar attendees, too numerous to mention individually, who have expressed support for the ideas contained herein. We would also like to thank our reviewers for their careful and constructive comments on the manuscript. Finally, we are grateful to our editors Elisabeth Beller, Diane Cerra, Joan Flaherty, and Lothlórien Homet, and to all of the staff at Morgan Kaufmann, for their assistance and their high standards of professionalism. It has been a pleasure to work with them.

Nikos A. Lorentzos adds: I would like to thank my mother, Efrosini, who knows better than anyone how endlessly busy my work keeps me, and Aliki Galati who has always encouraged me in my research. I would also like to express a strong debt of gratitude to Mike Sykes, the first person to express an interest in my work on temporal databases. Thanks to Mike, I came in contact with Hugh Darwen, with whom I have had many fruitful discussions on this topic. And thanks to Hugh, I finally met Chris Date. This book is the result of my collaboration with Hugh and Chris.

Hugh Darwen adds: I began my study of temporal database issues in the mid 1990s in connection with my work in UKDBL, the working group that formulates U.K. contributions to the development of the international SQL standard. I was joined in that study by my UKDBL colleague Mike Sykes, and together we began to search for alternatives to the temporal proposals then being considered by the SQL standards committee. It was Mike who first discovered the work of Nikos Lorentzos, and I am profoundly grateful to him for realizing that it was not only exactly what he had been looking for but also what he knew *I* had been looking for. (Mike had been looking for an approach based on intervals in general rather than just time intervals in particular. I had been looking for an approach that did not depart from the relational model.)

Various university contacts in the U.K. were helpful during my initial study period. I would especially like to thank Babis Theodoulidis of the University of Manchester Institute of Science and Technology for setting up a meeting between academics (including Nikos Lorentzos) and members of UKDBL. My subsequent education in the temporal field benefited greatly from discussions with people at IBM's Almaden Research Center, especially Cliff Leung (now at the IBM Silicon Valley Laboratory) and later Bob Lyle. Finally, I must mention the participants at the June 1997 workshop on temporal databases in Dagstuhl, Germany, whose output was reference [46]. There were too many for me to name them individually, but I am grateful to them all for what struck me as a most informative, productive, stimulating, lively, and friendly event.

Chris Date adds: I would just like to acknowledge the debt I owe my coauthors: Nikos, for doing such a good job in laying the theoretical foundations for the approach described in this book; Hugh, for his persistence in trying to persuade me that I ought to take an interest in temporal database matters in general and Nikos's work in particular; and both Nikos and Hugh for their efforts in reviewing the numerous iterations this manuscript went through and their patience in correcting my many early errors and misconceptions.

C. J. Date—Healdsburg, California
Hugh Darwen—Shrewley, England
Nikos A. Lorentzos—Athens, Greece

Part I

PRELIMINARIES

This first part of the book consists of two "groundwork" chapters (both fairly formal in nature), as follows:

1. A Review of Relational Concepts
2. An Overview of **Tutorial D**

Chapter 1 consists of a detailed review of the principal components and concepts of the relational model. Chapter 2 presents the syntax and semantics of a relational language called **Tutorial D,** which is the language we use in our coding examples in Parts II and III of the book. You might prefer just to skim these chapters on a first reading, coming back to them later if you find you lack some specific piece of required background knowledge. In particular, if you are familiar with reference [39] or [43], then you probably do not need to read these two chapters in detail. However, Section 1.2 in Chapter 1 does introduce the suppliers-and-shipments database, which serves as the basis for almost all of the examples in later chapters, so you ought at least to take a look at that database before moving on to the rest of the book.

Chapter

1

A REVIEW OF RELATIONAL CONCEPTS

1.1 INTRODUCTION

This book assumes a basic familiarity with the relational model. This preliminary chapter is meant to serve as a quick refresher course on that model; in effect, it summarizes what you will be expected to know in later chapters. A detailed tutorial on this material, and much more, can be found in reference [39], and a more formal treatment can be found in reference [43]; thus, if you are familiar with either of those references, you probably do not need to read this chapter in detail. However, if your knowledge of the relational model derives from other sources (especially ones based on SQL), then you probably do need to read this chapter fairly carefully, because it emphasizes numerous important topics that other sources typically do not. Such topics include

- domains as types

- "possible representations"

- selectors and THE_ operators

- relation values vs. relation variables
- predicates and propositions
- relation-valued attributes
- the fundamental role of integrity constraints

and many others.

1.2 THE RUNNING EXAMPLE

Most of the examples in this book are based on the well-known suppliers-and-parts database—or, rather, on a simplified version of that database that we refer to as *suppliers and shipments*. Figure 1.1 shows a set of sample values for that simplified database. NOTE: In case you are familiar with the more usual version of this example as discussed in, for example, reference [39], we briefly explain what the simplifications consist of:

- First of all, we have dropped the parts relvar P entirely—hence the revised name, suppliers and shipments. (The term *relvar* is short for *relation variable*. Both terms are explained in Section 1.5.)

- Second, we have removed attribute QTY from the shipments relvar SP, leaving just attributes S# and P#.

- Third, we interpret that revised SP relvar thus: "Supplier S# is *currently able* to supply part P#." In other words, instead of standing for *actual* shipments of parts by suppliers, as it did, for example, in reference [39], relvar SP now stands for what might be termed *potential* shipments—that is, the *ability* of certain suppliers to supply certain parts.

FIGURE 1.1

Suppliers-and-shipments database (original version)—sample values.

S

S#	SNAME	STATUS	CITY
S1	Smith	20	London
S2	Jones	10	Paris
S3	Blake	30	Paris
S4	Clark	20	London
S5	Adams	30	Athens

SP

S#	P#
S1	P1
S1	P2
S1	P3
S1	P4
S1	P5
S1	P6
S2	P1
S2	P2
S3	P2
S4	P2
S4	P4
S4	P5

Overall, then, the database is meant to be interpreted as follows:

- Relvar S denotes *suppliers* who are currently under contract. Each such supplier has a supplier number (S#), unique to that supplier; a supplier name (SNAME), not necessarily unique (though the sample SNAME values shown in Figure 1.1 do happen to be unique); a rating or status value (STATUS); and a location (CITY).

- Relvar SP denotes *potential shipments* of parts by suppliers. For example, the sample values in Figure 1.1 indicate among other things that supplier S1 is currently capable of supplying, or shipping, part P1. Clearly, the combination of S# value and P# value for a given "potential shipment" is unique to that shipment. NOTE: Here and elsewhere, we take the liberty of referring to "potential shipments"—somewhat inaccurately, but very conveniently—as simply shipments, unqualified. Also, we assume for the sake of the example that it is possible for a given supplier to be under contract at a given time and yet not be able to supply any part at that time (supplier S5 is a case in point, given the sample values of Figure 1.1).

Figure 1.2 shows the corresponding database definition, expressed in a language called **Tutorial D**—or, to be more accurate, in a slightly simplified version of that language that is described in Chapter 2.[1] Note the KEY and FOREIGN KEY constraints in particular. Note too that, for simplicity, attributes STATUS and CITY are defined in terms of built-in or **system-defined** types—INTEGER (integers) and CHAR (character strings of arbitrary length), respectively—while other attributes are defined in terms of **user**-defined types. Definitions of those latter types are also shown in the figure, albeit in outline only.

FIGURE 1.2

Suppliers-and-shipments database (original version)—data definition.

```
TYPE S#   ... ;
TYPE NAME ... ;
TYPE P#   ... ;

VAR S RELATION
    { S#     S#,
      SNAME  NAME,
      STATUS INTEGER,
      CITY   CHAR }
    KEY { S# } ;

VAR SP RELATION
    { S#     S#,
      P#     P# }
    KEY { S#, P# }
    FOREIGN KEY { S# } REFERENCES S ;
```

---

1. **Tutorial D** is a computationally complete programming language with fully integrated database functionality and (we hope) more or less self-explanatory syntax. It was introduced in reference [43] as a vehicle for teaching database concepts.

1.3 TYPES

Relations in the relational model are defined over **types** (also known as *data types* or *domains*—we use the terms interchangeably, but favor *types*). Types are discussed in this section, relations are discussed in the next few sections.

What is a type? Among other things, it is *a finite set of values* (finite because we are concerned with computer systems specifically, which are finite by definition). Examples include the set of all integers (type INTEGER), the set of all character strings (type CHAR), and the set of all supplier numbers (type S#). NOTE: Instead of saying, for example, that type INTEGER is the set of *all* integers, it would be more correct to say that it is the set of all integers that are capable of representation in the computer system under consideration (there will obviously be some integers that are beyond the representational capability of any given computer system). In what follows, however, we will not usually bother to be quite so precise.

Every **value** has, or is of, some type; in fact, every value is of *exactly one* type.[2] Moreover:

- Every **variable** is explicitly declared to be of some type, meaning that every possible value of the variable in question is a value of the type in question.

- Every **attribute** of every relation is explicitly declared to be of some type, meaning that every possible value of the attribute in question is a value of the type in question.

- Every **operator** that returns a result is explicitly declared to be of some type, meaning that every possible result that can be returned by an invocation of the operator in question is a value of the type in question.

- Every **parameter** of every operator is explicitly declared to be of some type, meaning that every possible argument that can be substituted for the parameter in question is a value of the type in question. (Actually, this statement is not quite precise enough. Operators in general fall into two disjoint classes, read-only and update operators [43]; read-only operators return a result, while update operators update one or more of their arguments instead. For an update operator, any argument that is subject to update is required to be a *variable*, not a *value*, of the same type as the corresponding parameter.)

- More generally, every **expression** is at least implicitly declared to be of some type—namely, the type declared for the outermost operator involved in the expression in question.

---

2. Except possibly if type inheritance is supported, in which case a given value might have more than one type. Even then, however, the value still has exactly one *most specific* type. See Chapter 16, Section 16.2, for further discussion of this possibility.

NOTE: The remarks here concerning operators and parameters need some slight refinement if the operators in question are *polymorphic*. An operator is said to be polymorphic if it is defined in terms of some parameter *P* and the arguments corresponding to *P* can be of different types on different invocations. The equality operator "=" is an obvious example: We can test *any* two values for equality (just so long as the two values are of the same type), and so "=" is polymorphic—it applies to integers, and to character strings, and to supplier numbers, and in fact to values of every possible type. Analogous remarks apply to the assignment operator ":="; indeed, we follow reference [43] in requiring both "=" and ":=" to be defined for every type. Further examples of polymorphic operators include the *aggregate* operators such as MAX and COUNT (discussed in Section 1.7), the operators of the relational algebra such as UNION and JOIN (also discussed in Section 1.7), and the operators defined for intervals in Part II of this book.

Any given type is either *system-defined* or *user-defined;* of the three types mentioned earlier (INTEGER, CHAR, and S#), INTEGER and CHAR are system-defined—at least, we will assume so—and S# is user-defined. Any type whatsoever, regardless of whether it is system-defined or user-defined, can be used as the basis for defining variables, attributes, operators, and parameters.

Any given type is also either scalar or nonscalar. A **nonscalar** type is a type that has *a set of user-visible components;* in particular, relation types are nonscalar, because every relation type does indeed have a set of user-visible components (namely, the applicable set of attributes). A **scalar** type—also known as an *encapsulated* type, though for reasons explained in reference [38] we do not use this term ourselves—is a type that is not nonscalar (!), meaning it does not have a set of user-visible components; for example, the system-defined type INTEGER is a scalar type.

Following on from the foregoing, we must immediately add that even though scalar types have no user-visible components, they do have what are called **possible representations** [43], and those possible representations in turn can have user-visible components, as we will see in a moment. Do not be misled, however: The components in question are not components of the type, they are components of the possible representation. The type itself is still scalar in the sense previously explained.

By way of illustration, suppose we have a user-defined scalar type called QTY ("quantity"). Assume for the sake of the example that a possible representation is declared for this type that says, in effect, that quantities can "possibly be represented" by nonnegative integers. Then that possible representation certainly does have user-visible components—in fact, it has exactly one such, of type INTEGER—but, to repeat, quantities per se do not.

Here is a slightly more complicated example to illustrate the same point (**Tutorial D** syntax again):

```
TYPE POINT      /* geometric points in two-dimensional space */
     POSSREP CARTESIAN { X NUMERIC, Y NUMERIC }
     POSSREP POLAR { R NUMERIC, THETA NUMERIC } ;
```

The definition of type POINT here includes declarations of two distinct possible representations, CARTESIAN and POLAR, reflecting the fact that points in two-dimensional space can indeed "possibly be represented" by either Cartesian or polar coordinates. Each of those possible representations in turn has two components, both of which are of type NUMERIC. Note carefully, however, that (to spell it out once again) type POINT per se is still scalar—it has no user-visible components.

NOTE: Type NUMERIC in the foregoing example stands (we assume) for fixed-point numbers, but for reasons of simplicity we have omitted the precision and scale factor specifications that would certainly be needed in practice, at least implicitly. For example, the definition of coordinate X might be, not just NUMERIC, but (say) NUMERIC(3,1), meaning that X values are decimal numbers with precision three and scale factor one—which is to say, those values are precisely –99.9, –99.8, …, –00.1, 00.0, 00.1, …, 99.9. We will have quite a lot more to say regarding such matters in Chapter 16.

To return to the example of type POINT: It is important to understand in that example that the *physical* representation of values of type POINT in the particular implementation at hand might be Cartesian coordinates, or it might be polar coordinates, or it might be something else entirely. In other words, possible representations (which are, to repeat, user-visible) are indeed only *possible* ones; *physical* representations are merely an implementation matter and should never be user-visible.

Each possible-representation declaration causes automatic definition of the following more or less self-explanatory operators:

- A **selector** operator, which allows the user to specify or *select* a value of the type in question by supplying a value for each component of the possible representation

- A set of **THE_** operators (one such operator for each component of the possible representation), which allow the user to access the corresponding possible-representation components of values of the type in question

NOTE: When we say declaration of a possible representation causes "automatic definition" of the foregoing operators, what we mean is that (1) whatever agency—possibly the system, possibly some human user—is responsible for implementing the type in question is also responsible for implementing those operators, and further that (2) until those operators have been implemented, the process of implementing the type cannot be regarded as complete.

Here are some sample selector and THE_ operator invocations for type POINT (**Tutorial D** syntax once again):

```
CARTESIAN ( 5.0, 2.5 )
/* selects the point with x = 5.0, y = 2.5 */

CARTESIAN ( X1, Y1 )
/* selects the point with x = X1, y = Y1, where */
/* X1 and Y1 are variables of type NUMERIC      */

POLAR ( 2.7, 1.0 )
/* selects the point with r = 2.7, θ = 1.0 */

THE_X ( P )
/* denotes the x coordinate of the point value in */
/* P, where P is a variable of type POINT          */

THE_R ( P )
/* denotes the r coordinate of the point value in P */

THE_Y ( exp )
/* denotes the y coordinate of the point denoted  */
/* by the expression exp (which is of type POINT) */
```

As the first three of these examples suggest, selectors—or, more precisely, selector *invocations*—are a generalization of the more familiar concept of a **literal**.[3] Briefly, all literals are selector invocations, but not all selector invocations are literals; in fact, a selector invocation is a literal if and only if all of its arguments are literals in turn. We adopt the convention that selectors have the same name as the corresponding possible representation. We also adopt the convention that if a given type *T* has a possible representation with no explicitly declared name, then that possible representation is named *T* by default. Taken together, these two conventions mean that, for example, the expression S#('S1') is a valid selector invocation for type S# (see the definition of that type in Section 1.6).

Finally, the foregoing discussion of selectors and THE_ operators touches on another crucial issue, namely, the fact that the type concept includes the associated

---

3. The concept might be familiar, but it seems to be very hard to find a good definition for it in the literature! Here is our own preferred definition [43]: A literal is a symbol that denotes a value that is fixed and determined by the particular symbol in question (and the type of that value is also fixed and determined by the symbol in question). Loosely, we can say that a literal is *self-defining*. Here are some **Tutorial D** examples:

```
FALSE                     /* a literal of type BOOLEAN */
4                         /* a literal of type INTEGER */
2.7                       /* a literal of type NUMERIC */
'ABC'                     /* a literal of type CHAR    */
S# ('S1')                 /* a literal of type S#       */
CARTESIAN ( 5.0, 2.5 )    /* a literal of type POINT    */
```

notion of the *operators* that apply to values and variables of the type in question (values and variables of a given type can be operated upon *solely* by means of the operators defined in connection with that type). For example, in the case of the system-defined type INTEGER:

- The system defines operators "=", ">", and so on, for comparing integers.

- It also defines operators "+", "∗", and so on, for performing arithmetic operations on integers.

- It does *not* define operators "||" (concatenate), SUBSTR (substring), and so on, for performing string operations on integers. In other words, string operations on integers are not supported.

By way of another example, consider the user-defined type S#. Here we would certainly define an "=" operator, and perhaps ">" and "<" operators and so forth, for comparing supplier numbers. However, we would probably not define operators "+", "∗", and so forth, which would mean that arithmetic operations on supplier numbers would not be supported.

We see, therefore, that users will certainly need the ability to define their own operators. This fact is not particularly relevant to the primary topic of this book—at least, not until we get to Chapter 16—but we show a few examples here in order to give some idea of what such a capability might look like. First, here is the definition for a user-defined operator, ABS ("absolute value"), for the system-defined type INTEGER:

```
OPERATOR ABS ( I INTEGER ) RETURNS INTEGER ;
   RETURN ( IF I ≥ 0 THEN +I ELSE -I END IF ) ;
END OPERATOR ;
```

This operator is of declared type INTEGER (i.e., it returns an integer when it is invoked), and it has just one parameter, I, which is also of declared type INTEGER. Incidentally, note the use of an IF ... END IF expression in this example.

By way of a second example, here is the definition for a user-defined operator, DIST ("distance between"), for the user-defined type POINT:

```
OPERATOR DIST ( P1 POINT, P2 POINT ) RETURNS NUMERIC ;
   RETURN ( SQRT ( ( THE_X ( P1 ) - THE_X ( P2 ) ) ** 2
                 + ( THE_Y ( P1 ) - THE_Y ( P2 ) ) ** 2 ) ) ;
END OPERATOR ;
```

This operator is of declared type NUMERIC; it has two parameters, P1 and P2, both of declared type POINT.

Now, ABS and DIST are both read-only operators. Here by contrast is an example of an update operator definition:

```
OPERATOR REFLECT ( P POINT ) UPDATES P ;
   THE_X ( P )   :=   - THE_X ( P ) ,
   THE_Y ( P )   :=   - THE_Y ( P ) ;
END OPERATOR ;
```

This operator has just one parameter P, of declared type POINT; when invoked, it updates the argument variable corresponding to that parameter as indicated. It does not return a result. NOTE: This example also illustrates the use of both (1) multiple assignment and (2) THE_ operators on the left side of an assignment ("THE_ pseudo-variables"). Both of these issues will be revisited in Chapter 14.

By the way, note that ABS, DIST, and indeed most of the operators mentioned in this chapter so far, are scalar operators; that is, they return scalar values or update scalar variables. In later sections, by contrast, we will be discussing a number of *relational* operators (update operators in Section 1.5 and read-only operators in Section 1.7); relational update operators update relation variables, not scalar ones, and relational read-only operators return relation values, not scalar ones. (Relation values are discussed in the section immediately following; relation variables are discussed in Section 1.5.)

1.4 RELATION VALUES

Given a collection of types Ti ($i = 1, 2, …, n$), not necessarily all distinct, r is a **relation** (or **relation value**) on those types if it consists of two parts, a *heading* and a *body,* where:

- The **heading** is a set of n **attributes,** one for each Ti. Each attribute consists of an *attribute name Ai* and the corresponding *type name Ti*. Within any given heading, the attribute names Ai are all distinct.

- The **body** is a set of m **tuples,** where each tuple in turn is a set of n components, one for each attribute in the heading. Let t be such a tuple; then each component of t consists of the applicable attribute name Ai and a corresponding value vi of type Ti. The value vi is the *attribute value* for attribute Ai within tuple t.

The values m and n are called the **cardinality** and the **degree,** respectively, of relation r.

Points arising from this definition:

1. In terms of the usual tabular picture of a relation—see, for example, the two examples in Figure 1.1—the heading is the row of column names and the body is the set of data rows. Note therefore that, strictly speaking, the row of column names and the data rows in such pictures should include the relevant type and attribute names, respectively; in practice, however, it is usual to omit those type and attribute names as we did in Figure 1.1 (and will continue to do throughout the rest of the book).

2. Observe next that there is (of course) a *logical difference*[4] between an attribute name and an attribute per se. Informally, we often use expressions such as "attribute *A*"—indeed, we have done so many times in this chapter already—but such expressions must be understood to mean the attribute whose *name* is *A* (and whose type name has been left unspecified).

3. Observe that (again strictly speaking) a relation does not contain tuples—it contains a body, and that body in turn contains tuples. Informally, however, it is convenient to talk as if relations contained tuples directly, and we follow this simplifying convention throughout this book.

4. A relation of degree one is said to be *unary*, a relation of degree two *binary*, a relation of degree three *ternary*, …, and a relation of degree *n n-ary*. A relation of degree zero is said to be *nullary*.

   Perhaps we should say a little more about the possibility of nullary relations, since the concept might be unfamiliar to you. In fact, there are precisely two such relations: one that contains just one tuple (necessarily with no components, and hence a *0-tuple*), and one that contains no tuples at all. Following reference [25], we refer to these two relations colloquially as TABLE_DEE and TABLE_DUM, respectively. We will meet these two relations again (especially TABLE_DEE) later in this chapter, also in Chapters 7 and 8.

5. The term *n-tuple* is sometimes used in place of *tuple* (and so we sometimes speak of, e.g., 2-tuples, 4-tuples, 0-tuples, etc.). However, it is usual to drop the *n-* prefix and speak of just *tuples*, unqualified. The terms *pair*, *triple*, and so on, are also used on occasion.

6. No relation ever contains any duplicate tuples.[5] N O T E : We should explain precisely what we mean by the term *duplicate tuples*. Here is a definition:

   > Tuples *t1* and *t2* are **duplicates** of one another if and only if they involve exactly the same attributes *A1, A2, …, An* and, for all *i* ($i = 1, 2, …, n$), the value for *Ai* in *t1* is equal to the value for *Ai* in *t2*. Furthermore—this might seem obvious but it needs to be said—tuples *t1* and *t2* are *equal* (i.e., "*t1* = *t2*" is true) if and only if they are duplicates of each other (meaning they are in fact the very same tuple).

   The concept of duplicate tuples or tuple equality is relevant in numerous contexts, including, for example, the definitions of *candidate key* and *foreign key* (see Section 1.5) and the definition of relational operators such as *join* (see Section 1.7).

---

4. This useful term comes from the dictum (due, we believe, to Wittgenstein) that *all logical differences are big differences*. For further discussion, see reference [43].

5. As you probably know, SQL tables are allowed to contain duplicate rows; SQL tables are thus not relations, in general. For this reason, we emphasize the fact that in this book we *always* use the term *relation* to mean a relation—without duplicate tuples, by definition—and not an SQL table. What is more, relational operations (projection and union in particular) *always* produce a result without duplicate tuples, again by definition.

Incidentally, note that it is an immediate consequence of the foregoing definition that all 0-tuples are duplicates of one another! For this reason, we are justified in talking in terms of *the* 0-tuple instead of *a* 0-tuple, and indeed we usually do.

7. There is no top-to-bottom ordering to the tuples of a relation (figures like Figure 1.1 notwithstanding).

8. There is no left-to-right ordering to the attributes of a relation (figures like Figure 1.1 notwithstanding).

9. Every tuple of every relation contains exactly one value for each attribute of that relation; that is, relations are always *normalized* or, equivalently, in *first normal form*, 1NF.

   In connection with this point, it needs to be said that much of the literature talks about—and SQL products generally support—the use of what are called "nulls" in attribute positions to indicate that some value is missing for some reason. However, since by definition nulls are not values, the notion of a "tuple" containing nulls is a contradiction in terms. A "tuple" that contains nulls is not a tuple!—and a "relation" that contains such a "tuple" is not a relation. Thus, *relations never contain nulls*. (In fact, we categorically reject the concept of nulls, at least as that concept is usually understood. A detailed justification for this position can be found in reference [39] and elsewhere.)

10. Let {*H*} be the heading {*A1 T1, A2 T2, …, An Tn*}. To say that relation *r* has heading {*H*} is to say, precisely, that **relation *r* is of type RELATION{*H*}** (and the name of that type is, precisely, "RELATION{*H*}"). In fact, RELATION here is a **type generator** (see Section 1.5), and RELATION{*H*} is a specific **relation type** that is produced by a specific *invocation* of that type generator. And if relation *r* is of type RELATION{*H*}, then that type RELATION{*H*} is said to have the same heading, degree, and attributes that relation *r* has.

11. Note carefully that, by definition, a relation is a *value* (a nonscalar value, of course, with user-visible components). Figure 1.1, for example, shows two such values. For emphasis, we sometimes speak of "relation values" explicitly, but we usually abbreviate that term to simply *relations* (just as we usually abbreviate, e.g., "integer values" to simply *integers*).

    N o t e : All of the remarks in the foregoing paragraph apply equally to tuples, *mutatis mutandis*.[6]

---

6. In case you are not familiar with this useful expression, we offer a brief explanation here. Essentially, it means *with all necessary changes having been made* (and it can save a great deal of writing). In the case at hand, for example, the "necessary changes" are as follows:
   1. In the first sentence, replace relation by tuple.
   2. Delete the second sentence.
   3. In what was the third sentence (now the second), replace "relation values" by "tuple values" and *relations* by *tuples*.

12. Finally, to say that tuple *t* involves exactly the attributes that constitute heading {*H*} is to say, precisely, that **tuple *t* is of type TUPLE{*H*}** (and the name of that type is, precisely, "TUPLE{*H*}"). We also say, somewhat informally, that tuple *t* "conforms to" heading {*H*}. Note in particular, therefore, that if relation *r* is of type RELATION{*H*}, then every tuple in *r* is of type TUPLE{*H*} and conforms to heading {*H*}. In fact, TUPLE here—like RELATION (see point 10 above)—is a **type generator** (see Section 1.5), and TUPLE{*H*} is a specific **tuple type** that is produced by a specific *invocation* of that type generator.[7] And if tuple *t* is of type TUPLE{*H*}, then both that tuple *t* and that type TUPLE{*H*} are said to have the same heading, degree, and attributes as type RELATION{*H*} does.

Relation-Valued Attributes

Remember that any type whatsoever can be used as the basis for defining attributes of relations. It follows that, since they are certainly types, relation types in particular can be used as the basis for defining attributes of relations; in other words, attributes can be **relation-valued,** meaning we can have relations with attributes whose values are relations in turn (and this fact will turn out to be important when we discuss temporal databases in Parts II and III of this book—in Chapter 8 in particular). An example of such a relation is shown, in outline, in Figure 1.3.

FIGURE 1.3

A relation with a relation-valued attribute.

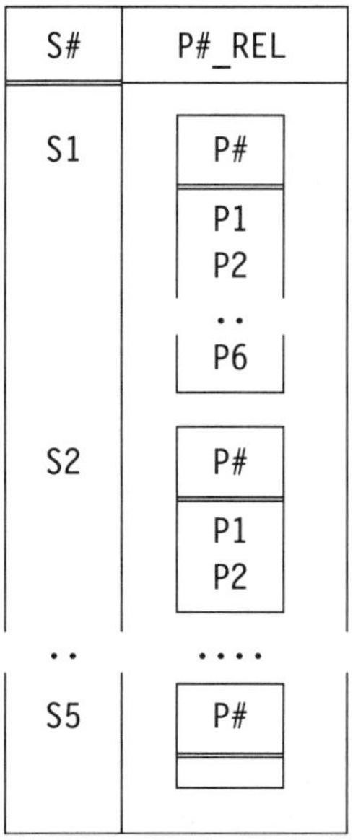

7. For simplicity, however, the grammar shown for **Tutorial D** in Chapter 2 does not include the TUPLE type generator, though the one given in reference [43] does.

Relations and Their Meaning

NOTE: *The topic of this subsection is of crucial importance. As you will quickly find in Chapter 3 and later chapters, we will be appealing to it repeatedly in the pages to come.*

Given a relation *r,* the heading of *r* can be regarded as denoting a certain **predicate** (i.e., a function, with a set of parameters, that returns a truth value—TRUE or FALSE in **Tutorial D**—when it is invoked). The predicate corresponding to relation *r* is the **relation predicate** for that relation. Further, each tuple in the body of *r* can be regarded as denoting a certain **proposition** (i.e., a statement that is unconditionally either true or false). The propositions correspond to invocations or "instantiations" of the relation predicate; they are obtained from that predicate by substituting arguments of the appropriate type for the parameters of the predicate. In the case of the suppliers relation in Figure 1.1, for example, the relation predicate looks something like this:

Supplier S# is under contract, is named SNAME, has status STATUS, and is located in city CITY

(the parameters are S#, SNAME, STATUS, and CITY, corresponding of course to the four attributes of the relation). And the corresponding propositions are:

Supplier S1 is under contract, is named Smith, has status 20, and is located in city London

(obtained by substituting the S# value S1, the NAME value Smith, the INTEGER value 20, and the CHAR value London for the appropriate parameters);

Supplier S2 is under contract, is named Jones, has status 10, and is located in city Paris

(obtained by substituting the S# value S2, the NAME value Jones, the INTEGER value 10, and the CHAR value Paris for the appropriate parameters); and so on.

More generally, we can say that the predicate corresponding to a given relation is **the intended interpretation,** or meaning, for that relation, and the propositions corresponding to tuples of that relation are understood by convention to be ones that evaluate to true. Furthermore, we subscribe, noncontroversially, to the **Closed World Assumption** [87], which says that if a given tuple conforms to the relation heading but does not in fact appear in the relation body, then the corresponding proposition is understood by convention to be one that evaluates to false. In other words, the body of the relation contains *all* and *only* the tuples that correspond to propositions that evaluate to true.

NOTE: Reference [43] refers to predicates such as those we have been discussing as *external* predicates, to stress the fact that they have to do with what relations mean to the user, rather than to the system. By contrast, *integrity constraints*—see Section 1.6— have to do with what relations mean to the system; such constraints can be thought of, loosely, as the internal counterpart to external predicates. Throughout this book, we will take the term *predicate* to mean an external predicate specifically, barring explicit statements to the contrary.

By the way, it is important to understand that *every* relation has an associated predicate, including in particular relations that are derived from others by means of relational operators such as projection and join. For example, suppose we project the suppliers relation shown in Figure 1.1 over the S#, SNAME, and STATUS attributes (thereby effectively removing the CITY attribute). Then the predicate for the relation that results looks something like this:

There exists some city CITY such that supplier S# is under contract, is named SNAME, has status STATUS, and is located in city CITY.

Observe that—as required—this predicate does have three parameters, not four, corresponding to the three attributes of the relation (CITY is now no longer a parameter but a *bound variable* instead,[8] thanks to the fact that it is **quantified** by the phrase "there exists some city").

Another, perhaps clearer, way of making the same point (i.e., that the predicate has three parameters, not four) is to observe that the predicate as stated is logically equivalent to this one:

Supplier S# is under contract, is named SNAME, has status STATUS, and is located in some city.

This version of the predicate very clearly has just three parameters.

1.5 RELATION VARIABLES

Consider the suppliers-and-shipments database as shown in Figure 1.1 once again. As noted in the previous section, that figure shows two relation **values**—namely, the relation values that happen to appear in the database at some particular time. But, of course, if we were to look at the database at some different time, we would probably see two *different* relation values. In other words, S and SP in that database are really **variables:** *relation* variables, to be precise, or in other words variables whose permitted values are relation values (different relation values at different times, in general). For example, suppose relation variable S currently has the value (the *relation* value, that is) shown in Figure 1.1, and suppose we delete the tuples for suppliers in Paris:

```
DELETE S WHERE CITY = 'Paris' ;
```

(**Tutorial D** syntax again). The result is shown in Figure 1.4.

---

8. Bound variables are not variables in the usual programming language sense, they are variables in the sense of logic. See reference [39] for further explanation of quantifiers, bound variables, and related matters.

FIGURE 1.4

S

S#	SNAME	STATUS	CITY
S1	Smith	20	London
S4	Clark	20	London
S5	Adams	30	Athens

Conceptually, what has happened here is that *the old relation value of S has been replaced* en bloc *by an entirely new relation value.* Of course, the old value (with five tuples) and the new one (with three) are somewhat similar, but they certainly are different values. Indeed, the DELETE just shown is basically shorthand for the following **relational assignment:**

```
S := S WHERE NOT ( CITY = 'Paris' ) ;
```

As in all assignments, what is happening here, conceptually speaking, is that

1. the **source expression** on the right side is evaluated, and then

2. the result of that evaluation is assigned to the **target variable** on the left side.

As already stated, the net effect is thus to replace the "old" value of S by a "new" one, or in other words to update the variable S.[9]

In analogous fashion, of course, relational INSERT and UPDATE operators are also basically just shorthand for certain relational assignments. In the case of INSERT, for example, the expression on the right side of that assignment involves a *union* of (1) the current value of the target relation variable and (2) a relation value containing just the tuples to be inserted. Thus, while **Tutorial D** certainly does support the familiar INSERT, DELETE, and UPDATE operators on relation variables, it expressly recognizes that those operators are really just shorthands (albeit convenient ones) for certain relational assignments. NOTE: We follow convention throughout this book in using the generic term *update* to refer to the INSERT, DELETE, and UPDATE operators considered collectively (indeed, we have already begun to do this, as you might have noticed). When we want to refer to the UPDATE operator specifically, we will set it in all uppercase as just shown.

Back to relation variables. It is an unfortunate fact that most of the literature uses the term *relation* when what it really means is a relation *variable* (as well as when it means a relation per se—in other words, a relation value). Historically, however, this practice has certainly led to confusion. In this book, therefore, we will distinguish very carefully between relation variables and relations per se; following references [39] and [43], in fact, we will use the term **relvar** as a convenient shorthand for "relation variable," and we

---

9. Of course, the left side of an assignment must identify a variable specifically. Variables are updatable by definition (values, of course, are not); in the final analysis, in fact, to say that *V* is a variable is to say precisely that *V* can serve as the target for an assignment operation, no more and no less.

will take care to phrase our remarks in terms of relvars, not relations, when it really is relvars that we mean (and in terms of relations, not relvars, when it really is relations that we mean).

Here then is an example of a relvar definition (repeated from Figure 1.2):

```
VAR S RELATION
    { S#     S#,
      SNAME  NAME,
      STATUS INTEGER,
      CITY   CHAR }
    KEY { S# } ;
```

Any given relvar is defined to be of some *relation type* (and all possible values of that relvar are of that same type). For example, the type of relvar S is, precisely,

```
RELATION { S# S#, SNAME NAME, STATUS INTEGER, CITY CHAR }
```

As noted in Section 1.4, in fact, RELATION is a type generator[10] (much as, e.g., "array" is a type generator in conventional programming languages), and the expression just shown can be regarded as an invocation of that type generator, yielding a specific relation type.

NOTE: Relvars come in two varieties, called *real* and *virtual* in reference [43] and corresponding to what are more usually called "base tables" and "views," respectively. In this book, however, we will have little to say regarding virtual relvars or "views" (until we get to Chapter 13, at any rate); prior to that point, therefore, we will adopt the pretense that all relvars are real ones ("base tables") specifically, barring explicit statements to the contrary. In particular, we will simplify the syntax of such relvar definitions by omitting the keyword REAL that reference [43] would require.

Finally, we observe that the terms *heading, body, attribute, tuple, cardinality,* and *degree,* defined for relation values in Section 1.4, can all be interpreted in the obvious way to apply to relation variables, or relvars, as well. (In the case of *body, tuple,* and *cardinality,* the terms must be understood as applying to the specific relation that happens to be the current value of the relvar in question.) Furthermore, relvars, like relation values, also have a corresponding *predicate* (called the **relvar predicate** for the relvar in question)—namely, the predicate that is common to all of the relations that are possible values of the relvar in question. In the case of the suppliers relvar S, for example, the relvar predicate is

Supplier S# is under contract, is named SNAME, has status STATUS, and is located in city CITY

(as we already know).

---

10. Many terms can be found in the literature for this construct: *type constructor, parameterized type, type template, generic type,* and others. We will stay with the term *type generator.*

A Remark on Updating

We return for a moment to the issue of updating relvars, because there is another point to be made in connection with that issue: *Relational assignment and the INSERT, DELETE, and UPDATE shorthands are all **set-level** operators.* UPDATE, for example, updates a *set* of tuples in the target relvar, loosely speaking (more precisely, it replaces one set of tuples in the target relvar by another such set of tuples). Informally, we often talk of, for example, updating some individual tuple, but it must be clearly understood that (1) such talk really means that the set of tuples we are updating just happens to have cardinality one, and (2) sometimes updating a set of tuples of cardinality one is impossible!

Suppose, for example, that the suppliers relvar S is subject to the integrity constraint that suppliers S1 and S4 are always located in the same city. Then any "single-tuple" UPDATE on S that attempts to change the city for just one of those two suppliers must necessarily fail. Instead, both must be updated simultaneously, as here:

```
UPDATE S WHERE S# = S# ('S1') OR S# = S# ('S4')
       { CITY := some value } ;
```

To pursue the point a moment longer, we now observe that to talk, as we have just been doing, about "updating a tuple" (or set of tuples) is really rather imprecise—not to say sloppy!—as well. Rembember that tuples, like relations, are values and cannot be updated (by definition, the one thing we cannot do to a value of *any* kind is update it). In order to be able to "update tuples," therefore, we would need some notion of a *tuple variable* or "tuplevar"—a notion that is not part of the relational model at all. Thus, what we really mean when we talk of, for example, "updating tuple t to t'" is that we are **replacing** the tuple t (the tuple *value t,* that is) by another tuple t' (which is, again, a tuple *value*). Analogous remarks apply to phrases such as "updating attribute A" (within some tuple). In this book, we will continue to talk from time to time in terms of updating tuples or attributes thereof—the practice is convenient—but it must be understood that such talk is only shorthand, and rather sloppy shorthand at that.

Keys

Let K be a subset of the set of attributes of relvar R. Then K is said to be a **candidate key** (or just *key*) for R if and only if it possesses both of the following properties:

- *Uniqueness:* No possible value of R contains two distinct tuples with the same value for K.

- *Irreducibility:* No proper subset of K has the uniqueness property.

NOTE: Throughout this book, we take statements of the form "B is a subset of A" and "A is a superset of B"—in accordance with normal mathematical usage—to include the possibility that A and B might be equal. If we wish to exclude that possibility, we will talk explicitly in terms of *proper* subsets and supersets.

Back to candidate keys. In the case of suppliers and shipments, the only such keys are {S#} for relvar S and {S#,P#} for relvar SP. *Note the enclosing braces:* It is important to understand that candidate keys are always *sets* of attributes, not just attributes per se (even when the set in question involves just one attribute, as it does in the case of relvar S). For that reason, we always enclose the relevant attribute name(s) in braces, as in the examples at hand. (In fact, we generally use braces in **Tutorial D** when we wish to indicate that whatever is enclosed by those braces denotes a set of some kind.)

It should be clear that any given relvar always has at least one candidate key (why?). Now, if it has two or more, the relational model has historically required that one of those candidate keys be chosen as the *primary* key, and the others are then said to be *alternate* keys. For reasons given in reference [36], we do not insist on this practice; however, we do not prohibit it, either, and indeed we usually adopt it in our examples. In particular, we assume—where it makes any difference—that {S#} is the primary key for relvar S and {S#,P#} is the primary key for relvar SP. And in figures like Figure 1.1, we adopt the convention of identifying attributes that participate in primary keys by *double underlining.*

Now let *R1* and *R2* be relvars, not necessarily distinct. Let *K* be a candidate key for *R1*. Let *FK* be a subset of the attributes of *R2* that—after any attribute renaming that might be required (see Chapter 2)—involves exactly the same attributes as *K*. Then *FK* is said to be a **foreign key** if and only if, for all time, every tuple in the current value of *R2* has a value for *FK* that is equal to the value of *K* in some (necessarily unique) tuple in the current value of *R1*. In the case of suppliers and shipments in particular, the only foreign key is {S#} in relvar SP, which matches—or *references*—the sole candidate key (in fact, the primary key) of relvar S.

It follows immediately from the foregoing that *no database is ever allowed to contain any unmatched foreign key values*—where an "unmatched foreign key value" is a foreign key value within the current value of some referencing relvar for which there does not exist an equal value of the pertinent candidate key within the current value of the pertinent referenced relvar. This rule is known as the **referential integrity rule**.

Functional Dependencies

Let *A* and *B* be subsets of the set of attributes of relvar *R*. Then the **functional dependency** $A \rightarrow B$ holds for *R* if and only if, in every possible value of *R*, whenever two tuples have the same value for *A*, they also have the same value for *B*. For example, suppose there were a rule on the suppliers-and-shipments database to the effect that if two suppliers are located in the same city at the same time, then they must also have the same status at that time. Then the functional dependency

```
{ CITY } → { STATUS }
```

would hold for the suppliers relvar S. Points arising:

- If *K* is a candidate key for *R* and *A* is any set of attributes of *R,* then the functional dependency $K \rightarrow A$ necessarily holds for *R.*

- Functional dependencies are the basis of *normalization theory,* up to and including *Boyce/Codd normal form.* (Higher levels of normalization do exist, but they involve additional kinds of dependencies, over and above functional dependencies per se [47]. A detailed tutorial on such matters can be found in reference [39]. See also Chapter 10, Section 10.4.)

1.6 Integrity Constraints

An integrity constraint, or *constraint* for short, can be thought of, loosely, as a *boolean expression*—also known as a *logical, conditional,* or *truth-valued* expression—that is required to evaluate to true. We classify such constraints into database, relvar, attribute, and type constraints (though we should say immediately that the distinction between database and relvar constraints is primarily a matter of pragma, not logic). In essence:

- A **database constraint** is a constraint on the values a given database is permitted to assume.

- A **relvar constraint** is a constraint on the values a given relvar is permitted to assume.

- An **attribute constraint** is a constraint on the values a given attribute is permitted to assume.

- A **type constraint** is, precisely, a definition of the set of values that constitute a given type.

It suits our purposes to explain them in reverse order, however. Here first, then, is an example of a *type* constraint:

```
TYPE S# POSSREP { C CHAR
              CONSTRAINT SUBSTR ( C, 1, 1 ) = 'S'
              AND LENGTH ( C ) ≥ 2
              AND LENGTH ( C ) ≤ 5 } ;
```

This type definition constrains supplier numbers to be such that they can be represented by a character string C consisting of from two to five characters, of which the first must be an "S".[11] (Just as an aside, note that the specified possible representation is named S# by default, and the corresponding selector is therefore named S# as well.)

---

11. In practice we might additionally want to specify that every character after the first is a decimal digit. We do not bother to do so here for reasons of simplicity.

Second, an *attribute* constraint is essentially no more than a statement to the effect that a specified attribute of a specified relvar is of a specified type. For example, the specification

```
STATUS INTEGER
```

(part of the definition of relvar S) constrains values of attribute STATUS to be of type INTEGER.

Third, a *relvar* constraint is a constraint on an individual relvar (it is expressed in terms of the relvar in question only and does not mention any others). Here are some examples (note the constraint names—RC1, RC2, and RC3—and the appeals to the self-explanatory operators IS_EMPTY and COUNT,[12] which we assume are system-defined):

```
CONSTRAINT RC1 IS_EMPTY ( S WHERE STATUS < 1
                            OR    STATUS > 100 ) ;
```

MEANING: Supplier status values must be in the range 1 to 100 inclusive. In practice, some shorthand syntax might well be available to express simple constraints of this kind; for example, the expression "IN 1..100" might be attached to the declaration of attribute STATUS within the definition of relvar S. But such considerations are mostly beyond the purview of this book.

```
CONSTRAINT RC2 IS_EMPTY ( S WHERE CITY = 'London'
                            AND   STATUS ≠ 20 ) ;
```

MEANING: Suppliers in London must have status 20.

```
CONSTRAINT RC3 COUNT ( S ) = COUNT ( S { S# } ) ;
```

MEANING (APPROXIMATE): {S#} is a candidate key for relvar S. The **Tutorial D** syntax KEY {S#} might be regarded as shorthand for the longer expression; thus, if K is a candidate key for R, then that fact is a relvar constraint on R. In like manner, if the functional dependency $A \rightarrow B$ holds for R, then that fact is also a relvar constraint on R.

NOTE: It would be more accurate to say that Constraint RC3 means that {S#} is a **superkey** for relvar S. A superkey is a superset—not necessarily a proper superset, of course—of a candidate key; thus, all candidate keys are superkeys, but some superkeys are not candidate keys. Superkeys satisfy the uniqueness requirement for candidate keys but not necessarily the irreducibility requirement. In the case at hand, of course, the superkey does satisfy the irreducibility requirement and is thus a candidate key after all.

---

12. IS_EMPTY and COUNT are both scalar operators (they both return scalar results). COUNT is also an aggregate operator (see the remarks on this latter subject following the discussion of the SUMMARIZE operator near the end of Section 1.7).

Finally, a *database* constraint is a constraint that interrelates two or more distinct relvars. Here are some examples (again, note the constraint names):

```
CONSTRAINT DBC1 IS_EMPTY ( ( S JOIN SP )
                           WHERE STATUS < 20
                           AND   P# = P# ('P6') ) ;
```

MEANING: No supplier with status less than 20 can supply part P6.

```
CONSTRAINT DBC2 SP { S# } ⊆ S { S# } ;
```

MEANING: Every supplier number in the shipments relvar must also exist in the suppliers relvar. Note that this example involves a *relational comparison;* to be specific, it requires that the body of the relation that is the projection of SP on {S#} be a subset of the body of the relation that is the projection of S on {S#}. Of course, the constraint in question is basically just the necessary referential (foreign key) constraint from shipments to suppliers; thus, the **Tutorial D** syntax

```
FOREIGN KEY { S# } REFERENCES S
```

might be regarded as shorthand for the slightly longer formulation shown as Constraint DBC2.

In general, constraints are required to be satisfied *at statement boundaries* [43]; that is, constraints are conceptually checked at the end of any statement that might cause them to be violated ("immediate checking"). If any such check fails, the statement in question is effectively undone and an exception is raised. NOTE: By the term *statement* here, we basically mean just a *relational assignment* (possibly multiple—see Chapters 2 and 14—and possibly expressed in terms of the INSERT, DELETE, or UPDATE shorthands); fundamentally, relational assignment is the *only* operator that can update the database.[13] In **Tutorial D,** statements are delimited by semicolons, and thus we can say, very informally, that "checking is done at semicolons."

1.7 RELATIONAL OPERATORS

The relational model includes an open-ended set of generic operators known collectively as the **relational algebra** (the operators are generic because they apply to all possible relations, loosely speaking). In this section, we define those operators that we will be relying on most heavily in the pages to come; we also give a few examples, but only where we think the operators in question might be unfamiliar to you. Each of the

---

13. For simplicity, we ignore relvar definitions and similar statements that cause updates to be made to the database *catalog.* Of course, all such statements are really just relational assignments anyway—to be specific, they are relational assignments in which the target relvars happen to be relvars in the catalog.

operators we discuss takes either one relation or two relations as operand(s) and returns another relation as result. NOTE: The—very important!—fact that the result is always another relation is referred to as the (relational) **closure property**. It is that property that, among other things, allows us to write *nested relational expressions*.

Rename

Let *A* be a relation with an attribute *X* and no attribute *Y*. Then the **renaming**

```
A RENAME X AS Y
```

yields a relation that differs from *A* only in that the name of the specified attribute is *Y* instead of *X*.

Union, Intersect, and Difference

Let *A* and *B* be relations of the same relation type. Then:

- The **union** of those relations, *A* UNION *B,* is a relation of the same type, with body consisting of all tuples *t* such that *t* appears in *A* or *B* or both.

- The **intersection** of those relations, *A* INTERSECT *B,* is a relation of the same type, with body consisting of all tuples *t* such that *t* appears in both *A* and *B*.

- The **difference** between those relations, *A* MINUS *B* (in that order), is a relation of the same type, with body consisting of all tuples *t* such that *t* appears in *A* and not *B*.

NOTE: Union and intersection are both associative, and **Tutorial D** thus allows unnecessary parentheses to be omitted from an uninterrupted sequence of unions or intersections. For example, the expressions

```
A UNION ( B UNION C )
```

and

```
( A UNION B ) UNION C
```

can both be unambiguously abbreviated to just

```
A UNION B UNION C
```

Furthermore, it turns out to be desirable, at least from a conceptual point of view, to define both (1) unions and intersections of just a single relation and (2) unions and intersections of no relations at all (even though **Tutorial D** provides no direct syntactic support for such operations). Let S be a set of relations all of the same relation type, RT. Then:

1. If S contains just one relation r, then the union and intersection of all relations in S are both defined to be simply r.

2. If S contains no relations at all, then:

   - The union of all relations in S is defined to be the empty relation of type RT.
   - The intersection of all relations in S is defined to be the "universal" relation of type RT—that is, that unique relation of type RT that contains all possible tuples of type TUPLE{H}, where {H} is the heading of relation type RT.

Restrict

Let relation A have attributes X and Y (and possibly others), and let θ be an operator—typically "=", "≠", ">", "<", and so on—such that the expression $X \theta Y$ is well-formed and, given particular values for X and Y, evaluates to a truth value (true or false). Then the **θ-restriction,** or just *restriction* for short, of relation A on attributes X and Y (in that order)—

```
A WHERE X θ Y
```

—is a relation with the same heading as A and with body consisting of all tuples of A such that the expression $X \theta Y$ evaluates to true for the tuple in question.

NOTE: The foregoing is essentially the definition given for the restriction operator in most of the literature (including reference [39] in particular). However, it is of course possible to generalize it, as follows. Let relation A have attributes $X, Y, ..., Z$, and let p be a predicate—necessarily an internal predicate (see Section 1.4)—whose parameters are, precisely, some subset of $X, Y, ..., Z$. Then the restriction of relation A according to p—

```
A WHERE p
```

—is a relation with the same heading as A and with body consisting of all tuples of A such that the predicate p evaluates to true for the tuple in question.

Project

Let relation A have attributes $X, Y, ..., Z$ (and possibly others). Then the **projection** of relation A on $X, Y, ..., Z$—

```
A { X, Y, ..., Z }
```

—is a relation with:

- A heading derived from the heading of *A* by removing all attributes not mentioned in the set $\{X, Y, ..., Z\}$, and

- A body consisting of all tuples $\{X\ x, Y\ y, ..., Z\ z\}$ such that a tuple appears in *A* with *X* value *x*, *Y* value *y*, ..., and *Z* value *z*.

Join

Let relations *A* and *B* have attributes

```
X1, X2, ..., Xm, Y1, Y2, ..., Yn
```

and

```
Y1, Y2, ..., Yn, Z1, Z2, ..., Zp
```

respectively; that is, the *Y* attributes *Y1, Y2, ..., Yn* (only) are common to the two relations, the *X* attributes *X1, X2, ..., Xm* are the other attributes of *A*, and the *Z* attributes *Z1, Z2, ..., Zp* are the other attributes of *B*. Observe that:

- We can (and do) assume without loss of generality—thanks to the availability of the attribute RENAME operator—that no attribute Xi ($i = 1, 2, ..., m$) has the same name as any attribute Zj ($j = 1, 2, ..., p$).

- Every attribute Yk ($k = 1, 2, ..., n$) has the same type in both *A* and *B* (for otherwise it would not be a common attribute, by definition).

Now consider $\{X1, X2, ..., Xm\}$, $\{Y1, Y2, ..., Yn\}$, and $\{Z1, Z2, ..., Zp\}$ as three *composite* attributes *X*, *Y*, and *Z*, respectively. Then the **join** of *A* and *B*—

```
A JOIN B
```

—is a relation with heading $\{X, Y, Z\}$ and body consisting of all tuples $\{X\ x, Y\ y, Z\ z\}$ such that a tuple appears in *A* with *X* value *x* and *Y* value *y* and a tuple appears in *B* with *Y* value *y* and *Z* value *z*.

Observe that if $n = 0$, join degenerates to (relational) Cartesian product; if $m = p = 0$, it degenerates to (relational) intersection.

Like union and intersection, join is associative, and **Tutorial D** thus allows unnecessary parentheses to be omitted from an uninterrupted sequence of joins. For example, the expressions

```
A JOIN ( B JOIN C )
```

and

```
( A JOIN B ) JOIN C
```

can both be unambiguously abbreviated to just

```
A JOIN B JOIN C
```

Furthermore, it turns out to be desirable to define both (1) joins of just a single relation and (2) joins of no relations at all (even though **Tutorial D** provides no direct syntactic support for such operations). Let S be a set of relations. Then:

- If S contains just one relation r, then the join of all relations in S is defined to be simply r.

- If S contains no relations at all, then the join of all relations in S is defined to be TABLE_DEE.

NOTE: You might notice an apparent contradiction here: Given that INTERSECT is a special case of JOIN, you might have expected both operators to give the same result when applied to no relations at all. But INTERSECT is defined only if its operand relations are all of the same type, while no such limitation applies to JOIN. It follows that, when there are no operands at all, we can define the result for JOIN *generically,* but we cannot do the same for INTERSECT—we can only define the result for *specific* INTERSECT operations (i.e., INTERSECT operations that are specific to some particular relation type). In fact, when we say that INTERSECT is a special case of JOIN, what we really mean is that every *specific* INTERSECT is a special case of some *specific* JOIN. Let S_JOIN be such a specific JOIN. Then S_JOIN and JOIN are not the same operator, and it is reasonable to say that the S_JOIN and the JOIN of no relations at all give different results.

Extend

Let A be a relation. Then the **extension**

```
EXTEND A ADD exp AS Z
```

is a relation with:

- A heading consisting of the heading of A extended with the attribute Z, and

- A body consisting of all tuples t such that t is a tuple of A extended with a value for attribute Z that is computed by evaluating exp on that tuple of A.

Relation A must not have an attribute called Z, and exp must not refer to Z. Observe that the result has cardinality equal to that of A and degree equal to that of A plus one. The type of Z in that result is whatever the type of exp is.

Here is a simple example of EXTEND:

```
EXTEND S ADD ( STATUS * 3 ) AS TRIPLE
```

The result of this operation, given our usual sample data values, is shown in Figure 1.5.

FIGURE 1.5

Extending S (as shown in Figure 1.1) to add a "triple status" attribute.

S#	SNAME	STATUS	CITY	TRIPLE
S1	Smith	20	London	60
S2	Jones	10	Paris	30
S3	Blake	30	Paris	90
S4	Clark	20	London	60
S5	Adams	30	Athens	90

NOTE: Do not make the mistake in this example of thinking that relvar S has been changed in the database. EXTEND is not an SQL-style "ALTER TABLE." Rather, the result of the EXTEND expression is simply a derived relation, just as (for example) the result of the expression S JOIN SP is a derived relation. Analogous remarks apply to all of the other relational algebra operators, of course—in particular, to RENAME (see earlier).

Summarize

Let *A* and *B* be two relations. Then the **summarization**

```
SUMMARIZE A PER B ADD summary AS Z
```

is a relation defined as follows:

- First, *B* must be of the same type as some projection of *A;* that is, every attribute of *B* must be an attribute of *A*. Let the attributes of that projection (equivalently, of *B*) be *A1, A2, ..., An*.

- The heading of the result consists of the heading of *B* extended with the attribute *Z*.

- The body of that result consists of all tuples *t* such that *t* is a tuple of *B* extended with a value for attribute *Z*. That *Z* value is computed by evaluating *summary* over all tuples of *A* that have the same value for attributes {*A1, A2, ..., An*} as tuple *t* does. (Of course, if no tuples of *A* have the same value for {*A1, A2, ..., An*} as tuple *t* does, then *summary* is evaluated over an empty set of tuples.)

Relation *B* must not have an attribute called *Z*, and *summary* must not refer to *Z*. Observe that the result has cardinality equal to that of *B* and degree equal to that of *B* plus one. The type of *Z* in that result is whatever the type of *summary* is.

Here is a simple example of SUMMARIZE:

```
SUMMARIZE SP PER S { S# } ADD COUNT AS P_COUNT
```

The result of this operation, given our usual sample data values, is shown in Figure 1.6. Observe in particular that the result includes a tuple for supplier S5. If you happen to be familiar with SQL, it might help to point out that (by contrast) the SQL expression—

```
SELECT S#, COUNT(*) AS P_COUNT
FROM   SP
GROUP  BY S#
```

—yields a result containing no tuple for supplier S5, because relvar SP as shown in Figure 1.1 contains no such tuple either. In other words, it might be thought that the expression just shown is an SQL analog of the SUMMARIZE expression earlier, but in fact it is not, not quite.[14]

FIGURE 1.6

Summarizing SP (as shown in Figure 1.1) to obtain "number of shipments per supplier."

S#	P_COUNT
S1	6
S2	2
S3	1
S4	3
S5	0

Here is another SUMMARIZE example:

```
SUMMARIZE S PER S { CITY } ADD AVG ( STATUS ) AS AVG_STATUS
```

In this second example, "the B relation" is not just of the same type as some projection of "the A relation," it actually *is* such a projection. The result is shown in Figure 1.7.

FIGURE 1.7

Summarizing S (as shown in Figure 1.1) to obtain "average status per city."

CITY	AVG_STATUS
London	20
Paris	20
Athens	30

14. While we are talking about SQL, we should mention that the character "#" is not included in what the SQL standard calls *the standard character set* and thus cannot appear in what that standard calls a *regular identifier* [42, 52]. We choose to overlook this fact, both here and throughout the rest of this book.

Note carefully that the "summary" in SUMMARIZE is not the same thing as an aggregate operator invocation. An aggregate operator invocation is a scalar expression and is allowed wherever a literal of the appropriate type would be allowed. A summary, by contrast, is merely an operand within a SUMMARIZE invocation; it is not a scalar expression, it has no meaning outside the context of a SUMMARIZE invocation, and in fact it cannot appear outside that context.

So what then is an aggregate operator invocation? Well, an aggregate operator is, very loosely, an operator that derives a scalar value from the "aggregate" of values appearing in some specified relation or in specified attribute(s) of some specified relation. Typical examples include COUNT, SUM, AVG, MAX, MIN, ALL, and ANY. A detailed discussion of such operators is beyond the scope of this book, but we give below a few illustrative examples, together with corresponding results (based on our usual sample data values). Another example involving the aggregate operator COUNT was given in Section 1.6.

```
COUNT ( S )                           /* result    5 */

COUNT ( S { CITY } )                  /* result    3 */

AVG ( S { STATUS }, STATUS )          /* result   20 */

AVG ( S, STATUS )                     /* result   22 */

MAX ( S, STATUS )                     /* result   30 */

SUM ( EXTEND S
      ADD ( ( 2 * STATUS ) + 1 )
      AS XYZ, XYZ )                   /* result  225 */

ANY ( EXTEND S
      ADD ( STATUS > 20 )
      AS TEST, TEST )                 /* result TRUE */
```

Group and Ungroup

We devote a little more space to these two operators because they might be less familiar than the ones previously described. Consider the following two relation types:

```
RELATION { S# S#, P# P# }

RELATION { S# S#, P#_REL RELATION { P# P# } }
```

We will refer to these two types as *RT1* and *RT2*, respectively. Note that attribute P#_REL in *RT2* is relation-valued.

Now let SP and SP′ be relvars of types *RT1* and *RT2*, respectively (the relations in Figures 1.1 and 1.3, respectively, can be taken as examples of possible values for these two relvars). Then the expression

```
SP GROUP { P# } AS P#_REL
```

yields a relation defined as follows:[15]

- First, the heading looks like this:

  ```
  { S# S#, P#_REL RELATION { P# P# } }
  ```

  In other words, the heading contains a relation-valued attribute P#_REL (where P#_REL relation values in turn involve just one attribute, namely P#, of type P#), together with all of the other attributes of SP (of course, "all of the other attributes of SP" here just means attribute S#).

- Second, the body contains exactly one tuple for each distinct S# value in SP (and it does not contain any other tuples). Each tuple in that body consists of the applicable S# value (*s*, say), together with a P#_REL value (*ps*, say) obtained as follows:

  - Each SP tuple is replaced by a tuple (*x*, say) in which the P# component has been "wrapped" into a tuple-valued component (*y*, say).

  - The *y* components of all such tuples *x* in which the S# value is equal to *s* are then "grouped" into a relation, *ps*, and a result tuple with S# value equal to *s* and P#_REL value equal to *ps* is thereby obtained.

The overall result is thus of type *RT2*, and so, for example, the following relational assignment is valid:

```
SP'  :=  SP GROUP { P# } AS P#_REL ;
```

If the current value of relvar SP is as shown in Figure 1.1, the value of SP′ after this assignment is as shown in Figure 1.8. Note in particular that the result includes no tuple for supplier S5 (because relvar SP as shown in Figure 1.1 does not do so either).

---

15. If you happen to be familiar with SQL, it might help to point out that—*very* loosely speaking!—GROUP in **Tutorial D** specifies the attributes that are to be grouped together, whereas GROUP BY in SQL specifies the *other* attributes (i.e., the attributes that control the grouping). In other words, the expression SP GROUP {P#} AS P#_REL might loosely be read as "group SP *by* S#," since S# is the sole attribute of SP not mentioned in the GROUP specification.

FIGURE 1.8

S#	P#_REL
S1	P#
	P1
	P2
	P3
	P4
	P5
	P6
S2	P#
	P1
	P2
S3	P#
	P2
S4	P#
	P2
	P4
	P5

Observe that the result of R GROUP $\{A1, A2, \ldots, An\}$ AS B has degree equal to $nR - n + 1$, where nR is the degree of R.

Turning now to UNGROUP, the expression, for example,

```
SP' UNGROUP P#_REL
```

yields a relation defined as follows:

- First, the heading looks like this:

  ```
  { S# S#, P# P# }
  ```

  In other words, the heading contains attribute P# (derived from the relation-valued attribute P#_REL), together with all of the other attributes of SP′ (i.e., just attribute S#).

- Second, the body contains exactly one tuple for each combination of a tuple in SP′ and a tuple in the P#_REL value within that SP′ tuple (and it does not contain any other tuples). Each tuple in that body consists of the applicable S# value (s, say), together with a P# value (p, say) obtained as follows:

- Each SP′ tuple is replaced by an "ungrouped" set of tuples, one such tuple (x, say) for each tuple in the P#_REL value in that SP′ tuple. Each such tuple x contains an S# component (s, say) equal to the S# component from the SP′ tuple in question and a tuple-valued component (y, say) equal to some tuple from the P#_REL component from the SP′ tuple in question.
- The y components of each such tuple x in which the S# value is equal to s are then "unwrapped" into a P# component (p, say), and a result tuple with S# value equal to s and P# value equal to p is thereby obtained.

The overall result is thus of type *RT1,* and so the following relational assignment is valid:

```
SP  :=  SP' UNGROUP P#_REL ;
```

If the current value of relvar SP′ is as shown in Figure 1.8, the value of SP after this assignment is as shown in Figure 1.1.

Observe that the result of R UNGROUP B (where the relations that are values of the relation-valued attribute B have heading {A1, A2, ..., An}) has degree equal to $nR + n - 1$, where nR is the degree of R.

Incidentally, it follows from the definition of UNGROUP that if SP′ includes exactly one tuple with S# equal to s (say), and if the P#_REL value in that tuple is an empty relation, then the result of evaluating SP′ UNGROUP P#_REL will contain no tuple at all with S# equal to s. For example, if r denotes the relation shown in Figure 1.3 in Section 1.4, then the result of evaluating r UNGROUP P#_REL will contain no tuple at all for supplier S5.

Relational Operations on Relvars

As we have seen, the operators of the relational algebra apply, by definition, to relation *values* specifically. In particular, of course, they apply to the values that happen to be the current values of relation *variables.* As a consequence, it clearly makes sense to talk about—for example—"the projection over attribute A of relvar R," meaning the relation that results from taking the projection over that attribute A of the current value of that relvar R.

Occasionally, however, it is convenient to use expressions like "the projection over attribute A of relvar R" in a slightly different sense. By way of example, suppose we define a "view" or virtual relvar SC of the suppliers relvar S that consists of just the S# and CITY attributes of that relvar. In **Tutorial D,** that definition might look like this:

```
VAR SC VIRTUAL S { S#, CITY } ;
```

In this example, we might say, loosely but very conveniently, that relvar SC is "the projection over S# and CITY of relvar S"—meaning, more precisely, that the value of SC at all times is the projection over S# and CITY of the value of relvar S at the time in question. In a sense, therefore, we can talk in terms of projections of relvars per se, rather than just in terms of projections of current values of relvars. We hope this kind of dual usage does not cause any confusion.

NOTE: As the preceding example suggests, the **Tutorial D** statement for defining a virtual relvar takes the form

```
VAR <relvar name> VIRTUAL <relation exp> ;
```

Candidate key definitions can be included if desired [43].

1.8 THE RELATIONAL MODEL

NOTE: This section is based on material that previously appeared in reference [40], Appendix A (pages 141–142), copyright © 2001 Addison Wesley Longman, Inc. Reprinted by permission of Pearson Education, Inc.

For purposes of future reference, we close this chapter with a formal (and deliberately somewhat terse!) definition of the relational model. Briefly, the relational model consists of the following five components:

1. an open-ended collection of **scalar types** (including in particular the type *boolean* or *truth value*)

2. a **relation type generator** and an intended interpretation for relations of types generated thereby

3. facilities for defining **relation variables** of such generated relation types

4. a **relational assignment** operator for assigning relation values to such relation variables

5. an open-ended collection of generic **relational operators** for deriving relation values from other relation values

We offer the following additional comments on these five components:

1. The scalar types can be system-defined or user-defined, in general; thus, a means must be available for users to define their own scalar types (this requirement is implied, partly, by the fact that the set of such types is open-ended). A means must therefore also be available for users to define their own scalar operators, since types without operators are useless. The only *required* system-defined scalar type is the type BOOLEAN (the most fundamental type of all), but a real system will surely support other built-in scalar types (e.g., type INTEGER) as well.

2. The relation type generator allows users to specify any required relation type. The intended interpretation for a given relation (of a given relation type) is the corresponding *relation predicate.*

3. Facilities for defining relation variables must be available (of course). Relation variables are the *only* variables allowed in a relational database. NOTE: This latter requirement is in accordance with Codd's *Information Principle.* As you probably know, Codd was the inventor of the relational model (see references [20–22], also the overview in reference [40]), and he has stated his *Information Principle* in various forms and in various places over the years (indeed, he has been known to refer to it on occasion as the fundamental principle of the relational model). Here it is:

   All information in the database (at any given time) must be cast explicitly in terms of values in relations and in no other way.

4. Variables are updatable by definition; hence, every kind of variable is subject to *assignment,* and relation variables are no exception. INSERT, DELETE, and UPDATE shorthands are permitted and indeed useful, but strictly speaking they *are* only shorthands.

5. The generic relational operators are the operators that make up the relational algebra, and they are therefore built-in (though there is no inherent reason why users should not be able to define additional such operators of their own, if desired).

EXERCISES

NOTE: For definiteness, exercises throughout this book are expressed in terms of **Tutorial D** and/or require **Tutorial D** answers, except where there is an explicit statement to the contrary or where **Tutorial D** is not directly relevant to the issue at hand.

1. Explain the difference between

   a. values and variables in general

   b. relation values and variables (relvars) in particular

2. Define the terms *type, possible representation,* and *selector.*

3. Explain the difference between scalar and nonscalar types. Give examples of each.

4. What is a literal?

5. Using **Tutorial D,** define a read-only operator called DOUBLE that takes an integer and doubles it.

6. Repeat Exercise 5, but make the operator an update operator.

7. Define the terms *heading, attribute, body, tuple, cardinality,* and *degree.*

8. State as precisely as you can what it means for two tuples *t1* and *t2* to be duplicates of each other.

9. What is a type generator?

10. What is a relation-valued attribute?

11. What do you understand by the terms *proposition* and *predicate?* Give examples of each.

12. Explain the terms *relation predicate* and *relvar predicate.* Give examples. Distinguish between internal and external predicates.

13. Explain the Closed World Assumption.

14. State Codd's *Information Principle.*

15. What is a relational assignment?

16. Define the terms *candidate key* (*key* for short) and *foreign key.*

17. What is a functional dependency?

18. Using **Tutorial D,** write integrity constraints for the suppliers-and-shipments database to express the following requirements:

    a. The only valid cities are Athens, London, Oslo, Paris, and Rome.

    b. All London suppliers must have status 20.

    c. No two suppliers can be located in the same city.

    d. At most one supplier can be located in Athens at any one time.

    e. There must exist at least one London supplier.

    f. The average supplier status must be at least 10.

    g. Every London supplier must be capable of supplying part P2.

19. What is the closure property of the relational algebra?

20. Define the operators *extend, summarize, group,* and *ungroup.*

21. What is an aggregate operator?

22. Write **Tutorial D** expressions for the following queries on the suppliers-and-shipments database:

    a. Get all shipments.

    b. Get supplier numbers for suppliers who are able to supply part P1.

    c. Get suppliers with status in the range 15 to 25 inclusive.

    d. Get part numbers for parts available from a supplier in London.

    e. Get part numbers for parts not available from a supplier in London.

f. Get city names for cities in which at least two suppliers are located.

g. Get all pairs of part numbers such that some supplier is able to supply both the indicated parts.

h. Get the total number of parts available from supplier S1.

i. Get supplier numbers for suppliers with a status lower than that of supplier S1.

j. Get supplier numbers for suppliers whose city is first in the alphabetic list of such cities.

k. Get part numbers for parts available from all suppliers in London.

l. Get supplier-number/part-number pairs such that the indicated supplier is not able to supply the indicated part.

m. Get all pairs of supplier numbers, Sx and Sy say, such that Sx and Sy are able to supply exactly the same set of parts as each other.

23. Here is a **Tutorial D** definition for a courses-and-students database:[16]

```
VAR COURSE RELATION
    { COURSE#   COURSE#,
      CNAME     NAME,
      AVAILABLE DATE }
    KEY { COURSE# } ;

VAR STUDENT RELATION
    { STUDENT#   STUDENT#,
      SNAME      NAME,
      REGISTERED DATE }
    KEY { STUDENT# } ;

VAR ENROLLMENT RELATION
    { COURSE#  COURSE#,
      STUDENT# STUDENT#,
      ENROLLED DATE }
    KEY { COURSE#, STUDENT# }
    FOREIGN KEY { COURSE# } REFERENCES COURSE
    FOREIGN KEY { STUDENT# } REFERENCES STUDENT ;
```

The predicates are as follows:

- COURSE: *Course COURSE#, named CNAME, has been available at the university since date AVAILABLE.*

---

16. Many exercises in subsequent chapters are based on this database or on some variant of it.

- STUDENT: *Student STUDENT#, named SNAME, registered with the university on date REGISTERED.*

- ENROLLMENT: *Student STUDENT# enrolled in course COURSE# on date ENROLLED.*

Selector operators COURSE# and STUDENT#, each of which takes a single argument (of type CHAR), are available for types COURSE# and STUDENT#, respectively.

a. Write an integrity constraint to express the fact that no student can be enrolled in a course prior to that course's becoming available or prior to that student's registering with the university.

b. Write a query to obtain student number and name for every student who is enrolled in all of the courses that student ST2 is enrolled in.

c. Consider this expression:
```
( ( STUDENT WHERE STUDENT# = STUDENT# ('ST1') ) JOIN COURSE )
                            WHERE AVAILABLE > REGISTERED
```

Write a predicate for the relation produced by this expression. If the expression were used to define a (virtual) relvar, what key(s) would that relvar have?

Chapter

2

AN OVERVIEW
OF TUTORIAL D

2.1 INTRODUCTION

NOTE: This chapter is based on material that previously appeared in reference [43], Chapter 5 (pages 59–79), copyright © 2000 Addison Wesley Longman, Inc. Reprinted by permission of Pearson Education, Inc.

Coding examples in this book are expressed in a language called **Tutorial D**—or, to be more precise, in a version of that language that has been simplified slightly for the purpose. Those examples should mostly be self-explanatory, but we offer in this chapter a brief description of the most important features of the language, to serve as a convenient reference. Please note, however, that the chapter is not meant to be either definitive or exhaustive: It omits many features that are irrelevant to the purpose at hand, and it simplifies several others. The definitive description of the language is that given in reference [43].

The bulk of what follows consists of a BNF grammar for the version of **Tutorial D** that we will be using in our examples. The grammar is defined by means of what is essentially standard BNF notation, except for certain extensions of our own that we now explain. Let *<xyz>* denote an arbitrary syntactic category (i.e., anything that appears on the left side of some BNF production rule):

- The expression *<xyz list>* denotes a sequence of zero or more *<xyz>*s in which each *<xyz>* is separated from the next (if there is a next) by at least one space.

- The expression *<xyz commalist>* denotes a sequence of zero or more *<xyz>*s in which each *<xyz>* is separated from the next (if there is a next) by a comma, as well as, optionally, one or more spaces either before or after the comma (or both).

- The expression *<ne xyz list>* (where *ne* stands for "nonempty") denotes an *<xyz list>* that contains at least one *<xyz>*.

- The expression *<ne xyz commalist>* is defined analogously.

A few more preliminary remarks:

- First, all syntactic categories of the form *<... name>* are defined to be *<identifier>*s. The category *<identifier>* in turn is terminal and is not further defined here.

- Second, some of the BNF production rules are accompanied by a prose explanation of (among other things) certain additional syntax rules or the corresponding semantics or both—but only in cases where such further explanation seems necessary.

- Third, braces "{" and "}" in the grammar stand for themselves; that is, they are symbols in the language being defined, not, as they usually are, symbols of the metalanguage. To be more specific, braces are used to enclose commalists of items when the commalist in question is intended to denote a *set* of some kind (implying in particular that (1) the order in which items appear within that commalist is immaterial, and further that (2) no item appears within that commalist more than once).

- Certain features of **Tutorial D** are deliberately omitted from the grammar that follows. Such features include

  - features that we regard as self-explanatory, such as IF ... END IF and CASE ... END CASE expressions and their IF ... END IF and CASE ... END CASE statement analogs

  - features used only in passing or only very much later in the book or both (we will explain the syntax and semantics of such features when we actually come to use them)

  - features specific to the type inheritance discussions in Chapter 16 (we will explain the syntax and semantics of such features in that chapter)

  - features explicitly added to the language in subsequent discussions in this book, such as the interval type generator introduced in Chapter 5 (of course, we will explain the syntax and semantics of such features when we introduce them)

2.2 Scalar Type Definitions

```
<scalar type def>
    ::=    TYPE <scalar type name> <ne possrep def list> ;

<possrep def>
    ::=    POSSREP [ <possrep name> ]
                 { <ne possrep component def commalist>
                           [ <possrep constraint def> ] }
```

The *<possrep name>* can be omitted if and only if the *<possrep def>* is the only one within the applicable *<scalar type def>*. A *<possrep name>* is assumed for such a *<possrep def>* that is identical to the corresponding *<scalar type name>*.

```
<possrep component def>
    ::=    <possrep component name> <type>

<possrep constraint def>
    ::=    CONSTRAINT <bool exp>
```

A *<bool exp>* is any expression that yields a truth value; in particular, we assume the usual boolean operators (AND, OR, NOT, etc.) and literals (TRUE and FALSE) are available for use in connection with such expressions. In the context at hand—within a *<possrep constraint def>*—a *<bool exp>* is not allowed to mention variables, but *<possrep component name>*s from the containing *<possrep def>* can be used to denote the corresponding components of the applicable possible representation of an arbitrary value of the scalar type in question. Note that since truth values are scalar values (as we saw in Chapter 1, type BOOLEAN is a scalar type), it follows that a *<bool exp>* is a special case of a *<scalar exp>*.

```
<relation comp>
    ::=    <relation exp> <relation comp op> <relation exp>
```

A *<relation comp>* ("relation comparison") is an important special case of a *<bool exp>*. The relations denoted by the two *<relation exp>*s must be of the same type.

```
<relation comp op>
    ::=    = | ≠ | ⊆ | ⊂ | ⊇ | ⊃
```

NOTE: The symbols "⊆" and "⊂" denote "subset of" and "proper subset of," respectively; the symbols "⊇" and "⊃" denote "superset of" and "proper superset of," respectively.

2.3 Relational Definitions

```
<relvar def>
    ::=    VAR <relvar name>
           RELATION { <attribute commalist> }
               <ne candidate key def list>
                   <foreign key def list> ;
```

Recall from Chapter 1 that the relvar defined by a given *<relvar def>* is said to have type—more precisely, relation type—RELATION {*A1 T1, A2 T2, ..., An Tn*}, where *A1 T1, A2 T2, ..., An Tn* are the *<attribute>*s specified in the *<attribute commalist>* within that *<relvar def>*. NOTE: For reasons explained in reference [43], **Tutorial D** deliberately does not provide an explicit "define relation type" operator. Instead, relation types can simply be *used* "inline," as it were, typically (as here) as part of a *<relvar def>*.

```
<attribute>
    ::=    <attribute name> <attribute type>
```

The *<attribute type>* can be any type, system-defined or user-defined. In particular, it can be a relation type (i.e., relation-valued attributes are permitted).

```
<candidate key def>
    ::=    KEY { <attribute name commalist> }
```

We use the unqualified keyword KEY to mean a candidate key specifically, for reasons of simplicity. Every relvar is required to have at least one candidate key. For reasons explained in reference [36], we do not insist that the relvar definer select one of those candidate keys and make it primary (meaning it is somehow "more equal than the others"), though we do often follow that practice, informally, in our own examples. Note that **Tutorial D** provides no syntax for specifying that some given candidate key has been chosen as the primary one.

```
<foreign key def>
    ::=    FOREIGN KEY { <foreign key component commalist> }
               REFERENCES <relvar name>
```

Let the *<foreign key component>*s, after any required attribute renamings have been done, specify that the attributes of the foreign key being defined are called *A1, A2, ..., An*. Then the relvar identified by *<relvar name>* must include a set of attributes called *A1, A2, ..., An,* and that set of attributes must have been defined as a candidate key for that relvar.

```
<foreign key component>
    ::=    <attribute name>
         | RENAME ( <ne renaming commalist> )
```

In the second format, the individual *<renaming>*s are executed in sequence as written. The parentheses can be omitted if the commalist contains just one *<renaming>*.

```
<renaming>
    ::=   <attribute name> AS <attribute name>
```

2.4 RELATIONAL EXPRESSIONS

```
<relation exp>
    ::=   <relvar name>
        | <relation selector inv>
        | <other relation op inv>
        | <with exp>
        | <introduced name>
        | ( <relation exp> )

<relation selector inv>
    ::=   RELATION [ { <attribute commalist> } ]
                    { <tuple selector inv commalist> }
```

Chapter 1 did not mention the point explicitly, but of course relation types have corresponding selectors, just as scalar types do. In our simplified version of **Tutorial D,** a relation selector invocation for relation type *RT* usually consists just of the keyword RELATION, followed by a commalist of *tuple* selector invocations enclosed in braces (the intervening *<attribute commalist>* and enclosing braces, which together specify the heading of relation type *RT,* are required only if the *<tuple selector inv commalist>* is empty). Each of those tuple selector invocations must select a tuple of type TUPLE{*H*}, where {*H*} is the heading of relation type *RT*. NOTE: We also permit TABLE_DEE and TABLE_DUM to be used as shorthand for the relation selector invocations RELATION{}{TUPLE{}} and RELATION{}{}, respectively. See Section 1.4 for further explanation.

```
<tuple selector inv>
    ::=   TUPLE { <tuple component commalist> }

<tuple component>
    ::=   <attribute name> <exp>
```

Of course, the specified attribute and the *<exp>* must be of the same type; in particular, if the specified attribute is of some *relation* type, then the *<exp>* must be, specifically, a *<relation exp>* of that same type. NOTE: For a detailed explanation of the syntax and semantics of *<exp>*s in general, see reference [43].

```
<other relation op inv>
    ::=   <project>
        | <nonproject>
```

We distinguish between *<project>*s and *<nonproject>*s merely for reasons of operator precedence (it is convenient to assign a high precedence to projection).

```
<project>
    ::=   <relation exp>
                    { [ ALL BUT ] <attribute name commalist> }
```

The *<relation exp>* must not be a *<nonproject>*.

```
<nonproject>
    ::=   <rename>
        | <where>
        | <union>
        | <intersect>
        | <minus>
        | <join>
        | <extend>
        | <summarize>
        | <group>
        | <ungroup>
```

```
<rename>
    ::=   <relation exp> RENAME ( <ne renaming commalist> )
```

The *<relation exp>* must not be a *<nonproject>*. The individual *<renaming>*s are executed in sequence as written. The parentheses can be omitted if the commalist contains just one *<renaming>*.

```
<where>
    ::=   <relation exp> WHERE <bool exp>
```

The *<relation exp>* must not be a *<nonproject>*. A *<bool exp>* is any expression that yields a truth value; in the context at hand, such expressions are allowed to include a reference to an attribute of the relation denoted by the *<relation exp>* wherever a literal of the appropriate type would be allowed (thus, e.g., S WHERE CITY = 'London' is a valid *<where>*). NOTE: The **Tutorial D** *<where>* operator corresponds to the generalized version of the restriction operator of relational algebra, as defined in Chapter 1.

```
<union>
    ::=   <relation exp> UNION <relation exp>
```

The *<relation exp>*s must not be *<nonproject>*s, except that either or both can be another *<union>*. They must denote relations of the same type.

```
<intersect>
    ::=    <relation exp> INTERSECT <relation exp>
```

The *<relation exp>*s must not be *<nonproject>*s, except that either or both can be another *<intersect>*. They must denote relations of the same type.

```
<minus>
    ::=    <relation exp> MINUS <relation exp>
```

The *<relation exp>*s must not be *<nonproject>*s. They must denote relations of the same type.

```
<join>
    ::=    <relation exp> JOIN <relation exp>
```

The *<relation exp>*s must not be *<nonproject>*s, except that either or both can be another *<join>*. NOTE: As pointed out in Chapter 1, if the relations denoted by those *<relation exp>*s have exactly the same attributes (and hence the same heading), the *<join>* degenerates to an *<intersect>;* if they have no attributes in common, it degenerates to a Cartesian product (as that term is normally understood in a relational context; see, e.g., reference [39]). **Tutorial D** provides special syntax for the former case but not for the latter.

```
<extend>
    ::=    EXTEND <relation exp>
               ADD ( <ne extend add commalist> )
```

The *<relation exp>* must not be a *<nonproject>*. The individual *<extend add>*s are executed in sequence as written. The parentheses can be omitted if the commalist contains just one *<extend add>*.

```
<extend add>
    ::=    <exp> AS <attribute name>
```

The *<exp>* is allowed to include a reference to an attribute of the relation being extended wherever a literal of the appropriate type would be allowed.

```
<summarize>
    ::=    SUMMARIZE <relation exp> PER <relation exp>
               ADD ( <ne summarize add commalist> )
```

The *<relation exp>*s must not be *<nonproject>*s. The individual *<summarize add>*s are executed in sequence as written. The parentheses can be omitted if the commalist contains just one *<summarize add>*.

```
<summarize add>
    ::=    <summary> AS <attribute name>

<summary>
    ::=    <summary spec> [ ( <scalar exp> ) ]
```

A *<scalar exp>* is any expression that yields a scalar value. (In particular, scalar-valued selector and THE_ operator invocations are *<scalar exp>*s, though they would hardly be likely to appear as the *<scalar exp>* in the context of a *<summary>* specifically.) In the context at hand, the *<scalar exp>* and enclosing parentheses can and must be omitted if and only if the *<summary spec>* is COUNT. The *<scalar exp>* is allowed to include a reference to an attribute of the relation being summarized wherever a literal of the appropriate type would be allowed.

```
<summary spec>
    ::=    COUNT | SUM | AVG | MAX | MIN | ALL | ANY
           | SUMD | AVGD
```

The "D" ("distinct") in SUMD and AVGD means that redundant duplicate values are to be eliminated before the summing or averaging is done.

```
<group>
    ::=    <relation exp>
           GROUP { [ ALL BUT ] <attribute name commalist> }
           AS <attribute name>
```

The <relation exp> must not be a <nonproject>.

```
<ungroup>
    ::=    <relation exp> UNGROUP <attribute name>
```

The *<relation exp>* must not be a *<nonproject>*. The attribute identified by the *<attribute name>* must be of some relation type.

```
<with exp>
    ::=    WITH <ne name intro commalist> : <exp>
```

The *<with exp>*s we are primarily concerned with in this book are relational expressions (which is why we are discussing them in the present section specifically). However, scalar and tuple *<with exp>*s are supported too; in fact, a given *<with exp>* is a relational expression, a tuple expression, or a scalar expression according as the *<exp>* following the colon is a relational expression, a tuple expression, or a scalar expression in turn. In all cases, the individual *<name intro>*s are executed in sequence as written, and the semantics of the *<with exp>* are defined to be the same as those of a version of *<exp>* in which each occurrence of each introduced name is replaced by the text of the corresponding expression. In general, of course, those replacement expressions might involve further occurrences of introduced names; the replacement process is therefore performed repeatedly until no such occurrences remain. (Examples of WITH expressions are given in Chapter 6 and several subsequent chapters. And in Chapter 14, we will discuss a WITH *statement,* which effectively allows introduced names to be used and reused across statements instead of just within an individual expression.)

```
<name intro>
    ::=    <exp> AS <introduced name>
```

The *<introduced name>* can be used within the containing *<with exp>* wherever the *<exp>* (enclosed in parentheses if necessary) would be allowed.

2.5 RELATIONAL ASSIGNMENTS

```
<relation assignment>
    ::=    <ne relation assign commalist> ;
```

Observe that a *<relation assignment>* in **Tutorial D** is a **multiple** assignment (in general).[1] The semantics are as follows: First, all of the source expressions on the right sides of the individual *<relation assign>*s are evaluated; second, all of the individual *<relation assign>*s are then executed in sequence as written. See Chapter 14, Section 14.4, for further discussion and several examples.

```
<relation assign>
    ::=    <relvar name> := <relation exp>
        |  <relation insert>
        |  <relation delete>
        |  <relation update>
```

In the first format, the relations denoted by the *<relvar name>* and the *<relation exp>* must be of the same type.

```
<relation insert>
    ::=    INSERT <relvar name> <relation exp>
```

---

1. In fact, all assignments in **Tutorial D** are multiple assignments, in general. A nonrelational example appeared in the definition of the update operator REFLECT in Chapter 1.

The relvar denoted by the *<relvar name>* and the relation denoted by the *<relation exp>* must be of the same type.

```
<relation delete>
    ::=   DELETE <relvar name> [ WHERE <bool exp> ]
```

The *<bool exp>* is allowed to include a reference to an attribute of the relvar denoted by the *<relvar name>* wherever a literal of the appropriate type would be allowed.

```
<relation update>
    ::=   UPDATE <relvar name> [ WHERE <bool exp> ]
                        { <ne attribute update commalist> }
```

The *<bool exp>* is allowed to include a reference to an attribute of the relvar denoted by the *<relvar name>* wherever a literal of the appropriate type would be allowed. "For each tuple to be updated"—speaking very loosely!—(1) all of the source expressions on the right sides of the individual *<attribute update>*s are evaluated; (2) all of the individual *<attribute update>*s are then executed in sequence as written. The braces can be omitted if the commalist contains just one *<attribute update>*.

```
<attribute update>
    ::=   <attribute name> := <exp>
```

The specified attribute and the *<exp>* must be of the same type; also, the *<exp>* is allowed to include a reference to an attribute of the relvar being updated wherever a literal of the appropriate type would be allowed.

2.6 CONSTRAINT DEFINITIONS

```
<constraint def>
    ::=   CONSTRAINT <constraint name> <bool exp> ;
```

The *<bool exp>* must not mention any variables other than relvars. In terms of the constraint classification scheme described in Chapter 1 (Section 1.6), **Tutorial D** *<constraint def>*s correspond to relvar and database constraints (only). NOTE: A special form of *<bool exp>*, IS_EMPTY (*<relation exp>*), which evaluates to true if the body of the relation denoted by *<relation exp>* is empty (i.e., contains no tuples) and false otherwise, is particularly useful in the context of a *<constraint def>*. See Chapter 1 for several examples.

EXERCISES

1. What do you understand by the terms *<xyz list>* and *<xyz commalist>?* What about *<ne xyz list>* and *<ne xyz commalist>?*

2. What is a *<bool exp>?*

3. What does the unqualified keyword KEY denote?

4. What is a relation selector?

5. Why do you think **Tutorial D** provides two formats for each of *<project>* and *<group>?*

6. What is SUMD?

7. Explain the term *multiple assignment.*

8. The operators INSERT, DELETE, and UPDATE are all really just shorthand: True or false?

9. What does the IS_EMPTY operator do?

Part II

LAYING THE FOUNDATIONS

The purpose of this part of the book is to explain basic temporal principles—that is, the basic concepts and fundamental theory underlying temporal data and databases. It consists of the following chapters (which, as stated in the preface, are *definitely* meant to be read in sequence as written):

3. Time and the Database

4. What Is the Problem?

5. Intervals

6. Operators on Intervals

7. The EXPAND and COLLAPSE Operators

8. The PACK and UNPACK Operators

9. Generalizing the Relational Operators

The titles give some idea as to the scope of each chapter. Further specifics are given in the body of Chapter 3, near the end of Section 3.1.

Chapter

3

Time and the Database

3.1 Introduction

A **temporal database** can be thought of, very loosely, as a database that contains histor-ical data instead of or in addition to current data. Such databases have been under active investigation since the early 1980s (possibly earlier). Some of those investigations have taken the extreme position that data in such a database, once inserted, should never be deleted or changed in any way, in which case the database can be thought of, again loosely, as containing historical data only. (Some *data warehouse* systems adopt this approach, at least to a first approximation [45].) Conventional databases, by con-trast, are typically at the other extreme; such a database typically contains current data only, and data in such a database is changed or deleted as soon as the propositions rep-resented by that data cease to be ones that evaluate to true. In what follows, we will occasionally refer to such a database explicitly as **nontemporal,** in order to emphasize the fact that it contains current data only.

(As an aside, we note that nontemporal databases are sometimes called *snapshot* databases in the literature. We do not care for this term, however, because "snapshot" has been much used in the past—and still is used—to refer to the database as it appears or appeared at some specific point in time; in other words, the term can very reasonably be, and is, applied to *any* database, temporal or nontemporal.)

The suppliers-and-shipments database of Chapter 1 is a nontemporal database in the foregoing sense. Consider Figure 1.1 once again, which shows a set of sample values for that database. That figure indicates among other things that the status of supplier S1 is currently 20. By contrast, a temporal version of that database might indicate not only that the status of that supplier is currently 20, but also that it has been 20 ever since July 1st last year, and perhaps that it was 15 from April 5th to June 30th last year, and so on.

The propositions in a nontemporal database are generally taken to be true "now"—that is, at the time the database is inspected. In fact, even if they are thought of as being true at some time other than "now," it makes no material difference to the way the data is managed and used. As we will see over the next several chapters, however, the way the data is managed and used in a temporal database differs in a variety of important ways from the way it is managed and used in a nontemporal one (a fact that accounts for the existence of this book, of course).

Now, the distinguishing feature of a temporal database is, obviously enough, time itself. Temporal database research has therefore involved a certain amount of investigation into the nature of time itself. Here are some of the questions that have been explored:

- Does time have a beginning or an end?

- Is time a continuum or is it divided into discrete quanta?

- What is the best way to characterize the important concept "now" (sometimes known as "the moving point now")?

But these questions, interesting though they might be, are not intrinsically database questions as such, and we therefore do not delve very deeply into them in this book; instead, we simply make what we hope are reasonable assumptions at appropriate points as we proceed. This approach allows us to concentrate on matters that are more directly relevant to our overall aim. However, we note that parts of that temporal research do possess certain interesting generalizations; that is, ideas developed originally or primarily to support temporal data specifically have been found to have application in other important areas as well. We will touch on this point again from time to time in subsequent chapters.

Out of all that research, the ideas we focus on in this book represent what we regard—naturally enough, since the ideas in question are due primarily to one of the authors (Lorentzos)—as the most satisfactory and the most promising part.[1] What do we mean when we say "most promising"? Well, it is a fact that the research community has been divided for some time over the best way to address the temporal database problem. In a nutshell:

- Some researchers have proposed a very specialized approach to the problem, one that treats temporal data as special and involves some departure from relational principles.

- Others—the present authors included—have favored an approach that most definitely does not depart from those same relational principles but treats temporal data (as far as possible) just like data of any other kind.

---

1. Be warned, however, that over questions of nomenclature and similar matters we depart (quite extensively, in fact) from previous publications by Lorentzos on the same subject.

The "departure from relational principles" in question consists in representing time-stamps—to be discussed in the next section—not by means of attributes in relations in the usual way, but rather by means of what might be thought of as *hidden attributes* instead. We believe such a scheme is unwise. (The attributes are hidden in the sense that they are not directly visible to the user in the usual way; in particular, they cannot be referenced by simple names in the usual way.) Indeed, it is clear that "hidden attributes" are not true relational attributes, "relations" that contain such "attributes" are not true relations, and the overall approach constitutes a clear violation of Codd's *Information Principle.* Some of the consequences of such violation are explored in reference [107].

We should warn you, however, that few if any of the ideas we describe have yet been implemented in any commercial DBMS. Possible reasons for this state of affairs include the following:

- It was not until the 1990s that disk storage became cheap enough to make the keeping of large volumes of historical data a practical possibility. Precisely because it is now a practical possibility, however, data warehouses have recently become widespread, as is well known [45]. As a direct consequence of this fact, users have increasingly begun to find themselves faced with temporal database problems, and they have begun to need solutions to those problems.

- Although features analogous to most of those we describe have in fact been implemented, at least in prototype form, their incorporation into existing products—especially SQL products, where SQL's departures from the relational model will have to be catered for—is likely to prove a daunting prospect. Besides, DBMS vendors typically have their hands full at the time of writing with attempts to support the World Wide Web and "e-business," attempts to provide "object/relational" support, and other such matters.

Now, if data in general can be regarded as an encoded representation of propositions, then temporal data in particular can be regarded as an encoded representation of **time-stamped** propositions—by which we mean propositions that involve one or more arguments of some timestamp type. It follows that in a temporal database (under the extreme interpretation of that term, according to which *all* of the data is temporal), every proposition is timestamped in the foregoing sense. We might therefore define a **temporal relation** to be one in which each tuple includes at least one timestamp (i.e., the relation heading contains at least one attribute of some timestamp type). We might further define a **temporal relvar** to be one whose heading is that of some temporal relation. Finally, we might define a **temporal database** to be one in which all of the relvars are temporal ones. (We are being deliberately vague here as to what the timestamps we are talking about might look like in actual practice. We will take up this issue in the next couple of chapters.)

Having just offered a reasonably precise definition of the concept "temporal database" (in its extreme form), we now dismiss that definition as not very useful! We dismiss it because even if the original relvars in the database are all temporal, many relations that can be derived from that database will *not* be temporal in the foregoing sense. For example, the answer to the query "Get the names of all employees we have ever hired" might be obtained from some temporal database, but the result is not itself a temporal relation. And it would be a strange DBMS indeed—certainly not a relational one—that would let us obtain results that could not themselves be kept in the database.

From this point forward, therefore, we take a temporal database to be one that does include some temporal data but is not necessarily limited to such data. The next few chapters discuss such databases in detail. The plan for those chapters is as follows:

- The remainder of the present chapter and Chapter 4 together set the scene for subsequent chapters. In particular, Chapter 4 shows why temporal data seems to require special treatment.

- Chapter 5 introduces *intervals* as a convenient basis for timestamping certain kinds of data (i.e., as a basis for defining what we have been referring to in the last few paragraphs as "timestamp types").

- Chapters 6 and 7 then discuss a variety of operators for dealing with such intervals and sets containing such intervals.

- Finally, Chapters 8 and 9 introduce some important new operators for dealing with relations with interval-valued attributes.

By the way, it is important to understand that—with just one exception, the *interval type generator* introduced in Chapter 5, along with its associated operators—all of the new constructs to be discussed in Parts II and III of this book are essentially just shorthand. That is, they can all be expressed (albeit only very longwindedly, in most cases) in terms of features already available in a relationally complete language such as **Tutorial D**. In other words, the approach to temporal databases that we advocate involves *no* changes to the classical relational model!—though it does involve certain generalizations, as we will see in Chapter 9 and subsequent chapters, and (as already indicated) it does also involve the introduction of a new *type generator*. With regard to this latter point, however, we note that in any case the question as to which types and type generators are supported is essentially orthogonal to the question of support for the relational model itself [43]. The relational model merely requires that *some* types be available, in order that relations might be defined over them; nowhere does it prescribe exactly what types have to be supported.[2]

3.2 TIMESTAMPED PROPOSITIONS

We are now in a position to begin our investigation into some of the issues surrounding temporal databases. We start by appealing to the way people typically express timestamped propositions in natural language. Here are three examples (labeled *T1, T2,* and *T3* for purposes of subsequent reference):

---

2. Except of course for the scalar type BOOLEAN and the type generator RELATION, both of which must be supported for obvious reasons. See Chapter 1, Section 1.8.

T1: Supplier S1 was appointed—that is, placed under contract—**on** July 1st, 1999.

T2: Supplier S1 has been under contract **since** July 1st, 1999.

T3: Supplier S1 was under contract **during** the interval from July 1st, 1999, to the present day.

Each of these three propositions represents a possible interpretation for a tuple that looks like this:

S#	FROM
S1	July 1st, 1999

(As you can see, the tuple has two attributes, S# and FROM, with values the supplier number S1 and the timestamp July 1st, 1999, respectively.) Moreover, any of the three interpretations might be appropriate of this tuple if it appeared in some database representing the current state of affairs in some enterprise. The boldface prepositions **on, since,** and **during** characterize the three interpretations. N O T E : We are using the terms *since* and *during* here in the strong senses of "**ever** since" and "**throughout** (the interval in question)," respectively.

Now, although we have mentioned three possible interpretations, it might be argued that propositions *T1, T2,* and *T3* are really all saying the same thing in slightly different ways. Indeed, we do take *T2* and *T3* to be equivalent, but not *T1* and *T2* (or *T1* and *T3*). For consider:

- *T1* clearly implies that supplier S1 was not under contract on the date (June 30th, 1999) immediately preceding the specified appointment date;[3] *T2* neither states that fact nor implies it.

- Suppose today ("the present day") is May 1st, 2000. Then *T2* clearly states that supplier S1 was under contract on every day from July 1st, 1999, to May 1st, 2000, inclusive; *T1* neither states *that* fact, nor implies it.

Thus, neither of *T1* and *T2* implies the other, and they are certainly not equivalent.

That said, tuples in conventional databases often do include things like "date of appointment," and propositions like *T2* (or *T3*) often are the intended interpretation. If such is the case here, however (i.e., if *T1* is meant to be equivalent to *T2* and *T3* after all), then the present formulation is not quite adequate to the task. We can improve it by rephrasing it thus:

---

3. Or, at least, such would be the normal interpretation. But natural language is so often imprecise! The appointment on July 1st might have been a renewal, and supplier S1 might have been under contract on June 30th after all. For the sake of the present discussion, we assume the normal interpretation is the correct one.

T1: Supplier S1 was most recently appointed on July 1st, 1999, and the contract has not subsequently been terminated.

What is more, if this version of *T1* really is what our hypothetical 2-tuple is supposed to mean, then *T2* in its present form is not adequate either—it needs to be rephrased thus:

T2: Supplier S1 was not under contract on June 30th, 1999, but has been so ever since July 1st, 1999.

Of course, *T3* needs an analogous clarification:

T3: Supplier S1 was not under contract on June 30th, 1999, but has been so during the interval from July 1st, 1999, to the present day.

Observe now that *T1* expresses a time **at** which a certain event took place, while *T2* and *T3* express an interval of time **during** which a certain state persisted. We have deliberately chosen an example in which a certain *state* might be inferred from information regarding a certain *event:* Since the event—the most recent appointment of supplier S1—occurred on July 1st, 1999 (and the contract has not subsequently been terminated), that supplier has been in the state of being under contract from that date to the present day. Conventional database technology can handle time instants (times at which events occur) reasonably well; however, it cannot handle time intervals (intervals of time during which states persist) very well at all, as we will see in the next chapter.

As an aside, we note that events from which states cannot be inferred are not very interesting from the viewpoint of temporal data in general. For example, the statement "Lightning struck at 2:30 PM last Tuesday" is certainly a timestamped proposition, but—from the viewpoint of temporal data in general, at least—it is not a very interesting one. To be more specific, the timestamp in this example has almost none of the special properties, and displays almost none of the special kinds of behavior, that apply to temporal data in general. For this reason, we will have very little to say from this point forward regarding propositions like the one in the lightning example.

To return to propositions *T1, T2,* and *T3:* Observe now that, although *T2* and *T3* are logically equivalent, they are significantly *different in form;* that is, the predicates of which they are instantiations are significantly different. To be specific, *T3* explicitly refers to a time *interval* (with a specific begin point and end point), while *T2* refers only to a specific time *instant.* As a consequence, the form of *T2* cannot be used for historical records, while that of *T3* can—provided, of course, that we replace the phrase "the present day" in that proposition by some explicit date, say May 1st, 2000.[4] (Of course, *T3* would then correspond to a 3-tuple, not a 2-tuple.) The corresponding predicates look something like this:

---

4. These remarks are based on the empirical observation that most interesting historical records do involve intervals, not instants (see the lightning example once again).

T2: Supplier S*x* has been under contract since date *d*.

T3: Supplier S*x* was under contract during the interval from date *b* to date *e*.

(For simplicity, we ignore for the moment the various clarifications discussed earlier, although those clarifications would certainly be needed in practice. See the remarks on this subject at the very end of this chapter.)

We conclude from the foregoing that the concept of "during" is very important for historical records. Indeed, that concept pervades the next few chapters, as we will soon see.[5]

We close this section by noting that, despite our repeated use of terms such as "historical data" and "historical records," temporal databases might quite reasonably contain information regarding the future as well as the past. For example, we might wish to document the fact that supplier S1 *will be* under contract during the interval from date *b* to date *e,* where *e* is a date in the future (and *b* might be as well). Thus, we will take the term *temporal* to include the future in this way throughout this book, barring explicit statements to the contrary. We will also offer some specific comments regarding the possibility of recording information about the future at suitable points in the text.

3.3 VALID TIME VERSUS TRANSACTION TIME

In a conventional (i.e., nontemporal) database, anything can be updated, barring explicit constraints to the contrary. But if *historical* data can be updated, we find ourselves faced with the possibility that, apparently, history can be changed! What of this possibility?

Well, it is important to understand that the database does not contain "the real world," it contains only our *knowledge of* or *beliefs about* the real world.[6] And while it is perfectly reasonable to assert that the past is immutable and history as such can never change, it is equally reasonable to assert that our beliefs about it *can* change (indeed, they often do). In a database context, therefore, when we speak of "updating history," what we really mean is updating our *beliefs about* history, not updating history as such—though the distinction is often blurred, and even confused, in informal contexts, as you might imagine.

In the temporal database literature, the terms *valid time* and *transaction time* are used in an attempt to get at the foregoing distinction [87]. Because the meanings of these terms can hardly be said to "leap off the page," we will not be using them much in the chapters to come; however, the distinction per se is important, and it does merit some discussion. So consider the following simple example. Let *p* be the proposition "Supplier S1 was under contract." Suppose it is our current understanding that this

---

5. Perhaps we might describe those chapters as an investigation into the possibility of building a During Machine …

6. More precisely, it contains a *representation* of those beliefs. For simplicity, we will talk throughout this book as if the database (and relations in the database) contained not just representations of information but information per se, though we freely admit that such talk is more than a little loose.

state of affairs obtained from July 1st, 1999, to May 1st, 2000, and we therefore insert the following tuple into the database:

S#	FROM	TO
S1	July 1st, 1999	May 1st, 2000

Note very carefully that this tuple does *not* correspond to proposition *p*. Rather, it corresponds to what might be called a *timestamped extension* of proposition *p* that can be stated thus: "Supplier S1 was under contract *from July 1st, 1999, to May 1st, 2000.*" And the literature would refer to the timestamp here—the interval from July 1st, 1999, to May 1st, 2000—as the **valid time** for the original proposition *p*. Thus, the valid time for *p* in this example is the interval of time during which (according to our current beliefs) *p* was in fact true. NOTE: We are assuming for simplicity that the specified interval (from July 1st, 1999, to May 1st, 2000) is the *only* valid time for *p*. More generally, the valid time for a given proposition is a *set* of intervals, not just a single interval. For example, if it is our understanding that supplier S1 was also under contract previously from January 1st, 1998, to April 1st, 1998, then the relevant valid time would clearly involve two intervals, not just one. But we will assume for simplicity throughout the remainder of this section that valid times are indeed just single intervals.

Suppose we now learn that supplier S1's contract in fact began on June 1st, not July 1st, and we therefore replace the original tuple by one that looks like this:

S#	FROM	TO
S1	June 1st, 1999	May 1st, 2000

This change has no effect on proposition *p* as such, of course—it merely changes the associated timestamp (i.e., it reflects our revised understanding that supplier S1 was in fact under contract from June 1st, 1999, to May 1st, 2000). Thus, the valid time for proposition *p* is now the interval from June 1st, 1999, to May 1st, 2000. In other words, we have just "updated our belief about history." What we have certainly not done, however, is update history as such; the update we have just performed does not and cannot change the historical fact that the database previously showed supplier S1 as under contract from July (not June) 1st, 1999.

Finally, suppose we discover that a mistake has been made and supplier S1 was never under contract at all. We therefore delete the tuple for supplier S1 entirely. Proposition *p* is now known to be false; as a consequence, there is now no valid time associated with it at all. (Equivalently, we could say that the valid time is now an *empty* set of intervals.)

Now suppose the original tuple was inserted at time *t1* and replaced at time *t2*, and that replacement tuple was then deleted at time *t3*. Then the literature would say that the interval from *t1* to *t2* was the **transaction time**, not for proposition *p* as such, but rather for the *timestamped extension* of *p* with "valid-time timestamp" July 1st, 1999, to May 1st, 2000. That is, the interval from *t1* to *t2* is the time during which the database asserted that this particular timestamped extension of *p* was true. Likewise, the literature would also say that the interval from *t2* to *t3* was the transaction time for the timestamped extension of *p* with valid-time timestamp June 1st, 1999, to May 1st, 2000; that is, the interval from *t2* to *t3* is the time during which the database asserted that *that* particular timestamped extension of *p* was true.[7] NOTE: Again we are simplifying matters somewhat; in general, transaction times (like valid times) are sets of intervals, not just individual intervals per se. For example, if the database additionally showed the first of the foregoing timestamped extensions of *p* as being true during the interval from *t4* to *t5*, then the relevant transaction time would clearly involve two intervals, not just one.

We will have a great deal more to say about the foregoing concepts in Chapter 15. Until then, it is sufficient to stress the point that—as our examples have suggested— *valid times can be updated, but transaction times cannot.* (Valid times reflect our beliefs about history, and those beliefs can change; transaction times, by contrast, reflect history as such, and history cannot change. Indeed, transaction times are managed by the system, not by some human user.) Largely for such reasons, all of our discussions from this point forward will concern themselves with valid times only (and what is more, they will do so *implicitly,* for the most part), until we get to Chapter 15.

3.4 SOME FUNDAMENTAL QUESTIONS

The references in previous sections of this chapter to intervals of time tacitly introduce a simple but fundamental idea: namely, the idea that an interval with begin time *b* and end time *e* can be thought of as *the set of all times t such that* $b \leq t \leq e$ (where "<" means "earlier than," of course). Though "obvious," this simple notion has numerous far-reaching consequences, as we will see in the chapters to come. It also leads directly to a series of fairly fundamental questions! Indeed, some of those questions might have occurred to you already. Regardless of whether they did so or not, we now raise them explicitly ourselves and try to answer them.

1. Does not the expression "all times *t* such that $b \leq t \leq e$" raise the specter of infinite sets and all of the conceptual and computational difficulties such sets suffer from?

   ANSWER: Well, yes, it does appear to, but we dismiss the specter and circumvent the difficulties by adopting the assumption that the "timeline" consists of a finite sequence of discrete, indivisible *time quanta* (where a time quantum is the smallest time unit the system is capable of representing). The interval with begin time *b* and end time *e* thus involves a finite number of such quanta, *a fortiori.*

---

7. As you will surely realize, the transaction time for the first of these two timestamped extensions of *p* is not exactly the interval from *t1* to *t2* but, rather, the interval from *t1* to "just before" *t2* (and similarly for the second). We ignore such niceties here for simplicity.

NOTE: Much of the literature refers to a time quantum as a *chronon*. However, it then typically goes on to define a chronon as an *interval* (see, e.g., reference [53]), implying that chronons have a begin point and an end point, and perhaps further points in between, and so are not indivisible after all. (What exactly are those various "points" in such an interval? What else can they be but chronons?) We find some confusion here and therefore choose to avoid the term.

2. Propositions *T1*, *T2*, and *T3* from Section 3.2 seem to assume that time quanta are *days*, but surely the system supports time units down to tiny fractions of a second. If S1 was a supplier on July 1st, 1999, but not on June 30th, 1999, what is to be done about the presumed interval of time from the beginning of the day July 1st, 1999, up to the very instant of appointment, during which S1 was still not officially under contract?

ANSWER: We need to distinguish carefully between time quanta as such, which are the smallest time units the system is capable of representing, and the time units that are relevant for some particular purpose, which might be days or months or milliseconds (etc., etc.). We call these latter units **time points** (or just *points* for short) in order to stress the fact that *for the purpose at hand* they too are considered to be indivisible. Now, we might say, informally, that a time point is "a section of the timeline"—in other words, the set of time quanta—that stretches from one "boundary" quantum to the next (e.g., from midnight on one day to midnight on the next). We might therefore say, again informally, that time points have a duration (one day, in the example). Formally, however, time points are indeed points—they are indivisible, and the concept of duration strictly does not apply.

NOTE: Much of the literature uses the term *granule* to refer to something like a time point as just defined (see, e.g., reference [6]). As with the term *chronon*, however, it then typically goes on (unfortunately) to say that a granule is an *interval*. We therefore choose to avoid the term *granule* also.[8] We do, however, sometimes make informal use of the term **granularity,** which refers to the "size" or duration of the applicable time point, or equivalently to the "size" or duration of the gap between adjacent points. Thus, we might say in our example that the granularity is one day, meaning that we are casting aside (in this context) our usual notion of a day being made up of hours, which are made up of minutes, and so on. Such notions can be expressed only by recourse to finer levels of granularity.

By the way, the term *granularity* tends to suggest that all points and gaps are the same size. This assumption is not necessarily valid when we extend our temporal ideas to nontemporal data; in fact, it is not always valid for temporal data, either (for example, different months are of different duration). See Chapter 16 for further discussion.

---

8. It seems to us that the confusion over whether chronons and granules are intervals stems from a confusion over intuition vs. formalism. An intuitive belief about the way the world works is one thing; a formal model is something else entirely. In particular, we might *believe* the timeline is continuous and infinite, but we nevertheless *model* it for computing purposes as discrete and finite.

3. Given, then, that the timeline can be regarded (for some specific purpose) as a finite sequence of time points, we can refer unambiguously to the time point immediately succeeding or preceding any given point. Is that right?

ANSWER: Yes, up to a point—the point in question being, of course, the end of time! And down to a point, too—the beginning of time. As far as we are concerned, the beginning of time is a time point that has no predecessor (it might perhaps correspond to cosmologists' best estimate of the very moment of the putative Big Bang), and the end of time is a time point that has no successor. (To repeat, the timeline is a *finite* sequence of points.)

NOTE: In Chapter 16, we will briefly consider the possibility of a "timeline" that is *cyclic* and thus has no beginning and no end. Throughout the rest of the book, however, we will assume that time does indeed have a beginning and an end.

4. If some relation includes a 3-tuple representing the fact that supplier S1 was under contract from July 1st, 1999, to May 1st, 2000, does not the Closed World Assumption demand that the same relation also include, for example, a 3-tuple representing the fact that supplier S1 was under contract from July 2nd, 1999, to April 30th, 2000, and a whole host of additional 3-tuples representing other trivial consequences of the original 3-tuple?

ANSWER: Good point! Clearly, we need a more constraining predicate as our general interpretation of such 3-tuples:

Supplier Sx was under contract on every day from date b to date e, but not on the day immediately before b, nor on the day immediately after e.

This more constraining interpretation, in its general form, provides the motivation and basis for many of the constructs we introduce and describe in the next few chapters.

NOTE: Such more constraining interpretations also mean we need to tighten up our use of the terms *since* and *during* once again. To be specific, henceforth we take *since* to mean "**ever since and not immediately before** (the point in question)," and *during* to mean "**throughout and not immediately before or immediately after** (the interval in question)"—barring explicit statements to the contrary in both cases, of course.

We close this section (and this chapter) with some final remarks regarding the running example. To be specific, from this point forward we assume, realistically enough, that:

1. No supplier can end one contract on one day and begin another on the very next day.

2. No supplier can be under two distinct contracts at the same time.

3. Supplier contracts can be open-ended—that is, a supplier can be currently under contract and the end date for that contract can be currently unknown.

1. What is a timestamped proposition? Give some examples.

2. Distinguish between "valid time" and "transaction time."

3. What is a time quantum? What is a time point?

4. What do you understand by the term *granularity*?

5. What do you understand by the terms *beginning of time* and *end of time*?

Chapter

4

WHAT IS THE PROBLEM?

4.1 INTRODUCTION

In this chapter, we use the suppliers-and-shipments database as a basis for illustrating some of the problems that arise when we try to add temporal features to a conventional (i.e., nontemporal) database. We deliberately add those temporal features in a piece-meal fashion.

Actually, the first change we introduce is not a temporal one at all (nor is it an addition); rather, it is a matter of simplification. To be specific, we simplify relvar S, the suppliers relvar, by dropping all of the attributes except attribute S#. The predicate for this revised—and dramatically simplified!—relvar is just:

Supplier S# is currently under contract.

Figure 4.1, which is based on Figure 1.1, shows a set of sample values for the database after this simplification. As already indicated, this revised database is still a purely conventional one—it involves no temporal aspects at all, as yet. NOTE: For ease of reference, Figure 4.1 is repeated in Endpaper Panel 1 at the front of the book.

FIGURE 4.1

Simplified suppliers-and-shipments database— sample values.

S

S#
S1
S2
S3
S4
S5

SP

S#	P#
S1	P1
S1	P2
S1	P3
S1	P4
S1	P5
S1	P6
S2	P1
S2	P2
S3	P2
S4	P2
S4	P4
S4	P5

Now, you might be thinking the simplified database of Figure 4.1 is much *too* simple. However, it is perfectly adequate as a basis for illustrating almost all of the points we want to make in this part of the book, and we will stay with it until further notice. In fact, *not* simplifying the database in the manner indicated would lead to problems that we do not wish to get into at this juncture.

We now proceed to consider some simple constraints and queries against this revised database. In the next two sections (also in the next chapter, to some extent), we will see what happens to those constraints and queries when the database is extended to incorporate various temporal features.

Constraints (original database): The only constraints we want to consider here are the various *key* constraints. Just to remind you, {S#} and {S#,P#} are the primary keys for relvars S and SP, respectively, and {S#} is a foreign key in SP that references the primary key of S. NOTE: In terms of the classification scheme described in Chapter 1 (Section 1.6), the primary key constraints are both *relvar* constraints and the foreign key constraint is a *database* constraint.

Queries (original database): We consider just two queries, both of them very simple:

- **Query A:** Get supplier numbers for suppliers who are currently able to supply at least one part.

   Here is a **Tutorial D** formulation of this query:

   SP { S# }

- **Query B:** Get supplier numbers for suppliers who are currently unable to supply any parts at all.

Tutorial D formulation:

```
S { S# } MINUS SP { S# }
```

Observe that Query A involves a simple projection and Query B involves the difference between two such projections.[1] When we get to consider temporal analogs of these two queries in Chapter 8, we will find that they involve "temporal" analogs of these two operators—and you will probably not be surprised to learn in Chapter 9 that temporal analogs of other relational operators can be defined as well.

4.2 "SEMITEMPORALIZING" SUPPLIERS AND SHIPMENTS

To repeat, we want to proceed gently and make our temporal revisions to the suppliers-and-shipments database in a piecemeal fashion. The first such revision involves "semitemporalizing" (so to speak) relvars S and SP by adding a timestamp attribute, SINCE, to each and renaming the two relvars accordingly. See Figure 4.2 (repeated in Endpaper Panel 2 at the front of the book).

FIGURE 4.2

Suppliers-and-shipments database (semitemporal version)—sample values.

S_SINCE

S#	SINCE
S1	d04
S2	d07
S3	d03
S4	d04
S5	d02

SP_SINCE

S#	P#	SINCE
S1	P1	d04
S1	P2	d05
S1	P3	d09
S1	P4	d05
S1	P5	d04
S1	P6	d06
S2	P1	d08
S2	P2	d09
S3	P2	d08
S4	P2	d06
S4	P4	d04
S4	P5	d05

For simplicity, we do not show real timestamps in Figure 4.2; instead, we use symbols of the form *d01, d02,* and so forth, where the *d* can conveniently be pronounced "day," a convention to which we adhere throughout the book. (Most examples in the

---

1. In the case of Query B, the first projection is actually an *identity* projection (the expression "S{S#}" is logically equivalent to just "S"). We show it as an explicit projection for reasons of clarity.

next few chapters use time points that are days specifically; the applicable granularity in all of those examples is thus one day.) We assume that day 1 immediately precedes day 2, day 2 immediately precedes day 3, and so on; also, we drop insignificant leading zeros from expressions such as "day 1" (as you can see).

The predicate for relvar S_SINCE is:

Ever since day SINCE (and not on the day immediately before day SINCE), supplier S# has been under contract.

And the predicate for relvar SP_SINCE is:

Ever since day SINCE (and not on the day immediately before day SINCE), supplier S# has been able to supply part P#.

NOTE: We are deliberately spelling these predicates out fairly precisely here, just to remind you of the need to be careful when stating intended interpretations. We will not always bother to be quite so precise, however, appealing instead for the most part to our tightened-up definitions of the terms *since* and *during* as explained at the very end of Chapter 3.

Constraints (semitemporal database): The primary and foreign keys for the semitemporal database of Figure 4.2 are the same as they were for the original database of Figure 4.1. Hence, the relvar definitions might look as follows, in **Tutorial D**. Note that we have defined the two SINCE attributes to be of type DATE, which represents (let us assume) Gregorian dates—by which we mean dates that are accurate to the day and are constrained by the rules of the Gregorian calendar (implying among other things that, e.g., "April 31st, 2005" and "February 29th, 2100" are not valid dates).

```
VAR S_SINCE RELATION { S# S#, SINCE DATE }
    KEY { S# } ;

VAR SP_SINCE RELATION { S# S#, P# P#, SINCE DATE }
    KEY { S#, P# }
    FOREIGN KEY { S# } REFERENCES S_SINCE ;
```

However, we need an additional constraint, over and above the foreign key constraint from SP_SINCE to S_SINCE, to express the fact that no supplier can supply any part before that supplier is placed under contract:

```
CONSTRAINT XST1    /* "extra semitemporal constraint no. 1" */
    IS_EMPTY ( ( ( S_SINCE  RENAME SINCE AS SS  ) JOIN
                 ( SP_SINCE RENAME SINCE AS SPS ) )
               WHERE SPS < SS ) ;
```

The intuition behind this formulation is that if tuple *sp* in SP_SINCE references tuple *s* in S_SINCE, then the SINCE value in *sp* must not be less than that in *s*. We observe that, given a semitemporal database like that of Figure 4.2, we will probably have to state many constraints of the same general and rather cumbersome nature as Constraint XST1, and we will soon begin to wish we had some convenient shorthand for the purpose.

Queries (semitemporal database): We now consider semitemporal analogs of Queries A and B.

- **Query A:** Get supplier numbers for suppliers who are currently able to supply at least one part, showing in each case the date since when they have been able to do so.

If supplier S*x* is currently able to supply several different parts, then S*x* has been able to supply at least one part since the earliest SINCE date shown for S*x* in relvar SP_SINCE (e.g., if S*x* is S1, then the earliest SINCE date is *d04*). Here then is a **Tutorial D** formulation of the query:

```
SUMMARIZE SP PER SP { S# } ADD MIN ( SINCE ) AS SINCE
```

The result looks like this:

S#	SINCE
S1	*d04*
S2	*d08*
S3	*d08*
S4	*d04*

- **Query B:** Get supplier numbers for suppliers who are currently unable to supply any parts at all, showing in each case the date since when they have been unable to do so.

In our sample data there is just one supplier—namely, supplier S5—who is currently unable to supply any parts at all. However, we cannot discover the date since when S5 has been unable to supply any parts, because there is insufficient information in the database; to say it again, the database is still only *semi*temporal. For example, suppose the current day is day 10. Then it might be the case that S5 was able to supply at least one part from as early as day 2, when S5 was first placed under contract, right up to as late as day 9; or, going to the other extreme, it might be the case that S5 has never been able to supply anything at all.

In order to have any hope of answering Query B, we must complete the "temporalizing" of our database, or at least the SP portion of it. To be more precise, we must keep *historical records* in the database that show which suppliers were able to supply which parts when.

4.3 Fully Temporalizing Suppliers and Shipments

Figure 4.3 (repeated in Endpaper Panel 3 at the front of the book) shows a "fully temporalized" version of suppliers and shipments. Observe that the SINCE attributes have become FROM attributes, and each relvar has acquired an additional timestamp attribute called TO (and for that reason we have replaced _SINCE by _FROM_TO in the relvar names). The FROM and TO attributes together express the notion of an interval of time during which (according to our current beliefs) some proposition was true. NOTE: We have assumed for definiteness that "today" is day 10, and so we have shown *d10* as the TO value for each tuple that pertains to the current state of affairs. However, that assumption might—and indeed should!—immediately lead you to wonder what mechanism could cause all of those *d10*'s to be replaced by *d11*'s on the stroke of midnight, as it were, on day 10. Unfortunately, we will have to set this issue aside for the time being. We will return to it in Chapter 10.

FIGURE 4.3

Suppliers-and-shipments database (first fully temporal version, using explicit FROM and TO attributes)—sample values.

S_FROM_TO

S#	FROM	TO
S1	d04	d10
S2	d02	d04
S2	d07	d10
S3	d03	d10
S4	d04	d10
S5	d02	d10

SP_FROM_TO

S#	P#	FROM	TO
S1	P1	d04	d10
S1	P2	d05	d10
S1	P3	d09	d10
S1	P4	d05	d10
S1	P5	d04	d10
S1	P6	d06	d10
S2	P1	d02	d04
S2	P1	d08	d10
S2	P2	d03	d03
S2	P2	d09	d10
S3	P2	d08	d10
S4	P2	d06	d09
S4	P4	d04	d08
S4	P5	d05	d10

Because we are now keeping historical records, there are more tuples in this database than there were in either of its predecessors, as you can see. In fact, the fully temporal database of Figure 4.3 includes all of the information from the semitemporal one of Figure 4.2—except that, purely for the sake of the example, we have shown the TO value for two of supplier S4's shipments as a date prior to the current date (i.e., we have converted those two shipments from "current" to "historical" information). That fully temporal database also includes historical information concerning an earlier interval of time, from *d02* to *d04*, during which supplier S2 was previously under contract and able to supply certain parts. The predicate for relvar S_FROM_TO is:

From day FROM (and not on the day immediately before FROM) to day TO (and not on the day immediately after TO), inclusive, supplier S# was under contract.

The predicate for relvar SP_FROM_TO is:

From day FROM (and not on the day immediately before FROM) to day TO (and not on the day immediately after TO), inclusive, supplier S# was able to supply part P#.

NOTE: We will occasionally refer to this version of suppliers and shipments, with explicit FROM and TO attributes, as the *first* fully temporal version, because we will be discussing a second fully temporal version in the next chapter. That second (and superior) version will use intervals instead of explicit FROM and TO values for timestamping tuples.

Constraints (first fully temporal database): First of all, we need to guard against the absurdity of a FROM-TO pair appearing in which the TO value is less than the FROM value:

```
CONSTRAINT S_FROM_TO_OK
    IS_EMPTY ( S_FROM_TO WHERE TO < FROM ) ;

CONSTRAINT SP_FROM_TO_OK
    IS_EMPTY ( SP_FROM_TO WHERE TO < FROM ) ;
```

Next, observe from the double underlining in Figure 4.3 that we have included the FROM attribute in the primary key for both relvar S_FROM_TO and relvar SP_FROM_TO. Indeed, the primary key for S_FROM_TO (for example) clearly cannot be just {S#}, because if it were we would not be able to deal with a supplier like supplier S2 who has been under contract during two or more separate intervals. A similar observation applies to SP_FROM_TO.

NOTE: We could have included the TO attributes in the primary keys instead of the FROM attributes; in fact, relvars S_FROM_TO and SP_FROM_TO both have two candidate keys and are good examples of relvars for which there is no obvious reason to choose one of those candidate keys as primary [36]. We make the choices we do purely for reasons of definiteness.

Here then are possible relvar definitions, expressed once again in **Tutorial D**:

```
VAR S_FROM_TO RELATION { S# S#, FROM DATE, TO DATE }
    KEY { S#, FROM }
    KEY { S#, TO } ;

VAR SP_FROM_TO RELATION { S# S#, P# P#, FROM DATE, TO DATE }
    KEY { S#, P#, FROM }
    KEY { S#, P#, TO } ;
```

However, the constraints we have discussed so far—the two "_FROM_TO_OK" constraints and the four KEY constraints—are still inadequate to capture everything we would like them to. Consider relvar S_FROM_TO, for example. Obviously, if there is a tuple for supplier S*x* in that relvar with FROM value *f* and TO value *t,* then we want there *not* to be a tuple for supplier S*x* in that same relvar indicating that S*x* was under contract on the day immediately before *f* or the day immediately after *t.* By way of example, consider supplier S1, for whom we have just one S_FROM_TO tuple, with FROM = *d04* and TO = *d10.* The mere fact that {S#,FROM} is a candidate key for this relvar is clearly insufficient to prevent the appearance of an additional "overlapping" S1 tuple with (say) FROM = *d02* and TO = *d06,* which would indicate among other things that S1 *was* under contract on the day immediately before day 4. Clearly, what we would like is that those two S1 tuples be combined into a single tuple with FROM = *d02* and TO = *d10.*

Now, you might have already guessed that this idea of combining tuples is going to turn out to be very important. Indeed, *not* combining the two tuples in the foregoing example would be almost as bad as permitting duplicates! Duplicates amount to "saying the same thing twice." And those two tuples for supplier S1 with overlapping FROM-TO intervals do indeed "say the same thing twice"; to be specific, they both say supplier S1 was under contract on days 4, 5, and 6. Indeed, if those two tuples did both appear, then relvar S_FROM_TO would be in violation of its own predicate.

Next, the fact that {S#,FROM} is a candidate key for S_FROM_TO is also insufficient to prevent the appearance of an "abutting" S1 tuple with (say) FROM = *d02* and TO = *d03,* which would indicate again that S1 was under contract on the day immediately before day 4. As before, what we would like is that the two tuples in question be combined into one; otherwise, again, relvar S_FROM_TO would be in violation of its own predicate.[2]

Here then is a constraint that does prohibit such overlapping and abutting:

```
CONSTRAINT XFT1
    IS_EMPTY
        ( ( ( S_FROM_TO RENAME ( FROM AS F1, TO AS T1 ) ) JOIN
            ( S_FROM_TO RENAME ( FROM AS F2, TO AS T2 ) ) )
                WHERE ( T1 ≥ F2 AND T2 ≥ F1 ) ) OR
                       ( F2 = T1+1 OR F1 = T2+1 ) ) ;
```

With this example, we begin to see the problem. This constraint is quite complicated!—not to mention the fact that we have taken the gross liberty of writing, for example, T1+1 to designate the immediate successor of the day denoted by T1, a point we will come back to in the next chapter. Furthermore, we observe that, given a fully temporal database like that of Figure 4.3, we will probably have to state many con-

---

2. In Chapter 11, we refer to the possibility of overlapping tuples and the possibility of abutting tuples as a *redundancy* problem and a *circumlocution* problem, respectively. That chapter also discusses a third, related problem which it calls a *contradiction* problem. Our running example in its present form is too simple to illustrate this third problem.

straints of the same general nature as Constraint XFT1, and again we will surely wish we had some good shorthand for the purpose.[3]

Next, note that the attribute combination {S#,FROM} in relvar SP_FROM_TO is *not* a foreign key from that relvar to relvar S_FROM_TO, even though it does involve the same attributes as the primary key of relvar S_FROM_TO. (It is not a foreign key because it is possible for an {S#,FROM} value to appear in SP_FROM_TO and not in S_FROM_TO, as a glance at Figure 4.3 will quickly confirm.) But we certainly do need to ensure that if a given supplier is represented in relvar SP_FROM_TO, then that supplier is represented in relvar S_FROM_TO as well:

```
CONSTRAINT XFT2
    SP_FROM_TO { S# } ⊆ S_FROM_TO { S# } ;
```

This constraint is an example of an *inclusion dependency* [10] (note that, like Constraint DBC2 in Chapter 1, Section 1.6, it involves a relational comparison). Inclusion dependencies can be regarded as a generalization of referential constraints. And it should be clear that any fully temporal database like that of Figure 4.3 is likely to involve a large number of such dependencies, at least implicitly.

Constraint XFT2 is still not enough, however; we also need to ensure that if relvar SP_FROM_TO shows some supplier as being able to supply some part during some interval of time, then relvar S_FROM_TO shows that same supplier as being under contract throughout that same interval of time. Two attempts at formulating this constraint (the first of which is incorrect) are shown below. *We recommend strongly that you try to produce a formulation of your own before reading further.*

Here then is a first attempt:

```
CONSTRAINT XFT3                         /* Warning--inadequate! */
    IS_EMPTY
        ( ( S_FROM_TO RENAME ( FROM AS SF, TO AS ST ) ) JOIN
          ( SP_FROM_TO RENAME ( FROM AS SPF, TO AS SPT ) ) )
        WHERE SPF < SF OR SPT > ST ) ;
```

The intuition behind this formulation is that if tuples *s* and *sp,* from relvars S_FROM_TO and SP_FROM_TO, respectively, correspond to the same supplier, then the FROM-TO interval in *s* must encompass that in *sp.* As the comment indicates, however, the intuition and the formulation are both incorrect, or at least incomplete. To see why, let relvar S_FROM_TO be as shown in Figure 4.3, and let relvar SP_FROM_TO include a tuple for supplier S2 with (say) FROM = *d03* and TO = *d04*. Such an arrangement is clearly consistent, and yet Constraint XFT3 as stated would prohibit it (because the result of the join would include a tuple for supplier S2 with SF = *d07*, ST = *d10*, SPF = *d03*, and SPT = *d04*, thereby causing the IS_EMPTY test to give false).

---

3. In fact, there is yet another problem with Constraint XFT1 as stated: namely, what happens to the expression T1+1 if T1 happens to denote "the end of time"?

Here by contrast is a correct formulation:

```
CONSTRAINT XFT3
   COUNT ( SP_FROM_TO { ALL BUT P# } ) =
   COUNT ( ( ( SP_FROM_TO RENAME ( FROM AS SPF, TO AS SPT ) )
                                                    { ALL BUT P# }
            JOIN
            ( S_FROM_TO RENAME ( FROM AS SF, TO AS ST ) ) )
          WHERE SF ≤ SPF AND ST ≥ SPT ) ;
```

The (correct) intuition here is that if relvar SP_FROM_TO includes a tuple showing supplier S*x* as able to supply some specific part from day *spf* to day *spt*, then relvar S_FROM_TO must include exactly one tuple showing supplier S*x* as being under contract throughout that interval. (Note that we are assuming here that all of the constraints discussed previously are in effect!) A detailed explanation follows:

- The constraint as stated asserts that two counts must be equal.

- The first is a count of the number of distinct propositions of the form "S*x* supplies some part from day *spf* to day *spt*" implied by relvar SP_FROM_TO. Let that count be *N*.

- The second is a count of the number of tuples contained in a certain restriction of a certain join. The join in question should contain at least one tuple for each of the *N* propositions of the form "S*x* supplies some part from day *spf* to day *spt*" implied by relvar SP_FROM_TO. The subsequent restriction should eliminate all but one of those tuples for each of those *N* propositions.

Incidentally, note the use in Constraint XFT3 of expressions of the form "{ALL BUT …}" to specify a projection of some relation over all attributes *apart from* those specified.

Now, you might have had some difficulty in following the foregoing explanation. Even if you did not, you will surely recognize that once again the constraint is quite complex, and yet once again we will certainly have to state many constraints of the same general nature, given a fully temporal database like that of Figure 4.3. Once again, therefore, we will surely wish we had some good shorthand available.

Queries (first fully temporal database): Here now are fully temporal analogs of Queries A and B:

- **Query A:** Get S#-FROM-TO triples for suppliers who have been able to supply at least one part during at least one interval of time, where FROM and TO together designate a maximal interval during which supplier S# was in fact able to supply at least one part. NOTE: We use the term "maximal" here as a convenient shorthand to mean (in the case at hand) that supplier S# was unable to supply any part at all on the day immediately before FROM or immediately after TO. Note too that the result of the query might contain several tuples for the same supplier (but with different intervals, of course; moreover, those intervals will neither abut nor overlap).

- **Query B:** Get S#-FROM-TO triples for suppliers who have been unable to supply any parts at all during at least one interval of time, where FROM and TO together designate a maximal interval during which supplier S# was in fact unable to supply any part at all. (Again the result might contain several tuples for the same supplier.)

Well, you might like to take a little time to convince yourself that, like us, you would really prefer not even to attempt these queries! If you do make the attempt, however, the fact that they *can* be expressed, albeit exceedingly laboriously, will eventually emerge, but it will surely be obvious that some kind of shorthand is highly desirable.

In a nutshell, then, the problem of temporal data is that it quickly leads to constraints and queries (not to mention updates—see Chapter 14) that are unreasonably complex to express: unreasonably complex, that is, unless the system provides some well-designed shorthands, which commercially available DBMSs currently do not. In the next chapter, therefore, we will begin our search for such a set of "well-designed shorthands."

EXERCISES

1. State as precisely as you can the predicates for the following:

    a. Relvars S and SP as illustrated in Endpaper Panel 1

    b. Relvars S_SINCE and SP_SINCE as illustrated in Endpaper Panel 2

    c. Relvars S_FROM_TO and SP_FROM_TO as illustrated in Endpaper Panel 3

2. Explain the redundancy and circumlocution problems in your own words.

3. Write **Tutorial D** expressions for the following queries on the database illustrated in Endpaper Panel 2:

    a. Get supplier numbers for suppliers who are currently able to supply at least two different parts, showing in each case the date since when they have been able to do so.

    b. Get supplier numbers for suppliers who are currently unable to supply at least two different parts, showing in each case the date since when they have been unable to do so.

What about analogs of these two queries on the database illustrated in Endpaper Panel 3? At least try to state such analogs in natural language, even if you decide you would rather not attempt to come up with any corresponding **Tutorial D** formulations.

Chapter

5

INTERVALS

5.1   INTRODUCTION

We are now ready to embark on our development of an appropriate set of constructs for dealing with temporal data. The first and most fundamental step is to recognize the need to deal with intervals as such—that is, the need to treat intervals as values in their own right, instead of treating them as pairs of separate values as we did in the previous chapter.

What exactly is an interval?[1] Take another look at Figure 4.3 in Chapter 4 (or Endpaper Panel 3 at the front of the book). According to that figure, supplier S1 was able to supply part P1 during the interval from day 4 to day 10. But what does "from day 4 to day 10" mean? It is clear that days 5, 6, 7, 8, and 9 are included—but what about days 4 and 10? It turns out that, given an interval specified (perhaps rather loosely) as stretching "from p to q," we sometimes want to regard the points p and q as included in the interval and sometimes not. If we do want to include the point p, we say the expression "from p to q" is **closed** at its beginning, otherwise we say it is **open** at its beginning. Likewise, if we want to include the point q, we say the expression is closed at its end, otherwise we say it is open at its end.

---

1. Two caveats here. First, if you happen to be familiar with SQL, we should warn you that intervals as we use the term are nothing to do with intervals as understood in SQL—which are not really intervals in the usual sense, but rather *durations*. Second, we assume until further notice that the intervals we are interested in are, specifically, intervals that are defined over what are called *discrete point types*.

Conventionally, therefore, we denote an interval by a pair of points *p* and *q* separated by a colon,[2] preceded by an opening bracket or parenthesis and followed by a closing bracket or parenthesis. A bracket is used where we want the closed interpretation, a parenthesis where we want the open one. Thus, for example, there are four distinct ways to denote the specific interval that runs from the **begin point** day 4 to the **end point** day 10, inclusive:

[d04:d10]
[d04:d11)
(d03:d10]
(d03:d11)

By the way, you might think it odd to use, say, an opening bracket with a closing parenthesis; the fact is, however, there are good reasons to allow all four styles. Indeed, the so-called closed-open style—closed at the beginning and open at the end, as in *[d04:d11)*—is the one most often used in practice. But the closed-closed style, as in *[d04:d10]*, is surely the most intuitive, and we will favor it in what follows. NOTE: To see why the closed-open style might be advantageous, consider the operation of splitting the interval *[d04:d11)* immediately before, say, day 7. The result is the abutting pair of intervals *[d04:d07)* and *[d07:d11)*.

Now, given that an interval such as *[d04:d10]* can be considered as a value in its own right, it clearly makes sense to combine the FROM and TO attributes of each of the relvars in Figure 4.3 into a single attribute, DURING, whose values are drawn from some **interval type** (see Section 5.3). Figure 5.1 (opposite) shows what happens to our running example if we adopt this approach (note the relvar name changes). NOTE: The figure is repeated in Endpaper Panel 4 at the front of the book.

The predicate for relvar S_DURING is:

From the day that is the begin point of DURING (and not on the day immediately before that day) to the day that is the end point of DURING (and not on the day immediately after that day), inclusive, supplier S# was under contract.

And the predicate for relvar SP_DURING is:

From the day that is the begin point of DURING (and not on the day immediately before that day) to the day that is the end point of DURING (and not on the day immediately after that day), inclusive, supplier S# was able to supply part P#.

The idea of replacing the pair of attributes FROM and TO by the single attribute DURING in each of the two relvars brings with it a number of immediate advantages. Here are some of them:

---

2. Other separators—for example, commas, dashes, and so on—are also used in the literature. We prefer colons because commas can make intervals look like subscripts, and dashes can look like minus signs.

FIGURE 5.1

Suppliers-and-
shipments database
(second fully
temporal version,
using intervals)—
sample values.

S_DURING

S#	DURING
S1	[d04:d10]
S2	[d02:d04]
S2	[d07:d10]
S3	[d03:d10]
S4	[d04:d10]
S5	[d02:d10]

SP_DURING

S#	P#	DURING
S1	P1	[d04:d10]
S1	P2	[d05:d10]
S1	P3	[d09:d10]
S1	P4	[d05:d10]
S1	P5	[d04:d10]
S1	P6	[d06:d10]
S2	P1	[d02:d04]
S2	P1	[d08:d10]
S2	P2	[d03:d03]
S2	P2	[d09:d10]
S3	P2	[d08:d10]
S4	P2	[d06:d09]
S4	P4	[d04:d08]
S4	P5	[d05:d10]

- It avoids the problem of having to make an arbitrary choice as to which of two candidate keys should be regarded as primary. For example, relvar S_FROM_TO had two candidate keys, {S#,FROM} and {S#,TO}, but relvar S_DURING has just one, {S#,DURING}, which we can therefore designate as primary (if we wish) without any undesirable arbitrariness. Similarly, relvar SP_FROM_TO also had two candidate keys but relvar SP_DURING has just one, {S#,P#,DURING}, which again we can designate as primary if we wish.

- It also avoids the problem of having to decide whether the FROM-TO intervals in the previous version of the database (Figure 4.3) are to be interpreted as closed or open with respect to FROM and TO. In Chapter 4 those intervals were implicitly taken to be closed with respect to both FROM and TO. But now, for example, [d04:d10], [d04:d11), (d03:d10], and (d03:d11) are four distinct *possible representations* of the very same interval, and we have no need to know which, if any, is the actual physical representation.

- Yet another advantage is that integrity constraints "to guard against the absurdity of a FROM-TO pair appearing in which the TO value is less than the FROM value" (as we put it in the previous chapter) are no longer necessary, because the constraint "FROM ≤ TO" is implicit in the very notion of an interval type, so to speak. That is, constraints of the form "FROM ≤ TO" are effectively replaced by a *generic* constraint that implicitly applies to every individual interval type. Those individual interval types are defined by means of invocations of the interval *type generator* (see Section 5.3); the generic constraint can thus be thought of as being associated with that type generator, just as the generic interval operators discussed later in this chapter (and in the next) can also be thought of as being associated with that type generator.

- Suppose relations *r1* and *r2* were both to include distinct FROM and TO attributes (albeit with different names in each case), instead of a single DURING attribute, and suppose we were to join *r1* and *r2* to produce *r3*. Then *r3* would contain two FROM-TO attribute pairs, and it would be the user's responsibility, not the system's, to match up the FROMs and TOs appropriately. Clearly, this problem (though admittedly psychological, not logical, in nature) will only get worse as the number of joins increases, and it could give rise to serious human errors. What is more, the difficulties would be compounded if we were to discard some of the FROMs and/or TOs by means of projections. Such problems do not arise—or, at least, are much less severe—with DURING attributes.

Other advantages will become clearer over the next several chapters.

As for the constraints and queries discussed in the previous chapter, in Section 4.3, it should be clear that direct analogs of those constraints and queries can be formulated against the database of Figure 5.1, just so long as we have a way to access the begin and end points of any given interval. We do not bother to show such formulations, however, since it is part of our goal to come up with a better way to express such constraints and queries—a way, that is, that involves something better than just direct analogs of those earlier formulations. We will discuss such a better way in subsequent chapters; to be specific, we will deal with queries in Chapters 8 and 9 (also Chapter 13) and constraints in Chapters 11 and 12.

One last preliminary point: We should stress the fact (implicit in much of what we have been saying already) that intervals as discussed in this chapter are **scalar values**— they have no user-visible components. (The begin and end points are components of *possible representations* of intervals, not components of intervals as such.) Another way of saying the same thing is to say that intervals are *encapsulated* (but see reference [38]).

5.2 APPLICATIONS OF INTERVALS

The interval concept is the key to addressing the problems raised in Section 4.3 in the previous chapter. In other words, intervals are the fundamental abstraction we need for dealing with temporal data satisfactorily. Before we delve into details of temporal intervals as such, however, we should make it clear that the interval concept is actually of much wider applicability; that is, there are many other applications for intervals, applications in which the intervals are not necessarily temporal ones (see, e.g., reference [65]). Here are a few examples:

- Tax brackets are represented by taxable-income ranges—in other words, intervals whose begin and end points (and all points in between, of course) are money values.

- Machines are built to operate within certain temperature and voltage ranges—in other words, intervals whose contained points are temperatures and voltages, respectively.

- Animals vary in the range of frequencies of light and sound waves to which their eyes and ears are receptive.

- Various natural phenomena occur and can be measured in ranges in depth of soil or sea or height above sea level.

Although our focus in this book is, for the most part, on temporal intervals specifically, many of our discussions are relevant to intervals in general.

NOTE: All of the intervals discussed so far can be thought of as *one-dimensional*. However, we might want to combine two one-dimensional intervals to form a *two*-dimensional interval. For example, a rectangular plot of ground might be thought of as a two-dimensional interval, because it is, by definition, an object with length and width, each of which is basically a one-dimensional interval measured along some axis. And, of course, we can extend this idea to any number of dimensions. For example, a (rather simple!) building might be regarded as a three-dimensional interval: It is an object with length, width, and height, or in other words a *cuboid*. (More realistically, a building might be regarded as a set of several such cuboids that overlap in various ways.) And so on. In what follows, however, we will restrict our attention to one-dimensional intervals specifically, barring explicit statements to the contrary, and we will omit the "one-dimensional" qualifier for simplicity.

5.3 POINT TYPES AND INTERVAL TYPES

Our discussion of intervals has so far been mostly intuitive in nature. Now we need to address the issue more formally. We begin by considering the interval value [*d04:d10*] once again; let us refer to it as *the interval value i*, or just interval *i* for short. In accordance with our running convention, the points that make up interval *i*—namely, *d04*, *d05*, …, and *d10*—are all *days*. For the sake of the example, therefore, let us assume that those points are all values of type DATE, where type DATE represents Gregorian dates. Then type DATE is said to be the **point type** for interval *i*.

But how exactly do we know the points in interval *i* are the ones we said they were (i.e., *d04*, *d05*, …, *d10*)? Well, we certainly know that *i* includes its begin and end points *d04* and *d10*, by definition. We also know that *i* consists of a set of points arranged in accordance with some agreed ordering. So if we are to determine the complete set of points in *i*, we first need to determine the point—for simplicity, let us refer to it as *d04*+1—that immediately follows the begin point *d04* according to that agreed ordering. That point *d04*+1 is the **successor** of *d04* according to that ordering, and the function by which that successor is determined is the corresponding **successor function**. In the case at hand, where the point type is DATE, the successor function is basically "next day" (meaning "add one day to the given date"); that is, it is a function that, given a DATE value *d*, returns the DATE value that is the immediate successor of *d* according to the normal rules of the Gregorian calendar. NOTE: If *d*+1 is the successor of *d* in some ordering, then (of course) *d* is the **predecessor** of *d*+1 in that same ordering. For simplicity, we sometimes refer to the predecessor of *d* as *d*–1.

Having determined that *d04*+1 is the successor of *d04*, we must next determine whether or not *d04*+1 comes after the end point *d10* according to that ordering. If it does not, then *d04*+1 is indeed a point in *i* = [*d04:d10*], and we must now consider the next point, *d04*+2. Repeating this process until we come to the first point *d04*+*n* (actually *d04*+7, or in other words *d11* = *d10*+1) that comes after *d10*—or, just possibly, until we come to "the last day" (see below)—we will discover every point in *i* = [*d04:d10*].

More generally, let interval *i* = [*b:e*], where *b* and *e* are again values of type DATE, and the same "next day" successor function applies. Then there are, of course, a couple of special cases to consider:

- *b* = "the first day" (i.e., the point corresponding to "the beginning of time," which has no predecessor). The expression *b*–1 is undefined in this case.

- *e* = "the last day" (i.e., the point corresponding to "the end of time," which has no successor). The expression *e*+1 is undefined in this case.

As the foregoing discussion should suggest, a given type *T* is usable as a point type if all of the following are defined for it:

- A **total ordering,** according to which the infix operator ">" (greater than) is defined for every pair of values *v1* and *v2* of type *T*; if *v1* and *v2* are distinct, exactly one of the expressions "*v1* > *v2*" and "*v2* > *v1*" returns true and the other returns false. NOTE: As we know from Chapter 1, the "=" operator is certainly defined for *T*. Given that ">" is defined as well, therefore (and given also the availability of the boolean NOT operator), we can legitimately assume that all of the usual comparison operators—"=", "≠", ">", "≥", "<", and "≤"—are available for all pairs of values of type *T*.

- Niladic **"first"** and **"last"** operators, which return the smallest and the largest value of *T*, respectively, according to the aforementioned ordering.

- Monadic **"next"** and **"prior"** operators, which return the successor and the predecessor, respectively, of any given value of type *T*, according to the aforementioned ordering. Of course, the "next" operator is the successor function. As already pointed out, the "next" and "prior" operators are undefined if the given value of type *T* is in fact the "last" or "first" value, respectively, of that type.

As an aside, we remark that the *empty* scalar type (called *omega* in reference [43]) satisfies the foregoing requirements and is thus a valid point type!—vacuously so, however, because if the point type is empty, then the corresponding interval type (see later in this section) is necessarily empty as well. Of course, the "first," "last," "next," and "prior" operators will all be undefined if the point type is empty. EXERCISE FOR THE READER: Is a singleton scalar type—that is, one containing just a single scalar value—a valid point type?

To return to the main thread of our discussion: *We now need to make a crucial assumption.* To be specific, we assume until further notice that the successor function is unique (i.e., if *T* is a point type, then *T* has *exactly one* successor function). Now, this assumption might seem reasonable at first glance—but is it? Consider type DATE once again. In practice, we do not always want to deal with dates that are accurate to the day. For example, U.S. presidential administrations are usually specified in terms of dates that are accurate only to the year (e.g., "Gerald R. Ford, 1974–1977"), and the same is true for reigns of monarchs and the like. It follows that we might want to consider two distinct successor functions for type DATE, "next day" and "next year" (note that these two functions correspond informally to two distinct DATE *granularities*). Such considerations muddy the picture considerably, as you might expect! We therefore defer detailed discussion of them to a later chapter (Chapter 16); until then, we will simply stay with our "unique successor function" assumption.

To return to the interval value *i* = [*d04:d10*], we can now pin down the type of that value precisely, as follows:

- First, of course, it is of some interval type, and that fact by itself is sufficient to determine the generic interval operators that are applicable to the interval value in question (just as to say that, e.g., some value is of some relation type is sufficient to determine the generic relational operators—restrict, project, and so on—that are applicable to the relation value in question). A few such operators are discussed later in this section, and many more are discussed in Chapter 6.

- Second, the interval value in question is, very specifically, an interval from one Gregorian date to another, and—thanks to our "unique successor function" assumption—that fact is sufficient to determine the specific set of values that together constitute the interval type in question. (Recall from Chapter 1 that a type is, among other things, a set of values.) In the case at hand, of course, that specific set of values is the set of all possible intervals of the form [*b:e*], where *b* and *e* are values of type DATE and *b* ≤ *e*.

In other words, we can say that the specific type of the interval value *i* = [*d04:d10*] is **INTERVAL_DATE,** where:

- INTERVAL is a **type generator,** like RELATION in **Tutorial D** (see Chapters 1 and 2) or "array" in conventional programming languages. Specific interval types are produced by *invoking* that type generator.

- DATE is the point type for this specific interval type; that is, intervals of this specific interval type are made up of points of this specific point type.

Here are two more examples of interval types:

- `INTERVAL_INTEGER`
  The point type here is INTEGER; the successor function is "next integer" (i.e., "add one"), and values of this interval type are intervals of the form [*b:e*], where *b* and *e* are values of type INTEGER and *b* ≤ *e*.

- INTERVAL_MONEY

  MONEY here is—let us assume—a type that represents monetary amounts measured in dollars and cents. The successor function is "add one cent." Values of this interval type are intervals of the form [b:e], where b and e are values of type MONEY and $b \leq e$.

And here (at last!) is a reasonably precise definition of the term *interval:*

Let *T* be a point type. Then an **interval** (or **interval value**) *i* of type INTERVAL_T is a scalar value for which two monadic operators, BEGIN and END, and one dyadic operator, $\in$, are defined, such that:

1. BEGIN(*i*) and END(*i*) both return a value of type *T.*

2. BEGIN(*i*) $\leq$ END(*i*).

3. If *p* is a value of type *T,* then $p \in i$ is true if and only if BEGIN(*i*) $\leq p$ and $p \leq$ END(*i*) are both true. NOTE: Of course, the operator "$\in$" is basically just the conventional set membership operator. The expression "$p \in i$" can be pronounced as "*p* belongs to *i*" or "*p* is a member of *i*" or, more simply, just "*p* [is] in *i*."

Points arising from this definition:

1. Observe that intervals are always *nonempty*—that is, there is always at least one point in any given interval.

2. Two intervals *i1* and *i2* of the same interval type are *equal*—that is, *i1* = *i2* is true—if and only if BEGIN(*i1*) = BEGIN(*i2*) and END(*i1*) = END(*i2*) are both true (see Chapter 6 for further discussion).

3. As pointed out in Section 5.1, the begin and end points together constitute a possible representation for interval values. It follows from this latter fact that in **Tutorial D** we would normally refer to the operators BEGIN and END as THE_BEGIN and THE_END, respectively. However, we use BEGIN and END, here and elsewhere in this book, for consistency with other writings in this field.

4. It is convenient to introduce the term *unit interval.* A **unit interval** is an interval *i* for which BEGIN(*i*) = END(*i*). For example, the interval value *i* = [d04:d04] is a unit interval of type INTERVAL_DATE.

We round off this section by giving possible **Tutorial D** definitions for relvars S_DURING and SP_DURING:

```
VAR S_DURING RELATION
  { S# S#, DURING INTERVAL_DATE }
  KEY { S#, DURING } ;
```

```
VAR SP_DURING RELATION
  { S# S#, P# P#, DURING INTERVAL_DATE }
  KEY { S#, P#, DURING } ;
```

Note, however, that these definitions are still very incomplete! We will elaborate on them in Chapter 11.

5.4 A More Searching Example

Relvars S_DURING and SP_DURING both involve just one interval attribute, called DURING in both cases. However, it is certainly possible for a relvar to involve two or more such attributes. For example, suppose, not unreasonably, that there is a total ordering on part numbers, say P1 < P2 < P3 (etc.), and suppose further that we wish our database to show that certain suppliers were able to supply certain *ranges* of parts during certain intervals of time. Then relvar SP_DURING might well have two interval attributes, DURING and PARTS (say), where DURING is as before and PARTS indicates the corresponding part ranges. To avoid confusion, let us refer to this revised version of the relvar as S_PARTS_DURING instead of SP_DURING. A sample value is shown in Figure 5.2.

Please note that the sample value in Figure 5.2 is not meant to correspond in any particular way to the sample value shown for relvar SP_DURING in Figure 5.1. Indeed, you might have noticed that the sample value of Figure 5.2 does suffer—deliberately, of course—from certain problems; for example, it tells us twice that supplier S3 was able to supply part P4 on days 1 to 4 inclusive. We will take up such issues in later chapters (in Chapter 11 in particular).

We will occasionally make use of examples based on relvar S_PARTS_DURING instead of our more usual SP_DURING in the chapters to come.

FIGURE 5.2

A relvar with two interval attributes (S_PARTS_DURING)— sample value.

S_PARTS_DURING

S#	PARTS	DURING
S1	[P1:P3]	[d01:d04]
S1	[P2:P4]	[d07:d08]
S1	[P5:P6]	[d09:d09]
S2	[P1:P1]	[d08:d09]
S2	[P1:P2]	[d08:d08]
S2	[P3:P4]	[d07:d08]
S3	[P2:P4]	[d01:d04]
S3	[P3:P5]	[d01:d04]
S3	[P2:P4]	[d05:d06]
S3	[P2:P4]	[d06:d09]
S4	[P3:P4]	[d05:d08]

Some final points to close this chapter:

- Although relvar S_PARTS_DURING does involve two interval attributes, only one of the two involves temporal intervals specifically. Here by contrast is a relvar with two distinct interval attributes, both of which represent temporal intervals specifically:

```
EMP { EMP#, PRIMARY, SECONDARY }
```

Here attributes PRIMARY and SECONDARY show the intervals of time during which the employee identified by EMP# received his or her primary and secondary education, respectively.

- Second, note that we would need to consider *relations*—that is, relation *values*—with two or more interval attributes even if we had no *relvars* (like EMP or S_PARTS_DURING) with two or more such attributes. For example, as soon as we join the two relations *R1{A,B}* and *R2{A,C}*, where *B* and *C* are interval attributes, we obtain a relation that has two interval attributes.

- Third, we could extend the S_PARTS_DURING example to include three interval attributes by replacing attribute S# by an attribute SUPPLIERS showing supplier number ranges (assuming there is a total ordering defined for supplier numbers, of course). Here is a sample value:

SUPPLIERS	PARTS	DURING
[S1:S2]	[P2:P3]	[d03:d04]
[S2:S3]	[P3:P4]	[d04:d05]

Exercises

1. State as precisely as you can the predicates for relvars S_DURING and SP_DURING as illustrated in Endpaper Panel 4.

2. List as many advantages as you can in favor of replacing FROM-TO attribute pairs by individual DURING attributes.

3. Give some examples of nontemporal intervals, over and above the ones listed in Section 5.2.

4. Define the terms *point type* and *interval type*. Complete the following sentence in your own words: "A type *T* is usable as a point type if ... ."

5. (Repeated from Section 5.3) Is a singleton scalar type—that is, one containing just a single scalar value—a valid point type?

6. Let *i* be an interval. Define the operators BEGIN(*i*), END(*i*), and $p \in i$.

7. What is a unit interval?

8. Give your own examples of (a) a relation or relvar with two interval attributes and (b) a relation or relvar with three.

9. Here is a revised and extended version of the courses-and-students database from Exercise 23 in Chapter 1:

```
VAR COURSE RELATION
    { COURSE#   COURSE#,
      CNAME     NAME,
      AVAILABLE DATE }
    KEY { COURSE# } ;

VAR CANCELED_COURSE RELATION
    { COURSE# COURSE#,
      CANCELED DATE }
    KEY { COURSE# }
    FOREIGN KEY { COURSE# } REFERENCES COURSE ;

VAR STUDENT RELATION
    { STUDENT#   STUDENT#,
      SNAME      NAME,
      REGISTERED DATE }
    KEY { STUDENT#, REGISTERED } ;

VAR UNREG_STUDENT RELATION
    { STUDENT#     STUDENT#,
      UNREGISTERED DATE }
    KEY { STUDENT#, UNREGISTERED } ;

VAR ENROLLMENT RELATION
    { COURSE#  COURSE#,
      STUDENT# STUDENT#,
      ENROLLED DATE }
    KEY { COURSE#, STUDENT# }
    FOREIGN KEY { COURSE# } REFERENCES COURSE
    FOREIGN KEY { STUDENT# } REFERENCES STUDENT ;

VAR COMPLETED_COURSE RELATION
    { COURSE#   COURSE#,
      STUDENT#  STUDENT#,
      COMPLETED DATE,
      GRADE     GRADE }
    KEY { COURSE#, STUDENT# }
    FOREIGN KEY { COURSE# } REFERENCES COURSE ;
```

The predicates are as follows:

- COURSE: *Course COURSE#, named CNAME, became available on date AVAILABLE.*

- CANCELED_COURSE: *Course COURSE# ceased to be available on date CANCELED.*

- STUDENT: *Student STUDENT#, named SNAME, registered with the university on date REGISTERED.*

- UNREG_STUDENT: *Student STUDENT# left the university on date UNREGISTERED.*

- ENROLLMENT: *Student STUDENT# enrolled in course COURSE# on date ENROLLED.*

- COMPLETED_COURSE: *Student STUDENT# completed course COURSE# on date COMPLETED, achieving grade GRADE.*

Selector operator GRADE, which takes a single argument of type INTEGER (with value in the range 1 through 5), is available for type GRADE.

a. Assuming this database constitutes a record of the relevant part of a typical university's business, what additional constraints (expressed in natural language) might be required?

b. Suppose the following relvar is added, with the intent (eventually) of using it to replace relvar COMPLETED_COURSE:

```
VAR STUDIED RELATION
    { COURSE#   COURSE#,
      STUDENT#  STUDENT#,
      DURING    INTERVAL_DATE,
      GRADE     GRADE }
    KEY { COURSE#, STUDENT# }
    FOREIGN KEY { COURSE# } REFERENCES COURSE ;
```

The predicate is: *Student STUDENT# studied course COURSE# during interval DURING, achieving grade GRADE.* Write a **Tutorial D** query, making use of relvars ENROLLMENT and COMPLETED_COURSE, whose result corresponds to exactly this predicate (and can therefore usefully be assigned to relvar STUDIED).

c. Write a **Tutorial D** definition for a relvar called COURSE_AVAILABILITY that combines relvars COURSE and CANCELED_COURSE analogously to the way STUDIED combines relvars ENROLLMENT and COMPLETED_COURSE. Include at least one KEY specification and all appropriate FOREIGN KEY specifications.

Chapter

6

OPERATORS ON INTERVALS

6.1 INTRODUCTION

In this chapter we introduce a number of useful operators that apply to interval values. Most but not all of the operators in question are described in the literature; however, we have taken the liberty of changing many of their names to ones that we find intuitively preferable, for one reason or another.

For the purpose of explaining the operators, we adopt the same informal notation as we did in Chapter 5:

- First, let T be a point type, and let p be a value of type T. Then we use the expressions $p+1$, $p+2$, and so on, to denote the value that is the successor of p, the value that is the successor of $p+1$, and so on. Of course, the foregoing notation is only informal; a real language would have to provide some kind of explicit *next* operator. When we need to refer to that formal operator explicitly, we will call it NEXT_T—thus, NEXT_$T(p)$ returns $p+1$, NEXT_T(NEXT_$T(p)$) returns $p+2$, and so on. Observe, therefore, that the formal *next* operator includes an explicit "_T" qualifier (and the same is true for the formal *prior, first, last,* and *interval selector* operators, as we will see in a moment). We will explain why that qualifier is necessary in Chapter 16.

- We also use (again informally) the expressions $p-1$, $p-2$, and so on, to denote the value whose successor is p, the value whose successor is $p-1$, and so on. A real language would have to provide an explicit *prior* operator, which we will call PRIOR_*T*; PRIOR_*T*(*p*) returns *p*–1, PRIOR_*T*(PRIOR_*T*(*p*)) returns *p*–2, and so on.

- We also need FIRST_*T* and LAST_*T* operators; FIRST_*T*() and LAST_*T*() return the "first" value and the "last" value of type *T*, respectively.

- The interval type corresponding to point type *T* is INTERVAL_*T*. We use the expression [*p1:pn*] to denote the interval whose contained points are exactly *p1*, *p1*+1, *p1*+2, ..., *pn* (1 ≤ *n*). Observe that the expression [*p1:pn*] can be regarded as an informal example of an *interval selector invocation*. A real language would have to provide some kind of explicit syntax for such invocations, as in, for example, INTERVAL_*T* ([*p1:pn*]).[1]

- We occasionally make use of the other informal notational styles for intervals (closed-open, open-closed, and open-open). As a reminder, let the point type be INTEGER, and consider the corresponding interval type INTERVAL_ INTEGER. Then the expressions [3:5], [3:6), (2:5], and (2:6) all informally denote the very same interval: namely, that interval whose contained points are exactly 3, 4, and 5. The formal analogs of these expressions are INTERVAL_ INTEGER ([3:5]), INTERVAL_INTEGER ([3:6)), INTERVAL_INTEGER ((2:5]), and INTERVAL_INTEGER ((2:6)), respectively.

We also remind you of the operators BEGIN, END, and ∈ from Chapter 5. For completeness, we repeat the definitions here (slightly reworded in each case). Let *i* be the interval [*b:e*] of type INTERVAL_*T* and let *p* be a value of type *T*. Then:

- BEGIN(*i*) returns *b*.

- END(*i*) returns *e*.

- *p* ∈ *i* returns true if and only if *b* ≤ *p* and *p* ≤ *e* both return true.

We additionally define the operators PRE(*i*) and POST(*i*), which return *b*–1 and *e*+1, respectively, and the operator *i* ∋ *p* (read "*i* contains *p*"), which returns true if and only if *p* ∈ *i* returns true. Note that PRE is undefined if *b* is the "first" value of type *T*, and POST is undefined if *e* is the "last" value of type *T*. Of course, PRE(*i*) and POST(*i*) are effectively just shorthand for PRIOR_*T*(BEGIN(*i*)) and NEXT_*T*(END(*i*)), respectively.

NOTE: POST has been called STOP in the literature [53]. PRE might thus analogously be called START, but does not usually seem to be defined at all. We prefer the names PRE and POST because they are more obviously distinct from BEGIN and END and because they are intuitively clearer as well.

---

1. We will use this explicit syntax in many examples later in the book. Please do not be confused by the fact that we used brackets "[" and "]" in the **Tutorial D** grammar shown in Chapter 2 to enclose material that was optional! In Chapter 2, brackets were not part of the language being defined but were, rather, part of the metalanguage. In an interval selector invocation, by contrast, the brackets are very definitely part of the language as such.

Finally, we introduce the POINT FROM operator. Let *i* be the *unit interval* [*p:p*] of type INTERVAL_T. Then POINT FROM *i* returns the value *p* (which is of type *T*, of course). Note that the argument to POINT FROM *must* be a unit interval.

6.2 COMPARISON OPERATORS

A variety of operators can be defined for testing whether two intervals are equal, whether they overlap, and so on. In this section, we describe some of the most useful of those operators, giving in each case a formal definition together with an intuitive picture to illustrate the functionality. NOTE: The operators to be discussed are known collectively as **Allen's operators**, most of them having first been proposed by Allen in reference [2].

Here and throughout the remainder of this chapter, we take *i1* and *i2* to be the intervals [*b1:e1*] and [*b2:e2*], respectively, both of the same type INTERVAL_T. Note that, in order for the various operators to be defined in the first place, the two intervals must indeed be of the same interval type, and hence *a fortiori* must be defined over the same point type. We remark without further elaboration that many of the operators to be discussed can be defined in several different (but of course equivalent) ways.

Equals (=): As explained in the previous chapter, *i1* = *i2* is true if and only if *b1* = *b2* and *e1* = *e2* are both true.

```
b1                e1
├───────i1───────┤

b2                e2
├───────i2───────┤
```

Includes (⊇) and included in (⊆): *i1* ⊇ *i2* is true if and only if *b1* ≤ *b2* and *e1* ≥ *e2* are both true; *i2* ⊆ *i1* is true if and only if *i1* ⊇ *i2* is true. NOTE: The "⊇" operator was first defined in reference [60], not reference [2], and was there called CONTAINS. By contrast, the "⊆" operator *was* defined in reference [2], but was there called DURING.

```
b1                        e1
├──────────────i1─────────┤

    b2              e2
    ├───────i2──────┤
```

It is also convenient to define "proper" versions of "⊇" and "⊆", as follows: *i1* ⊃ *i2* is true if and only if *i1* ⊇ *i2* is true and *i1* = *i2* is false; *i2* ⊂ *i1* is true if and only if *i1* ⊃ *i2* is true.

BEFORE and AFTER: *i1* BEFORE *i2* is true if and only if *e1* < *b2* is true; *i2* AFTER *i1* is true if and only if *i1* BEFORE *i2* is true.

```
b1              e1    b2                        e2
├──────i1──────┤     ├────────────i2───────────┤
```

MEETS: *i1* MEETS *i2* is true if and only if *b2* = *e1*+1 is true or *b1* = *e2*+1 is true (it follows that *i2* MEETS *i1* is true if and only if *i1* MEETS *i2* is true). NOTE: The keyword MEETS presumably derives from the closed-open notation—it makes good intuitive sense to think of the intervals [*x*:*y*) and [*y*:*z*) as meeting at *y*. The keyword is not quite so apt with the closed-closed notation, where "abuts" or "touches" might be intuitively more acceptable.

```
b1              e1b2                        e2
├──────i1──────┤├────────────i2───────────┤
```

OVERLAPS: *i1* OVERLAPS *i2* is true if and only if *b1* ≤ *e2* and *b2* ≤ *e1* are both true (it follows that *i2* OVERLAPS *i1* is true if and only if *i1* OVERLAPS *i2* is true).

```
b1                e1
├────────i1───────┤
        b2                        e2
        ├────────────i2───────────┤
```

MERGES: *i1* MERGES *i2* is true if and only if *i1* OVERLAPS *i2* is true or *i1* MEETS *i2* is true (it follows that *i2* MERGES *i1* is true if and only if *i1* MERGES *i2* is true). NOTE: This operator was first defined in reference [60], not reference [2]. The keyword MERGES is perhaps not very good from the standpoint of intuition, but it is hard to find a word that catches the sense better and yet is equally succinct. That sense is, of course, "overlaps or meets" (or, if you prefer, "overlaps or abuts").

```
b1                e1
├────────i1───────┤
        b2                        e2
        ├────────────i2───────────┤
```

Or:

```
b1              e1b2                        e2
├──────i1──────┤├────────────i2───────────┤
```

BEGINS: *i1* BEGINS *i2* is true if and only if *b1* = *b2* and *e1* ≤ *e2* are both true. NOTE: Reference [2] uses the keyword STARTS in place of BEGINS.

```
b1              e1
├──────i1──────┤

b2                    e2
├──────────i2──────────┤
```

ENDS: *i1* ENDS *i2* is true if and only if *e1* = *e2* and *b1* ≥ *b2* are both true. NOTE: Reference [2] uses the keyword FINISHES in place of ENDS.

```
        b1           e1
        ├──────i1──────┤

b2                     e2
├──────────i2──────────┤
```

6.3 OTHER OPERATORS

The operator COUNT(*i*) returns a count of the number of points in interval *i* (in other words, the cardinality—sometimes called the *length*—of the interval in question). For example, if *i* is the interval [*d03:d07*], of type INTERVAL_DATE, then COUNT(*i*) is 5. NOTE: The keyword DURATION is sometimes used in place of COUNT. We prefer COUNT because it is more neutral (DURATION is somewhat temporal in tone).

Now let *p1* and *p2* be values of type *T*. Then we define MAX(*p1,p2*) to return *p2* if *p1* < *p2* is true and *p1* otherwise, and MIN(*p1,p2*) to return *p1* if *p1* < *p2* is true and *p2* otherwise. We use these operators in the definition of certain useful dyadic operators on intervals: namely, interval analogs of the familiar set operators UNION, INTERSECT, and MINUS. Each of these operators takes two intervals of the same type as its operands and returns another interval of the same type as its result.

UNION: *i1* UNION *i2* returns [MIN(*b1,b2*):MAX(*e1,e2*)] if *i1* MERGES *i2* is true and is otherwise undefined.

```
b1              e1
├──────i1──────┤

        b2                   e2
        ├──────────i2──────────┤

b1                             e2
├──────────i1 UNION i2──────────┤
```

INTERSECT: *i1* INTERSECT *i2* returns [MAX(*b1*,*b2*):MIN(*e1*,*e2*)] if *i1* OVERLAPS *i2* is true and is otherwise undefined.

```
b1                e1
├───────i1───────┤

        b2                      e2
        ├──────────i2──────────┤

        b2   e1
        ├────┤
             └──────── i1 INTERSECT i2
```

MINUS: *i1* MINUS *i2* returns [*b1*:MIN(*b2*−1,*e1*)] if *b1* < *b2* and *e1* ≤ *e2* are both true, [MAX(*e2*+1,*b1*):*e1*] if *b1* ≥ *b2* and *e1* > *e2* are both true, and is otherwise undefined. Note, therefore, that *i1* MINUS *i2* is undefined if either *i1* BEGINS *i2* or *i1* ENDS *i2* is true or if either of *i1* and *i2* is properly included in the other.

```
b1                e1
├───────i1───────┤

        b2                      e2
        ├──────────i2──────────┤

b1      b2-1
├───────┤
        └──────── i1 MINUS i2
```

NOTE: Given that intervals are sets (sets of points, to be specific), it might be thought that the set operators UNION, INTERSECT, and MINUS would apply directly. However:

- The general set union of *i1* and *i2* would not require *i1* and *i2* to be such that *i1* MERGES *i2* is true.

- The general set intersection of *i1* and *i2* would not require *i1* and *i2* to be such that *i1* OVERLAPS *i2* is true.

- The general set difference between *i1* and *i2* (in that order) would not require *i1* and *i2* to be such that *i1* BEGINS *i2*, *i1* ENDS *i2*, *i1* ⊃ *i2*, and *i1* ⊂ *i2* are all false.

These requirements are imposed on the interval versions of the operators in order to guarantee that the result is a proper interval in every case.[2]

---

2. Since we have now defined the UNION, INTERSECT, and MINUS operators to apply to intervals as well as relations, we can say those operators are *polymorphic* (see Chapter 1, Section 1.3). The particular kind of polymorphism involved is known as *overloading* polymorphism; other kinds exist, but further details are beyond the scope of the present discussion (see Chapter 16, Section 16.2).

Note: Reference [60] calls the interval UNION and INTERSECT operators MERGE and INTERVSECT, respectively (it does not discuss an interval MINUS operator). Observe that if *i1* INTERSECT *i2* is defined, then *i1* UNION *i2* is certainly defined, but the converse is not true (some pairs of intervals—which ones, exactly?—have a union but no intersection). Observe also that *i1* MINUS *i2* is sometimes defined when *i1* UNION *i2* and *i1* INTERSECT *i2* are not, and vice versa.

6.4 Sample Queries

The scalar operators discussed in the preceding sections are of course available for use within scalar expressions in all of the usual places. In particular, therefore, they can appear

- within the *<bool exp>* following the keyword WHERE in a *<relation delete>* or *<relation update>*

- within the *<bool exp>* in a *<where>*

- within an *<extend add>* or *<summarize add>*

Note: The various possibilities are phrased in terms of **Tutorial D** syntax. Refer to Chapters 1 and 2 if you need to refresh your memory regarding any of the constructs mentioned.

Consider the database of Fig. 5.1 or Endpaper Panel 4 at the front of the book once again (the fully temporal version involving intervals and relvars S_DURING and SP_DURING). Here is a possible query against that database ("Get supplier numbers for suppliers who were able to supply part P2 on day 8"):

```
( SP_DURING WHERE P# = P# ('P2')
            AND    d08 ∈ DURING ) { S# }
```

Explanation: The expression within the outer parentheses restricts the set of tuples appearing in relvar SP_DURING to just those for which the P# value is P2 and day 8 is contained in the interval that is the DURING value. The final "{S#}" then causes those tuples to be projected over attribute S#, thereby producing the desired result. Note: In practice, the expression "*d08*" in the comparison *d08* ∈ DURING would have to be replaced by an appropriate DATE selector invocation.

By way of another example, here is a possible formulation of the query "Get pairs of suppliers who were able to supply the same part at the same time":

```
WITH ( SP_DURING RENAME ( S# AS X#, DURING AS XD ) ) AS T1 ,
     ( SP_DURING RENAME ( S# AS Y#, DURING AS YD ) ) AS T2 ,
     ( T1 JOIN T2 ) AS T3 ,
     ( T3 WHERE XD OVERLAPS YD ) AS T4 ,
     ( T4 WHERE X# < Y# ) AS T5 :
T5 { X#, Y# }
```

EXPLANATION: This example is the first we have seen to use the WITH construct to introduce names for subexpressions. Relation T1 is the relation that is the current value of relvar SP_DURING, except that attributes S# and DURING are renamed as X# and XD, respectively; relation T2 is the same, except that the new attribute names are Y# and YD instead. Relation T3 is the join of T1 and T2 over part numbers. Relation T4 is the restriction of T3 to just those tuples where the XD and YD intervals overlap (meaning the suppliers were not just able to supply the same part but in fact were able to supply the same part *at the same time,* as required). Relation T5 is the restriction of T4 to just those tuples where supplier number X# is less than supplier number Y#. (The purpose of this step is twofold: It eliminates pairs of supplier numbers of the form (x,x), and it guarantees that the pairs (x,y) and (y,x) will not both appear. Of course, the operator "<" must be defined for type S# in order for this step to be legitimate.) The final projection over X# and Y# produces the desired result.

As a third example, suppose we want to get, not just pairs of suppliers who were able to supply the same part at the same time, but also the parts and times in question. Here is a possible formulation:

```
WITH ( SP_DURING RENAME ( S# AS X#, DURING AS XD ) ) AS T1 ,
     ( SP_DURING RENAME ( S# AS Y#, DURING AS YD ) ) AS T2 ,
     ( T1 JOIN T2 ) AS T3 ,
     ( T3 WHERE XD OVERLAPS YD ) AS T4 ,
     ( T4 WHERE X# < Y# ) AS T5 ,
     ( EXTEND T5 ADD ( XD INTERSECT YD ) AS DURING ) AS T6 :
T6 { X#, Y#, P#, DURING }
```

EXPLANATION: Relations T1, T2, T3, T4, and T5 are exactly as in the previous example. The EXTEND ... ADD then computes the relevant intervals, and the final projection produces the desired result.

As a final example, suppose we are given the following relvars (in outline):

```
FEDERAL_GOVT { PRESIDENT, PARTY, DURING }
STATE_GOVT   { GOVERNOR, STATE, PARTY, DURING }
```

The semantics are meant to be self-explanatory (the two DURING attributes are each assumed to be of type INTERVAL_DATE; for the sake of the example, we ignore the fact that presidential and gubernatorial administrations are usually expressed in terms of years, not days). Now suppose we want to obtain a result that looks like this:

```
RESULT { PRESIDENT, GOVERNOR, STATE, PARTY, DURING }
```

A tuple is to appear in this result if and only if the specified president and specified state governor both belong to the specified party and have overlapping periods of administration (and DURING specifies exactly the overlap in question). Writing a suitable relational expression to obtain this result is left as an exercise.

6.5 A Final Remark

It is worth pointing out that all of the operators on intervals discussed in this chapter—BEGIN, END, PRE, POST, POINT FROM, $\in$ and $\ni$, Allen's operators, COUNT, and interval UNION, INTERSECT, and MINUS—are *generic,* loosely speaking, in the sense that they apply to all possible intervals (i.e., intervals of any possible interval type). Also, most but not all—which, exactly?—make implicit use of the applicable successor function.

Exercises

1. Let i be an interval. Define the operators PRE(i), POST(i), and p FROM i.

2. If a and b are relations (or sets), then it is a fact that

   a INTERSECT b $\equiv$ a MINUS (a MINUS b)

   Is the same true if a and b are intervals?

3. Let i be a value of type INTERVAL_INTEGER. Write an expression to obtain the interval that results from extending i by its own length in both directions (e.g., [5:7] becomes [2:10]). In what circumstances will evaluation of your expression fail at run time?

4. Again, let i be a value of type INTERVAL_INTEGER. Write an expression to obtain the interval that is the middle third of i. You can assume that COUNT(i) is a multiple of three.

5. Let $i1$, $i2$, and $i3$ be intervals such that there is a single interval $i4$ consisting of every point p such that $p \in i1$ or $p \in i2$ or $p \in i3$. Write an expression, using operators defined in this chapter, that when evaluated yields $i4$. (Beware of the trap!)

6. Given the relvar STUDIED from Exercise 9 in Chapter 5, write a **Tutorial D** query whose result shows for every grade the average length of study for all students who achieved that grade. (We are assuming for the sake of this exercise that the university's courses are "self-study" ones and are completed at the student's own pace.)

7. Given the relvars STUDENT and ENROLLMENT from Exercise 9 in Chapter 5, write a query whose result is a relation pairing the student number of each student who has enrolled in at least two courses with the interval from that student's earliest registration date to the date of that student's second enrollment. Note that there might be several enrollments for the same student on the same date.

8. (Repeated from Section 6.4) Suppose we are given the following relvars (in outline):

   ```
   FEDERAL_GOVT { PRESIDENT, PARTY, DURING }
   STATE_GOVT   { GOVERNOR, STATE, PARTY, DURING }
   ```

The semantics are meant to be self-explanatory (the two DURING attributes are each assumed to be of type INTERVAL_DATE; for the sake of the example, we ignore the fact that presidential and gubernatorial administrations are usually expressed in terms of years, not days). Now suppose we want to obtain a result that looks like this:

```
RESULT { PRESIDENT, GOVERNOR, STATE, PARTY, DURING }
```

A tuple is to appear in this result if and only if the specified president and specified state governor both belong to the specified party and have overlapping periods of administration (and DURING specifies exactly the overlap in question). Write a suitable relational expression to obtain this result.

Chapter

7

THE EXPAND AND COLLAPSE OPERATORS

7.1   INTRODUCTION

In Chapters 5 and 6 we encountered a variety of generic scalar operators—BEGIN, PRE, OVERLAPS, MERGES, UNION, and so on—that apply to intervals (or pairs of intervals, rather, in most cases). In this chapter we will meet two more generic operators, which we call EXPAND and COLLAPSE.[1] Unlike those earlier operators, however, EXPAND and COLLAPSE are not scalar: They apply to *sets* of intervals instead of individual intervals (or pairs of intervals) per se, and they produce another such set of intervals as their result. More specifically, they take a set of intervals all of the same type as their input, and they return another set of intervals of that same type as their result. In each case, that result can be regarded as a particular **canonical form** for the input set—and the two canonical forms in question have important roles to play in the solutions we are at last beginning to approach to the temporal database problems we identified in Chapters 3 and 4.

---

1.   In references [28] and [39], we called these operators UNFOLD and COALESCE, respectively.

NOTE: The notion of canonical form is central to many branches of mathematics and related disciplines. It can be explained as follows: Given a set S of objects and a notion of equivalence among such objects, subset C of S is said to be a *set of canonical forms* for S (under the stated definition of equivalence) if and only if every object s in S is equivalent to just one object c in C. The object c is said to be the *canonical form* for the object s. All "interesting" properties that apply to the object s also apply to its canonical form c; thus, it is sufficient to study just the small set C, not the large set S, in order to obtain or prove a variety of "interesting" results regarding the objects in question.

The applicability of the foregoing ideas to sets of intervals in particular is explained in the next two sections.

7.2 EXPANDED FORM

As already indicated, the objects we wish to study are **sets of intervals,** where all of the intervals in question are of the same interval type (and are therefore necessarily defined over the same point type). Let $X1$ and $X2$ be two such sets. Then we define the necessary notion of **equivalence** thus:

> $X1$ and $X2$ are **equivalent** if and only if the set of all points contained in intervals in $X1$ is equal to the set of all points contained in intervals in $X2$.

By way of example, let $X1$ and $X2$ be the sets

    { [d01:d01], [d03:d05], [d04:d06] }

and

    { [d01:d01], [d03:d04], [d05:d05], [d05:d06] }

respectively. Clearly, sets $X1$ and $X2$ are not equal—that is, they are not the same set. However, it is easy to see that they are at least equivalent (under the foregoing definition of equivalence), because the set of all points p such that p is contained in some interval in $X1$ is equal to the set of all points p such that p is contained in some interval in $X2$. The set of points in question is, obviously enough, the set

    { d01, d03, d04, d05, d06 }

For reasons that will soon become apparent, however, we are interested not so much in this set of points as such, but rather in the corresponding set of *unit intervals* (let us call it $X3$):

    { [d01:d01], [d03:d03], [d04:d04], [d05:d05], [d06:d06] }

X3 is clearly equivalent to each of *X1* and *X2*. It is said to be the *expanded form* of each of those sets. More generally, if *X* is a set of intervals all of the same type, then the **expanded form** of *X* is the set of all intervals—more precisely, the set of all *unit* intervals—of the form [*p*:*p*], where *p* is a point in some interval in *X*. Given this definition, it should be clear that:

- Given any set *X* of intervals all of the same type, a corresponding expanded form of *X* always exists.

- That expanded form is equivalent to *X*.

- That expanded form is unique.

Note in particular that if *X* is empty, then the expanded form of *X* is empty too.

The expanded form of *X* is one possible canonical form for *X*. To be precise, it is that unique equivalent set whose contained intervals are all of the minimum possible length (i.e., one). Intuitively, the expanded form of *X* allows us to focus on the information content of *X* at an atomic level, without having to worry about the many ways in which that information might be bundled into "clumps."

By the way, note how the concept of expanded form relies on the successor function for the underlying point type. To be specific, the successor function is needed in order to determine the set of points in any given interval in the given set *X* (and hence to determine the corresponding set of unit intervals). Note too that the concept of expanded form allows us to restate our original definition of equivalence more succinctly, as follows:

Two sets of intervals are equivalent if and only if they have the same expanded form.

As an exercise, consider the two sets of intervals shown as values of the DURING attribute in relvars S_DURING and SP_DURING in Figure 5.1 (or Endpaper Panel 4). Are those two sets equivalent? What are the corresponding expanded forms?

7.3 COLLAPSED FORM

The sets *X1*, *X2*, and *X3* discussed in the previous section all have different cardinalities. In fact, it so happens in that particular example that *X3* (the expanded form) is the one whose cardinality is the greatest; however, it is easy to find another set *X4* that has the same expanded form—that is, it is equivalent to *X1* and *X2*—but has cardinality greater than that of *X3*. One such set *X4* (not the only one possible) is:

{ [d01:d01], [d03:d03], [d03:d04], [d03:d05], [d03:d06],
                [d04:d04], [d04:d05], [d04:d06] }

It is also easy to find the much more interesting set *X5* that has the same expanded form and the **minimum possible** cardinality:

{ [d01:d01], [d03:d06] }

X5 is said to be the *collapsed form* of *X1* (and also of *X2, X3,* and *X4*). More generally, if *X* is a set of intervals all of the same type, then the **collapsed form** of *X* is the set *Y* of intervals of the same type such that:

- *X* and *Y* have the same expanded form.

- No two distinct intervals *i1* and *i2* in *Y* are such that *i1* MERGES *i2* is true (recall that MERGES means "overlaps or abuts"). Equivalently, no two distinct intervals *i1* and *i2* in *Y* are such that *i1* UNION *i2* is defined.

It follows from this last point that *Y* can be computed from *X* by successively replacing pairs of intervals in *X* by their union until no further such replacements are possible. It further follows that no two distinct intervals *i1* and *i2* in *Y* are such that *i1* INTERSECT *i2* is defined, either. NOTE: The intersection *i1* INTERSECT *i2* is likewise not defined for any pair of intervals *i1* and *i2* in the *expanded* form of *X;* however, the union *i1* UNION *i2* might be. To be specific, *i1* UNION *i2* will be defined for such a pair of intervals if and only if the—necessarily unique—points *p1* and *p2* in *i1* and *i2,* respectively, are such that one is the immediate successor of the other.

The collapsed form of *X* is another possible canonical form for *X*. To be precise, it is that unique equivalent set that has the minimum possible cardinality. Intuitively, the collapsed form of *X* allows us to focus on the information content of *X* in a compressed ("clumped") form, without having to worry about the possibility that distinct "clumps" might meet or overlap.

By the way, note how the concept of collapsed form relies on the successor function for the underlying point type. To be specific, it relies on the MERGES operator, that operator in turn relies on the MEETS operator, and *that* operator relies on the successor function. Note too that (as we have already seen) many distinct sets can have the same collapsed form. Also, it should be clear that:

- Given any set *X* of intervals all of the same type, a corresponding collapsed form of *X* always exists.

- That collapsed form is equivalent to *X*.

- That collapsed form is unique.

Note in particular that if *X* is empty, then the collapsed form of *X* is empty too. The following is also a true statement:

Two sets of intervals are equivalent if and only if they have the same collapsed form.

As an exercise, consider again the two sets of intervals shown as values of the DUR-ING attribute in relvars S_DURING and SP_DURING in Figure 5.1 (or Endpaper Panel 4). What are the corresponding collapsed forms of those sets?

7.4 OPERATING ON SETS OF INTERVALS

We can now define the EXPAND and COLLAPSE operators. Let X be a set of intervals all of the same type. Then EXPAND(X) returns the expanded form of X and COLLAPSE(X) returns the collapsed form of X. Note in particular that:

- If X has cardinality zero, the result does too (for both EXPAND and COLLAPSE).
- If X has cardinality one, the result is equal to X for COLLAPSE, but not for EXPAND (unless the single interval in X happens to be a unit interval).

By the way, do not make the mistake of thinking that EXPAND and COLLAPSE are inverses of each other. For example, let $X1$ be the set

{ [d01:d01], [d03:d05], [d04:d06] }

(as before). If we expand this set and then collapse the result, we necessarily obtain the collapsed form $X5$:

{ [d01:d01], [d03:d06] }

And if we collapse the original set $X1$ and then expand the result, we (again necessarily) obtain the expanded form $X3$:

{ [d01:d01], [d03:d03], [d04:d04], [d05:d05], [d06:d06] }

In other words, neither EXPAND(COLLAPSE(X)) nor COLLAPSE(EXPAND(X)) is identically equal to X, in general (though they are both equivalent to X, of course). Indeed, it is easy to see that the following identities hold:

- EXPAND (COLLAPSE (X)) ≡ EXPAND (X)
- COLLAPSE (EXPAND (X)) ≡ COLLAPSE (X)

It follows that the first operation in a collapse-then-expand or expand-then-collapse sequence on some set X can simply be ignored, a fact that could be useful for optimization purposes (especially when that first operation is EXPAND).

Formal Definitions

NOTE: This subsection is included primarily for reasons of completeness. It requires an elementary understanding of the quantifiers of predicate logic (see Chapter 1). However, it can safely be skipped without interfering with the overall flow.

We now give formal definitions of the EXPAND and COLLAPSE operators, in order to show that—like so much else discussed in this book—they really are just shorthand. First EXPAND. Let X be a set of intervals all of the same type, IT say, and let i and j be intervals of type IT. Let $i = [b{:}e]$. Then we have:

```
EXPAND ( X )  ≡  { i : b = e AND
                        ( EXISTS j ∈ X ) ( b ∈ j ) }
```

In other words, EXPAND(X) is the set of all intervals i of type IT such that (1) the begin and end points of i are equal and (2) the point in question is contained within at least one interval in X. Note that we have extended our use of the set membership operator "∈" to apply not just to a point and an interval ("$b \in j$"), but also to an interval and a set of intervals ("$j \in X$"); in fact, we are *overloading* the " ∈ " operator (see the footnote on this topic in Chapter 6, page 94).

COLLAPSE is a little more complicated. Again, let X be a set of intervals all of the same type IT; also, let the underlying point type be T. Let $i, i1, i2, j,$ and k be intervals of type IT, and let t be a point of type T. Let $i = [b{:}e], i1 = [b1{:}e1],$ and $i2 = [b2{:}e2]$. Then we have:

```
 0  COLLAPSE ( X )  ≡
 1      { i : ( EXISTS i1 ∈ X )
 2          ( ( EXISTS i2 ∈ X )
 3              ( b = b1 AND e = e2 AND b1 ≤ b2 AND e1 ≤ e2 AND
 4                ( FORALL t < b )
 5                  ( NOT ( EXISTS j ∈ X )
 6                         ( PRIOR_T ( b ) ∈ j ) )
 7              AND
 8                ( FORALL t > e )
 9                  ( NOT ( EXISTS j ∈ X )
10                         ( NEXT_T ( e ) ∈ j ) )
11              AND
12                ( FORALL t )
13                  ( IF t > e1 AND t < b2 THEN
14                         ( EXISTS k ∈ X ) ( t ∈ k )
15                      END IF )
16              )
17          )
18      }
```

EXPLANATION: Note first of all that if i appears in COLLAPSE(X), then the begin point of i must be the begin point of at least one interval $i1$ in X and the end point of *i* must be the end point of at least one interval *i2* in *X* (see lines 1 through 3; *i1* and *i2* are not necessarily distinct, of course). We require that $b1 \leq b2$ AND $e1 \leq e2$ (line 3 again) in order to ensure that *i1* neither begins nor ends after *i2* does, so that we can say definitively that BEGIN(*i*) is *b1*, not *b2*, and END(*i*) is *e2*, not *e1*. Lines 4 through 6 guarantee that there is no interval in *X* that contains the predecessor *b*–1 of BEGIN(*i*)—for if such an interval existed, it would have to be combined with *i*. (Line 4 is necessary to ensure that the *b* in line 6 does not denote the first value of type *T*; if it did, then the PRIOR_*T* invocation in that line would be undefined.) Likewise, lines 8 through 10 guarantee that there is no interval in *X* that contains the successor *e*+1 of END(*i*), for the same reason. Finally, lines 12 through 15 guarantee that if there is a "gap" between *i1* and *i2* (i.e., if *i1* MEETS *i2* is false), then every point in that gap is contained in some interval in *X*, and hence is justifiably included in *i*.

Some questions:

1. What happens to the foregoing definition if *X* is empty?

   ANSWER: COLLAPSE(*X*) is equal to *X* in this case.

2. What happens if *X* contains just one interval?

   ANSWER: COLLAPSE(*X*) is equal to *X* in this case too.

3. What happens if *X* contains an interval with begin point equal to FIRST_*T*() or end point equal to LAST_*T*()?

   ANSWER: See the explanation above, fourth sentence.

7.5 TREATING SETS AS UNARY RELATIONS

You might have noticed that we have been indulging in a little sleight of hand in this chapter so far. To be specific, we have been describing two operators, EXPAND and COLLAPSE, that apply to sets (sets of intervals, to be specific[2]); however, the relational model deals specifically with relations, not with sets in general, and thus EXPAND and COLLAPSE as described so far are not a very good fit with the relational model. So we have some tidying up to do, and that is the purpose of this section.

We begin with the fundamental observation that any set of values all of the same type can easily be converted into a unary relation. That is, if *v1, v2, ..., vn* are values all of the same type *T* (and all distinct, of course), then the *relation selector invocation*—

```
RELATION { A T } { TUPLE { A v1 } ,
                   TUPLE { A v2 } ,
                   .......
                   TUPLE { A vn } }
```

—will produce a relation that looks like this:

---

2. Actually it is possible to generalize the operators to apply to sets in which the contained values are of some other type (i.e., not intervals). We will investigate this possibility in Appendix B.

```
 A
───
 v1
 v2
 ..
 vn
```

Just to remind you, the specification {A *T*} in the selector invocation defines the heading for the relation being selected. Such a specification can always be omitted from a given relation selector invocation unless the given set of values *v1, v2, ..., vn* is empty. If such were the case in this example, the relation selector invocation would degenerate to the form RELATION {A *T*} {}.

In order to stay within the framework of the relational model, therefore, what we need to do—and of course what we can do, without any loss of generality—is replace the EXPAND and COLLAPSE operators as previously described by versions in which the argument is specified as a unary relation instead of just a set. (We adopted the fiction we did—that the operators applied to sets, not unary relations—in earlier sections of this chapter purely for pedagogic reasons.)

Replacing the operators as just suggested is straightforward, of course. In the case of EXPAND, the unary-relation form of the operator is similar to the set form as previously described, except that the input and output, instead of just being sets of intervals, are now unary relations whose tuples contain those intervals as such. For example, suppose the input relation (*r*, say) looks like this:

```
 DURING
─────────
[d06:d09]
[d04:d08]
[d05:d10]
[d01:d01]
```

Then EXPAND(*r*) produces a result that looks like this:

```
 DURING
─────────
[d01:d01]
[d04:d04]
[d05:d05]
[d06:d06]
[d07:d07]
[d08:d08]
[d09:d09]
[d10:d10]
```

Likewise, the unary-relation form of COLLAPSE is similar to the set form as previously described, except that the input and output, instead of just being sets of intervals, are unary relations whose tuples contain those intervals as such. For example, if the unary relation *r* is as for the preceding EXPAND example, COLLAPSE(*r*) produces a result that looks like this:

We can also define a notion of equivalence for such unary relations: Two such relations are equivalent if and only if they have the same expanded form (or the same collapsed form).

Finally, please note carefully that we will take all references to EXPAND and COLLAPSE throughout the remainder of this book as references to the unary-relation versions as just defined—barring explicit statements to the contrary, of course. However, please note also that some of those "explicit statements to the contrary" appear in the very next section!

7.6 OPERATING ON NULLARY RELATIONS

For reasons that will become clear in the next two chapters, it is highly desirable to define versions of the EXPAND and COLLAPSE operators that work on *nullary* relations instead of unary ones. Recall from Chapter 1 that a nullary relation is one that has no attributes, and that there are exactly two such:

- TABLE_DEE, which contains just one tuple (necessarily the "0-tuple," that is, the tuple with no components);
- TABLE_DUM, which contains no tuples at all.

It follows that a nullary relation cannot possibly contain intervals—more precisely, it cannot contain tuples that contain intervals—but this fact need not deter us from our goal. To be specific:

- We define the result of expanding or collapsing a nullary relation, reasonably enough, to be equal to the input in both cases. Thus, for example, COLLAPSE (TABLE_DEE) returns TABLE_DEE, and COLLAPSE (TABLE_DUM) returns TABLE_DUM.
- We also define two nullary relations to be equivalent, again reasonably enough, if and only if they are equal.

We close this section, and this chapter, by observing that the EXPAND and COLLAPSE operators as we have defined them are still not quite what we need to deal with temporal databases; they are just another stepping-stone on the way, so to speak. The point is, those operators work on unary (or nullary) relations, and we are going to need operators that work on general n-ary relations instead (in particular, on n-ary relations that include interval attributes). We will introduce such operators in Chapter 8.

EXERCISES

1. (Repeated from Section 7.2) Consider the two sets of intervals shown as values of the DURING attribute in relvars S_DURING and SP_DURING in Endpaper Panel 4. Are those two sets equivalent? What are the corresponding expanded and collapsed forms?

2. Let MOD3 be the type whose values are the integers 0, 1, and 2.[3] Consider the type RELATION { DURING INTERVAL_MOD3 }. How many relations xr of this type satisfy the condition EXPAND(xr) = xr? List every relation cr of this type that satisfies the condition COLLAPSE(cr) = cr.

---

3. MOD3 is in fact a *subtype* of type INTEGER (see Chapter 16).

Chapter

8

THE PACK AND UNPACK OPERATORS

8.1   INTRODUCTION

The purpose of this chapter is to introduce and describe certain relational operators that build on the operators COLLAPSE and EXPAND discussed in Chapter 7. The operators in question are called PACK and UNPACK.[1] The following examples should help you understand the detailed discussions that appear in subsequent sections. Suppose relation *r* looks like this (this relation is not meant to correspond in any particular way to our usual sample data values):

---

1. In references [28] and [39], we used the names COALESCE and UNFOLD for PACK and UNPACK, respectively (as well as for COLLAPSE and EXPAND).

S#	DURING
S2	[d02:d04]
S2	[d03:d05]
S4	[d02:d05]
S4	[d04:d06]
S4	[d09:d10]

Packing this relation "on DURING"—which we will express formally as PACK *r* ON DURING—gives:

S#	DURING
S2	[d02:d05]
S4	[d02:d06]
S4	[d09:d10]

Informally, this result represents the same information as the original relation *r*, but *packed* or rearranged in such a way that no two DURING intervals for a given supplier either meet or overlap. The effect of that packing is thus to let us view the information content of *r* in a clumped form, without having to worry about the possibility that distinct clumps might meet or overlap; in fact, the original relation and the packed version are *equivalent*, in a sense we will explain in the final section of this chapter. The relevance of COLLAPSE to such packing should be obvious.

Analogously, **unpacking** that same original relation *r* "on DURING," which we will express formally as UNPACK *r* ON DURING, gives:

S#	DURING
S2	[d02:d02]
S2	[d03:d03]
S2	[d04:d04]
S2	[d05:d05]
S4	[d02:d02]
S4	[d03:d03]
S4	[d04:d04]
S4	[d05:d05]
S4	[d06:d06]
S4	[d09:d09]
S4	[d10:d10]

Informally, this result also represents the same information as the original relation *r*, but *unpacked* or rearranged in such a way that every DURING value is a unit interval specifically. The effect of that unpacking is thus to let us view the information content of *r* at an atomic level, without having to worry about the many ways in which that information might be bundled into clumps (as you will surely expect, the original relation is equivalent to the unpacked version, just as it is to the packed version). The relevance of EXPAND to such unpacking should be obvious.

In the next two sections, we will explain the PACK and UNPACK operators in detail. Our explanations are based on examples that in turn are based on Queries A and B from the very end of Chapter 4. For convenience, we repeat those queries here:

- **Query A:** Get S#-FROM-TO triples for suppliers who have been able to supply at least one part during at least one interval of time, where FROM and TO together designate a maximal interval during which supplier S# was in fact able to supply at least one part. NOTE: We use the term "maximal" here as a convenient shorthand to mean (in the case at hand) that supplier S# was unable to supply any part at all on the day immediately before FROM or immediately after TO. Note too that the result of the query might contain several tuples for the same supplier (but with different intervals, of course; moreover, those intervals will neither abut nor overlap).

- **Query B:** Get S#-FROM-TO triples for suppliers who have been unable to supply any parts at all during at least one interval of time, where FROM and TO together designate a maximal interval during which supplier S# was in fact unable to supply any part at all. (Again the result might contain several tuples for the same supplier.)

8.2 PACKING RELATIONS

We concentrate first on Query A. Following is a restatement of that query in terms of the database of Figure 5.1 (i.e., the version of the database—repeated in Endpaper Panel 4 at the front of the book—that contains intervals as such instead of explicit FROM-TO pairs):

- **Query A:** Get S#-DURING pairs for suppliers who have been able to supply at least one part during at least one interval of time, where DURING designates a maximal interval during which supplier S# was in fact able to supply at least one part.

You will probably recall that an earlier version of this query (also discussed in Chapter 4) required the use of certain operations of a grouping nature; more specifically, it involved a relational SUMMARIZE operator. You will probably not be surprised to learn, therefore, that this restated version is also going to require certain operations of a grouping nature. However, we will build up our formulation of that query one small step at a time, and the grouping per se will not come into the picture until the second step. Here then is the first step:

```
WITH SP_DURING { S#, DURING } AS T1 :
```

(There is more of this expression to come, as the colon suggests.) This step merely "projects away" part numbers, which are irrelevant to the query under consideration, and introduces a name for the result of that projection. Given our usual sample data values, T1 looks like this:

S#	DURING
S1	[d04:d10]
S1	[d05:d10]
S1	[d09:d10]
S1	[d06:d10]
S2	[d02:d04]
S2	[d08:d10]
S2	[d03:d03]
S2	[d09:d10]
S3	[d08:d10]
S4	[d06:d09]
S4	[d04:d08]
S4	[d05:d10]

Observe now that this relation contains redundant information; for example, we are told no fewer than three times that supplier S1 was able to supply something on day 6. The desired result, eliminating all such redundancy, is clearly as follows (let us call it RESULT):

S#	DURING
S1	[d04:d10]
S2	[d02:d04]
S2	[d08:d10]
S3	[d08:d10]
S4	[d04:d10]

We call this result the **packed form** of T1 **on** DURING. Note very carefully that a DURING value for a given supplier in this packed form need not exist as an explicit DURING value for that supplier in the relation T1 from which the packed form is derived; in our example, this remark applies to supplier S4 in particular (but to supplier S4 only, as it happens).

Now, we will eventually reach a point where we can obtain this result by means of a simple expression of the form

```
PACK T1 ON DURING
```

As already indicated, however, we want to build up to that point gradually. The next step is as follows:

```
WITH ( T1 GROUP { DURING } AS X ) AS T2 :
```

T2 looks like this:

S#	X
S1	DURING
	[d04:d10]
	[d05:d10]
	[d09:d10]
	[d06:d10]
S2	DURING
	[d02:d04]
	[d08:d10]
	[d03:d03]
	[d09:d10]
S3	DURING
	[d08:d10]
S4	DURING
	[d06:d09]
	[d04:d08]
	[d05:d10]

Note in particular that attribute X of T2 is relation-valued.

Next, we apply the COLLAPSE operator from the previous chapter to the unary relations that are values of the relation-valued attribute X:

```
WITH ( EXTEND T2 ADD COLLAPSE ( X ) AS Y )
                              { ALL BUT X } AS T3 :
```

T3 looks like this (note that attribute X has been projected away, thanks to the specification "{ALL BUT X}"):

S#	Y
S1	DURING [d04:d10]
S2	DURING [d02:d04] [d08:d10]
S3	DURING [d08:d10]
S4	DURING [d04:d10]

Finally, we ungroup:

```
T3 UNGROUP Y
```

This expression yields the relation we earlier called RESULT. In other words, now showing all of the steps together (and simplifying slightly), RESULT is the result of evaluating the following overall expression:

```
WITH SP_DURING { S#, DURING } AS T1 ,
    ( T1 GROUP { DURING } AS X ) AS T2 ,
    ( EXTEND T2 ADD COLLAPSE ( X ) AS Y ) { ALL BUT X } AS T3 :
T3 UNGROUP Y
```

Obviously, it would be desirable to be able to get from T1 to RESULT in a single operation. To that end, we introduce (at last!) our new PACK operator, with syntax as follows:

```
PACK R ON A
```

Here R is a relational expression and A is an interval attribute of the relation r denoted by that expression. The semantics are defined by obvious generalization of the grouping, extension, projection, and ungrouping operations by which we obtained RESULT from T1:

```
PACK R ON A  ≡  WITH ( R GROUP { A } AS X ) AS R1 ,
                   ( EXTEND R1 ADD COLLAPSE ( X ) AS Y )
                                        { ALL BUT X } AS R2 :
             R2 UNGROUP Y
```

PACK is thus obviously just shorthand. NOTE: It might help to point out that—as should be clear from the definition—packing a relation *on* some attribute A involves grouping that relation *by* all of its attributes apart from that attribute A. (Recall that the expression "T1 GROUP {DURING} ..." can be read "group T1 *by* S#," S# being the sole attribute of T1 apart from the one mentioned in the GROUP specification.) However, note that, while R GROUP $\{A\}$ ... is guaranteed to return a result with exactly one tuple for each distinct value of B (where B is all of the attributes of R apart from A), PACK R ON A might return a result with several tuples for any given value of B. By way of illustration, refer to the PACK result shown in Section 8.1, which has two tuples for supplier S4.

To get back to Query A, we can now offer the following as a reasonably concise formulation of that query:

```
PACK SP_DURING { S#, DURING } ON DURING
```

The overall operation denoted by this expression is an example of what is sometimes called *temporal projection* (see, e.g., reference [53]). To be specific, it is a "temporal projection" of SP_DURING over S# and DURING. (Recall that the original version of this query—see Chapter 4, Section 4.1—involved a *regular* projection of SP over S#.) We will have quite a lot more to say about temporal projection and other "temporal" operators in the next chapter.

8.3 UNPACKING RELATIONS

We now turn to Query B. Following is a restatement of that query in terms of the database of Figure 5.1 or Endpaper Panel 4:

- **Query B:** Get S#-DURING pairs for suppliers who have been unable to supply any parts at all during at least one interval of time, where DURING designates a maximal interval during which supplier S# was in fact unable to supply any part at all.

Recall now that the original version of this query involved a relational difference operation. Thus, if you are expecting to see something that might be called a *temporal difference*, then of course you are correct. As you might also be expecting, while temporal projection involves the relational PACK operator, temporal difference involves the relational UNPACK operator. (Actually it involves the PACK operator as well, as we will soon see.)

Like the regular difference operation, temporal difference involves two relation operands. In the example, in fact, it should be intuitively clear that what we need to do, in essence, is look for S#-DURING pairs that appear in or are implied by S_DURING and do *not* appear in and are *not* implied by SP_DURING. This brief characterization should be sufficient to suggest (correctly) that, again in essence, what we need to do is perform a couple of unpack operations and then take the difference between the results. So let us first introduce the UNPACK operator:

```
UNPACK R ON A  ≡  WITH ( R GROUP { A } AS X ) AS R1 ,
                       ( EXTEND R1 ADD EXPAND ( X ) AS Y )
                                        { ALL BUT X } AS R2 :
              R2 UNGROUP Y
```

This definition is identical to that for PACK, except for the appearance of EXPAND rather than COLLAPSE in the second line. We call the result of the expression the **unpacked form** of R on A.

Returning to Query B, we can now obtain the left operand we need (i.e., S#-DURING pairs that appear in or are implied by S_DURING) as follows:

```
UNPACK S_DURING { S#, DURING } ON DURING
```

For purposes of subsequent reference, here is the expanded form of this expression:

```
WITH S_DURING { S#, DURING } AS T1 ,
   ( T1 GROUP { DURING } AS X ) AS T2 ,
   ( EXTEND T2 ADD EXPAND ( X ) AS Y ) { ALL BUT X } AS T3 :
T3 UNGROUP Y
```

Working through this expression in detail, step by step, is left as an exercise. Given the sample data of Figure 5.1, however, the overall result—let us call it U1—looks like this:

S#	DURING
S1	[d04:d04]
S1	[d05:d05]
S1	[d06:d06]
S1	[d07:d07]
S1	[d08:d08]
S1	[d09:d09]
S1	[d10:d10]
S2	[d02:d02]
S2	[d03:d03]
S2	[d04:d04]
S2	[d07:d07]
S2	[d08:d08]
S2	[d09:d09]
S2	[d10:d10]
S3	[d03:d03]
S3	[d04:d04]
S3	[d05:d05]
S3	[d06:d06]
S3	[d07:d07]
S3	[d08:d08]
S3	[d09:d09]
S3	[d10:d10]
S4	[d04:d04]
S4	[d05:d05]
S4	[d06:d06]
S4	[d07:d07]
S4	[d08:d08]
S4	[d09:d09]
S4	[d10:d10]
S5	[d02:d02]
S5	[d03:d03]
S5	[d04:d04]
S5	[d05:d05]
S5	[d06:d06]
S5	[d07:d07]
S5	[d08:d08]
S5	[d09:d09]
S5	[d10:d10]

So now we have the left operand for the difference operation we are gradually building up to. Of course, the right operand (i.e., S#-DURING pairs that appear in or are implied by SP_DURING) is obtained in like fashion:

```
UNPACK SP_DURING { S#, DURING } ON DURING
```

Let us call the result of this expression U2. That result looks like this:

S#	DURING
S1	[d04:d04]
S1	[d05:d05]
S1	[d06:d06]
S1	[d07:d07]
S1	[d08:d08]
S1	[d09:d09]
S1	[d10:d10]
S2	[d02:d02]
S2	[d03:d03]
S2	[d04:d04]
S2	[d08:d08]
S2	[d09:d09]
S2	[d10:d10]
S3	[d08:d08]
S3	[d09:d09]
S3	[d10:d10]
S4	[d04:d04]
S4	[d05:d05]
S4	[d06:d06]
S4	[d07:d07]
S4	[d08:d08]
S4	[d09:d09]
S4	[d10:d10]

Now we can apply (regular) relation difference:

```
U1 MINUS U2
```

The result of this expression, U3 say, looks like this:

S#	DURING
S2	[d07:d07]
S3	[d03:d03]
S3	[d04:d04]
S3	[d05:d05]
S3	[d06:d06]
S3	[d07:d07]
S5	[d02:d02]
S5	[d03:d03]
S5	[d04:d04]
S5	[d05:d05]
S5	[d06:d06]
S5	[d07:d07]
S5	[d08:d08]
S5	[d09:d09]
S5	[d10:d10]

Finally, we pack U3 on DURING to obtain the desired overall result:

```
PACK U3 ON DURING
```

The final result looks like this:

S#	DURING
S2	[d07:d07]
S3	[d03:d07]
S5	[d02:d10]

Here then is a formulation of Query B as a single nested expression:

```
PACK
  ( ( UNPACK S_DURING { S#, DURING } ON DURING )
    MINUS
    ( UNPACK SP_DURING { S#, DURING } ON DURING ) )
ON DURING
```

As already indicated, the overall operation denoted by this expression is an example of what is sometimes called *temporal difference*. More precisely, it is a temporal difference between (1) the projection of S_DURING over S# and DURING[2] and (2) the projection of SP_DURING over S# and DURING (in that order). Again, we will have much more to say on such matters in the next chapter; here we content ourselves with a few additional remarks on the semantics of the PACK and UNPACK operators. Here first is a repeat of the formal definition of UNPACK:

```
UNPACK R ON A  ≡  WITH ( R GROUP { A } AS X ) AS R1 ,
                       ( EXTEND R1 ADD EXPAND ( X ) AS Y )
                                            { ALL BUT X } AS R2 :
                  R2 UNGROUP Y
```

Now observe the following:

- Unpacking R on A (just like packing R on A) involves grouping R by all of the attributes of R apart from A.

- Like PACK, UNPACK is really just shorthand; in particular, it is defined in terms of the EXPAND operator from the previous chapter.

- The following identities hold (obviously enough):

```
UNPACK R ON A  ≡  UNPACK ( PACK R ON A ) ON A
PACK R ON A    ≡  PACK ( UNPACK R ON A ) ON A
```

It follows that the first operation in a pack-then-unpack or unpack-then-pack sequence on some given relation can simply be ignored, a fact that could be useful for optimization purposes (especially when that first operation is UNPACK).

- Like the operators COLLAPSE and EXPAND on which they are based, PACK and UNPACK are not inverses of each other. That is, neither of the expressions UNPACK (PACK R ON A) ON A and PACK (UNPACK R ON A) ON A is guaranteed to return a result that is equal to R, in general.

8.4 SAMPLE QUERIES

In this section we give further examples of the use of PACK and UNPACK in formulating queries. We assume, reasonably enough, that the result is required in suitably packed form in every case.

Our first example is deliberately not a temporal one. Suppose we are given a relvar NHW, with attributes NAME, HEIGHT, and WEIGHT, giving the height and weight of certain persons. Consider the query "For each weight represented in NHW, get every

---

2. The projection of S_DURING over S# and DURING is an *identity* projection, of course (i.e., the expression "S_DURING {S#,DURING}" is logically equivalent to just "S_DURING").

range of heights such that for each such range *r* and for each height in *r* there is at least one person represented in NHW who is of that height and that weight." Here is a possible formulation:

```
PACK
    ( ( EXTEND NHW { HEIGHT, WEIGHT }
        ADD INTERVAL_HEIGHT ( [ HEIGHT : HEIGHT ] ) AS HR )
      { WEIGHT, HR } )
ON HR
```

EXPLANATION: We begin by projecting NHW over HEIGHT and WEIGHT, thereby obtaining all height-weight pairs in the original relation (i.e., all height-weight pairs such that there is at least one person of that height and weight). We then extend that projection by introducing another attribute, HR, whose value in any given tuple is a unit interval of the form [*h:h*], where *h* is the HEIGHT value in that same tuple (note the invocation of the interval selector INTERVAL_HEIGHT). We then project away the HEIGHT attribute and pack the result on HR. The final result is a relation with two attributes, WEIGHT and HR, and predicate as follows:

For all heights h in HR—but not for h = PRE(HR) or h = POST(HR)—there exists at least one person p such that p has weight WEIGHT and height h.

Note that this example is indeed, as previously stated, not a temporal one—the intervals involved represent ranges of heights, not temporal intervals (in other words, they are of type INTERVAL_HEIGHT, where HEIGHT is the applicable point type).

By way of a second example, consider relvar SP_DURING once again (see Endpaper Panel 4). At any given time, if there are any shipments at all at that time, then there is some part number *pmax* such that no supplier is able to supply any part at that time with a part number greater than *pmax*. (Obviously we are assuming here that the operator ">" is defined for values of type P#.) So consider the query "For each part number that has ever been such a *pmax* value, get that part number together with the interval(s) during which it actually was that *pmax* value." Here is a possible formulation:

```
WITH ( UNPACK SP_DURING ON DURING ) AS SP_UNPACKED ,
     ( SUMMARIZE SP_UNPACKED
       PER SP_UNPACKED { DURING }
       ADD MAX ( P# ) AS PMAX ) AS SUMMARY :
PACK SUMMARY ON DURING
```

Our third and last example is based on relvar S_PARTS_DURING from Section 5.4 (the one with two interval attributes). For convenience, we show a sample value for that relvar in Figure 8.1 (a repeat of Figure 5.2). Consider the query "For each part that has ever been capable of being supplied by supplier S3, get the part number and the applicable intervals of time." (Given the values shown in Figure 8.1, the desired result is as shown in Figure 8.2.) Here is a possible formulation:

```
WITH ( S_PARTS_DURING WHERE S# = S# ('S3') ) AS T1 ,
     T1 { PARTS, DURING } AS T2 ,
     ( UNPACK T2 ON PARTS ) AS T3 ,
     ( EXTEND T3 ADD POINT FROM PARTS AS P# ) AS T4 ,
     T4 { P#, DURING } AS T5 :
PACK T5 ON DURING
```

Note the use of POINT FROM in this example to extract the single point from a unit interval. EXERCISE: Give a formulation of this same query using our usual relvar SP_DURING instead of S_PARTS_DURING. Also, give formulations of the query "For each day on which some part has been capable of being supplied by supplier S3, get that day and the applicable ranges of parts," using (1) relvar S_PARTS_DURING, (2) relvar SP_DURING. What conclusions do you draw from this exercise?

FIGURE 8.1

Relvar
S_PARTS_DURING
(sample value).

S_PARTS_DURING

S#	PARTS	DURING
S1	[P1:P3]	[d01:d04]
S1	[P2:P4]	[d07:d08]
S1	[P5:P6]	[d09:d09]
S2	[P1:P1]	[d08:d09]
S2	[P1:P2]	[d08:d08]
S2	[P3:P4]	[d07:d08]
S3	[P2:P4]	[d01:d04]
S3	[P3:P5]	[d01:d04]
S3	[P2:P4]	[d05:d06]
S3	[P2:P4]	[d06:d09]
S4	[P3:P4]	[d05:d08]

FIGURE 8.2

Sample result.

P#	DURING
P2	[d01:d09]
P3	[d01:d09]
P4	[d01:d09]
P5	[d01:d04]

8.5 PACKING AND UNPACKING ON NO ATTRIBUTES

Up to this point, we have considered the packing and unpacking of relations on just a single attribute of the relation in question. However, it is possible to generalize the operators in such a way as to allow packing and unpacking to be done on *any subset* of the attributes of the relation in question, including the empty set of attributes in particular (since the empty set is a subset of every set)—just so long as every attribute in the set of attributes in question is interval-valued, of course. We consider the empty set of attributes in this section and other (i.e., nonempty) sets of attributes in the next section.

As we will see in the next chapter, the ability to pack or unpack a relation on no attributes at all turns out to be very important. The syntax is as follows:

- PACK R ON ()

- UNPACK R ON ()

We define the result of both of these expressions to be, simply, the relation r that is the result of evaluating the specified relational expression R. We justify this position as follows. First, PACK R ON () is defined, reasonably enough, to be shorthand for the expression

```
WITH ( R GROUP { } AS X ) AS R1 ,
     ( EXTEND R1 ADD COLLAPSE ( X ) AS Y )
              { ALL BUT X } AS R2 :
R2 UNGROUP Y
```

This expression is identical to the expansion for PACK R ON A, except that the first step (the grouping step) specifies "GROUP {}" instead of "GROUP {A}." Thus, the semantics are as follows:

- The grouping step gives an intermediate result R1 with the same cardinality as r and with the same heading as r except that it contains one additional attribute, X, which is relation-valued. (Recall from Chapter 1 that, in general, the result of R GROUP {A1,A2,...,An} AS B has degree nR−n+1, where nR is the degree of R. If $n = 0$, therefore, the—possibly counterintuitive—effect is indeed to *add* an attribute to the heading.) Relations that are values of X have degree zero; that is, they are nullary relations. Furthermore, each of those relations is TABLE_DEE, not TABLE_DUM, because every tuple t in r effectively includes the 0-tuple as its value for that subtuple of t that corresponds to the empty set of attributes. Thus, each tuple in R1 effectively consists of the corresponding tuple from r extended with the X value TABLE_DEE.

- The next step gives an intermediate result R2 that is identical to R1 except that attribute X is renamed Y. (Recall from Chapter 7 that collapsing TABLE_DEE returns TABLE_DEE.)

- The final step then effectively replaces each tuple *t* in *R2* by its concatenation with the 0-tuple, discards the attribute *Y*, and then returns the relation thereby obtained as the overall result. But concatenating any tuple *t* with the 0-tuple simply yields that same tuple *t*. Thus, the final result is identical to relation *r*.

Turning now to UNPACK, we define UNPACK *R* ON (), again reasonably, to be shorthand for the expression

```
WITH ( R GROUP { } AS X ) AS R1 ,
      ( EXTEND R1 ADD EXPAND ( X ) AS Y )
            { ALL BUT X } AS R2 :
R2 UNGROUP Y
```

This expression is readily seen to evaluate to *r* as well.

NOTE: Two obvious but far-reaching consequences of the foregoing definitions are that (1) packing *r* on no attributes and then unpacking the result, also on no attributes, returns *r*, and (2) unpacking *r* on no attributes and then packing the result, again on no attributes, also returns *r*. The significance of these seemingly rather trivial observations will become apparent in the final section of the next chapter, as well as in the section immediately following.

8.6 PACKING AND UNPACKING ON SEVERAL ATTRIBUTES

Now we turn to the question of packing and unpacking relations on two or more attributes (all of them necessarily interval-valued) of the relation in question. For reasons that will become clear later, when we get to the subsection on PACK, it is convenient to deal with UNPACK first, and so we will.

UNPACK

We begin by considering the case of unpacking on two attributes specifically. Let *r* be a relation with two distinct interval attributes A1 and A2 (and possibly other attributes as well). Just to be definite, suppose *r* looks like this:

A1	A2
[P1:P1]	[d08:d09]
[P1:P2]	[d08:d08]
[P3:P4]	[d07:d08]

This relation is in fact the restriction of the relation shown in Figure 8.1 to just those tuples for supplier S2, projected over PARTS and DURING, except that we have renamed the two attributes A1 and A2, respectively. (Actually, we could have retained the S# attribute if we had wanted to—it would have made essentially no difference to the analysis that follows.)

Now we consider the expression

```
UNPACK ( UNPACK r ON A1 ) ON A2
```

The inner expression UNPACK r ON A1 yields:

A1	A2
[P1:P1]	[d08:d09]
[P1:P1]	[d08:d08]
[P2:P2]	[d08:d08]
[P3:P3]	[d07:d08]
[P4:P4]	[d07:d08]

Unpacking this relation on A2 then yields:

A1	A2
[P1:P1]	[d08:d08]
[P1:P1]	[d09:d09]
[P2:P2]	[d08:d08]
[P3:P3]	[d07:d07]
[P3:P3]	[d08:d08]
[P4:P4]	[d07:d07]
[P4:P4]	[d08:d08]

Now we consider what happens if we do the two unpackings in the opposite order—that is, we consider the expression

```
UNPACK ( UNPACK r ON A2 ) ON A1
```

The inner expression UNPACK r ON A2 yields:

A1	A2
[P1:P1]	[d08:d08]
[P1:P1]	[d09:d09]
[P1:P2]	[d08:d08]
[P3:P4]	[d07:d07]
[P3:P4]	[d08:d08]

Unpacking this relation on A1 then yields:

A1	A2
[P1:P1]	[d08:d08]
[P1:P1]	[d09:d09]
[P2:P2]	[d08:d08]
[P3:P3]	[d07:d07]
[P4:P4]	[d07:d07]
[P3:P3]	[d08:d08]
[P4:P4]	[d08:d08]

And this overall result is readily seen to be the same as before. In fact, it is easy to see that, more generally, if *r* is *any* relation with interval attributes *A1* and *A2*, then

```
UNPACK ( UNPACK r ON A1 ) ON A2  ≡
UNPACK ( UNPACK r ON A2 ) ON A1
```

(Working through the foregoing example should be sufficient to give you the necessary insight as to why this identity must be valid.) In fact, it is easy to see that, more generally, if *r* has interval attributes *A1, A2, ..., An*, then unpacking *r* on those attributes *in any order whatsoever* will always yield the same overall result. We therefore propose the following shorthand syntax:

```
<unpack>
    ::=   UNPACK <relation exp>
              ON ( <attribute name commalist> )
```

The semantics are as follows:

```
UNPACK r ON ( A1, A2, ..., An )  ≡
UNPACK ( ... ( UNPACK ( UNPACK r ON B1 ) ON B2 ) ... ) ON Bn
```

where the sequence of attribute names *B1, B2, ..., Bn* is some arbitrary permutation of the specified sequence of attribute names *A1, A2, ..., An*. The parentheses can be omitted if the specified sequence contains just one attribute name.

NOTE: In fact, the specified sequence *A1, A2, ..., An* really denotes a *set* of attribute names; in **Tutorial D,** therefore, we would normally enclose it in braces, not parentheses. As we will see in the next subsection, however, parentheses are *required* in the case of PACK—that is, the sequence in which the attribute names are specified is significant for PACK (even though it is still the case that no attribute name can be specified more than once). We thus felt it would be more user-friendly to use parentheses instead of braces, but then to state explicitly that the sequence is arbitrary, in the case of UNPACK as well.

PACK

We turn now to PACK. Here we proceed somewhat differently, for reasons that will be made clear in the next section. We begin by defining an operator that we will refer to for the time being as PACK+ ("pack plus"),[3] which operates by first *unpacking* the specified relation on all specified attributes, and then (re)packing that unpacked relation on those same attributes in the order in which they are specified. Thus, for example, the expression

```
PACK+ r ON ( A1, A2 )
```

is defined to be shorthand for the expression

```
PACK ( PACK ( UNPACK r ON ( A1, A2 ) ) ON A1 ) ON A2
```

In other words, the original PACK+ invocation PACK+ *r* ON (*A1,A2*) is evaluated by first unpacking relation *r* on *A1* and *A2,* then packing the result on *A1,* and finally packing *that* result on *A2.*

As a basis for examining this definition more closely, suppose relation *r* looks like this:

A1	A2
[P2:P4]	[d01:d04]
[P3:P5]	[d01:d04]
[P2:P4]	[d05:d06]
[P2:P4]	[d06:d09]

This relation is in fact the restriction of the relation shown in Figure 8.1 to just those tuples for supplier S3, projected over PARTS and DURING, except that we have renamed the two attributes A1 and A2, respectively. (As in the case of the UNPACK dis-

---

3. We say "for the time being" because (as we will see in a while) it is possible, and desirable, to use the unqualified name PACK to refer unambiguously to both PACK+ and the PACK operator as originally defined (and so we will). But first things first.

cussion in the previous subsection, we could have retained the S# attribute if we had wanted to—it would have made essentially no difference to the analysis that follows.)

We now consider the expression PACK+ *r* ON (A1,A2). First, here is the result of evaluating the implicit UNPACK *r* ON (A1,A2) that lies at the heart of the expansion of that expression:

A1	A2
[P2:P2]	[d01:d01]
[P2:P2]	[d02:d02]
[P2:P2]	[d03:d03]
[P2:P2]	[d04:d04]
[P3:P3]	[d01:d01]
[P3:P3]	[d02:d02]
[P3:P3]	[d03:d03]
[P3:P3]	[d04:d04]
[P4:P4]	[d01:d01]
[P4:P4]	[d02:d02]
[P4:P4]	[d03:d03]
[P4:P4]	[d04:d04]
[P5:P5]	[d01:d01]
[P5:P5]	[d02:d02]
[P5:P5]	[d03:d03]
[P5:P5]	[d04:d04]
[P2:P2]	[d05:d05]
[P2:P2]	[d06:d06]
[P3:P3]	[d05:d05]
[P3:P3]	[d06:d06]
[P4:P4]	[d05:d05]
[P4:P4]	[d06:d06]
[P2:P2]	[d07:d07]
[P2:P2]	[d08:d08]
[P2:P2]	[d09:d09]
[P3:P3]	[d07:d07]
[P3:P3]	[d08:d08]
[P3:P3]	[d09:d09]
[P4:P4]	[d07:d07]
[P4:P4]	[d08:d08]
[P4:P4]	[d09:d09]

Packing this relation on A1 yields:

A1	A2
[P2:P5]	[d01:d01]
[P2:P5]	[d02:d02]
[P2:P5]	[d03:d03]
[P2:P5]	[d04:d04]
[P2:P4]	[d05:d05]
[P2:P4]	[d06:d06]
[P2:P4]	[d07:d07]
[P2:P4]	[d08:d08]
[P2:P4]	[d09:d09]

Packing *this* relation on A2 then yields:

A1	A2
[P2:P5]	[d01:d04]
[P2:P4]	[d05:d09]

Now we consider what happens if we do the two packings in the opposite order—that is, we consider the expression PACK+ *r* ON (A2,A1). First, the implicit UNPACK yields the same relation as before, of course. Packing that relation on A2 yields:

A1	A2
[P2:P2]	[d01:d09]
[P3:P3]	[d01:d09]
[P4:P4]	[d01:d09]
[P5:P5]	[d01:d04]

Packing *this* relation on A1 then yields:

A1	A2
[P2:P4]	[d01:d09]
[P5:P5]	[d01:d04]

And this overall result is clearly different from before. Hence, we have that if *r* is a relation with interval attributes *A1* and *A2*, then

```
PACK+ r ON ( A1, A2 )  ≢  PACK+ r ON ( A2, A1 )
```

(in general). In other words, although we might (and effectively do) propose the following shorthand syntax—

```
<pack+>
    ::=   PACK+ <relation exp>
          ON ( <attribute name commalist> )
```

—it is important to understand that (1) a preliminary unpacking on all specified attributes is required before any packings are done, and (2) the individual packings must be done in the sequence specified by the parenthesized commalist of attribute names. (As usual, the parentheses can be omitted if the commalist contains just one attribute name.) Thus, the semantics are as follows:

```
PACK+ r ON ( A1, A2, ... An )  ≡
PACK ( ... ( PACK ( PACK r' ON A1 ) ON A2 ) ... ) ON An
```

where r' is

```
UNPACK r ON ( A1, A2, ..., An )
```

Note clearly that this definition for PACK+ on n attributes explicitly relies on the definition of PACK given in Section 8.2 for packing on just one attribute.

Now let us consider the special cases $n = 1$ and $n = 0$. If $n = 1$, we are performing the PACK+ operation on a single attribute A, and we have:

```
PACK+ r ON A  ≡   PACK ( UNPACK r ON A ) ON A
              ≡   PACK r ON A
```

(thanks to one of the identities stated near the very end of Section 8.3). Similarly, if $n = 0$, we are performing the PACK+ operation on no attributes at all, and we have:

```
PACK+ r ON ()  ≡   PACK ( UNPACK r ON () ) ON ()
               ≡   PACK r ON ()
```

(thanks to the definition given for unpacking on no attributes in Section 8.5). It follows that PACK+ reduces to PACK as previously defined for the cases $n = 0$ and $n = 1$. Thus, PACK+ on n attributes for $n > 1$ is a straightforward generalization of PACK as previously defined for $n = 0$ and $n = 1$. As a consequence, we can rename PACK+ as simply PACK (i.e., we can drop the "+") without risk of ambiguity, and so we will from this point forward.

8.7 FURTHER POINTS

The idea of packing a relation on two or more of its attributes has a number of consequences and ramifications, all of them important and some of them not immediately obvious. In this final section, we explore some of those consequences.

First of all, a simple but useful general observation is the following: If some relation *r* is in packed form (on attributes *A1, A2, ..., An,* say), then every restriction of *r* is also in that same packed form, *a fortiori.*

Next, note that the expressions

```
PACK r ON ( A1, A2, ... An )
```

and

```
PACK ( ... ( PACK ( PACK r ON A1 ) ON A2 ) ... ) ON An
```

are not logically equivalent, in general—the first is equivalent to

```
PACK ( ...
        ( PACK
          ( PACK
            ( UNPACK ...
              ( UNPACK
                ( UNPACK r
                  ON A1 )
                ON A2 ) ...
              ON An )
            ON A1 )
          ON A2 )
        ...    )
ON An
```

and the second is equivalent to

```
PACK
  ( UNPACK
    ( ...
      ( PACK
        ( UNPACK
          ( PACK
            ( UNPACK r
              ON A1 )
            ON A1 )
          ON A2 )
        ON A2 )
```

```
    ...   )
  ON An )
ON An
```

By way of example, consider again the relation *r* introduced at the beginning of the PACK discussion in the previous section:

A1	A2
[P2:P4]	[*d01*:*d04*]
[P3:P5]	[*d01*:*d04*]
[P2:P4]	[*d05*:*d06*]
[P2:P4]	[*d06*:*d09*]

Then it turns out that, whereas the expressions

```
PACK r ON ( A1, A2 )
```

and

```
PACK ( PACK r ON A1 ) ON A2
```

do happen to produce the same result, the expressions

```
PACK r ON ( A2, A1 )
```

and

```
PACK ( PACK r ON A2 ) ON A1
```

do not. *We recommend strongly that you verify these claims for yourself;* however, we observe that in the case in which the results differ, the second expression produces a result that involves some redundancy, whereas the first does not. This fact explains why we defined the operator the way we did in the previous section (with a preliminary UNPACK on all specified attributes) instead of—as might seem on the face of it more logical—simply as a sequence of PACKs: We did so because our definition is guaranteed to eliminate redundancy, whereas the apparently "more logical" definition is not.

NOTE: If you do verify the foregoing claims for yourself as recommended, you will find the difference is as follows: Where the relation produced by the first expression—PACK *r* ON (A2,A1)—has the interval [P5:P5], the relation produced by the second expression—PACK (PACK *r* ON A2) ON A1—has the interval [P3:P5] instead. As a consequence, the result produced by the second expression effectively tells us twice that parts P3 and P4 appear in combination with days 1, 2, 3, and 4.

Equivalence of Relations

The next point we wish to make is as follows. Using the same sample relation *r* once more, here again are the results of PACK *r* ON (A1,A2) and PACK *r* ON (A2,A1), now shown side by side (relation *left* corresponds to packing on A1-then-A2, relation *right* to packing on A2-then-A1):

left

A1	A2
[P2:P5]	[d01:d04]
[P2:P4]	[d05:d09]

right

A1	A2
[P2:P4]	[d01:d09]
[P5:P5]	[d01:d04]

Observe now that, although relations *left* and *right* are certainly not equal, they are at least *equivalent,* in the sense that they both represent the same information. In other words, the two relations merely correspond to *slightly different points of view* regarding that information—one might be interpreted as showing the ranges of parts corresponding to given time intervals, while the other might be interpreted as showing the time intervals corresponding to given ranges of parts. (In the case at hand, the relations are so simple that it might not be immediately obvious which interpretation applies to which; in fact, however, the first interpretation applies to relation *left* and the second to relation *right*.)

By the way, you might have noticed in the example that relation *left* has at most one tuple for any given day while relation *right* has at most one tuple for any given part. This state of affairs is a fluke, however. To be more precise, if *r* is a relation with interval attributes *A1*, ..., *An*, and if *An* values are defined over point type *PTn*, then it is *not* the case that the result of PACK *r* ON (*A1*,...,*An*) is guaranteed to include at most one tuple for any given value of type *PTn*. We will see a counterexample in the next subsection.

Of course, the foregoing difference in interpretation between *left* and *right* is more of a psychological difference than it is a logical one. Also, of course, it is a trivial matter (conceptually speaking, at any rate) to convert either relation into the other. For example, the following expression will convert *left* into *right*:

```
PACK left ON ( A2, A1 )
```

We now use the foregoing discussions as motivation for a definition of equivalence for *n*-ary relations, analogous to (but not the same as) the definitions of equivalence given for nullary and unary relations in the previous chapter. Let *r1* and *r2* be relations of the same relation type, and let attributes *A1, A2, ..., An* of those two relations be interval-valued. Then *r1* and *r2* are **equivalent** (with respect to attributes *A1,A2,...,An*) if and only if the results of UNPACK *r1* ON (*A1,A2,...,An*) and UNPACK *r2* ON (*A1,A2,...,An*) are equal. Note that if two relations are equal, they are certainly equivalent—with respect to every possible subset of their interval attributes, in fact.

Eliminating Redundancy

Here is another example that bears close examination. Suppose relation *r* is as follows:

A1	A2
[P3:P8]	[d01:d04]
[P5:P9]	[d03:d08]
[P1:P7]	[d07:d10]

Then (as again we recommend you verify for yourself) the results of PACK *r* ON (A1,A2) and PACK *r* ON (A2,A1) are as follows:

PACK `r` ON `(A1,A2)`

A1	A2
[P3:P8]	[d01:d02]
[P3:P9]	[d03:d04]
[P5:P9]	[d05:d06]
[P1:P9]	[d07:d08]
[P1:P7]	[d09:d10]

PACK `r` ON `(A2,A1)`

A1	A2
[P3:P4]	[d01:d04]
[P1:P4]	[d07:d10]
[P5:P7]	[d01:d10]
[P8:P8]	[d01:d08]
[P9:P9]	[d03:d08]

The interesting thing about this example is not so much that the two packed forms are distinct (as in the *left/right* example discussed earlier), but rather that—perhaps somewhat counterintuitively—they are both of cardinality greater than that of the original relation! Thus, while the original relation certainly involves some redundancy (e.g., it tells us twice that part P5 appears in combination with day 3), it is in a certain sense *more compact* than the two packed forms, even though those packed forms do not involve the same kind of redundancy.

NOTE: Given the truth of the foregoing, one conclusion we might draw is that "pack" is not the best name for the operator we have been discussing, since packing a relation is not guaranteed to make it smaller (as it were). However, we will stay with the term in this book.

So let us try to pin down exactly what we mean when we say that a certain packed form "eliminates redundancy." Let *r* be a relation with interval attributes A1, A2, ..., An. Let *u* be the relation that results from unpacking *r* on all of those attributes A1, A2, ..., An. Then, if every tuple in *u* derives from exactly one tuple in *r*, we can say that *r* is **redundancy-free**. For example, the relation *r* shown at the beginning of this subsection is *not* redundancy-free in this sense, because if we unpack it on A1 and A2, then the result includes (among other things) the tuple

A1	A2
[P5:P5]	[d03:d03]

and this tuple derives from both of the following tuples of *r:*

A1	A2
[P3:P8]	[d01:d04]

A1	A2
[P5:P9]	[d03:d08]

By contrast, PACK *r* ON (A1,A2) and PACK *r* ON (A2,A1)—that is, both of the "fully packed" forms of *r*—*are* redundancy-free in the foregoing sense. (EXERCISE: Check this claim.) In general, in fact, any "fully packed" form of any relation is guaranteed to be redundancy-free in the foregoing sense.

By the way, the foregoing example raises a couple of further points. First, note that the result of PACK *r* ON (A2,A1) includes two distinct tuples corresponding to part number P3 (also two distinct tuples corresponding to part number P4). Thus, we have here an example to show that if *r* is a relation with interval attributes *A1, ..., An,* and if *An* values are defined over point type *PTn,* then it is *not* the case that the result of PACK *r* ON (*A1,...,An*) is guaranteed to include at most one tuple for any given value of type *PTn.*

Second, although the two fully packed forms in the example are of greater cardinality than the original relation, they do happen both to be of the *same* cardinality. Again, however, this state of affairs is a fluke. By way of a counterexample, suppose relation *r* is as follows:

A1	A2
[P1:P2]	[d01:d02]
[P1:P4]	[d03:d04]
[P3:P4]	[d05:d06]

Packing this relation on (A1,A2) returns the original relation *r,* of cardinality three. By contrast, packing it on (A2,A1) returns a relation of cardinality two:

A1	A2
[P1:P2]	[d01:d04]
[P3:P4]	[d03:d06]

Considering this example and the previous one in combination, we see that if *r* is a relation and *FP* is the set of all "fully packed" forms of *r*, then there is not, in general, just one relation *fp* in *FP* with *minimum* cardinality—that is, with cardinality less than that of all other relations *fp′* (*fp′* ≠ *fp*) in *FP*. It follows that, if we regard each *fp* in *FP* as a canonical form of *r*, there is (in general) no canonical form *fp* that is somehow "more canonical than all the rest."

An Extended Example

We conclude this section (and this chapter) by looking at an example involving *three* interval attributes. Consider the following relation *r* (which is identical to the relation shown at the very end of Section 5.4, except that we have renamed the attributes A1, A2, and A3, for simplicity):

A1	A2	A3
[S1:S2]	[P2:P3]	[d03:d04]
[S2:S3]	[P3:P4]	[d04:d05]

Note that there are six logically distinct "fully packed" forms of this relation, which we now proceed to show:

PACK r ON (A1,A2,A3)

A1	A2	A3
[S1:S2]	[P2:P3]	[d03:d03]
[S1:S2]	[P2:P2]	[d04:d04]
[S1:S3]	[P3:P3]	[d04:d04]
[S2:S3]	[P3:P4]	[d05:d05]
[S2:S3]	[P4:P4]	[d04:d04]

PACK r ON (A1,A3,A2)

A1	A2	A3
[S1:S2]	[P2:P3]	[d03:d03]
[S1:S2]	[P2:P2]	[d04:d04]
[S1:S3]	[P3:P3]	[d04:d04]
[S2:S3]	[P3:P4]	[d05:d05]
[S2:S3]	[P4:P4]	[d04:d04]

PACK *r* ON (A2,A1,A3)

A1	A2	A3
[S1:S2] [S2:S3] [S3:S3]	[P2:P3] [P3:P4] [P3:P4]	[*d03*:*d04*] [*d05*:*d05*] [*d04*:*d04*]

PACK *r* ON (A2,A3,A1)

A1	A2	A3
[S1:S1] [S2:S2] [S2:S2] [S2:S2] [S3:S3]	[P2:P3] [P2:P3] [P2:P4] [P3:P4] [P3:P4]	[*d03*:*d04*] [*d03*:*d03*] [*d04*:*d04*] [*d05*:*d05*] [*d04*:*d05*]

PACK *r* ON (A3,A1,A2)

A1	A2	A3
[S1:S2] [S1:S1] [S2:S2] [S2:S3] [S3:S3]	[P2:P2] [P3:P3] [P3:P3] [P4:P4] [P3:P3]	[*d03*:*d04*] [*d03*:*d04*] [*d03*:*d05*] [*d04*:*d05*] [*d04*:*d05*]

PACK *r* ON (A3,A2,A1)

A1	A2	A3
[S1:S1] [S2:S2] [S2:S2] [S2:S2] [S3:S3]	[P2:P3] [P2:P2] [P3:P3] [P4:P4] [P3:P4]	[*d03*:*d04*] [*d03*:*d04*] [*d03*:*d05*] [*d04*:*d05*] [*d04*:*d05*]

Of these six fully packed relations, the first two happen to be the same, but the rest are all distinct. And the third happens to be (uniquely) of the smallest cardinality, though it still has cardinality greater than that of the original relation *r*. All six are, of course, redundancy-free.

Exercises

1. What exactly does it mean to say that some relation is redundancy-free?

2. Let relation *r* be as follows:

A1	A2
[P2:P4]	[d05:d06]
[P3:P5]	[d01:d04]
[P1:P4]	[d06:d08]
[P2:P4]	[d01:d04]

Show the result of PACK *r* ON (A1,A2) and PACK *r* ON (A2,A1).

3. Let relation *r* be as follows:

A1	A2	A3
[S2:S4]	[P2:P3]	[d03:d04]
[S2:S3]	[P3:P5]	[d04:d05]
[S3:S4]	[P3:P4]	[d03:d04]

Show all possible "fully packed" forms of *r* (where by "fully packed" we mean the relation is packed on all of its attributes A1, A2, and A3, in some order).

4. (Repeated from Section 8.4)

   a. Write a **Tutorial D** expression making use of relvar SP_DURING (as illustrated in Endpaper Panel 4) for the query "For each part that has ever been capable of being supplied by supplier S3, get the part number and the applicable intervals of time."

   b. Give formulations of the query "For each day on which some part has been capable of being supplied by supplier S3, get that day and the applicable ranges of parts," using (1) relvar S_PARTS_DURING from Section 5.4 and (2) relvar SP_DURING.

5. Let *T* be a type consisting of all positive integers in the range 1 to *n*. Find the smallest value for *n* such that relations *r1* and *r2* of type RELATION { A1 INTERVAL_*T*, A2 INTERVAL_*T* } exist that satisfy all of the following conditions (a) through (f):

   a. *r1* ≠ *r2*

   b. UNPACK *r1* ON (A1, A2) = UNPACK *r2* ON (A1, A2)

   c. *r1* ≠ PACK *r1* ON (A1, A2)

   d. *r2* ≠ PACK *r2* ON (A1, A2)

e. COUNT (*r1*) = COUNT (*r2*)

f. There does not exist a relation *r3* such that

```
UNPACK r3 ON ( A1, A2 ) = UNPACK r1 ON ( A1, A2 )
AND COUNT ( r3 ) < COUNT ( r1 )
```

What do you conclude from this exercise?

6. In the body of the chapter, we saw several examples of packing and unpacking a relation *r* on all of its attributes. What happens if that relation *r* is of degree one?

Chapter

9

GENERALIZING THE RELATIONAL OPERATORS

9.1 INTRODUCTION

Recall this query from Chapter 8, Section 8.3:

- **Query B:** Get S#-DURING pairs for suppliers who have been unable to supply any parts at all during at least one interval of time, where DURING designates a maximal interval during which supplier S# was in fact unable to supply any part at all.

Here again is the formulation of this query as a "temporal difference" expression against the database of Figure 5.1 (or Endpaper Panel 4):

```
PACK
  ( ( UNPACK S_DURING { S#, DURING } ON DURING )
    MINUS
    ( UNPACK SP_DURING { S#, DURING } ON DURING ) )
ON DURING
```

It turns out that expressions like this one are needed so often in practice that the idea of defining a shorthand for them seems worthwhile (a further shorthand, that is!—they are basically just shorthand already, of course, as we know). To be specific, it seems worth capturing as a single operation the sequence:

1. Unpack both operands.

2. Take the difference.

3. Pack the result.

As a bonus, moreover, such a shorthand offers the opportunity of *better performance.* When long intervals of fine granularity[1] are involved, the output from an unpack operation can be very large in comparison to the input. And if the system were actually to materialize the result of both unpackings, compute the difference between them, and then pack the result, the query might "execute forever" or run out of memory. By contrast, expressing the overall requirement as a single operation might allow the optimizer to choose a more efficient implementation, one that does not require materialization of unpacked intermediate results.

More generally, in fact, we can define analogous shorthands for all of the usual relational operators. Such is the aim of the present chapter. NOTE: For obvious reasons, however, there is no point in defining an analogous shorthand for RENAME, and we do not bother to do so.

9.2 UNION, INTERSECT, AND DIFFERENCE

Since we began this chapter with a brief look at "temporal difference," let us complete our treatment of that operator first. Here then is our proposed further shorthand:

```
USING ( ACL ) ◀ R1 MINUS R2 ▶
```

---

1. In Chapter 3 we defined the term *granularity* in connection with points, not intervals (informally, the term refers to the "size" of the points in question, or equivalently to the size of the "gap" between adjacent points). Clearly, however, we can use the term in connection with intervals as well. To be specific, the granularity of a given interval is simply the granularity of the points within the interval in question, or equivalently of the gap between adjacent points within the interval in question (if any such gaps exist).

R1 and *R2* here are relational expressions denoting relations *r1* and *r2* of the same relation type, and *ACL* is a commalist of attribute names in which every attribute mentioned (1) is of some interval type and (2) appears in both relations. (Of course, since *r1* and *r2* are required to be of the same relation type, if an attribute mentioned in *ACL* appears in either *r1* or *r2*, then it certainly appears in the other as well.) The overall expression is defined to be semantically equivalent to—that is, shorthand for—the following longer expression:

```
PACK
    ( ( UNPACK R1 ON ( ACL ) )
      MINUS
      ( UNPACK R2 ON ( ACL ) ) )
ON ( ACL )
```

Points arising:

- Although we have been referring, informally, to the operator just defined as "temporal difference," we have to say that we do not much care for this terminology, because the operator is not peculiar to temporal intervals. Until further notice, therefore, we will refer to it as **U_difference**—U for USING[2]—or simply **U_MINUS** for short.

- As usual, the parentheses surrounding the commalist of attribute names in the USING specification can be omitted if the commalist contains just one attribute name. NOTE: This remark applies to all of the shorthands we will be defining in this chapter, and we will not bother to repeat it every time.

- In the remaining sections of this chapter, then, we will define several further contexts in which a USING specification can appear. In all of those contexts, solid arrowheads ◀ and ▶ are used, as in the case of U_MINUS, to delimit the operational expression to which the USING specification applies. The operational expression in question represents either an invocation of some relational algebra operator—this is the more usual case—or else a relational comparison.

- As an aside, for readers who might be familiar with **temporal statement modifiers** as defined in reference [8], we stress the point that our USING specifications are not the same thing. Loosely speaking, temporal statement modifiers affect every operator within the statement—or expression—they apply to. Our USING specifications, by contrast, affect only the *outermost* operator within the expression they apply to (i.e., the expression between the solid arrowheads).

---

2. Or for "unpacking," if you like—unpacking being, in a sense, the most important component of the sequence "unpack the operands, take the difference, pack the result."

Here then is a shorthand formulation for Query B from the beginning of the previ-ous section:

```
USING DURING ◀ S_DURING { S#, DURING }
                MINUS
                SP_DURING { S#, DURING } ▶
```

EXPLANATION: First, the projections of S_DURING and SP_DURING over {S#, DURING} are computed. (Note carefully that those projections are indeed regular pro-jections, not U_projections.) Those two projections are then unpacked on DURING, their difference is computed, and the result is then packed on DURING again.

It is interesting to note, by the way, that (unlike the regular MINUS operator) U_MINUS can actually produce a result whose cardinality is greater than that of its left operand! For example, let R1 and R2 be as follows:

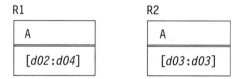

Then USING A ◀ R1 MINUS R2 ▶ gives:

A
[d02:d02]
[d04:d04]

We turn now to UNION, and define the "U_UNION" expression

```
USING ( ACL ) ◀ R1 UNION R2 ▶
```

to be shorthand for

```
PACK
    ( ( UNPACK R1 ON ( ACL ) )
      UNION
      ( UNPACK R2 ON ( ACL ) ) )
ON ( ACL )
```

R1, R2, and *ACL* are as for U_MINUS; that is, *R1* and *R2* must be of the same relation type, and every attribute mentioned in *ACL* must be of some interval type and must appear in both *R1* and *R2*.

Actually, there is no need to perform the preliminary UNPACKs in the case of U_UNION. That is, the U_UNION expansion can be further simplified in this case to just

```
PACK ( R1 UNION R2 ) ON ( ACL )
```

It is not hard to see why this simplification is possible, but you can try working through an example if you need to convince yourself that it is indeed valid. (In fact, similar simplifications are possible with several of the other "U_" operators as well. We will not bother to spell out the specifics in this chapter, however; instead, we will discuss such matters in detail in Appendix A.)

By the way, just as U_MINUS, slightly counterintuitively, can increase the cardinality (loosely speaking), so U_UNION can decrease it. For example, let R1 and R2 be as follows:

R1

A
[d02:d02]
[d04:d04]

R2

A
[d03:d03]

Then USING A ◀ R1 UNION R2 ▶ gives:

A
[d02:d04]

In fact, the result might well have cardinality less than that of *either* operand! Such would be the case, for example, if relation R2 above additionally contained a tuple in which the interval value was [d04:d04].

Turning now to INTERSECT, the "U_INTERSECT" expression

```
USING ( ACL ) ◀ R1 INTERSECT R2 ▶
```

(where R1, R2, and ACL are as for U_MINUS and U_UNION) is defined to be shorthand for

```
PACK
    ( ( UNPACK R1 ON ( ACL ) )
      INTERSECT
      ( UNPACK R2 ON ( ACL ) ) )
ON ( ACL )
```

For example, let R1 and R2 be as follows:

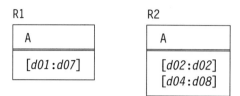

R1

A
[d01:d07]

R2

A
[d02:d02]
[d04:d08]

Then USING A ◄ R1 INTERSECT R2 ► gives:

A
[d02:d02]
[d04:d07]

Observe that the cardinality of this result is greater than that of R1 (contrast the situation with the regular INTERSECT operator). In fact, as you might be expecting by now, the result can have cardinality greater than that of *either* operand. E X E R C I S E : Check this claim.

A N O T E O N S Y N T A X : Although it is the best we have managed to come up with at this time, we have to say we are not entirely satisfied with the syntax we have been using above for our various "U_" operators. For example, the expression

```
USING ( ACL ) ◄ R1 MINUS R2 ►
```

would be better—certainly more logical—if it looked something like this:

```
R1 U_MINUS ( ACL ) R2
```

After all, U_MINUS is basically a dyadic relational operator; since we use infix notation for the regular MINUS operator, it would be more consistent to do the same for U_MINUS (and likewise for U_UNION and U_INTERSECT). However, at least two difficulties arise immediately:

- The "U_" versions of MINUS, UNION, and INTERSECT each involve what might be thought of as a third operand (namely, the commalist *ACL* of attribute names), and "third operands" do not fit well with an infix syntactic style.

- In the case of the monadic operators restrict and project (see the next section) and the monadic operator EXTEND (see Section 9.5), it is even harder to come up with syntax for "U_" versions that is simultaneously logical and consistent with the syntax of the regular versions (try it and you will see!).

For such reasons, we decided to adopt the style already illustrated, involving a prefix USING specification, in every case. That decision does at least mean that all of the "U_" operators follow the same syntactic style, more or less. What is more, it also extends fairly gracefully to certain further "U_" constructs that we will be introducing and discussing in later chapters.

9.3 RESTRICT AND PROJECT

We turn now to the monadic operators *restrict* and *project*. For these operators, of course, there is (by definition) only one relation to be unpacked in the initial step. In the case of restrict, for example, we define the expression

```
USING ( ACL ) ◄ R WHERE p ►
```

to be shorthand for

```
PACK ( ( UNPACK R ON ( ACL ) ) WHERE p ) ON ( ACL )
```

Every attribute mentioned in *ACL* must be an attribute of *R* and must be of some interval type.[3]

Here is an example to illustrate the use of U_restrict:

```
USING DURING ◄ S_DURING WHERE
              INTERVAL_DATE ( [ d04 : d04 ] ) = DURING ►
```

Note the difference between this U_restrict and the following regular restrict:

```
S_DURING WHERE INTERVAL_DATE ( [ d04 : d04 ] ) = DURING
```

Suppose, for example, that relvar S_DURING currently contains just two tuples, as follows:

S#	DURING
S2	[d02:d04]
S2	[d07:d10]

Then the regular restrict just shown will return a result of cardinality zero, while the original U_restrict will return a result of cardinality one.

---

3. Perhaps we should say that we doubt whether "U_restrict" will be much used in practice. We include it primarily for reasons of completeness. Similar remarks apply to U_EXTEND, which we discuss in Section 9.5.

It is worth pointing out explicitly that U_restrict, unlike the regular restrict operation, can actually return a result with cardinality greater than that of its input. For example, suppose again that relvar S_DURING contains just the two tuples for supplier S2 shown above, and consider the following U_restrict:

```
USING DURING ◄ S_DURING WHERE
                  DURING = INTERVAL_DATE ( [ d02 : d02 ] )
               OR DURING = INTERVAL_DATE ( [ d04 : d04 ] )
               OR DURING = INTERVAL_DATE ( [ d07 : d07 ] ) ►
```

The result looks like this:

S#	DURING
S2	[d02:d02]
S2	[d04:d04]
S2	[d07:d07]

Turning now to projection, we define the expression

```
USING ( ACL ) ◄ R { BCL } ►
```

to be shorthand for

```
PACK ( ( UNPACK R ON ( ACL ) ) { BCL } ) ON ( ACL )
```

Every attribute mentioned in *ACL* must be of some interval type and must be mentioned in *BCL* (and hence *a fortiori* must be an attribute of *R*). By way of an example, recall this query from Chapter 8, Section 8.2:

- **Query A:** Get S#-DURING pairs for suppliers who have been able to supply at least one part during at least one interval of time, where DURING designates a maximal interval during which supplier S# was in fact able to supply at least one part.

Here is a "U_project" formulation for this query:

```
USING DURING ◄ SP_DURING { S#, DURING } ►
```

9.4 Join

We define the "U_JOIN" expression

```
USING ( ACL ) ◄ R1 JOIN R2 ►
```

to be shorthand for

```
PACK
    ( ( UNPACK R1 ON ( ACL ) )
      JOIN
      ( UNPACK R2 ON ( ACL ) ) )
ON ( ACL )
```

Every attribute mentioned in *ACL* must be of some interval type and must appear in both *R1* and *R2* (and so the join is to be done on all of the attributes mentioned in *ACL*, as well as possibly others). NOTE: If *R1* and *R2* are of the same relation type, then U_JOIN degenerates, as would surely be expected, to U_INTERSECT.

In order to illustrate the use of U_JOIN, suppose we have another relvar in the database, S_CITY_DURING, with attributes S#, CITY, and DURING, with candidate key {S#,DURING}, and with predicate as follows:

> *From the day that is the begin point of DURING (and not on the day immediately before that day) to the day that is the end point of DURING (and not on the day immediately after that day), inclusive, supplier S# was located in city CITY.*

Now consider the query "Get S#-CITY-P#-DURING tuples such that supplier S# was located in city CITY and was able to supply part P# throughout interval DURING, where DURING contains day 4." Here is a possible formulation of that query:

```
( USING DURING ◄ S_CITY_DURING JOIN SP_DURING ► )
                                        WHERE d04 ∈ DURING
```

Observe that this formulation involves a U_join followed by a *regular* restrict.

NOTE: If we were to project attribute DURING away from the result of the foregoing query, the resulting projection would represent what is sometimes called a *snapshot* of the database—or of a certain portion of the database, rather—as of a certain point in time (namely, day 4). Such *snapshot queries* are needed quite often in practice. (By the way, do not confuse "a snapshot of the database" with "a snapshot database"! See the introduction to Chapter 3 for a discussion of this latter term.)

9.5 EXTEND AND SUMMARIZE

By now the pattern should be familiar ... We define the "U_EXTEND" expression

```
USING ( ACL ) ◄ EXTEND R ADD exp AS B ▶
```

to be shorthand for

```
PACK
    ( EXTEND ( UNPACK R ON ( ACL ) ) ADD exp AS B )
ON ( ACL )
```

Every attribute mentioned in *ACL* must be of some interval type and must be an attribute of *R*.

Unlike the regular EXTEND operator, U_EXTEND can return a result with cardinality either greater or less than that of its input. Suppose relvar S_DURING, for example, currently contains just the following two tuples:

S#	DURING
S2	[d01:d05]
S2	[d03:d04]

Then the first of the following U_EXTENDs will return a relation of cardinality five and the second will return a relation of cardinality one:

1. USING DURING ◄ EXTEND S_DURING ADD BEGIN (DURING) AS X ▶

2. USING DURING ◄ EXTEND S_DURING ADD COUNT (DURING) AS X ▶

Note the trap for the unwary here: The expression in the ADD specification is evaluated against each tuple in the *unpacked* form of the pertinent relation. Thus, for example, the first of the foregoing U_EXTENDs does *not* return a relation containing just two tuples, one with an X value of *d01* and the other with an X value of *d03*. (In fact, the expression BEGIN(DURING) in that U_EXTEND is logically equivalent to—and might more clearly have been written as—POINT FROM DURING.)

Turning now to SUMMARIZE, we define the "U_SUMMARIZE" expression

```
USING ( ACL ) ◄ SUMMARIZE R1 PER R2 ADD summary AS B ▶
```

to be shorthand for

```
PACK
    ( SUMMARIZE ( UNPACK R1 ON ( ACL ) )
      PER ( UNPACK R2 ON ( ACL' ) )
      ADD summary AS B ) )
ON ( ACL' )
```

Every attribute mentioned in *ACL* must be of some interval type and must be an attribute of *R1*; *ACL´* is the same as *ACL,* except that any attribute in *ACL* that does not appear in *R2* is simply ignored.

In order to illustrate the use of U_SUMMARIZE, we return to the following example from Chapter 8. Consider relvar SP_DURING once again. At any given time, if there are any shipments at all at that time, then there is some part number *pmax* such that no supplier is able to supply any part at that time with a part number greater than *pmax*. So consider the query "For each part number that has ever been such a *pmax* value, get that part number together with the interval(s) during which it actually was that *pmax* value." Here is a formulation of this query that makes use of U_SUMMARIZE:

```
USING DURING ◄ SUMMARIZE SP_DURING
                PER SP_DURING { DURING }
                ADD MAX ( P# ) AS PMAX ►
```

Unlike the regular SUMMARIZE operator, U_SUMMARIZE can return a result with cardinality greater than that of its input (exercise for the reader).

9.6 GROUP AND UNGROUP

For completeness, we need "U_" versions of GROUP and UNGROUP. We therefore define the "U_GROUP" expression

```
USING ( ACL ) ◄ R GROUP { BCL } AS C ►
```

to be shorthand for

```
PACK
    ( ( UNPACK R ON ( ACL ) ) GROUP { BCL } AS C )
ON ( ACL )
```

Every attribute mentioned in *ACL* must be of some interval type, must be an attribute of *R*, and must *not* be mentioned in *BCL*.

By way of example, suppose the current value of relvar SP_DURING is as follows:

S#	P#	DURING
S2	P1	[*d08:d10*]
S2	P2	[*d09:d10*]
S4	P2	[*d07:d09*]
S4	P4	[*d07:d08*]

Consider the expression

```
USING DURING ◄ SP_DURING GROUP { P# } AS P#_REL ►
```

Here is the result of the initial UNPACK:

S#	P#	DURING
S2	P1	[*d08:d08*]
S2	P1	[*d09:d09*]
S2	P1	[*d10:d10*]
S2	P2	[*d09:d09*]
S2	P2	[*d10:d10*]
S4	P2	[*d07:d07*]
S4	P2	[*d08:d08*]
S4	P2	[*d09:d09*]
S4	P4	[*d07:d07*]
S4	P4	[*d08:d08*]

Now the GROUP:

S#	P#_REL	DURING
S2	P# P1	[d08:d08]
S2	P# P1 P2	[d09:d09]
S2	P# P1 P2	[d10:d10]
S4	P# P2 P4	[d07:d07]
S4	P# P2 P4	[d08:d08]
S4	P# P2	[d09:d09]

Finally the PACK:

S#	P#_REL	DURING
S2	P# P1	$[d08:d08]$
S2	P# P1 P2	$[d09:d10]$
S4	P# P2 P4	$[d07:d08]$
S4	P# P2	$[d09:d09]$

This last relation is the overall result.

Now we turn to UNGROUP. We define the "U_UNGROUP" expression

```
USING ( ACL ) ◀ R UNGROUP C ▶
```

to be shorthand for

```
PACK
    ( ( UNPACK R ON ( ACL ) ) UNGROUP C )
ON ( ACL )
```

Every attribute mentioned in *ACL* must be of some interval type and must be an attribute of *R*. *ACL* must not mention *C*.

As an exercise, show that, if *r* is the result of the U_GROUP example just shown, then the expression

```
USING DURING ◀ r UNGROUP P#_REL ▶
```

returns the relation shown as the value of SP_DURING earlier in this section.

9.7 RELATIONAL COMPARISONS

In Chapter 2 we introduced relational comparisons as a special case of boolean expressions in general, but we have made almost no use of relational comparisons prior to this point.[4] Just to remind you, here is the syntax:

```
<relation comp>
    ::=    <relation exp> <relation comp op> <relation exp>

<relation comp op>
    ::=    = | ≠ | ⊆ | ⊂ | ⊇ | ⊃
```

The relations denoted by the two relational expressions must be of the same relation type, of course.

Now, relational comparisons are strictly speaking not relational operations as such, because they return a truth value, not a relation. Nevertheless, we can subject them to the same kind of treatment we have been applying to the relational operators, and indeed it is desirable to do so. The point is, when the relations in question involve interval attributes, what we often want to do is compare certain *unpacked counterparts* of those relations, not those relations per se. To that end, we introduce, first, a "U_" counterpart to the regular "relation equality" comparison. To be specific, we define the expression

```
USING ( ACL ) ◀ R1 = R2 ▶
```

to be shorthand for

```
( UNPACK R1 ON ( ACL ) ) = ( UNPACK R2 ON ( ACL ) )
```

Every attribute mentioned in *ACL* must be an interval attribute and must appear in both *R1* and *R2*. Note that the question of a final PACK step does not arise, because (as already indicated) the result of "=" is a truth value, not a relation.

By way of example, let R1 and R2 be as follows:

R1

A
[d01:d03]
[d02:d05]
[d04:d04]

R2

A
[d01:d02]
[d03:d05]

---

4   The only exceptions are Constraint DBC2 (see Chapter 1, Section 1.6) and Constraint XFT2 (see Chapter 4, Section 4.3).

Then R1 = R2 is clearly false, but USING A ◄ R1 = R2 ► is true.

We will refer to the foregoing operator as "U_=" for brevity (in fact, it is precisely the *equivalence* operator as defined for *n*-ary relations in Section 8.7). In the same way, we can define "U_" analogs of all of the other relational comparison operators (≠, ⊂, ⊆, ⊃, and ⊇). For example, if R1 and R2 are as for the "U_=" example above, then USING A ◄ R1 ⊆ R2 ► is true, but USING A ◄ R1 ⊂ R2 ► is false.

By the way, the following point is worth making explicitly: Let R1 be a relation, and let the packed and unpacked forms of R1 on some specified set of attributes be PR1 and UR1, respectively. Likewise, let R2 be a relation of the same type as R1, and let the packed and unpacked forms of R2 on that same set of attributes be PR2 and UR2, respectively. Finally, let UR1 ⊂ UR2 be true. Then it certainly does not follow that PR1 ⊂ PR2 is also true. Development of an example to illustrate this point is left as an exercise.

9.8 THE UNDERLYING INTUITION

In this section, we briefly discuss an alternative way of thinking about relations with interval attributes and the "U_" operators on such relations (such as U_JOIN) discussed in the foregoing sections. Suppose the current value of relvar S_DURING is the relation shown here (let us call it *r*):

S#	DURING
S1	[d04:d06]
S2	[d02:d04]
S2	[d06:d07]
S3	[d05:d07]
S4	[d03:d05]

The intended interpretation for this relation, just to remind you, is that the indicated supplier was under contract during the indicated interval.

Observe now that every time point in every interval in relation *r* is taken from the following set:

{ d02, d03, d04, d05, d06, d07 }

The cardinality of this set is six. *Thus, we can think of r as effectively specifying the overall state of affairs (regarding who was under contract) at each of those six points in time.* That is, we can think of *r* as a kind of shorthand for a *sequence* of six separate relations, one for each of the six time points in question (where the sequence in question is determined by chronological ordering, of course). The six separate relations—let us label them *r02, r03, …, r07* in the obvious way—look like this:

r02	r03	r04	r05	r06	r07
S#	S#	S#	S#	S#	S#
S2	S2	S1	S1	S1	S2
	S4	S2	S3	S2	S3
		S4	S4	S3	

For example, relation *r03* shows that suppliers S2 and S4 (only) were under contract on day 3. And, of course, that relation is obtained from relation *r* by (1) restricting *r* to just those tuples in which the DURING interval contains the value *d03* and then (2) projecting the result of that restriction over all attributes but DURING.

It follows from the foregoing that we can imagine an operator that produces the sequence of relations *r02, r03, …, r07* from relation *r*. Similarly, we can imagine an inverse operator that will take the sequence of relations *r02, r03, …, r07* and give us back relation *r* once again. For definiteness, let us refer to those two operators as REL_TO_SEQ and SEQ_TO_REL, respectively.

Now we can explain the intuition behind U_JOIN and all of the other "U_" operators. The basic idea is that, first, for each *point* (each *time* point, in the foregoing example), the pertinent underlying operator—JOIN, in the case of U_JOIN—is applied to the pair of relations that correspond to that particular point value; second, the results of all of those individual operations are then put back together appropriately. Thus, the operation of (for example) U_JOIN can be thought of, very loosely, as doing a regular join *on a point-by-point basis*. In the same way, the operation of (for example) the "U_=" comparison can be thought of, again loosely, as doing a regular "=" comparison on a point-by-point basis.

In order to see how the foregoing works out in more detail, let us consider the case of U_JOIN specifically. Let the two relations to be "U_joined" be *r* and *s*. Conceptually, then, what happens is the following:

- REL_TO_SEQ is applied to *r* to yield a sequence *Qr* of relations, one for each point value in some set of such values, say *Pr*.

- REL_TO_SEQ is applied to *s* to yield a sequence *Qs* of relations, one for each point value in some set of such values, say *Ps*. Note that *Pr* and *Ps* will be distinct sets, in general.

- Let *P* be the union of *Pr* and *Ps*, and let the points in *P*, in sequence, be *p1, p2, …, pn*.

- For all *i* (*i* = 1, 2, …, *n*), if point *pi* appears in *Pr* and not in *Ps*, an empty relation of the same type as *s* and corresponding to *pi* is inserted into *Qs*; similarly, if point *pi* appears in *Ps* and not in *Pr*, an empty relation of the same type as *r* and corresponding to *pi* is inserted into *Qr*.

- For all *i* (*i* = 1, 2, ..., *n*), the relations in *Qr* and *Qs* corresponding to point *pi* are joined together. The net result is a sequence *Q* of joined relations.

- SEQ_TO_REL is applied to *Q* to yield the desired overall result.

9.9 THE REGULAR RELATIONAL OPERATORS REVISITED

Consider once again the operator U_MINUS. Just to remind you, we defined the expression

```
USING ( ACL ) ◄ R1 MINUS R2 ►
```

to be shorthand for the expression

```
PACK
    ( ( UNPACK R1 ON ( ACL ) )
      MINUS
      ( UNPACK R2 ON ( ACL ) ) )
ON ( ACL )
```

Suppose now that *ACL* is empty (i.e., specifies no attributes at all), thus:

```
USING ( ) ◄ R1 MINUS R2 ►
```

Then the expansion becomes

```
PACK
    ( ( UNPACK R1 ON ( ) )
      MINUS
      ( UNPACK R2 ON ( ) ) )
ON ( )
```

Recall now that UNPACK *R* ON () and PACK *R* ON () both reduce to just *R*. Thus, the entire expression reduces to just

```
R1 MINUS R2
```

In other words, the regular relational MINUS is essentially just a special case of U_MINUS! Thus, if we redefine the syntax of the regular MINUS operator as follows—

```
<minus>
    ::=    [ USING ( ACL ) ]
           ◀ <relation exp> MINUS <relation exp> ▶
```

—and allow the USING specification (and the solid arrowheads ◀ and ▶ enclosing the rest of the expression) to be omitted if and only if *ACL* is empty, then we no longer have any need to talk about a special "U_MINUS" operator at all—all MINUS invocations effectively become U_MINUS invocations, and we can generalize the meaning of MINUS accordingly.

Analogous remarks apply to all of the other relational operators (union, intersect, restrict, project, join, extend, summarize, group, and ungroup[5]), as well as to relational comparisons: In all cases, the regular operator is basically just that special case of the corresponding "U_" operator in which the USING specification mentions no attributes at all, and we can allow that specification (and the solid arrowheads enclosing the rest of the expression) to be omitted in that case. To put it another way, the "U_" operators are all just straightforward generalizations of their regular counterparts. Thus, we no longer need to talk explicitly about "U_" operators as such (and we no longer will, except occasionally for emphasis); instead, all we need to do is recognize that the regular operators permit, but do not require, an additional operand when they are applied to relations with interval attributes. *Please note carefully, therefore, that throughout the next part of the book, we will take all references to relational operators, and all references to relational comparisons, to refer to the generalized versions as described in the present chapter* (barring explicit statements to the contrary, of course). For clarity, however, we will occasionally use the explicit qualifiers *regular* (or *classical*) and *generalized,* as applicable, when referring to those operators and comparisons; as already noted, we will also sometimes use an explicit "U_" qualifier for the same reason.

EXERCISES

1. (Repeated from Section 9.2) Give:

   a. A U_INTERSECT example in which the result has cardinality greater than that of either of the relations being "U_intersected."

   b. A U_SUMMARIZE example in which the result has cardinality greater than that of the relation being "U_summarized."

2. (Repeated from Section 9.6) If *r* is the result of the U_GROUP example in Section 9.6, compute the result of the expression

   ```
   USING DURING ◀ r UNGROUP P#_REL ▶
   ```

---

5. For completeness we need to define "U_" versions of pack and unpack too. The details are left as an exercise.

3. (Repeated from Section 9.7) Find a pair of relations *r1* and *r2* of the same type such that the unpacked form of *r1* is a proper subset of the unpacked form of *r2* but the packed form of *r1* is not a proper subset of the packed form of *r2* (where the packings and unpackings are done on the basis of the same attributes in every case, of course).

4. Does the following identity hold?

```
USING ( ACL ) ◄ r1 INTERSECT r2 ►
≡  USING ( ACL ) ◄ r1 MINUS
                    ( USING ( ACL ) ◄ r1 MINUS r2 ► ) ►
```

5. Consider the operator U_JOIN. Assume for simplicity that the packing and unpacking is to be done on the basis of a single attribute *A*. Confirm that the following identity holds:

```
USING A ◄ r1 JOIN r2 ►
≡  WITH ( r1 RENAME A AS X ) AS T1 ,
        ( r2 RENAME A AS Y ) AS T2 ,
        ( T1 JOIN T2 ) AS T3 ,
        ( T3 WHERE X OVERLAPS Y ) AS T4 ,
        ( EXTEND T4 ADD ( X INTERSECT Y ) AS A ) AS T5 ,
        T5 { ALL BUT X, Y } AS T6 :
PACK T6 ON A
```

Confirm also that if *r1* and *r2* are both initially packed on *A*, then the final PACK step is unnecessary. NOTE: The INTERSECT operator in the EXTEND step here is the *interval* INTERSECT, not the relational one.

6. Write a query that makes use of relvars STUDENT and UNREG_STUDENT from Exercise 9 in Chapter 5 to obtain the entire student registration history of the university. The heading of the result should look like this:

```
{ STUDENT# STUDENT#, SNAME NAME, REG_DURING INTERVAL_DATE }
```

The value of END(REG_DURING) for current registrations should be as given by LAST_DATE().

Part III

BUILDING ON THE FOUNDATIONS

This part of the book uses the concepts introduced in Part II as a basis for investigating a variety of more advanced aspects of temporal database support: the question of temporal database design, the rather complicated (but vitally important) question of integrity constraints, and so on. It consists of the following chapters (which, as with Part II, are *definitely* meant to be read in sequence as written):

Chapter

10

DATABASE DESIGN

10.1 INTRODUCTION

Up to this point in the book, our sample relvars S_DURING and SP_DURING have served us well enough, clearly demonstrating the need for interval types and the desirability of special operators for dealing with interval data. Obviously enough, however, those two relvars are extremely simple in structure—and S_DURING, at least, is really *too* simple to serve as a basis for a proper investigation into the topic of the present chapter, namely, temporal database design.

Let us therefore go all the way back to our original *non*temporal relvars S and SP from Chapter 1. Here again are the **Tutorial D** definitions:

```
VAR S RELATION                    VAR SP RELATION
    { S#     S#,                      { S# S#,
      SNAME  NAME,                      P# P# }
      STATUS INTEGER,               KEY { S#, P# }
      CITY   CHAR }                 FOREIGN KEY { S# }
KEY { S# } ;                              REFERENCES S ;
```

Until further notice, let us focus on suppliers and ignore shipments. Just to remind you, the predicate for the suppliers relvar (i.e., relvar S) is:

Supplier S# is under contract, is named SNAME, has status STATUS, and is located in city CITY.

In an attempt to avoid any possible misunderstandings, let us state this predicate still more precisely, thus:

At any given time, the unique supplier identified by S# is under exactly one contract, has exactly one name SNAME, has exactly one status STATUS, and is located in exactly one city CITY.

We will not usually bother to be quite this precise in stating predicates, but we will certainly rely on the fact that such precise statements really are the intended interpretation, and hence that (for example) a given supplier does have exactly one status at any given time.

Now suppose we want to design a temporal analog of this simple nontemporal relvar. How can we do this? The most obvious approach, of course, is just to add an appropriate temporal attribute—a "since" attribute if we merely want to "semitemporalize" the design, or a "during" attribute if we want to temporalize it fully. Here is the semitemporal version:

```
VAR SSSC_SINCE RELATION
    { S#     S#,
      SNAME  NAME,
      STATUS INTEGER,
      CITY   CHAR,
      SINCE  DATE }
    KEY { S# } ;
```

(note the revised relvar name). And here is the fully temporal version:

```
VAR SSSC_DURING RELATION
    { S#     S#,
      SNAME  NAME,
      STATUS INTEGER,
      CITY   CHAR,
      DURING INTERVAL_DATE }
    KEY { S#, DURING } ;
```

Here, note the revised KEY specification as well as the revised relvar name. NOTE: In order to head off certain questions that might already be occurring to you, we should explain right away that we will have a great deal more to say about KEY specifications and related matters in the next two chapters.

Now we need to ask: Are relvars SSSC_SINCE and SSSC_DURING really *good* examples of what temporal relvars look like—or ought to look like—in practice? Are they well designed? If not, how can they be improved?

Well, to say it again, we "designed" these two relvars by simply adding a temporal attribute (a "since" attribute or a "during" attribute, as the case may be) to their non-temporal counterparts. So the question becomes: Is this a good approach to designing temporal relvars?

We answer this question in the negative. In fact, we will argue that relvars SSSC_SINCE and SSSC_DURING are both very *badly* designed! We will also show that the problem with SSSC_SINCE is easily fixed, but the problem with SSSC_DURING requires rather more thought and a rather more drastic solution. In fact, we will suggest that relvar SSSC_DURING should be *further decomposed*—by which we mean it should be decomposed beyond what pure classical normalization would require [39, 47]. In fact, we will recommend both of the following:

- Further *vertical* decomposition, to deal with the fact that—to use a sloppy but common manner of speaking—distinct "properties" of the same "entity" vary at different rates

- Further *horizontal* decomposition, to deal with the distinction between current and historical information

But first things first. In Section 10.2, we consider relvars like SSSC_SINCE that contain current information only, and we make some design recommendations for that comparatively simple case. In Section 10.3, we consider relvars like SSSC_DURING that contain historical information; that discussion leads to the proposed vertical decomposition (considered in depth in Section 10.4). Section 10.5 then discusses the special temporal problem, caused by what is usually referred to as "the moving point *now*" that arises in connection with historical relvars like SSSC_DURING even if we do vertically decompose them. Then, partly in an attempt to address that special temporal problem, we discuss in Section 10.6 the proposed horizontal decomposition, or in other words designs that involve both current and historical relvars. Finally, in Section 10.7, we offer a few concluding remarks.

One last preliminary point: The wording of the previous paragraph might be taken to suggest that a given database must follow one of the proposed approaches *exclusively* (current relvars only, historical relvars only, or a mixture). In practice, of course, any combination can be used; for example, we might want to represent some "entities" and their corresponding "properties" with "current relvars" only and others with "historical relvars" only. We ignore this nicety for reasons of simplicity, both in this chapter and in subsequent chapters in this part of the book. However, we remark that most of the research reported in the literature (on all aspects of temporal data, not just on design issues) has concentrated on databases that involve historical relvars only.

10.2 CURRENT RELVARS ONLY

We have used the term *current relvar* a couple of times now, but we have not really defined it. However, we hope it is obvious that we use the term to mean a relvar that is merely "semitemporal" and thus contains current information only. NOTE: We are speaking a little loosely here; in general, in fact, a current relvar does contain information about both the past and the future, at least implicitly, as we will soon see. In a sense, moreover, it also contains explicit information about the past—again as we will soon see—and it might even contain explicit information about the future! So to say that such a relvar contains "current" information is only an approximation to the true state of affairs. Nevertheless, we find the characterization useful from an intuitive point of view, and we will stay with it in what follows.

Here then, repeated from the previous section (but now shown in outline only, for simplicity), is the definition of the current relvar SSSC_SINCE:

```
SSSC_SINCE { S#, SNAME, STATUS, CITY, SINCE }
             KEY { S# }
```

The predicate for this relvar is as follows:

Ever since day SINCE (and not on the day immediately before day SINCE), all four of the following have been true:

1. *Supplier S# has been under contract.*

2. *Supplier S# has been named SNAME.*

3. *Supplier S# has had status STATUS.*

4. *Supplier S# has been located in city CITY.*

It should be immediately clear from this formulation of the predicate that the relvar is not very well designed! To see why, suppose it currently includes the following tuple:

S#	SNAME	STATUS	CITY	SINCE
S1	Smith	20	London	*d04*

Suppose too that today is day 10 and that, effective from today, the status of supplier S1 is to be changed to 30, and so we replace the tuple just shown by this one:

S#	SNAME	STATUS	CITY	SINCE
S1	Smith	30	London	*d10*

Now we have lost (among other things) the information that supplier S1 has been located in London since day 4!

It should be clear from this simple example that relvar SSSC_SINCE as currently designed is incapable of representing any information about a current supplier that predates the time of the most recent update to that supplier (speaking a little loosely). But this problem is easy to fix: We simply replace the existing "since" attribute by *four* such attributes, one for each of the other ("nonsince") attributes, thus:

```
SSSC_SINCE { S#,     S#_SINCE,
             SNAME,  SNAME_SINCE,
             STATUS, STATUS_SINCE,
             CITY,   CITY_SINCE }
          KEY { S# }
```

The predicate for this revised version of SSSC_SINCE is:

Supplier S# has been under contract ever since S#_SINCE, has been named SNAME ever since SNAME_SINCE, has had status STATUS ever since STATUS_SINCE, and has been located in city CITY ever since CITY_SINCE.

(We remind you that we take expressions of the form "ever since day *d*" to mean "ever since *and not immediately before* day *d*"). Here is a typical tuple for this revised design:

S#	S#_SINCE	SNAME	SNAME_SINCE	...
S1	d04	Smith	d04	...

...	STATUS	STATUS_SINCE	CITY	CITY_SINCE
...	30	d10	London	d04

This tuple shows among other things that supplier S1 has had status 30 since day 10 but has been located in London since day 4, and so we have solved the problem.

Of course, it is still the case that this revised design can represent "current" information only; in other words, the relvar is still just a current relvar, and the database is still only semitemporal. For example, if on day 10 supplier S1 moves to Paris, and we therefore replace the tuple just shown by another that has CITY = Paris and CITY_SINCE = *d10*, then we lose the information that supplier S1 was previously located in London. Thus we see that this semitemporal design cannot represent historical information (except as explained in the next paragraph). However, it could still be the *right* design in some circumstances. In particular, it could serve as part of an overall combined design involving both current and historical relvars, as discussed later in Section 10.6.

NOTE: When we say that relvars such as SSSC_SINCE cannot represent historical information, what we mean is that they cannot represent *purely* historical information (that is, information that was valid in the past but is no longer so). For example, if today is day 10 and the relvar states that supplier S1 has been located in London since day 4, then clearly it does contain historical information, of a kind. Thus, it would be more accurate to say that a current relvar cannot represent historical information *other than what can be inferred from the "since" values*. Those "since" values can be thought of as *explicit* historical information, and information inferred from them can be thought of as *implicit* historical information.

By the way, you might be thinking we could solve the problem mentioned above—that if we replace the tuple shown for supplier S1 by one with CITY = Paris and CITY_SINCE = *d10*, we lose the information that supplier S1 was previously located in London—by changing the KEY specification for relvar SSSC_SINCE in such a way as to allow two distinct tuples to appear for supplier S1, one showing S1 located in London since day 4 and the other showing S1 located in Paris since day 10. However, if you try to state the predicate for this revised version of the relvar, or if you try to write some queries against it, you will quickly see why we do not seriously suggest such an approach—especially when you realize that analogous changes would presumably have to be made for the SNAME and STATUS attributes as well as for the CITY attribute. (What is more, even if we did adopt such a design and thus be able, in a sense, to deal with supplier name and status and city histories, we would still not be able to deal with supplier *contract* histories.)

Further Points

A number of further points arise in connection with our revised design for relvar SSSC_SINCE, which we now proceed to discuss.

First of all, of course, it is clearly not necessary to have a "since" attribute for *every* "nonsince" attribute in the relvar. For example, if supplier names never change, or if they do change but we are simply not interested in knowing when such changes occur (i.e., we are interested only in what those names currently are), then attribute SNAME_SINCE is obviously not needed.

Second, let the S#_SINCE value in some SSSC_SINCE tuple be *d*, and let the value for any of the other "since" attributes in that same tuple be *d′*. Then it must be the case that $d′ \geq d$ (or, at least, we assume that such must be the case; that is, we assume, reasonably enough, that the current relvar SSSC_SINCE does not contain name, status, or city information for a supplier if that information predates the start of that supplier's current contract). In other words, the relvar is concerned with *current supplier contracts* specifically; although a supplier not currently under contract presumably does have a name and a status and a location, our database is not concerned with such matters. NOTE: We deliberately defer discussion of integrity constraints in general to Chapters 11 and 12, but this particular constraint ($d′ \geq d$) is such an obvious one that it seemed worth mentioning right away.

Third, although we have been referring to relvar SSSC_SINCE throughout our discussions as a "current" relvar, it might quite reasonably include information that explicitly pertains to the future. For example, the S#_SINCE value for some supplier S*x* might be some future date *d*, meaning that the indicated supplier *will be* placed under contract on that future date (in which case attribute S#_SINCE might better be named S#_FROM, where FROM means "effective from").

Fourth and last, we observe that, even if it includes no information that pertains to the future explicitly, a current relvar like SSSC_SINCE necessarily includes information that pertains to the future *implicitly*. For example, if relvar SSSC_SINCE contains a tuple indicating that supplier S1 has been under contract ever since day 4, that "ever since" must be understood to be *open-ended;* that is, the tuple must be understood to mean that supplier S1 was, is, or will be under contract on every day from day 4 until "the last day." In other words, the associated "valid time" is, currently, the interval from day 4 to the last day.[1] Of course, if we subsequently learn that supplier S1's contract actually terminated on some specific day, say on day 25 (and update the database accordingly), the valid time will then become the interval [*d04:d25*].

10.3 HISTORICAL RELVARS ONLY

We began our discussions in the previous section by examining the current or semi-temporal relvar SSSC_SINCE. Now we turn our attention to the *historical* or fully temporal relvar SSSC_DURING. NOTE: Again we are speaking a little loosely. It is clearly possible for a "historical" relvar such as SSSC_DURING to contain explicit information that pertains to the future. For example, relvar SSSC_DURING might include a tuple that indicates that the contract for supplier S*x* extends from *di* to *dj*, where *dj* is some date in the future, and *di* might be as well. (And if *dj* is in the future but *di* is not, or if *dj* is the date today, then the relvar contains current information as well.)

By way of another example, consider a relvar VACATION {EMP#, DURING}, with predicate:

Employee EMP# was, is, or will be on vacation throughout the interval DURING.

---

1. See Chapter 3, Section 3.3, for a brief explanation of the concept of valid time, and Chapter 15 for an extended discussion of the same concept. Here we just remind you that, strictly speaking, valid times are *sets* of intervals, not individual intervals per se. In the example, therefore, it would be more accurate to say that the valid time is initially {[*d04:d99*]} (where we assume for definiteness that *d99* is "the last day"), and subsequently becomes {[*d04:d25*]} instead. Note, moreover, that—because the database is merely semitemporal—this latter valid time will not actually be recorded in the database; rather, all information concerning supplier S1 will simply be deleted from the database when we learn that the contract has terminated. More generally, in fact, any valid time that involves an interval in which the end point is anything other than "the end of time," and/or involves two or more intervals, cannot be represented in a semitemporal database.

Here the end times certainly might be known, even for vacations that have not yet ended—possibly even for ones that have not yet begun. So to say that a "historical" (or "during") relvar contains historical information is only an approximation to the true state of affairs. As in the case of "current" (or "since") relvars, however, we find the characterization useful from a purely intuitive point of view, and we will stay with it in what follows.

Here then is the definition of relvar SSSC_DURING (in outline only, for simplicity):

```
SSSC_DURING { S#, SNAME, STATUS, CITY, DURING }
          KEY { S#, DURING }
```

The predicate for this relvar is as follows:

From the day that is the begin point of DURING (and not on the day immediately before that day) to the day that is the end point of DURING (and not on the day immediately after that day), inclusive, all four of the following were true:

1. *Supplier S# was under contract.*

2. *Supplier S# was named SNAME.*

3. *Supplier S# had status STATUS.*

4. *Supplier S# was located in city CITY.*

As with relvar SSSC_SINCE in the previous section (original version), it should be immediately clear from this predicate that the relvar is not very well designed. To see why, suppose it currently includes the following tuple:

S#	SNAME	STATUS	CITY	DURING
S2	Jones	10	Paris	[d02:d04]

Suppose we now learn that the status of supplier S2 was indeed 10 on days 2 and 3 (as shown) but became 15 on day 4. Then we have to make *two* changes to the relvar in order to reflect this change! To be specific, we have to delete the existing tuple and insert two new ones that look like this (or, equivalently, we have to replace the existing tuple by one of the two new ones and insert the other):

S#	SNAME	STATUS	CITY	DURING
S2	Jones	10	Paris	[d02:d03]

S#	SNAME	STATUS	CITY	DURING
S2	Jones	15	Paris	*[d04:d04]*

As this example suggests, the task of updating relvar S_DURING to reflect real-world changes is, in general, not entirely straightforward. Informally, the problem is that the timestamp attribute DURING in that relvar "timestamps too much"; in effect, it timestamps a combination of *four separate propositions* (supplier is under contract, supplier has name, supplier has status, supplier has city), instead of just a single proposition.[2] So the obvious idea suggests itself: Why not replace the original S_DURING relvar by four separate relvars, each with its own timestamp? The relvars in question would look like this (again in outline):

```
S_DURING            { S#, DURING }
                    KEY { S#, DURING }

S_NAME_DURING       { S#, SNAME, DURING }
                    KEY { S#, DURING }

S_STATUS_DURING { S#, STATUS, DURING }
                    KEY { S#, DURING }

S_CITY_DURING       { S#, CITY, DURING }
                    KEY { S#, DURING }
```

The example thus illustrates the proposed **vertical decomposition,**[3] as it applies to relvar SSSC_DURING. Relvar S_DURING shows which suppliers were under contract when; relvar S_NAME_DURING shows which suppliers had which name when; relvar S_STATUS_DURING shows which suppliers had which status when; and relvar S_CITY_DURING shows which suppliers were located in which city when. Here are some sample tuples (corresponding to the two new tuples we had to insert into relvar SSSC_DURING in our example a little while back):

---

2. The problems discussed in the previous section with the current relvar SSSC_SINCE (original version) could be characterized analogously: The timestamp attribute SINCE "timestamped too much." And we solved that problem by replacing that attribute by four separate "since" attributes. Clearly, however, we cannot solve the problem with relvar SSSC_DURING analogously; that is, we cannot just replace the single DURING attribute by four separate "during" attributes (why not?).

3. Vertical decomposition is discussed in the literature—under the name "horizontal splitting"!—in reference [48]. The concept seems to have originated in reference [55].

S#	DURING
S2	[d02:d04]

S#	SNAME	DURING
S2	Jones	[d02:d04]

S#	STATUS	DURING
S2	10	[d02:d03]

S#	STATUS	DURING
S2	15	[d04:d04]

S#	CITY	DURING
S2	Paris	[d02:d04]

Of the four relvars resulting from the vertical decomposition, relvar S_DURING in particular is, of course, the relvar on which we based a large part of our discussions in Part II of this book. In fact, however, that relvar is not 100 percent necessary in the overall design now under discussion. The reason is that—thanks to certain integrity constraints that will necessarily be in effect (see Chapter 12)—the information represented by that relvar can always be obtained from any of the other three. (To be more precise, the value of relvar S_DURING at any given time will be equal to the U_projection, using DURING, of the current value of any of the other three relvars on {S#,DURING}.) Nevertheless, we still prefer to include relvar S_DURING in our overall design, partly just for reasons of completeness, and partly because such inclusion avoids a certain degree of awkwardness and arbitrariness that would otherwise occur. NOTE: Analogous but more complicated considerations apply to the combined design to be discussed in Section 10.6.

10.4 SIXTH NORMAL FORM

The vertical decomposition of relvar SSSC_DURING into four separate relvars as discussed in the previous section is very reminiscent, in both rationale and effect, of the classical normalization process, and it is worth taking the time to examine the similarities in depth. In fact, of course, vertical decomposition is exactly what classical normalization theory has always been concerned with; the decomposition operator in that theory is *projection* (which is a vertical decomposition operator by definition), and the corresponding recomposition operator is *join*. Indeed, the ultimate normal form with respect to classical normalization theory, fifth normal form (abbreviated 5NF), is sometimes called **projection/join normal form** for these very reasons [37, 39, 47].

NOTE: Since the foregoing remarks are concerned with classical normalization specifically, the references to projection and join must be understood to mean the classical versions of those operators, not the generalized versions introduced in Chapter 9.

Now, even before temporal data was studied, some researchers (see, e.g., reference [51]) argued in favor of decomposing relvars as far as possible, instead of just as far as classical normalization would require. Some even argued that databases should contain binary relvars only. This extreme position is not really tenable, however. For one thing, unary relvars are sometimes needed. For another, some relvars of degree three or more simply *cannot* be decomposed into relvars of lower degree by taking projections—or, to be more precise, they cannot be so decomposed *in a nonloss way* (it is critically important that the decomposition in question be nonloss, of course). By way of an example, consider a ternary relvar SPJ, with attributes S#, P#, and J#, which represents a many-to-many-to-many relationship among suppliers, parts, and projects ("supplier S# supplies part P# to project J#"). This relvar cannot be nonloss-decomposed into projections of lower degree in any way whatsoever (unless a certain rather unlikely "cyclic" integrity constraint happens to be in effect [39]; for simplicity, we assume that such is not the case.)

Be that as it may, the idea of decomposing relvars as far as possible is motivated by a desire for reduction to the simplest possible terms (meaning no further nonloss decomposition is possible), or in other words a desire for reduction to **irreducible components** [51]. Now, the argument in favor of such decomposition is not very strong in the case of a nontemporal relvar like the original version of the suppliers relvar (i.e., relvar S from Chapter 1); however, it is much stronger in the case of a relvar like the fully temporal analog of that relvar (i.e., relvar SSSC_DURING from the previous section). A supplier's name, status, and city vary independently over time. Moreover, they probably vary at different rates as well. For example, it might be that a supplier's name hardly ever changes, while that same supplier's location changes occasionally and the corresponding status changes quite often—and we saw in the previous section (before we did the vertical decomposition) what a nuisance it is to have to repeat the name and location information every time the status changes. Besides, the name-history, status-history, and city-history concepts are surely more interesting and more digestible than the combined name-status-city-history concept is. Hence our proposed vertical decomposition.

There is another point to be made here, too. With SSSC_DURING as originally defined, we have to use a somewhat nontrivial expression to obtain, for example, suppliers and their city history:

```
USING DURING ◄ SSSC_DURING { S#, CITY, DURING } ►
```

At the same time, the expression to obtain suppliers and their much less interesting combined name-status-city history is far simpler, consisting as it does of just a reference to the relvar name:

```
SSSC_DURING
```

In a sense, therefore, the suggested vertical decomposition of SSSC_DURING levels the playing field for queries—or, rather, it makes it easier to express the more interesting ones and harder to express the less interesting ones. Of course, the "much less interesting" query to obtain suppliers and their combined name-status-history can still be expressed, thus:

```
USING DURING ◄ S_NAME_DURING JOIN
                ( USING DURING ◄ S_STATUS_DURING JOIN
                            S_CITY_DURING ► ) ►
```

By the way, it follows from the fact that this query is still expressible that our proposed vertical decomposition of SSSC_DURING is certainly nonloss.

As an aside, we remark that the foregoing example tends to suggest that some kind of prefix notation for join might be preferable to the traditional infix notation, thereby allowing us to formulate the query more symmetrically as, for example,

```
USING DURING ◄ JOIN ( S_NAME_DURING,
                      S_STATUS_DURING,
                      S_CITY_DURING ) ►
```

The point is, although join is fundamentally a dyadic operator, it is—as explained in Chapter 1—also *associative,* and so we can speak unambiguously of "the" join of n relations for any $n \geq 0$ (these remarks are true of both the classical join operation and its generalized counterpart). NOTE: The cases $n = 0$ and $n = 1$ were also explained in Chapter 1, in Section 1.7, in the subsection entitled "Join."

Back to vertical decomposition. With the foregoing discussion by way of motivation, we can now take a closer look at what is really going on. We begin by revisiting the classical normalization concept of fifth normal form (5NF), which as we said earlier is the ultimate normal form with respect to classical projection and join. Fifth normal form is based on the concept of *join dependency,* which can be defined thus:

Let R be a relvar, and let $A, B, \ldots, Z$ be subsets of the attributes of R. Then we say that R satisfies the **join dependency**

```
✳ { A, B, ..., Z }
```

(pronounced "star $A, B, \ldots, Z$") if and only if every legal value of R is equal to the join of its projections on $A, B, \ldots, Z$—that is, if and only if R can be nonloss-decomposed into those projections. NOTE: Again we are tacitly appealing to the fact that join is associative, meaning we can speak unambiguously of "the" join of n relations for any $n \geq 0$.

By way of example, consider the nontemporal suppliers relvar S, with attributes S#, SNAME, STATUS, and CITY. If we agree to use the name "SN" to refer to the subset

{S#,SNAME} of the set of attributes of S, and similarly for "ST" and "SC," then we can say that relvar S satisfies the join dependency ✳{SN,ST,SC}.

Now we can define fifth normal form:

A relvar R is in **fifth normal form** (abbreviated 5NF) if and only if every nontrivial join dependency that is satisfied by R is implied by the candidate key(s) of R, where:

- The join dependency ✳{A, B, ..., Z} on R is **trivial** if and only if at least one of A, B, ..., Z is the set of all attributes of R.

- The join dependency ✳{A, B, ..., Z} on R is **implied by the candidate key(s)** of R if and only if each of A, B, ..., Z is a superkey for R. (Recall from Chapter 1 that a *superkey* for relvar R is a superset—not necessarily a proper superset, of course—of some candidate key of relvar R; thus, all candidate keys are superkeys, but some superkeys are not candidate keys, in general.)

Now we proceed to generalize the foregoing ideas. First, we generalize the concept of join dependency by replacing the references to join and projection in the existing definition by references to the generalized versions of those operators, thus:

Let R be a relvar, let A, B, ..., Z be subsets of the attributes of R, and let $A1$, $A2$, ..., An be interval attributes of R. Then we say that R satisfies the (generalized) **join dependency**

```
USING ( A1, A2, ..., An ) ✳ { A, B, ..., Z }
```

if and only if the expression

```
USING ( A1, A2, ..., An ) ◄ R = R' ►
```

(where R' is the U_join of the U_projections of R on A, B, ..., Z, and the U_join and U_projections in question involve a USING specification identical to the one just shown) evaluates to true for every legal value of R. NOTE: We are tacitly appealing here to the fact that U_join, like join, is associative, meaning we can speak unambiguously of "the" U_join of any number of relations.[4] Note too that to say that the foregoing expression evaluates to true is to say that R and R' are *equivalent* (with respect to $A1$, $A2$, ..., An)—see the discussion of this concept in Section 8.7.

It should be clear that classical join dependencies are a special case of the generalized version as just defined, and so we can legitimately use the same term "join dependency" to refer to both.

---

4. Again we remark that some kind of prefix notation for join might be preferable to the traditional infix notation; in fact, the expression ✳{A, B, ..., Z} constitutes precisely such a prefix notation.

Now we can go on to define a new normal form, which we will call sixth normal form:

A relvar R is in **sixth normal form** (abbreviated 6NF) if and only if it satisfies no nontrivial join dependencies at all—where, as before, a join dependency is trivial if and only if at least one of the projections (possibly U_projections) involved is taken over the set of all attributes of the relvar concerned.

It is immediate from this definition that every relvar that is in 6NF is also in 5NF. It is also immediate that a given relvar is in 6NF if and only if it is irreducible in the sense explained earlier.

Now, relvar SSSC_DURING is clearly not in 6NF by this definition, because

- it satisfies the (generalized) join dependency USING DURING ✳{SND,STD,SCD} (where the name "SND" refers to the set of attributes {S#,SNAME,DURING}, and similarly for the names "STD" and "SCD"), and

- that join dependency is definitely nontrivial.[5]

At the same time, relvar SSSC_DURING *is* in 5NF, since the only nontrivial join dependencies it satisfies are ones that are implied by its sole candidate key {S#,DURING}. (In fact, all of the *classical* join dependencies it satisfies are either trivial or implied by that candidate key. But it additionally satisfies the *generalized* join dependency mentioned above.)

And now—as you must surely be expecting!—we suggest that a historical relvar that (1) is not in 6NF, and (2) can benefit from decomposition into a set of 6NF projections, be in fact so decomposed. Please understand, however, that the decomposition operator to be used in this process is not just the regular projection operator but, rather, the generalized version of that operator defined in the previous chapter. Likewise, the recomposition operator is not just the regular join operator but the generalized version of that operator, also defined in that previous chapter.

Let us make more precise the notion that a relvar R that is not in 6NF "can benefit from decomposition into a set of 6NF projections." To be specific, the benefits we have in mind occur if and only if

- R has at least one interval attribute I;

- R has at least one candidate key {K} that includes I;

- R has at least two additional attributes, over and above those included in {K}; and

---

5. In fact, it also satisfies the *classical* (and nontrivial) join dependency USING () ✳{SND,STD,SCD}—which we can abbreviate to just ✳{SND,STD,SCD}—because (1) the (sole) candidate key of SSSC_DURING is {S#,DURING}; (2) therefore every attribute of the relvar is functionally dependent on {S#,DURING}; hence, (3) the relvar can be nonloss-decomposed into its (regular) projections on {S#,SNAME,DURING}, {S#,STATUS,DURING}, and {S#,CITY,DURING}. (We should add, however, that while the combination {S#,DURING} would be a key for each of those regular projections, it would not be a U_key, in general. See the next chapter for further explanation of this point.)

- *R* is subject to the constraint PACKED ON *I*, and furthermore that constraint is nontrivial. (See the next chapter, Section 11.3, for an explanation of PACKED ON constraints in general, and Section 11.9 for an explanation of what it means for such a constraint to be nontrivial.)

To revert for a moment to the example of relvar SSSC_DURING: As we saw earlier, that relvar satisfies the nontrivial join dependency USING DURING ✻{SND,STD,SCD} (where the name "SND" refers to the set of attributes {S#,SNAME,DURING}, and similarly for the names "STD" and "SCD"). In fact, relvar SSSC_DURING also satisfies the nontrivial join dependency USING DURING ✻{SD,SND,STD,SCD} (where the name "SD" refers to the set of attributes {S#,DURING}—in other words, the sole candidate key). We could therefore nonloss-decompose the relvar into four projections (i.e., those on SD, SND, STD, and SCD), instead of just three. And indeed, for reasons explained earlier (in Section 10.3), we recommend doing exactly that—even though (as also noted in Section 10.3) the projection on SD is redundant, being identical at all times to the projection of any of the other three on S# and DURING (see the discussion of Requirements R3 and R6 in Chapter 12, Section 12.4).

We should add that if we switch from a database design like the one tacitly under discussion—that is, one that involves historical relvars only—to one that involves a mixture of both current and historical relvars (as we will be recommending in Section 10.6), then the projection on SD, as such, will no longer be redundant in the foregoing sense. Note, however, that even that recommended design will still involve *some* kind of redundancy. (This fact follows because (1) the mixed design includes, among other things, a current relvar called S_SINCE and two historical ones called S_DURING and S_STATUS_DURING, and (2) those three relvars together are logically equivalent to, and can be mapped into, relvars S_DURING and S_STATUS_DURING in the design involving historical relvars only. The mapping process is illustrated in Chapter 13, Section 13.5.)

One last point: Since regular projection is a special case of generalized projection and regular join is a special case of generalized join, it really does make sense to think of 6NF as another level of normalization, over and above 5NF; indeed, it makes sense to think of 6NF as a generalized projection/join normal form.

10.5 "THE MOVING POINT NOW"

Throughout our discussion of historical relvars prior to this point, we have assumed (reasonably enough) that history starts at "the beginning of time" and continues up until the present time. In particular, we have assumed that time intervals in those historical relvars can stretch from any point *b* to any point *e*, where $b \leq e$ and $e \leq$ the present time.[6] However, we have also assumed that the present time is represented as some

---

6. For simplicity, we are assuming here that those historical relvars do not include explicit information regarding the future; that is, no interval [*b*:*e*] is such that either *e* (or, *a fortiori, b*) is in the future. This simplifying assumption does not materially affect any of the discussions in this section. We note, however, that if *e* is in fact "the present time," then the historical relvar in question does include *current* information (i.e., information about the current state of affairs).

explicit value (which we have taken to be *d10*—day 10—whenever we needed to show concrete examples), and that assumption is not reasonable at all. In particular, it suggests that whenever time marches on, so to speak, the database must be updated accordingly; in the case at hand, it suggests that at midnight on day 10 every "present-time" appearance of *d10* must somehow be replaced by an appearance of *d11*, instantaneously (because those appearances of *d10* do not really mean day 10 per se, they really mean "until further notice"). A different example, involving intervals of finer granularity, might require such updates to be performed as often as every millisecond!

NOTE: Actually it should be obvious that using an explicit value such as *d10* to stand for "until further notice" makes no sense, because it leads to ambiguity. That is, there is no way to tell, in general, whether a given appearance of that value means what it says or whether it really means "until further notice."

Considerations such as these have led some writers (see, e.g., reference [19]) to propose the use of a special marker, which we will call NOW, to denote what in Chapter 3 we referred to as "the moving point *now*" (in other words, to stand for "until further notice"). The basic idea is to permit that special marker to appear wherever a value of the applicable point type is permitted and the intended interpretation is indeed "until further notice." Thus, for example, relvar S_DURING might include a tuple for supplier S1 with a DURING value of [*d04*:NOW] instead of [*d04*:*d10*]. (Of course, we are assuming in this example that the appearance of *d10* in the original interval [*d04*:*d10*] really was supposed to stand for "the moving point *now*" and not for day 10 as such.)

However, other writers, the present writers included, regard the introduction of the NOW marker as an incautious departure from sound relational principles. In fact, noting that NOW is really a *variable,* we observe that the approach involves the very strange—we would say logically indefensible—notion of *values* (interval values, to be specific) that contain *variables.* Indeed, the NOW construct bears a certain resemblance to the NULL construct of SQL, inasmuch as NULL too leads to the notion of values that contain something that is not a value. The present writers, among many others, have long argued that NULL is and always was a logical mistake (see, e.g., references [23–24], [31–33], and [75]), and we certainly do not want to make another such mistake if we can help it.

By the way, note that if the DURING value in (let us assume) the unique tuple for supplier S1 in relvar S_DURING really is [*d04*:NOW], then the result of the query "When does supplier S1's contract terminate?" must be NOW (= until further notice), not whatever happens to be the date today! For if the system actually evaluates that NOW at the time the query is executed and responds with (say) the value *d10,* then that response is clearly incorrect, since supplier S1's contract has not yet terminated. Furthermore, if the result is indeed NOW, then that NOW must be interpreted as meaning "some indefinite point in the future," an interpretation that does not fit very well with most people's intuitive understanding of the word *now.* Also, if the query is issued from within some application program, then that NOW will have to be returned to some program variable; so what exactly will the value of that variable be after that NOW has been assigned to it? What data type would that variable have to have?

Here are some more examples of the kinds of questions that arise from the notion of NOW that you might care to ponder:

- *The creeping delete problem:* Let i be the interval [NOW:*d14*], let t be a tuple containing i, and let today be day 10. Then tuple t can be thought of as a kind of shorthand for five separate tuples, containing intervals [*d10:d10*], [*d11:d11*], [*d12:d12*], [*d13:d13*], and [*d14:d14*], respectively. But when the clock reaches midnight on day 10, the first of these tuples is (in effect) automatically deleted! Likewise for day 11, day 12, and day 13 … and what exactly happens at midnight on day 14?

- What is the result of the comparison *d10* = NOW? NOTE: Some might suggest that the result should be *unknown* ("the third truth value")—a suggestion that takes us straight back into the NULL mess, of course, a possibility that we reject outright.

- What is the value of "NOW+1" or "NOW−1"?

- If *i1* and *i2* are the intervals [*d01*:NOW] and [*d06:d07*], respectively, do they meet, or overlap? That is, can we form their (interval) union or not?

- What is the result of unpacking a relation containing a tuple in which the interval attribute on which the unpacking is to be done has the value [*d04*:NOW]? In particular, does the result include a tuple in which that attribute has value [NOW:NOW]?

- What is the effect of assigning the interval [*d01*:NOW] to variable I1? And then (perhaps the next day) assigning it to I2? And then performing an "=" comparison on I1 and I2?

- What is the cardinality of the set {[*d01*:NOW],[*d01:d04*]}?

And so on (this is not an exhaustive list). We believe it is hard to give coherent answers to questions like these; clearly, we would prefer an approach that does not rely on any such suspect notions as the NOW marker and values that contain variables.

If we limit our design to historical relvars only, however, we must put *something* in the database to represent "until further notice" when "until further notice" is what we really mean. Once again, consider the case of a supplier whose contract has not yet terminated. As explained earlier, such a supplier can be regarded as having a contract that currently extends all the way into the future, right up to the very last day. Clearly, therefore, we can explicitly specify the END(DURING) value for such a supplier as the last day, and then replace that artificial value by the true value when the true value later becomes known. (Of course, we are assuming here that we do not know exactly when the contract will terminate; if we did know an explicit termination date, then clearly there would be no problem.) But note that this approach does mean that if "the last day" appears in the result of a query, then the user will—probably, but not necessarily—have to interpret that value to mean "until further notice," not the last day per se.

To conclude this section, we would like to emphasize that the foregoing paragraph merely describes one possible solution to the problem of "the moving point *now*." Describing is not the same as recommending! In general, it is a bad idea to place information in the database that is known to be incorrect—and, of course, an explicit statement to the effect that some contract will not terminate until "the end of time" is indeed incorrect, in general (!). In fact, including information in the database that is known to be incorrect could be regarded as a violation of another fundamental principle: namely, the principle that tuples in the database are supposed to correspond to propositions that are believed to be true. Don't tell lies! As already indicated, however, if our design consists of historical relvars only, we might be forced into telling this particular lie on occasion—a fact that in itself might be seen as a good reason to opt for the combination design to be discussed in the section immediately following.

10.6 BOTH CURRENT AND HISTORICAL RELVARS

In Section 10.2 we described a design approach based on current ("since") relvars only; the major problem with that approach turned out to be the fact that the database cannot really keep proper historical records (it is after all only *semi*temporal). Then, in Section 10.3, we described another design approach based on historical ("during") relvars only; and a big problem with *that* approach is it has to deal with the problem of "the moving point *now*" in an unpleasantly ad hoc way. In this section, by contrast, we describe an approach that can be characterized, loosely, as a combination of the approaches discussed in Sections 10.2 and 10.3. To be specific, we use "since" relvars to represent current information, and "during" relvars to represent historical information. This combination approach allows us to keep proper historical records while avoiding ad hoc solutions to the problem of "the moving point *now*."

We begin with the following fundamental observation: There is an important logical difference between historical information, on the one hand, and information regarding the current state of affairs, on the other. To spell out that difference:

- For historical information, the begin and end times are both known.

- For current information, by contrast, the begin time is known but the end time is not.

(Actually both of these statements are somewhat oversimplified, but we will stay with them for the time being.)

The foregoing difference strongly suggests that there should be two sets of relvars, one for the current state of affairs and one for the history (after all, there are certainly two sets of predicates). Refer to Figure 10.1. In that figure, observe the following:

- Relvar S_SINCE is the sole current relvar. It is *exactly* the same as relvar SSSC_SINCE (revised version with four "since" attributes, as discussed in Section 10.2), except that for simplicity we have abbreviated the name SSSC_SINCE to just S_SINCE. NOTE: Do not confuse this new S_SINCE relvar with the relvar of

```
S_SINCE   { S#,      S#_SINCE,
            SNAME,   SNAME_SINCE,
            STATUS,  STATUS_SINCE,
            CITY,    CITY_SINCE }
          KEY { S# }

S_DURING { S#, DURING }
          KEY { S#, DURING }

S_NAME_DURING { S#, SNAME, DURING }
          KEY { S#, DURING }

S_STATUS_DURING { S#, STATUS, DURING }
          KEY { S#, DURING }

S_CITY_DURING { S#, CITY, DURING }
          KEY { S#, DURING }
```

the same name from Chapter 4. Also, note that the new S_SINCE relvar is in 5NF but not 6NF. Note too that (as explained in Section 10.2) the relvar might contain explicit information concerning the future.

■ The relvars with DURING in their name are the historical ones, and they are as discussed in Section 10.2—with one crucial difference: They specifically do not include any tuples that pertain to either the current state of affairs or the future; rather, all information that would have been represented by such tuples in Section 10.3 is now represented by tuples in the current relvar S_SINCE instead.[7] Note in particular, therefore, that those historical relvars do not include any tuples with artificial end times as discussed in the previous section; thus, they do not violate the principle that tuples in the database are supposed to correspond to propositions that are believed to be true. As a consequence, we can tighten up the corresponding predicates slightly. For example, the predicate for relvar S_DURING now looks like this (note the new text following the semicolon):

From the day that is the begin point of DURING (and not on the day immediately before that day) to the day that is the end point of DURING (and not on the day immediately after that day), inclusive, supplier S# was under contract; furthermore, the day that is the end point of DURING is in the past.

---

7. This statement is slightly oversimplified. Suppose a tuple for some supplier Sx appears in relvar S_SINCE with some "since" value equal to *di*. Then that value *di* can be regarded as the beginning of an interval for which the corresponding end value is "the end of time." But if we happen to know (or, rather, if we currently believe or—better yet—*predict*) that the corresponding end value is some specific day *dj* in the future, then it would be better not to represent supplier Sx in relvar S_SINCE at all. Rather, such predictive information would be better represented in an entirely separate set of relvars, isomorphic to our familiar "during" relvars (but with different predicates, of course, both internal predicates and—*a fortiori*—external ones).

The process of separating current (and possibly future) information from historical information is the process of **horizontal decomposition** first mentioned in Section 10.1.[8] As you can see, that process is not nearly as cut and dried—not as formal—as the vertical decomposition process discussed in Sections 10.3 and 10.4; in our running example, however, we can think of it as working as follows. Suppose we start with the original fully temporal relvar SSSC_DURING from Section 10.1, which, we assume for generality, does include information about the future as well as the past (as well as information about the current state of affairs). Then:

- First, we introduce a current relvar S_SINCE with an attribute for every attribute of SSSC_DURING except for the DURING attribute itself.

- Second, for each attribute that appears in S_SINCE thanks to the first step, we add a corresponding "since" attribute to that relvar.

- Third, relvar SSSC_DURING is now to be understood as containing information that truly is historical only. (And now we can go on to decompose that relvar vertically into 6NF projections, as discussed earlier in the chapter.)

Now we return to the two statements that we admitted earlier were slightly oversimplified. The first was that the begin and end times are both known for historical information. Sometimes, however, we do not know the end time, or possibly even the begin time, for such information; for example, we might know that supplier S1 was once under contract, but not exactly when. Of course, such a state of affairs is basically just a specific example of the general (and generally vexing) problem of *missing information.* This book is not the place to get into a detailed discussion of that general problem; instead, we content ourselves by invoking Wittgenstein's famous dictum, *Wovon man nicht reden kann, darüber muss man schweigen* ("Whereof one cannot speak, thereon one must remain silent"), which we interpret to mean, in the context at hand, that another good general principle is that it is a bad idea to state explicitly in the database that you do not know something. Record only what you know![9]

The second of our slightly oversimplified statements was that, for current information, the begin time is known but the end time is not. However, sometimes we do know the end time after all, even for current information—see, for instance, the VACATION

---

8. Horizontal decomposition is also discussed (under the name "temporal partitioning") in reference [93]. The concept seems to have originated in reference [5], and an extensive discussion appears in reference [1]. However, the primary emphasis in those references seems to be on physical storage matters rather than on issues of logical database design; for example, the title of reference [1] is "Partitioned *Storage* Structures for Temporal Databases" (our italics). NOTE: The literature sometimes refers to current and historical information as "the current database" and "the temporal pool," respectively.

9. Perhaps we should stress once more the fact that we do *not* regard "nulls" as a suitable approach to the missing information problem. Indeed, as noted in Chapter 1, we do not regard nulls, as that term is usually understood, as part of the relational model at all.

example discussed briefly near the beginning of Section 10.3. In such a case, we can adopt the approach of that previous section and keep "historical" relvars only—"historical" in quotes because such relvars can now include information about the future—and discard the "current" relvars entirely. Of course, this approach does mean we might have to use explicit "end-of-time" values to denote "until further notice," as we know from Section 10.5.

Considerations like the foregoing show that the question of which design approach is best in any given situation will depend on circumstances. That said, however, we feel bound to say that the combination approach, involving both current and historical relvars, is our preferred approach overall. (And please note that, to say it again, the historical relvars in such a design truly do contain historical information *only*.) However, we cannot deny that our preferred approach does potentially complicate constraints, queries, and updates somewhat—essentially because those constraints, queries, and updates will often have to span current and historical relvars. In the next few chapters, we will explain some of those complications and offer some suggestions as to how the difficulties might be alleviated in practice.

10.7 CONCLUDING REMARKS

This chapter has been concerned, rather more than most of its predecessors, with temporal data specifically. The reason is that "the moving point *now*" is a concept that applies to temporal data specifically (other kinds of data for which the concepts of previous chapters apply—the interval concept in particular—typically have nothing analogous). And it is the concept of "the moving point *now*" that led us, eventually, to our preferred approach to design as described in the previous section. To summarize that preferred approach briefly:

- We suggest that horizontal decomposition be used to separate current and historical information into distinct relvars. We remark in passing that this distinction corresponds closely to the distinction found in many installations today between the operational database and the data warehouse.

- We suggest that current relvars be normalized in accordance with classical normalization theory to fifth normal form. We observe, however, that such relvars might require several "since" attributes, each of which is point-valued (i.e., denotes a time point), and we have found it necessary to give a very careful interpretation for such attributes.

- We suggest that vertical decomposition be used to separate historical relvars into irreducible (6NF) components, each with its own "during" attribute.

Next, there are a couple of small points that need to be made somewhere, and here is as good a place as any to make them:

- First, all of our examples of historical relvars in this chapter have involved candidate keys that in turn involved an interval attribute; the sole candidate key for relvar S_DURING, for example, is the combination {S#,DURING} (that relvar happens to be "all key"). But suppose suppliers never get a second chance; that is, once a supplier's contract terminates, that supplier is never placed under contract again. Then the sole candidate key for relvar S_DURING would be simply {S#}.

- Second, it is of course possible for a relvar to consist of interval attributes only. As a simple example, consider a relvar BLACKOUTS with a single attribute that shows intervals during which a certain airline's frequent-flyer program does not allow award travel this year.

Back to our running example. We close this section, and this chapter, with a brief discussion of shipments (all of our discussions in this chapter prior to this point have concentrated on suppliers). Without going into too much detail, it should be fairly obvious that our preferred design for shipments will involve two relvars, one current and one historical, that look like this (in outline):

```
SP_SINCE   { S#, P#, SINCE }
           KEY { S#, P# }
           FOREIGN KEY { S# } REFERENCES S_SINCE

SP_DURING { S#, P#, DURING }
           KEY { S#, P#, DURING }
```

Both of these relvars are in 6NF. (In other words, horizontal decomposition does apply to shipments but vertical decomposition does not.) Also, note the foreign key from relvar SP_SINCE to relvar S_SINCE, which reflects the fact that any supplier currently able to supply some part must be currently under contract. We will have a lot more to say about foreign keys and related matters in the next two chapters.

EXERCISES

1. Explain horizontal and vertical decomposition in your own words.

2. "Current" relvars can represent information about the past and future as well as the present. Explain this remark.

3. Define sixth normal form (6NF). When is 6NF recommended?

4. "The moving point *now*" is not a value but a variable. Discuss.

5. Give a realistic example of a relvar that consists of interval attributes only.

6. Consider the following revised version of the courses-and-students database from earlier chapters:

```
VAR CURRENT_COURSE RELATION
    { COURSE#   COURSE#,
      CNAME     NAME,
      AVAILABLE DATE }
    KEY { COURSE# } ;

VAR OLD_COURSE RELATION
    { COURSE#          COURSE#,
      CNAME            NAME,
      AVAILABLE_DURING INTERVAL_DATE }
    KEY { COURSE# } ;

VAR CURRENT_STUDENT RELATION
    { STUDENT#   STUDENT#,
      SNAME      NAME,
      REGISTERED DATE }
    KEY { STUDENT# } ;

VAR STUDENT_HISTORY RELATION
    { STUDENT#   STUDENT#,
      SNAME      NAME,
      REG_DURING INTERVAL_DATE }
    KEY { STUDENT#, REG_DURING } ;

VAR ENROLLMENT RELATION
    { COURSE#   COURSE#,
      STUDENT# STUDENT#,
      ENROLLED DATE }
    KEY { COURSE#, STUDENT# }
    FOREIGN KEY { COURSE# } REFERENCES CURRENT_COURSE
    FOREIGN KEY { STUDENT# } REFERENCES CURRENT_STUDENT ;

VAR COMPLETED_COURSE RELATION
    { COURSE#        COURSE#,
      STUDENT#       STUDENT#,
      STUDIED_DURING INTERVAL_DATE,
      GRADE          GRADE }
    KEY { COURSE#, STUDENT# } ;
```

The predicates are as follows:

- CURRENT_COURSE: *Course COURSE#, named CNAME, has been available since date AVAILABLE.*

- OLD_COURSE: *Course COURSE#, named CNAME, was available throughout interval AVAILABLE_DURING.*

- CURRENT_STUDENT: *Current student STUDENT#, named SNAME, registered with the university on date REGISTERED.*

- STUDENT_HISTORY: *Student STUDENT#, named SNAME, was registered with the university throughout interval REG_DURING.*

- ENROLLMENT: *Student STUDENT# enrolled on course COURSE# on date ENROLLED.*

- COMPLETED_COURSE: *Student STUDENT# studied course COURSE# throughout interval STUDIED_DURING, achieving grade GRADE.*

No course number appears in both CURRENT_COURSE and OLD_COURSE.

a. For each relvar, state whether it is in 6NF. If it is not, identify any problems that might be solved by decomposing it appropriately.

b. Write a query to obtain a relation showing, for each student, the number of courses completed during each registration interval for that student.

c. Assume that for each course there are zero or more offerings, each taking place over a given interval of time (possibly contiguous or overlapping). Some offerings have already taken place; others are currently under way (but have a scheduled completion date); others are scheduled to start at some future time (but, again, have a scheduled completion date). When students enroll in courses, they must specify which offering they are enrolling for. Each offering has a quota, and the number of students enrolled in that offering must not exceed that quota. Write the predicate and an appropriate **Tutorial D** definition for a relvar COURSE_OFFERING to reflect these requirements.

Chapter

11

INTEGRITY CONSTRAINTS I: CANDIDATE KEYS AND RELATED CONSTRAINTS

11.1 INTRODUCTION

In this chapter and the next, we turn our attention to the crucial question of the *integrity constraints* that might apply to temporal data. This chapter concerns itself with key (or "keylike") constraints in particular and Chapter 12 addresses temporal constraints in general. Now, in Chapter 4, we saw how difficult it was, in the absence of proper interval support, even to formulate such constraints correctly; in these two chapters, we will see how the concepts introduced in Chapters 5 through 9 might be used to alleviate the problem, somewhat. As we will also see, however, the solutions are not always as straightforward as they might be. This topic is surprisingly tricky!

We begin by assuming that the database has been designed as a combination of current and historical relvars and it therefore consists of the following seven relvars:

```
S_SINCE              SP_SINCE
S_DURING             SP_DURING
S_NAME_DURING
S_STATUS_DURING
S_CITY_DURING
```

(We leave discussion of designs involving current relvars only or historical relvars only to the next chapter.) With respect to this design, however, it should be clear that:

1. Within the current relvar S_SINCE, the attribute pairs {SNAME,SNAME_SINCE}, {STATUS,STATUS_SINCE}, and {CITY,CITY_SINCE} will all exhibit similar behavior.

2. The historical relvars S_NAME_DURING, S_STATUS_DURING, and S_CITY_ DURING will also all exhibit similar behavior.

Without loss of generality, therefore, we can clearly ignore both

- the attribute pairs {SNAME,SNAME_SINCE} and {CITY,CITY_SINCE} in relvar S_SINCE, and

- the relvars S_NAME_DURING and S_CITY_DURING.

For the purposes of the rest of this chapter, therefore (and—please note carefully— for the remainder of this part of the book, barring explicit statements to the contrary), we can simplify our database still further. To be specific, we can take our database to be as shown, in outline, in Figure 11.1 ("in outline" here meaning in particular that all

FIGURE 11.1

Simplified database design (outline).

```
S_SINCE { S#, S#_SINCE, STATUS, STATUS_SINCE }
        KEY { S# }

SP_SINCE { S#, P#, SINCE }
        KEY { S#, P# }
        FOREIGN KEY { S# } REFERENCES S_SINCE

S_DURING { S#, DURING }
        KEY { S#, DURING }

S_STATUS_DURING { S#, STATUS, DURING }
        KEY { S#, DURING }

SP_DURING { S#, P#, DURING }
        KEY { S#, P#, DURING }
```

integrity constraints other than KEY and FOREIGN KEY constraints have been omitted, because, of course, we are not yet in a position to say what those missing constraints should look like). Figures 11.2 and 11.3—which repay *very* careful study!—show a set of sample values for that database. NOTE: The specific values shown in those figures deliberately do not correspond exactly to our usual sample values as shown in Figure 5.1 and Endpaper Panel 4, though they are close. We should say too that very little in the present chapter actually depends on the specific values shown in Figures 11.2 and 11.3, but those specific values should help you understand the semantics of the database in general.

FIGURE 11.2

Relvars S_SINCE and SP_SINCE— sample values.

S_SINCE

S#	S#_SINCE	STATUS	STATUS_SINCE
S1	d04	20	d06
S2	d07	10	d07
S3	d03	30	d03
S4	d04	20	d08
S5	d02	30	d02

SP_SINCE

S#	P#	SINCE
S1	P1	d04
S1	P2	d05
S1	P3	d09
S1	P4	d05
S1	P5	d04
S1	P6	d06
S2	P1	d08
S2	P2	d09
S3	P2	d08
S4	P5	d05

FIGURE 11.3

Relvars S_DURING, S_STATUS_DURING, and SP_DURING— sample values.

S_DURING

S#	DURING
S2	[d02:d04]
S6	[d03:d05]

SP_DURING

S#	P#	DURING
S2	P1	[d02:d04]
S2	P2	[d03:d03]
S3	P5	[d05:d07]
S4	P2	[d06:d09]
S4	P4	[d04:d08]
S6	P3	[d03:d03]
S6	P3	[d05:d05]

S_STATUS_DURING

S#	STATUS	DURING
S1	15	[d04:d05]
S2	5	[d02:d02]
S2	10	[d03:d04]
S4	10	[d04:d04]
S4	25	[d05:d07]
S6	5	[d03:d04]
S6	7	[d05:d05]

Predicates

For reference, here are informal (re)statements of the predicates for the relvars of Figure 11.1. First the current relvars:

- S_SINCE: *Supplier S# has been under contract since S#_SINCE (and not the day immediately before S#_SINCE) and has had status STATUS since STATUS_SINCE (and not the day immediately before STATUS_SINCE).*

- SP_SINCE: *Supplier S# has been able to supply part P# since SINCE (and not the day immediately before SINCE).*

Now the historical relvars (and here we use *b* and *e* to denote BEGIN(DURING) and END(DURING), respectively):

- S_DURING: *Supplier S# was under contract from day b to day e inclusive (and not on the day immediately before b or after e).*

- S_STATUS_DURING: *Supplier S# had status STATUS from day b to day e inclusive (and not on the day immediately before b or after e).*

- SP_DURING: *Supplier S# was able to supply part P# from day b to day e inclusive (and not on the day immediately before b or after e).*

Remember too that when we say a given supplier has some status on a given day, we mean the supplier in question has *exactly one* status on that day (you might want to review the three assumptions at the end of Chapter 3). Moreover, in accordance with the discussions in Section 10.6, we assume that the "since" relvars contain current (and possibly future) data only, and the "during" relvars contain historical data only. Note in particular, therefore, that every END(DURING) value is less than the date today. Incidentally—you might like to check this point—it follows that if the sample values shown in Figures 11.2 and 11.3 are valid, today must be at least day 10.

Candidate and Foreign Keys

The candidate keys that apply to the database of Figure 11.1 are self-explanatory and are as indicated in that figure, and in the case of the "since" relvars, at least, there is little more to say about them. By contrast, there certainly is more to say in the case of the "during" relvars, and those discussions form the bulk of the rest of this chapter.

As for foreign keys, there is in fact only one such in our simplified database, and that is {S#} in the current relvar SP_SINCE, which is a foreign key referencing the sole candidate key—in fact the primary key, though Figure 11.1 did not explicitly define it as such[1]—{S#} in the current relvar S_SINCE:

---

1. In fact there is no way it could have done, because **Tutorial D** includes no specific support for primary keys.

```
FOREIGN KEY { S# } REFERENCES S_SINCE
```

This constraint, which appears as part of the definition of relvar SP_SINCE, reflects the fact that any supplier currently able to supply some part must be currently under contract. As we observed in Chapter 4, however (in Section 4.2, in connection with what we there called Constraint XST1), this foreign key constraint by itself is not sufficient; what we really need is something more general, in order to enforce the constraint that *whenever* a given supplier is, was, or will be able to supply some part, then that supplier is, was, or will be under contract at that same time. This more general constraint is not a regular foreign key constraint as such, however (and it is certainly not a *candidate* key constraint, of course), and we therefore defer further discussion of it to the next chapter.

We now proceed to examine, in the next three sections, three general problems that can occur with temporal databases like that of Figure 11.1 (in the absence of suitable constraints, that is). We refer to those problems as *the redundancy problem, the circumlocution problem,* and *the contradiction problem,* respectively (we mentioned these terms in passing in Chapter 4, as you might recall). NOTE: The current relvars S_SINCE and SP_SINCE are not discussed further in this chapter, except for a couple of brief mentions here and there; we will come back to them in Chapter 12.

11.2 THE REDUNDANCY PROBLEM

We begin by considering relvar S_STATUS_DURING specifically. Since {S#,DURING} is a candidate key for that relvar, a **Tutorial D** definition for that relvar might look as follows:

```
VAR S_STATUS_DURING RELATION
  { S# S#, STATUS INTEGER, DURING INTERVAL_DATE }
  KEY { S#, DURING } ;              /* Warning--inadequate! */
```

As the comment suggests, however, the KEY constraint here, though logically correct, is also inadequate. It is inadequate because it fails to prevent the relvar from containing (for example) both of the following tuples at the same time:

S#	STATUS	DURING
S4	25	[d05:d06]

S#	STATUS	DURING
S4	25	[d06:d07]

As you can see, these two tuples display a certain **redundancy,** inasmuch as the status for supplier S4 on day 6 is effectively stated twice. Clearly, it would be better if we were to replace the two tuples shown by the following single tuple:

S#	STATUS	DURING
S4	25	[d05:d07]

Observe now that if the two original tuples were the only tuples in some two-tuple relation and we packed that relation on DURING, we would wind up with a one-tuple relation containing the single tuple just shown. Loosely speaking, therefore, we might say the tuple just shown is a "packed" tuple, obtained by packing the two original tuples on attribute DURING (we say "loosely speaking" because packing is really an operation that applies to relations, not tuples). So we want to replace those two original tuples by that packed tuple. In fact, as pointed out in Chapter 4, *not* performing that replacement—that is, permitting both original tuples to appear—would be almost as bad as permitting duplicate tuples to appear (duplicate tuples, if allowed, would also constitute a kind of redundancy). Indeed, if both original tuples did appear, the relvar would be in violation of its own predicate! Consider the right tuple, for example (the one containing the interval [d06:d07]). That tuple says among other things that supplier S4 did *not* have status 25 on the day immediately before day 6 (check the predicate for relvar S_STATUS_DURING in Section 11.1 if you need to persuade yourself of this fact). But then the other tuple (the left one) says among other things that supplier S4 *did* have status 25 on day 5, and of course day 5 is the day immediately before day 6.

11.3 THE CIRCUMLOCUTION PROBLEM

The KEY constraint shown in the previous section for relvar S_STATUS_DURING is inadequate in another way also. To be specific, it fails to prevent the relvar from containing (for example) both of the following tuples at the same time:

S#	STATUS	DURING
S4	25	[d05:d05]

S#	STATUS	DURING
S4	25	[d06:d07]

Here there is no redundancy as such, but there is a certain **circumlocution,** inasmuch as we are taking two tuples to say what could be better said with just a single packed tuple (the same one as in the previous section, in fact):

S#	STATUS	DURING
S4	25	[d05:d07]

Indeed, not replacing the two original tuples by that packed tuple would mean, again, that the relvar would be in violation of its own predicate, as can easily be confirmed.

Fixing the Redundancy and Circumlocution Problems

Now, it should be clear that, in order to avoid redundancies and circumlocutions like those we have been discussing, what we need to do is enforce a constraint—let us call it Constraint A—along the following lines:

- **Constraint A:** If at any given time relvar S_STATUS_DURING contains two distinct tuples that are identical except for their DURING values *i1* and *i2*, then *i1* MERGES *i2* must be false.

Recall from Chapter 6 that, loosely speaking, MERGES is the logical OR of OVERLAPS and MEETS (or OVERLAPS and "abuts," if you prefer). Replacing MERGES by OVERLAPS in Constraint A gives the constraint we need to enforce in order to avoid the redundancy problem; replacing it by MEETS gives the constraint we need to enforce in order to avoid the circumlocution problem.

It should be clear too that there is a very simple way to enforce Constraint A: namely, by keeping the relvar packed at all times on attribute DURING. Let us therefore invent a new PACKED ON constraint that can appear in a relvar definition, as here:

```
VAR S_STATUS_DURING RELATION
   { S# S#, STATUS INTEGER, DURING INTERVAL_DATE }
   PACKED ON DURING                        /* Warning--still */
   KEY { S#, DURING } ;                    /* inadequate!    */
```

PACKED ON DURING here is a constraint—a relvar constraint, in fact, in terms of the classification scheme described in Chapter 1—on relvar S_STATUS_DURING. It is interpreted as follows: Relvar S_STATUS_DURING must at all times be kept packed on DURING;[2] in other words, it must at all times be identical to the result of the expression PACK S_STATUS_DURING ON DURING (implying among other things that this latter expression can always be replaced by the simpler one S_STATUS_DURING, an observation that could be of interest to the optimizer). This special syntax thus suffices to solve the redundancy and circumlocution problems; in other words, it solves the problem exemplified by the constraint we referred to as Constraint XFT1 in Chapter 4 (Section 4.3).

We remark in passing that an argument might be made for providing special syntax for solving just the redundancy problem and not the circumlocution problem (indeed, we will give an example in Section 11.7 of a relvar, TERM, that might be cited in support of such an argument). However, we have yet to see a truly *convincing* argument for such a position; for now, therefore, our preference is to kill two birds with one stone and avoid both problems at once.

---

2. In Chapter 14 we will meet some new operators that allow updates to be performed in such a way as to guarantee that such constraints cannot possibly be violated. See also the final section in this chapter, Section 11.10.

Note finally that (of course) a PACKED ON constraint should be allowed to specify two or more attributes, thus:

```
PACKED ON ( ACL )
```

where *ACL* is a commalist of attribute names. (We enclose that commalist in parentheses rather than braces because the sequence of attribute names is significant, for reasons explained in Chapter 8, Section 8.6. As usual, the parentheses can be omitted if the specified sequence contains just one attribute name.)

11.4 THE CONTRADICTION PROBLEM

We continue to discuss the relvar definition for S_STATUS_DURING specifically. Unfortunately, the PACKED ON and KEY constraints on that definition are still not quite adequate, even when taken together, for they fail to prevent the relvar from containing (for example) both of the following tuples at the same time:

S#	STATUS	DURING
S4	10	[d04:d06]

S#	STATUS	DURING
S4	25	[d05:d07]

Here supplier S4 is shown as having a status of both 10 and 25 on days 5 and 6—clearly an impossible state of affairs. In other words, we have a **contradiction** on our hands; in fact, the relvar is in violation of its own predicate once again, because (as you will recall) each supplier is supposed to have exactly one status on any given day.

NOTE: To say that each supplier is supposed to have exactly one status on any given day is to say, more formally, that if we were to unpack relvar S_STATUS_DURING on DURING, thereby producing a result in which every DURING value consists of a unit interval, the functional dependency {S#,DURING} → {STATUS} would hold in that result. We will have more to say about such matters in Section 11.8.

Fixing the Contradiction Problem

It should be clear that, in order to avoid contradictions like the one just discussed, we need to enforce a constraint—let us call it Constraint B—along the following lines:

- **Constraint B:** If at any given time relvar S_STATUS_DURING contains two tuples that have the same S# value but differ on their STATUS value, then their DURING values *i1* and *i2* must be such that *i1* OVERLAPS *i2* is false.

Note carefully that, as we have already seen, Constraint B is obviously not enforced by the mere fact that the relvar is kept packed on DURING. Even more obviously, it is also not enforced by the mere fact that {S#,DURING} is a candidate key. But suppose the relvar were kept unpacked at all times on attribute DURING (we ignore for the moment the fact that this supposition is an impossibility, given that the relvar is in fact to be kept *packed* on DURING). Then:

- As stated earlier, all DURING values in that unpacked form would be unit intervals and would thus effectively correspond to individual time points.

- The sole candidate key for that unpacked form would thus still be {S#,DURING}, because any given supplier under contract at any given time has just one status at that time. (No two distinct tuples in that unpacked form could possibly have the same S# value and "overlapping" unit intervals, because the only way such overlapping could occur would be if the two unit intervals were one and the same—meaning the two tuples would be duplicates of one another, and hence in fact the same tuple.)

It follows that if we were to enforce the constraint that {S#,DURING} is a candidate key for the unpacked form UNPACK S_STATUS_DURING ON DURING, then we would be enforcing Constraint B *a fortiori*. Let us therefore invent a new WHEN/THEN constraint that can appear in a relvar definition wherever a simple KEY constraint can appear, as here:

```
VAR S_STATUS_DURING RELATION
  { S# S#, STATUS INTEGER, DURING INTERVAL_DATE }
  PACKED ON DURING
  WHEN UNPACKED ON DURING THEN KEY { S#, DURING }
  KEY { S#, DURING } ;
```

WHEN UNPACKED ON DURING THEN KEY {S#,DURING} here is a constraint—a relvar constraint again, like the PACKED ON constraint discussed in the previous section—on relvar S_STATUS_DURING. It is interpreted as follows: Relvar S_STATUS_DURING must at all times be such that no two tuples in the result of the expression UNPACK S_STATUS_DURING have the same value for the attribute combination {S#,DURING} (loosely, "{S#,DURING} is a candidate key for UNPACK S_STATUS_DURING ON DURING"). This special syntax thus suffices to solve the contradiction problem.

It follows from the foregoing discussion that the WHEN/THEN, PACKED ON, and KEY specifications are together sufficient—at last—to fix all of the integrity problems we have been discussing in this chapter so far. However, it cannot be denied that those specifications do seem a little clumsy in combination; it therefore seems worth considering the possibility of simplifying the syntax, and so we will. But there are several other topics we need to get out of the way before we can consider such a possibility in any detail. Those topics are addressed in the next four sections.

One final point to close the present section: Of course, a WHEN/THEN constraint should be allowed to specify unpacking on two or more attributes, thus:

```
WHEN UNPACKED ON ( ACL ) THEN KEY { BCL }
```

(where *ACL* and *BCL* are both commalists of attribute names). NOTE: We enclose the commalist *ACL* in parentheses rather than braces, even though the sequence of attribute names is insignificant, for reasons explained in Chapter 8 (Section 8.6). As usual, the parentheses can be omitted if the specified sequence contains just one attribute name. Note that within any given WHEN/THEN constraint, every attribute mentioned in *ACL* must also be mentioned in *BCL* (i.e., *ACL* must be a subset of *BCL*). Note further that a WHEN/THEN constraint of the form WHEN ... THEN KEY {K+} effectively implies a conventional KEY specification of the form KEY {K}, where K is some subset of K+ (in other words, K+ is certainly a *superkey* for the relvar in question). We will revisit this point in Section 11.7.

11.5 COMBINING SPECIFICATIONS

We have now met three kinds of constraints that can appear in a relvar definition: KEY, PACKED ON, and WHEN/THEN constraints. At first sight, therefore, there are eight possible combinations of constraints that might make sense for any given relvar. But which ones actually do?

Well, we can simplify our investigation by first stipulating that (until further notice, at any rate) at least one explicit KEY constraint is *always* required. This stipulation immediately reduces the eight possibilities to four.

Now let *R* be a relvar with an interval attribute. Then we certainly know from the previous two sections that *R* might need both a PACKED ON constraint and a WHEN/THEN constraint. So the possibilities we still need to examine are:

- *R* has a PACKED ON constraint but no WHEN/THEN constraint;
- *R* has a WHEN/THEN constraint but no PACKED ON constraint;
- *R* has neither a PACKED ON constraint nor a WHEN/THEN constraint.

These three possibilities are the subject of the next three sections.

11.6 PACKED ON WITHOUT WHEN/THEN

Consider the historical relvar S_DURING, with attributes S# and DURING. It should be readily apparent without the need for detailed analysis that S_DURING is susceptible to problems of redundancy and circumlocution analogous to those discussed for relvar S_STATUS_DURING in Sections 11.2 and 11.3, respectively. However, it is *not* susceptible to the contradiction problem discussed in Section 11.4. (QUESTION: Why not? ANSWER: Because it is "all key"—its sole candidate key is the attribute combination {S#,DURING}—and so it cannot possibly contain two tuples that contradict each other.) Thus, the constraint PACKED ON DURING applies, but the constraint WHEN

UNPACKED ON DURING THEN KEY {S#,DURING} is unnecessary. The following thus serves as an adequate definition for this relvar:

```
VAR S_DURING RELATION
  { S# S#, DURING INTERVAL_DATE }
  PACKED ON DURING
  KEY { S#, DURING } ;
```

To repeat, a WHEN/THEN constraint is unnecessary for this relvar. However, it would not be logically wrong to specify one, as here:

```
VAR S_DURING RELATION
  { S# S#, DURING INTERVAL_DATE }
  PACKED ON DURING
  WHEN UNPACKED ON DURING THEN KEY { S#, DURING }
  KEY { S#, DURING } ;
```

Again, the WHEN/THEN constraint here is not incorrect, but it might lead to some inefficiency in implementation if the system blindly tried to enforce it. We will return to this point in the next section.

Remarks analogous to the foregoing apply to relvar SP_DURING as well and effectively dispose of that case also. Thus, the following is a possible definition for that relvar:

```
VAR SP_DURING RELATION
  { S# S#, P# P#, DURING INTERVAL_DATE }
  PACKED ON DURING
  KEY { S#, P#, DURING } ;
```

From these examples, we see that if the relvar is "all key," then no WHEN/THEN constraint is needed. But it does not follow that if no WHEN/THEN constraint is needed, then the relvar is all key! A counterexample is given in Section 11.8.

11.7 WHEN/THEN without PACKED ON

Suppose we are given a relvar TERM that represents U.S. presidential terms, with attributes DURING and PRESIDENT and sole candidate key {DURING}. A sample value is shown in Figure 11.4.

Before going any further, we remark that this example raises a number of interesting points, the following among them:

- First of all, presidential terms are usually stated in the form of *overlapping* intervals (e.g., "Ford, 1974–1977," "Carter, 1977–1981," etc.) instead of the way we have shown them in the figure. The truth is, however, that the *granularity* of those intervals as usually stated is wrong; presidential terms really stretch from

FIGURE 11.4
Relvar TERM—
sample value.

TERM	DURING	PRESIDENT
	[1974:1976]	Ford
	[1977:1980]	Carter
	[1981:1984]	Reagan
	[1985:1988]	Reagan
	[1993:1996]	Clinton
	[1997:2000]	Clinton

one Inauguration Day (a day in January) to the next, and so, for example, Ford was president for the first part of 1977 and Carter was president for the rest of that year.

- Second, last names of presidents are not necessarily unique—think of Roosevelt, for example, or Johnson—but we choose to overlook this fact for the purposes of this chapter.

- Third, over and above the key and "keylike" constraints that are the primary focus of this chapter, there are quite a few additional integrity constraints that apply to—and need to be stated and enforced for—relvar TERM. Here are some of them:

  a. There is exactly one president at any given time (this is an example of what in Chapter 12 we will call a *denseness* constraint).

  b. Nobody is allowed to serve as president for more than two terms (at least since 1951, when the 22nd Amendment to the U.S. Constitution was ratified).

  c. No term is allowed to exceed four years.

We leave it as an exercise for the reader to ponder the implications of such considerations.

Back to the main thread of our discussion. It should be clear that the constraint PACKED ON DURING must *not* be specified for relvar TERM, because (with reference to the sample value shown in Figure 11.4) such a constraint would cause the two Reagan tuples to be "packed" into one and the two Clinton tuples likewise. At the same time, it should be clear that a WHEN/THEN constraint *is* needed in order to avoid the possibility that (for example) the relvar might contain both of the following tuples at the same time:

DURING	PRESIDENT
[1985:1994]	Reagan

DURING	PRESIDENT
[1993:1996]	Clinton

Without such a constraint, relvar TERM would clearly be susceptible to the contradiction problem. Thus, the following might be an appropriate definition for this relvar:[3]

```
VAR TERM RELATION
  { DURING INTERVAL_... , PRESIDENT NAME }
  WHEN UNPACKED ON DURING THEN KEY { DURING }
  KEY { DURING } ;
```

There are further points to be made in connection with this example, however. First, note that we do want to avoid the possibility that the relvar might contain (for example) both of the following tuples at the same time:

DURING	PRESIDENT
[1993:1995]	Clinton

DURING	PRESIDENT
[1994:1996]	Clinton

(an example of the redundancy problem). However, we definitely do *not* want to avoid the possibility that the relvar might contain (for example) both of the following tuples at the same time:

DURING	PRESIDENT
[1993:1996]	Clinton

DURING	PRESIDENT
[1997:2000]	Clinton

On the face of it, therefore, it looks as if relvar TERM might be an example of a relvar for which we want to avoid the redundancy problem but not the circumlocution problem.

That said, however, we have to say that in our opinion the example intuitively fails. The point is, of course, that there actually is no circumlocution involved in the two tuples just shown; in fact, information would be lost if those tuples were to be replaced by a single packed tuple—namely, the information that one of the DURING intervals corresponds to Clinton's first term and the other to his second. The real problem is that "term number" has not been represented as an explicit attribute in the relvar (thus, if the relvar does not actually violate *The Information Principle*—see Chapter 1, Section 1.8—it certainly comes close to doing so). If we add such an attribute as indicated in Figure 11.5, the "circumlocution problem" goes away. (Well, not exactly; the relvar might still include a pair of tuples that would better be replaced by a single tuple. For example, it might include two tuples for Carter, one with a DURING value of [1977:1978] and the other with a DURING value of [1979:1980]. This state of affairs

---

3. Here and elsewhere in this chapter we use the syntax "INTERVAL_..." to denote an interval type that we do not want to get sidetracked into discussing in detail at this juncture.

FIGURE 11.5

FIGURE 11.5

Relvar TERM
with a TERM#
attribute—
sample value.

TERM

DURING	PRESIDENT	TERM#
[1974:1976]	Ford	1
[1977:1980]	Carter	1
[1981:1984]	Reagan	1
[1985:1988]	Reagan	2
[1993:1996]	Clinton	1
[1997:2000]	Clinton	2

really *is* an example of the circumlocution problem. But exactly the same situation could occur before we added the TERM# attribute! The trouble is, before we added that attribute, the system could not tell the difference between this genuine example of circumlocution and the previous example of what might be called "false circumlocution.")

Of course, this revised version of the TERM relvar still satisfies the candidate key constraint KEY {DURING} (as the double underlining in Figure 11.5 indicates, in fact). As you can probably see, however, the relvar is now susceptible to all three of our usual problems (redundancy, circumlocution, and contradiction). *Redundancy* will occur if the relvar contains, for example, both of the following tuples at the same time:

DURING	PRESIDENT	TERM#
[1977:1979]	Carter	1

DURING	PRESIDENT	TERM#
[1978:1980]	Carter	1

As already noted, *circumlocution* will occur if the relvar contains, for example, both of the following tuples at the same time:

DURING	PRESIDENT	TERM#
[1977:1978]	Carter	1

DURING	PRESIDENT	TERM#
[1979:1980]	Carter	1

And *contradiction* will occur if the relvar contains, for example, both of the following tuples at the same time:

DURING	PRESIDENT	TERM#
[1977:1980]	Carter	1

DURING	PRESIDENT	TERM#
[1974:1977]	Ford	1

Now, we can avoid the redundancy and circumlocution problems by specifying the constraint

```
PACKED ON DURING
```

Likewise, we can avoid the contradiction problem by specifying the constraint

```
WHEN UNPACKED ON DURING THEN KEY { DURING }
```

So a possible relvar definition to avoid all three problems is as follows:

```
VAR TERM RELATION
   { DURING INTERVAL_... , PRESIDENT NAME, TERM# INTEGER }
   PACKED ON DURING
   WHEN UNPACKED ON DURING THEN KEY { DURING }
   KEY { DURING } ;
```

However, this is not the end of the story. In fact, as you might have already realized, this relvar additionally satisfies the constraint

```
KEY { PRESIDENT, TERM# }
```

(i.e., the combination {PRESIDENT,TERM#} is a candidate key—no two distinct tuples ever have the same PRESIDENT and TERM# values). And this additional KEY constraint makes the PACKED ON constraint superfluous!—not actually incorrect, as it was with the original version of the relvar, but certainly unnecessary. The reason is that, since {PRESIDENT,TERM#} is a candidate key, packing the relvar on DURING cannot possibly have any effect. (More generally, in fact, the operation PACK *R* ON (*ACL*) cannot possibly have any effect if relvar *R* has a candidate key that does not include *ACL*. Thus, there is no point in specifying the constraint PACKED ON (*ACL*) for such a relvar.)

Here then is our final definition for relvar TERM (revised version):

```
VAR TERM RELATION
   { DURING INTERVAL_... , PRESIDENT NAME, TERM# INTEGER }
   WHEN UNPACKED ON DURING THEN KEY { DURING }
   KEY { DURING }
   KEY { PRESIDENT, TERM# } ;
```

In other words, relvar TERM, even with the addition of attribute TERM#, still serves as an example of a relvar for which we would probably want to specify WHEN/THEN and not PACKED ON.

By the way, it is worth pointing out that the introduction of attribute TERM#, while it does solve some problems, also introduces others: in particular, the problem of guaranteeing the uniqueness of a second candidate key.[4] For this reason, it might be argued that the original design (without TERM#) is preferable. However, we will stay with the revised design from this point forward, barring explicit statements to the contrary.

We now move on to examine another issue arising from the same example. In the TERM definition shown above (either version, in fact, but we assume the version with an explicit TERM# attribute for definiteness), the combination of constraints

```
WHEN UNPACKED ON DURING THEN KEY { DURING }
```

and

```
KEY { DURING }
```

certainly looks as if it might involve some redundant specification; that is, it looks as if it might somehow be saying the same thing twice. What of this possibility?

Well, the WHEN/THEN specification means that if relvar TERM were kept unpacked on DURING, then {DURING} would still be a candidate key. But if relvar TERM were kept unpacked on DURING, then each DURING value would be a unit interval; hence, each such interval would appear in that unpacked form in exactly one tuple, associated with exactly one combination of PRESIDENT and TERM# values. It follows that if we were now to pack that relvar on DURING, any given DURING value in the result, regardless of whether it is a unit interval or not, would also appear in exactly one tuple and be associated with exactly one combination of PRESIDENT and TERM# values. Clearly, then, the WHEN/THEN specification implies that {DURING} is a candidate key for TERM. NOTE: We are making a tacit but reasonable assumption here that relvar TERM is not constrained to contain at most one tuple (!), for otherwise the only candidate key would be the empty set [25].

---

4. Not to mention the problem of ensuring that, for a given president, a tuple with TERM# = 2 exists only if a tuple also exists with TERM# = 1, and ensuring moreover that BEGIN(DURING) in the tuple with TERM# = 2, if it exists, must be greater than END(DURING) in the tuple with TERM# = 1.

Before trying to draw any conclusions from this discussion, let us take a look at relvar S_STATUS_DURING once again, with definition as follows:

```
VAR S_STATUS_DURING RELATION
  { S# S#, STATUS INTEGER, DURING INTERVAL_DATE }
  PACKED ON DURING
  WHEN UNPACKED ON DURING THEN KEY { S#, DURING }
  KEY { S#, DURING } ;
```

This example is a little more general than the TERM example in that, in the WHEN/THEN specification, the "UNPACKED ON" attributes are not just a subset but a *proper* subset of the "KEY" attributes. If we perform the same kind of analysis as we did a few moments ago for the TERM example, we will see that the WHEN/THEN specification certainly implies that any given {S#,DURING} value appearing in relvar S_STATUS_DURING appears in exactly one tuple and is associated with exactly one STATUS value. However, we cannot conclude from this fact that {S#,DURING} is a candidate key for S_STATUS_DURING—we can conclude only that it is a *superkey* for that relvar (recall from Chapter 1 that a superkey is a superset of a candidate key).

In order to illustrate the foregoing point, suppose suppliers are subject to the— unlikely, but possible—additional constraints that (1) the status of a given supplier never changes and (2) no supplier is ever allowed to be under contract during two separate intervals (i.e., once a supplier's contract terminates, that supplier is never placed under contract again).[5] Then the relvar definition can be simplified to just:

```
VAR S_STATUS_DURING RELATION
  { S# S#, STATUS INTEGER, DURING INTERVAL_DATE }
  KEY { S# } ;
```

In other words, the sole candidate key for S_STATUS_DURING is now just {S#}, because for each supplier represented in that relvar there is just one corresponding status and one corresponding interval during which that supplier was under contract. At the same time, the sole candidate key for the unpacked form is the combination {S#,DURING}, because many suppliers can be under contract at the same time. (Indeed, the fact that S# values are unique in relvar S_STATUS_DURING clearly implies that {S#,DURING} values are unique in the unpacked form of that relvar on DURING; in other words, the constraint KEY {S#} clearly implies the constraint WHEN UNPACKED ON DURING THEN KEY {S#,DURING}.)

---

5. We note in passing that under these assumptions, (1) relvar S_DURING is unnecessary; (2) attributes S#_SINCE and STATUS_SINCE in relvar S_SINCE can be collapsed into a single SINCE attribute; and (3) relvar S_STATUS_DURING is no longer in 6NF, because it can be nonloss-decomposed into its projections on {S#,STATUS} and {S#,DURING} (where the projections in question are regular projections, not the generalized versions discussed in Chapter 9). We note too that if relvar S_STATUS_DURING *were* to be replaced by these two projections, then the one involving S# and STATUS could additionally be used to show the status for "potential" suppliers (that is, suppliers who have never as yet been under contract).

There seem to be two main conclusions we can draw from the foregoing examples and discussion:

- First, it seems unlikely in practice that a relvar would ever be subject to a constraint of the form WHEN ... THEN KEY {K} and not also subject to a constraint of the form KEY {K}.

- Second, if a relvar definition does include both a WHEN/THEN constraint of the form WHEN ... THEN KEY {K} and a KEY constraint of the form KEY {K}, then enforcing the first of these constraints will enforce the second automatically. Thus we might reasonably have a syntax rule to say that the KEY constraint can be omitted in such a situation. We choose not to adopt such a rule, however, for reasons that will become clear in Section 11.9.

  On the other hand, if a relvar definition includes a KEY constraint of the form KEY {K} and does *not* include a WHEN/THEN constraint of the form WHEN ... THEN KEY {K}, then that KEY constraint will definitely have to be enforced in its own right.

One final point to close this section: Just as a "regular" relvar—one without interval attributes—can be subject to two or more KEY constraints, so a relvar *with* interval attributes can be subject to two or more WHEN/THEN constraints. By way of an example, consider the following relvar (the semantics are meant to be obvious):

```
VAR MARRIAGE RELATION
  { HUSBAND NAME, WIFE NAME, DURING INTERVAL_... }
  PACKED ON DURING
  WHEN UNPACKED ON DURING THEN KEY { HUSBAND, DURING }
  WHEN UNPACKED ON DURING THEN KEY { WIFE, DURING }
  KEY { HUSBAND, DURING }
  KEY { WIFE, DURING } ;
```

11.8 NEITHER PACKED ON NOR WHEN/THEN

Suppose we are given a relvar INFLATION representing the inflation rate for a certain country during certain specified time intervals. The attributes are DURING and PERCENTAGE, and the sole candidate key is {DURING}. A sample value is given in Figure 11.6, showing that the inflation rate was 18 percent for the first three months of the year, went up to 20 percent for the next three months, stayed at 20 again for the *next* three months (but went up to 25 percent in month 7), ..., and averaged out at 20 percent for the year as a whole.

FIGURE 11.6

Relvar
INFLATION—
sample value.

INFLATION

DURING	PERCENTAGE
[m01:m03]	18
[m04:m06]	20
[m07:m09]	20
[m07:m07]	25
. . . . .	. .
[m01:m12]	20

It should be clear that the constraint PACKED ON DURING must *not* be specified for relvar INFLATION, because (in terms of the sample value shown in the figure) such a constraint would cause the three tuples with PERCENTAGE = 20 to be packed into one, and we would lose the information that the inflation rate for months 4 through 6 and months 7 through 9 (as well as for the year overall) was 20 percent.

At the same time, it should be clear that the only possible WHEN/THEN constraint that could sensibly be specified for this relvar is

```
WHEN UNPACKED ON DURING THEN KEY { DURING, PERCENTAGE }
```

And this specification tells us no more than that tuples are unique in the result of UNPACK INFLATION ON DURING (but of course a "constraint" analogous to this one applies to *every* relation).[6] So we can say that relvar INFLATION does not seem to be subject to any WHEN/THEN constraint, either—at least, not to any nontrivial one. Thus, a **Tutorial D** definition for this relvar might be simply:

```
VAR INFLATION RELATION
  { DURING INTERVAL_... , PERCENTAGE INTEGER }
  KEY { DURING } ;
```

In fact, this relvar is subject to none of our usual redundancy, circumlocution, and contradiction problems.

Now, a good question to ask is: Both relvar INFLATION and relvar TERM (either version) from the previous section seem not to need a PACKED ON constraint; so in what significant way do the two relvars differ from each other? *Do they differ significantly?*

Well, the two relvars do in fact resemble each other inasmuch as the functional dependency {DURING} → {PRESIDENT,TERM#} holds in relvar TERM—for definiteness, we assume the version of the relvar that includes an explicit TERM# attribute—and the functional dependency {DURING} → {PERCENTAGE} holds in relvar

---

6. In other words, this constraint is rather like a KEY constraint on a relvar for which every attribute participates in the key in question. Note that INFLATION is thus another example of a relvar for which a proper subset of the attributes that might be specified in the KEY portion of a WHEN/THEN constraint constitutes a true candidate key.

INFLATION. However, they also differ in an important respect, namely as follows. If we were to unpack each relvar on DURING, then:

- The functional dependency {DURING} → {PRESIDENT,TERM#} would still hold in the unpacked form of TERM.

- By contrast, the functional dependency {DURING} → {PERCENTAGE} would *not* still hold in the unpacked form of INFLATION.

Intuitively speaking, in other words, a given PERCENTAGE value in relvar INFLATION is a property of the corresponding DURING interval *taken as a whole*—it is not a property of the individual time points that make up that interval. To put it another way, just because the inflation rate for, say, the interval [*m07:m09*] was 20 percent, we cannot infer that the inflation rate for, say, the interval [*m07:m07*] was also 20 percent—and indeed it was not, as Figure 11.6 indicates.

That said, however, we feel bound to add that (like the first version of the TERM example in the previous section) the example intuitively fails, in our opinion. To be more specific, the fact that a PACKED ON constraint would be incorrect for relvar INFLATION is, obviously enough, a consequence of the way the relvar is designed. An alternative and arguably preferable design would recognize that if we want to represent certain "properties"—namely, percentages—for certain "entities"—namely, time intervals—then those time intervals are indeed distinct entities and should be given distinct IDs that can be used elsewhere in the database as references to the entities in question. Figure 11.7 is a revised version of Figure 11.6, showing what happens to relvar INFLATION if this approach is adopted. As you can see from that figure, {DURING}, though of course it is still a candidate key, is no longer the only one, and the idea of specifying the constraint PACKED ON DURING now *clearly* makes no sense. (It made no sense before, either, but for a different and less obvious reason.)

N O T E : It is true that the projection of (the current value of) relvar INFLATION over DURING and PERCENTAGE—

```
INFLATION { DURING, PERCENTAGE }
```

—yields a relation that we would not want to pack (and of course it *would* not be packed, given the semantics of the projection operation). The fact remains, however,

		ID	DURING	PERCENTAGE
FIGURE 11.7	INFLATION			
Relvar INFLATION				
with an ID attrib-		*h3*	[*m01:m03*]	18
ute—sample value.		*f7*	[*m04:m06*]	20
		x4	[*m07:m09*]	20
		z0	[*m07:m07*]	25
		..	.....	..
		q8	[*m01:m12*]	20

that we have yet to see a really convincing example of a *relvar*—as opposed to a relation value—for which PACKED ON might seem to apply but in fact does not. In other words, if a PACKED ON constraint seems to be necessary, then it probably is.

11.9 CANDIDATE KEYS REVISITED

Despite (or perhaps because of!) the discussions of the last three sections, it does seem likely in practice that relvars with interval attributes will often be subject to both a PACKED ON constraint and a WHEN/THEN constraint—not to mention the required KEY constraint. For that reason, it seems desirable to come up with some syntax that includes the functionality of all three. We therefore propose a shorthand; to be specific, we propose that the definition of any given relvar *R* should be allowed to include a specification of the form

```
USING ( ACL ) KEY { K }
```

Here:

- *ACL* and *K* are both commalists of attribute names, and every attribute mentioned in *ACL* must also be mentioned in *K*.

- As usual, the parentheses can be omitted if *ACL* contains just one attribute name.

- The specification is defined to be shorthand for the combination of the following three constraints:

```
PACKED ON ( ACL )

WHEN UNPACKED ON ( ACL ) THEN KEY { K }

KEY { K }
```

We refer to {*K*} as a "U_key" for short (but see below).[7] Using this shorthand, the definition of relvar S_STATUS_DURING, for example, might be simplified to just

```
VAR S_STATUS_DURING RELATION
  { S# S#, STATUS INTEGER, DURING INTERVAL_DATE }
  USING DURING KEY { S#, DURING } ;
```

Likewise, the definition of relvar MARRIAGE from Section 11.7 can be simplified to just

---

7. In Chapter 12 we will meet *foreign* "U_keys" as well.

```
VAR MARRIAGE RELATION
  { HUSBAND NAME, WIFE NAME, DURING INTERVAL_... }
  USING DURING KEY { HUSBAND, DURING }
  USING DURING KEY { WIFE, DURING } ;
```

Note that the two U_key specifications in this example have the same USING specification. We leave it as an exercise to consider what it would mean (if anything) for a relvar to have two or more U_keys with different USING specifications.

Suppose now that within a U_key specification the commalist of attribute names *ACL* is empty (i.e., contains no attribute names at all), thus:

```
USING ( ) KEY { K }
```

By definition, this specification is shorthand for the combination of constraints

```
PACKED ON ( )

WHEN UNPACKED ON ( ) THEN KEY { K }

KEY { K }
```

So:

- First, the pertinent relvar must be kept packed on no attributes. But packing a relation *r* on no attributes simply returns *r*, so the implied PACKED ON specification has no effect.

- Second, the pertinent relvar must be such that if it is unpacked on no attributes, then {*K*} is a candidate key for the result. But unpacking a relation *r* on no attributes simply returns *r*, so the implied WHEN/THEN specification simply means that {*K*} is a candidate key for the pertinent relvar, and the implied regular KEY constraint is thus redundant.

It follows that we can take a regular KEY constraint of the form KEY {*K*} to be shorthand for a certain U_key specification—namely, one of the form USING () KEY {*K*}. In other words, regular KEY constraints are essentially just a special case of our proposed new syntax! So, if we redefine the syntax of a regular KEY constraint (a *<candidate key def>*, in **Tutorial D** terms) thus—

```
<candidate key def>
    ::=   [ USING ( ACL ) ] KEY { K }
```

—and allow the USING specification to be omitted if and only if *ACL* is empty, then we have no need to talk about U_keys at all; all candidate keys effectively become U_keys, and we can generalize the meaning of "candidate key" (or just "key") accordingly. And so we will.

NOTE: It is occasionally useful to refer to PACKED ON and WHEN/THEN constraints that have (and can have) no logical effect as *trivial* constraints. In particular, the constraints PACKED ON () and WHEN UNPACKED ON () THEN ... are both trivial in this sense. So too are

- the constraint PACKED ON (*ACL*), if the set of attributes *not* included in *ACL* is a superkey for the relvar in question, and

- the constraint WHEN ... THEN KEY {*K*}, if *K* is the set of all attributes of the relvar in question.

Also, of course, a PACKED ON or WHEN/THEN constraint is *nontrivial* if and only if it is not trivial.

We close this chapter by showing the overall effect of the foregoing syntactic simplifications on our running example (see Figure 11.8). Note in particular that we have implicitly (but, we hope, harmlessly) specified a WHEN/THEN constraint for relvars S_DURING and SP_DURING, relvars that we claimed in Section 11.6 did not need such a constraint. By the same token, we could have expanded the KEY constraints for relvars S_SINCE and SP_SINCE, if we had wanted to, to include the specification USING ().

FIGURE 11.8

Revised and completed version of Figure 11.1.

```
S_SINCE { S#, S#_SINCE, STATUS, STATUS_SINCE }
        KEY { S# }

SP_SINCE { S#, P#, SINCE }
         KEY { S#, P# }
         FOREIGN KEY { S# } REFERENCES S_SINCE

S_DURING { S#, DURING }
         USING DURING KEY { S#, DURING }

S_STATUS_DURING { S#, STATUS, DURING }
              USING DURING KEY { S#, DURING }

SP_DURING { S#, P#, DURING }
          USING DURING KEY { S#, P#, DURING }
```

11.10 PACKED ON REVISITED

There is a little more to be said about the PACKED ON constraint. In Section 11.3, we described PACKED ON as just that, a constraint; if relvar *R* is subject to the constraint PACKED ON (*ACL*), then at all times relvar *R* must be kept packed on the attributes named in *ACL*, in the order in which they are named. And we also mentioned in that same section (in a footnote) that in Chapter 14 we would be describing some operators that allow updates to be performed in such a way as to guarantee that PACKED ON constraints cannot possibly be violated. However, there is another way to achieve the same effect—one that might be preferable in a real implementation, in that it might lay less direct responsibility on the user—which we now briefly explain.

In Chapter 1 we said that any update that, if performed, would cause some constraint to be violated will effectively be rejected. In the case of PACKED ON, however, it might be undesirable for updates to be rejected just because they happen to leave the target relvar in a state that is *not* packed on all of the pertinent attributes. Rather, it might be better to extend the semantics of PACKED ON in such a way as to cause an appropriate *compensating action*—in other words, any necessary (re)packing—to be performed by the system, automatically, after such an update. Keeping the relvar in the desired packed state would then be the responsibility of the system, not the user.

As an aside, we note that an analogy can be drawn here with "referential actions" such as *cascade delete*. Cascade delete is a compensating action that is performed automatically by the system whenever a certain referential constraint would otherwise be violated; its purpose is, in part, to make life easier for the user, inasmuch as it implies that less of the work needed to maintain the integrity of the database has to be done by the user. The parallels with the foregoing ideas should be obvious.

Since the primary focus of this book is on foundations, rather than on what might be regarded (comparatively speaking) as issues of pragma or syntax, we prefer not to get into detail here on the possibility of compensating actions. In the chapters to follow, therefore, we will continue to regard PACKED ON just as a constraint and nothing more (except for a few brief remarks in Chapter 14, Section 14.3).

EXERCISES

1. (This exercise expands on Exercise 2 in Chapter 4.) Explain the redundancy, circumlocution, and contradiction problems in your own words.

2. Explain in your own words:

   a. KEY constraints

   b. PACKED ON constraints

   c. WHEN/THEN constraints

   d. U_key constraints

3. Give examples of relvars that involve at least one interval attribute and require

   a. both a PACKED ON and a WHEN/THEN constraint

   b. a PACKED ON but no WHEN/THEN constraint

   c. a WHEN/THEN but no PACKED ON constraint

   d. neither a PACKED ON nor a WHEN/THEN constraint

   (where by "constraint" we mean a nontrivial one throughout).

4. Explain how classical keys can be regarded as a special case of U_keys.

5. Use **Tutorial D** to formulate as many (sensible!) constraints as you can think of for the second version of relvar TERM (i.e., the one with an explicit TERM# attribute).

6. Consider the revised version of courses-and-students from Exercise 6 in Chapter 10, with the following as an appropriate definition for relvar COURSE_OFFERING:

```
VAR COURSE_OFFERING RELATION
    { COURSE#          COURSE#,
      OFFERING#        POSINT,
      QUOTA            POSINT,
      OFFERED_DURING INTERVAL_DATE }
    KEY { COURSE#, OFFERING# } ;
```

(where POSINT is a type whose values are the integers greater than zero). The predicate is: *Offering OFFERING# of course COURSE# took place or is scheduled to take place during interval OFFERED_DURING.* Revise the database definition again to include all such PACKED ON, WHEN/THEN, and/or U_key constraints as you think necessary.

Chapter

12

INTEGRITY CONSTRAINTS II: GENERAL CONSTRAINTS

12.1 INTRODUCTION

In the previous chapter, we used the historical relvars from our "preferred design" of Figure 11.1—relvar S_STATUS_DURING in particular—to illustrate the need for and functionality of the PACKED ON and WHEN/THEN constraints, building up to the U_key shorthand and the fact that our regular KEY constraints can be regarded as a special case of that shorthand. In this chapter, we adopt a rather different strategy. To be specific, we stand back for a while from the specific design of Figure 11.1 and consider instead, in very general terms, *all* of the constraints that we might want a typical temporal database, like our running example involving suppliers and shipments, to satisfy. That discussion appears in Section 12.2. Then we consider, in Sections 12.3, 12.4, and 12.5, respectively, what happens to those constraints if the database contains (1) current ("since") relvars only, (2) historical ("during") relvars only, or (3) a mixture of both.

NOTE: We should say that, like Chapter 10 (but not Chapter 11), this chapter is concerned rather more than most of its predecessors with temporal data specifically. The principal reason is that temporal data, by its very nature, often has to satisfy certain "denseness" constraints—meaning, loosely, that certain conditions have to be satisfied *at every point* within certain intervals. For example, if the database shows supplier S1 as having been under contract ever since day 4, then it must also show supplier S1 as having had some status ever since day 4, and vice versa.[1] Such "denseness" constraints do not necessarily apply to other kinds of data for which the concepts of previous chapters, such as the interval concept, do apply.

We should also warn you that certain portions of this chapter—Section 12.5 in particular—might seem a little difficult, especially on a first reading. Unfortunately, the difficulties in question seem to be intrinsic; however, we do offer, in Section 12.6, some suggestions as to how it might be possible to conceal some of those difficulties from the user. Finally, in Section 12.7, we briefly discuss a few miscellaneous issues.

A NOTE ON TERMINOLOGY: In order to avoid confusion, from this point forward we will refer to the natural language versions of the constraints we need to discuss as *requirements,* and reserve the term *constraint* to mean, specifically, a formal statement of such a requirement in a relational language like **Tutorial D**. (We note in passing that some, though not all, of the requirements we will be discussing are in fact implied by the predicate(s) for the pertinent relvar(s). In fact, those requirements can be regarded as *design* requirements specifically; they can therefore be used to drive the database design process—database design in general being, in large part, precisely a process of pinning down the applicable predicates and constraints [41].)

12.2 THE NINE REQUIREMENTS

There are nine general requirements we want to consider. They fall nicely into three groups of three. The first three are all of the form "If the database shows a given supplier as being under contract on a given day or pair of consecutive days, then some other condition must also be satisfied":

- *Requirement R1:* If the database shows supplier Sx as being under contract on day *d,* then it must contain exactly one tuple that shows that fact.

- *Requirement R2:* If the database shows supplier Sx as being under contract on days *d* and *d*+1, then it must contain exactly one tuple that shows that fact.

- *Requirement R3:* If the database shows supplier Sx as being under contract on day *d,* then it must also show supplier Sx as having some status on day *d.*

Observe that Requirement R1 has to do with avoiding redundancy and Requirement R2 with avoiding circumlocution. Requirement R3 has to do with what we referred to in Section 12.1 as denseness.

---

1. By "some status" here, we do not mean some *fixed* status, of course—for example, supplier S1 might have had status 10 on days 4 and 5 and status 20 from day 6 onward. Analogous remarks apply to our use of phrases like "some status" throughout the chapter, barring explicit statements to the contrary.

The next three requirements are all of the form "If the database shows a given supplier as having a given status on some given day or pair of consecutive days, then some other condition must also be satisfied." They bear a strong family resemblance to Requirements R1 through R3, as you will immediately see:

- *Requirement R4:* If the database shows supplier Sx as having some status on day *d,* then it must contain exactly one tuple that shows that fact.

- *Requirement R5:* If the database shows supplier Sx as having the same status on days *d* and *d*+1, then it must contain exactly one tuple that shows that fact.

- *Requirement R6:* If the database shows supplier Sx as having some status on day *d,* then it must also show supplier Sx as being under contract on day *d.*

Requirement R4 has to do with avoiding redundancy and also with avoiding contradiction. Requirement R5 has to do with avoiding circumlocution, and Requirement R6 has to do with denseness.

The final three requirements are all of the form "If the database shows a given supplier as able to supply a given part on some given day or pair of consecutive days, then some other condition must also be satisfied":

- *Requirement R7:* If the database shows supplier Sx as able to supply some specific part Py on day *d,* then it must contain exactly one tuple that shows that fact.

- *Requirement R8:* If the database shows supplier Sx as able to supply the same part Py on days *d* and *d*+1, then it must contain exactly one tuple that shows that fact.

- *Requirement R9:* If the database shows supplier Sx as able to supply some part Py on day *d,* then it must also show supplier Sx as being under contract on day *d.*

Requirement R7 has to do with avoiding redundancy, Requirement R8 has to do with avoiding circumlocution, and Requirement R9 has to do with denseness. NOTE: In case you were wondering, we could simplify the phrase "some part Py" in Requirement R9 to just "some part" without changing the overall meaning. The explicit reference to Py is there purely to highlight the parallels between Requirement R9 and Requirements R7 and R8.

For ease of reference, the nine requirements are repeated in Endpaper Panel 5 at the back of the book. Note that:

1. Requirement R1 implies that no supplier can be under two distinct contracts at the same time.

2. Requirement R4 implies that no supplier can have two distinct status values at the same time.

3. Requirement R7 implies that no supplier can have two distinct "abilities to supply some specific part" at the same time.

Note too that Requirements R2, R5, and R8—or, rather, whatever analogs of those requirements apply to whatever temporal database we happen to be dealing with—cannot possibly be satisfied, in general, if full vertical decomposition into 6NF has not been performed (why not, exactly?).

12.3 CURRENT RELVARS ONLY

We now consider a temporal database that contains current relvars only. The database in question—see Figure 12.1—consists essentially of the two "since" relvars from Figure 11.1 (or, equivalently, Figure 11.8). Note in particular that those relvars, since they involve no interval attributes, do not involve any PACKED ON or WHEN/THEN constraints either (except for trivial ones, not shown). Some sample values are shown in Figure 12.2, a slightly modified version of Figure 11.2. (Figure 12.2 is repeated in Endpaper Panel 6 at the back of the book.)

Of course, this database is merely *semi*temporal: It cannot represent historical information at all (apart from what can be inferred from "since" values). By contrast, however, it certainly can represent future information. To be specific:

- Relvars S_SINCE and SP_SINCE both contain *implicit* information regarding the future—recall the discussion at the very end of Section 10.2 in Chapter 10, which said that if, for example, some S_SINCE tuple shows supplier S*x* as being under

FIGURE 12.1
Current relvars only.

```
S_SINCE  { S#, S#_SINCE, STATUS, STATUS_SINCE }
         KEY { S# }

SP_SINCE { S#, P#, SINCE }
         KEY { S#, P# }
         FOREIGN KEY { S# } REFERENCES S_SINCE
```

FIGURE 12.2
Current relvars only—sample values.

S_SINCE

S#	S#_SINCE	STATUS	STATUS_SINCE
S1	d04	20	d06
S2	d07	10	d07
S3	d03	30	d03
S4	d14	20	d14
S5	d02	30	d02

SP_SINCE

S#	P#	SINCE
S1	P1	d04
S1	P2	d05
S1	P3	d09
S1	P4	d05
S1	P5	d04
S1	P6	d06
S2	P1	d08
S2	P2	d09
S3	P2	d08
S4	P5	d14

contract since day *d*, then it means that supplier S*x* was, is, or will be under contract on every day from day *d* until "the last day" (pending future updates).

■ What is more, those relvars might contain *explicit* information regarding the future as well—again, recall the discussion near the end of Section 10.2, which said that, for example, the S#_SINCE value for some supplier S*x* might be some future date *d*, meaning that the indicated supplier will be placed under contract at that future date. Supplier S4 is a case in point in Figure 12.2 (once again we are assuming that today is day 10).

We now proceed to consider what formal versions of Requirements R1 through R9 might look like for this database.

Requirement R1: If the database shows supplier S*x* as being under contract on day *d*, then it must contain exactly one tuple that shows that fact.

The KEY constraint on relvar S_SINCE takes care of this requirement. Without it, the relvar might contain, for example, both of the following tuples at the same time:

S#	S#_SINCE	...
S1	d04	...

S#	S#_SINCE	...
S1	d06	...

Both of these tuples show among other things that supplier S1 was under contract on day 7 (assuming, of course, that today is at least day 7); if they both appeared, therefore, Requirement R1 would be violated.

Requirement R2: If the database shows supplier S*x* as being under contract on days *d* and *d*+1, then it must contain exactly one tuple that shows that fact.

The KEY constraint on relvar S_SINCE takes care of this requirement, too. Without it, the relvar might contain, for example, both of the following tuples at the same time:

S#	S#_SINCE	...
S1	d04	...

S#	S#_SINCE	...
S1	d05	...

Requirement R3: If the database shows supplier S*x* as being under contract on day *d*, then it must also show supplier S*x* as having some status on day *d*.

This requirement cannot be enforced on a database that is only semitemporal. The predicate for S_SINCE (slightly simplified) is:

Supplier S# has been under contract ever since S#_SINCE and has had status STATUS ever since STATUS_SINCE.

It is thus perfectly reasonable for S_SINCE to include a tuple in which the STATUS_SINCE value d' is greater than the S#_SINCE value d (see, e.g., the S_SINCE tuple for supplier S1 in Figure 12.2). And if supplier Sx is the supplier represented by that tuple, then the database shows supplier Sx as having been under contract throughout the interval $[d:d'-1]$ but does *not* show supplier Sx as having had some status throughout that interval. This latter is historical information that cannot be represented in this database.

We note in passing that the state of affairs just illustrated is quite typical of real-world "temporal" databases today (i.e., databases that include some temporal information but are implemented without direct temporal support from the system). For example, it would not be at all unusual to find a relvar like this one in such a database:

```
EMP { EMP#, DATE_OF_HIRE, SALARY, DATE_OF_LAST_INCREASE }
```

(The predicate here is meant to be obvious.) In such a relvar, there will probably be many tuples in which the DATE_OF_LAST_INCREASE value is greater than the DATE_OF_HIRE value.

Requirement R4: If the database shows supplier Sx as having some status on day d, then it must contain exactly one tuple that shows that fact.

The KEY constraint on relvar S_SINCE takes care of this requirement. Without it, the relvar might contain, for example, both of the following tuples at the same time:

S#	...	STATUS	STATUS_SINCE
S1	...	20	d06

S#	...	STATUS	STATUS_SINCE
S1	...	30	d06

Requirement R5: If the database shows supplier Sx as having the same status on days d and $d+1$, then it must contain exactly one tuple that shows that fact.

The KEY constraint on relvar S_SINCE takes care of this requirement, too. Without it, the relvar might contain, for example, both of the following tuples at the same time:

S#	...	STATUS	STATUS_SINCE
S1	...	20	d06

S#	...	STATUS	STATUS_SINCE
S1	...	20	d07

Requirement R6: If the database shows supplier S*x* as having some status on day *d*, then it must also show supplier S*x* as being under contract on day *d*.

We have encountered this requirement before, near the end of Section 10.2, where we observed that if the S#_SINCE and STATUS_SINCE values in some S_SINCE tuple are *d* and *d′*, respectively, then we must have *d′* ≥ *d*. Here is the formal statement:

```
CONSTRAINT CR6 IS_EMPTY
    ( S_SINCE WHERE STATUS_SINCE < S#_SINCE ) ;
```

Without this constraint, relvar S_SINCE might contain, for example, the following tuple:

S#	S#_SINCE	STATUS	STATUS_SINCE
S1	d04	20	d02

This tuple clearly shows among other things that supplier S1 had status 20 on day 2— and yet, because the database contains current relvars only (i.e., there is no historical record), it does not show that supplier S1 was under contract on day 2, thereby violating Requirement R6.

Requirement R7: If the database shows supplier S*x* as able to supply some specific part P*y* on day *d*, then it must contain exactly one tuple that shows that fact.

The KEY constraint on relvar SP_SINCE takes care of this requirement. Without it, the relvar might contain, for example, both of the following tuples at the same time:

S#	P#	SINCE
S1	P1	d04

S#	P#	SINCE
S1	P1	d02

Requirement R8: If the database shows supplier S*x* as able to supply the same part P*y* on days *d* and *d*+1, then it must contain exactly one tuple that shows that fact.

The KEY constraint on relvar SP_SINCE takes care of this requirement, too. Without it, the relvar might contain, for example, both of the following tuples at the same time:

S#	P#	SINCE
S1	P1	d04

S#	P#	SINCE
S1	P1	d05

Requirement R9: If the database shows supplier S*x* as able to supply some part P*y* on day *d*, then it must also show supplier S*x* as being under contract on day *d*.

The foreign key constraint from relvar SP_SINCE to relvar S_SINCE takes care of part of this requirement ("any supplier currently able to supply some part must be currently under contract"), but we also need:

```
CONSTRAINT CR9 IS_EMPTY
    ( ( S_SINCE JOIN SP_SINCE ) WHERE SINCE < S#_SINCE ) ;
```

("no supplier can supply any part before that supplier is under contract"). Without this constraint, relvars S_SINCE and SP_SINCE might respectively contain, for example, the following tuples at the same time:

S#	S#_SINCE	...
S1	d04	...

S#	P#	SINCE
S1	Py	d02

Compare and contrast Constraint XST1 in Chapter 4 (Section 4.2).

To complete this section, Figure 12.3 shows a revised and completed version of the original database design from Figure 12.1.

FIGURE 12.3
Current relvars
only—complete
design.

```
S_SINCE  { S#, S#_SINCE, STATUS, STATUS_SINCE }
            KEY { S# }

CONSTRAINT CR6 IS_EMPTY
    ( S_SINCE WHERE STATUS_SINCE < S#_SINCE )

SP_SINCE { S#, P#, SINCE }
            KEY { S#, P# }
            FOREIGN KEY { S# } REFERENCES S_SINCE

CONSTRAINT CR9 IS_EMPTY
    ( ( S_SINCE JOIN SP_SINCE ) WHERE SINCE < S#_SINCE )
```

12.4 HISTORICAL RELVARS ONLY

Now we turn to a temporal database that contains historical relvars only. The database in question—see Figure 12.4—consists essentially of the "during" relvars from Figure 11.1 (equivalently, from Figure 11.8); however, we now show the various PACKED ON and WHEN/THEN constraints that apply to those relvars (we deliberately do not use the U_key shorthand introduced in Section 11.9). The database is fully temporal, but does not separate current and historical information. Some sample values are shown in Figure 12.5, a considerably modified version of Figure 11.3. (Figure 12.5 is repeated in Endpaper Panel 7 at the back of the book.)

As we know from Chapter 10, one advantage of this design is that it can explicitly represent information about the future as well as the past. However, there is a disadvantage too: To be specific, we will probably have to use an artificial "end-of-time" value as the end value for any interval that refers to either the current or some future state of affairs (unless we do happen to know the actual end time, of course). Supplier S7 is a case in point in Figure 12.5 (we have assumed for the sake of the example that *d99* is "the last day").

<table>
<tr><td>FIGURE 12.4
Historical
relvars only.</td><td>

```
S_DURING { S#, DURING }
    PACKED ON DURING
    KEY { S#, DURING }

S_STATUS_DURING { S#, STATUS, DURING }
    PACKED ON DURING
    WHEN UNPACKED ON DURING THEN KEY { S#, DURING }
    KEY { S#, DURING }

SP_DURING { S#, P#, DURING }
    PACKED ON DURING
    KEY { S#, P#, DURING }
```

</td></tr>
</table>

FIGURE 12.5

Historical relvars only— sample values.

S_DURING

S#	DURING
S2	[d02:d04]
S6	[d03:d05]
S7	[d03:d99]

SP_DURING

S#	P#	DURING
S2	P1	[d02:d04]
S2	P2	[d03:d03]
S2	P5	[d03:d04]
S6	P3	[d03:d05]
S6	P4	[d04:d04]
S6	P5	[d04:d05]
S7	P1	[d03:d04]
S7	P1	[d06:d07]
S7	P1	[d09:d99]

S_STATUS_DURING

S#	STATUS	DURING
S2	5	[d02:d02]
S2	10	[d03:d04]
S6	5	[d03:d04]
S6	7	[d05:d05]
S7	15	[d03:d08]
S7	20	[d09:d99]

We now proceed to consider what formal versions of Requirements R1 through R9 might look like for this database.

Requirement R1: If the database shows supplier S*x* as being under contract on day *d*, then it must contain exactly one tuple that shows that fact.

The PACKED ON constraint on relvar S_DURING takes care of this requirement. Without it, the relvar might contain, for example, both of the following tuples at the same time:

S#	DURING
S2	[d02:d03]

S#	DURING
S2	[d03:d04]

By the way, there is a point here that might be bothering you. The database under discussion contains historical relvars only. As a consequence of this fact, the value of relvar S_DURING is always equal to the result of the expression

```
USING DURING ◄ S_STATUS_DURING { S#, DURING } ►
```

(as we saw in Chapter 10, Section 10.3).[2] Thus, it might be thought that if relvar S_DURING shows supplier S*x* as being under contract on day *d*, then relvar S_STATUS_DURING does so too, thereby violating Requirement R1. In fact, such is not the case. To be specific, the proposition "Supplier S*x* had some status on day *d*" does *not* logically imply the proposition "Supplier S*x* was under contract on day *d*," and relvar S_STATUS_DURING does *not* show that suppliers were under contract. NOTE: Analogous remarks apply to certain of the other discussions in this section as well. For a detailed discussion and analysis of such matters, see Chapter 15, Section 15.2.

Requirement R2: If the database shows supplier S*x* as being under contract on days *d* and *d*+1, then it must contain exactly one tuple that shows that fact.

The PACKED ON constraint on relvar S_DURING takes care of this requirement, too. Without it, the relvar might contain, for example, both of the following tuples at the same time:

S#	DURING
S2	[d02:d02]

S#	DURING
S2	[d03:d04]

---

2. You might like to check for yourself that the sample values in Figure 12.5 satisfy this property. As a matter of fact, we will be *insisting* later in this section that this property be satisfied (see the discussions of Requirements R3 and R6).

Requirement R3: If the database shows supplier *Sx* as being under contract on day *d*, then it must also show supplier *Sx* as having some status on day *d*.

Suppliers are shown as being under contract in relvar S_DURING and as having some status in relvar S_STATUS_DURING. Requirement R3 implies that every tuple that pairs supplier *Sx* with day *d* in the unpacked form of S_DURING must also appear in the unpacked form of the projection of S_STATUS_DURING on S# and DURING. Hence:

```
CONSTRAINT HR3 USING DURING
    ◄ S_DURING ⊆ S_STATUS_DURING { S#, DURING } ► ;
```

(Note that the foregoing expression involves a "U_⊆" comparison. See Chapter 9, Section 9.7.) Without this constraint, relvar S_DURING might contain, for example, the following tuple for supplier S7—

S#	DURING
S7	[*d03:d99*]

—while at the same time relvar S_STATUS_DURING contains, for example, just the following tuple and no other for supplier S7:

S#	STATUS	DURING
S7	20	[*d09:d99*]

Observe now that—as the applicable WHEN/THEN constraint in fact asserts—if relvar S_STATUS_DURING were actually kept unpacked on DURING, then {S#, DURING} would be a candidate key for that relvar. Furthermore, if relvar S_DURING were also kept unpacked on DURING, then {S#,DURING} would be a matching foreign key in S_DURING. Thus, if {S#,DURING} is regarded as a U_key for S_STATUS_DURING, then {S#,DURING} might be regarded as a matching *foreign* U_key in S_DURING! We therefore propose another shorthand. To be specific, we propose that the definition of any given relvar *R2* be allowed to include a specification of the form

```
USING ( ACL ) FOREIGN KEY { K } REFERENCES R1
```

As our discussion has more or less indicated already, the semantics are that if *R1* and *R2* were both to be kept unpacked on the attributes specified in *ACL*, then *K* in *R2* would be a foreign key matching the candidate key in *R1* that is implied by the corresponding U_key definition for *R1*. We skip further details here, except to note that—as by now you should surely be expecting—regular FOREIGN KEY constraints are basically just a special case of this proposed new syntax.

To get back to Requirement R3 specifically, we can now formulate that requirement thus:

```
USING DURING FOREIGN KEY { S#, DURING }
              REFERENCES S_STATUS_DURING
```

(part of the definition of relvar S_DURING).

Requirement R4: If the database shows supplier S*x* as having some status on day *d*, then it must contain exactly one tuple that shows that fact.

The PACKED ON and WHEN/THEN constraints on relvar S_STATUS_DURING take care of this requirement. Without the PACKED ON constraint, the relvar might contain, for example, both of the following tuples at the same time:

S#	STATUS	DURING
S7	15	[*d03:d06*]

S#	STATUS	DURING
S7	15	[*d05:d08*]

And without the WHEN/THEN constraint, the relvar might contain, for example, both of the following tuples at the same time:

S#	STATUS	DURING
S7	15	[*d03:d06*]

S#	STATUS	DURING
S7	20	[*d05:d08*]

Requirement R5: If the database shows supplier S*x* as having the same status on days *d* and *d*+1, then it must contain exactly one tuple that shows that fact.

The PACKED ON constraint on relvar S_STATUS_DURING takes care of this requirement. Without it, the relvar might contain, for example, both of the following tuples at the same time:

S#	STATUS	DURING
S7	15	[*d03:d06*]

S#	STATUS	DURING
S7	15	[*d07:d08*]

Requirement R6: If the database shows supplier S*x* as having some status on day *d*, then it must also show supplier S*x* as being under contract on day *d*.

Requirement R6 is effectively the inverse of Requirement R3. Hence:

```
USING DURING FOREIGN KEY { S#, DURING }
         REFERENCES S_DURING
```

(part of the definition of relvar S_STATUS_DURING). Without this constraint, relvar S_STATUS_DURING might contain, for example, the following tuple for supplier S7—

S#	STATUS	DURING
S7	20	[d09:d99]

—while at the same time relvar S_DURING contains, for example, just the following tuple and no other for supplier S7:

S#	DURING
S7	[d10:d99]

Note, therefore, that each of the relvars S_DURING and S_STATUS_DURING has a foreign U_key that references the other.

Requirement R7: If the database shows supplier Sx as able to supply some specific part Py on day d, then it must contain exactly one tuple that shows that fact.

The PACKED ON constraint on relvar SP_DURING takes care of this requirement. Without it, the relvar might contain, for example, both of the following tuples at the same time:

S#	P#	DURING
S2	P1	[d02:d03]

S#	P#	DURING
S2	P1	[d03:d04]

Requirement R8: If the database shows supplier Sx as able to supply the same part Py on days d and d+1, then it must contain exactly one tuple that shows that fact.

The PACKED ON constraint on relvar SP_DURING takes care of this requirement, too. Without it, the relvar might contain, for example, both of the following tuples at the same time:

S#	P#	DURING
S2	P1	[d02:d02]

S#	P#	DURING
S2	P1	[d03:d04]

Requirement R9: If the database shows supplier S*x* as able to supply some part P*y* on day *d*, then it must also show supplier S*x* as being under contract on day *d*.

The constraint

```
USING DURING FOREIGN KEY { S#, DURING }
          REFERENCES S_DURING
```

(part of the definition of relvar SP_DURING) takes care of this requirement. Without it, relvar SP_DURING might contain, for example, the following tuple for supplier S7—

S#	P#	DURING
S7	P1	*[d09:d99]*

—while at the same time relvar S_DURING contains, for example, just the following tuple and no other for supplier S7:

S#	DURING
S7	*[d10:d99]*

Compare and contrast Constraint XFT3 in Chapter 4 (Section 4.3).

To complete this section, Figure 12.6 shows a revised and completed version of the original database design from Figure 12.4. Observe that we now make use of the U_key shorthands.

FIGURE 12.6

Historical relvars only—complete design.

```
S_DURING { S#, DURING }
    USING DURING KEY { S#, DURING }
    USING DURING FOREIGN KEY { S#, DURING }
                REFERENCES S_STATUS_DURING

S_STATUS_DURING { S#, STATUS, DURING }
    USING DURING KEY { S#, DURING }
    USING DURING FOREIGN KEY { S#, DURING }
                REFERENCES S_DURING

SP_DURING { S#, P#, DURING }
    USING DURING KEY { S#, P#, DURING }
    USING DURING FOREIGN KEY { S#, DURING }
                REFERENCES S_DURING
```

12.5 BOTH CURRENT AND HISTORICAL RELVARS

In this section we consider the fully temporal database of Figure 11.1 (equivalently, of Figure 11.8). We show the database again in Figure 12.7, except that we now show all applicable PACKED ON and WHEN/THEN constraints explicitly (we deliberately do not use the U_key shorthand). This database keeps current information in the "since" relvars and historical information in the "during" relvars. Some sample values (copied from Figures 11.2 and 11.3) are shown in Figure 12.8. (That figure is repeated in Endpaper Panel 8 at the back of the book.)

As explained in Section 10.6, therefore, the "during" relvars do not contain any information regarding the present or the future; that is, every END(DURING) value—and *a fortiori* every BEGIN(DURING) value also—is less than the date today (which, for the sake of Figure 12.8, we assume once again is day 10). However, the "since" relvars certainly do include implicit information about the future, and they might include explicit information as well.

An aside regarding relvar S_SINCE: We remark that relvar S_SINCE is subject to the constraint (let us call it Constraint X) that if some S_SINCE tuple includes an S#_ SINCE value *d* that corresponds to some date in the future, then the STATUS_SINCE value in that tuple had better be *d* as well—for if it were greater than *d*, then Requirement R3 would be violated. (It cannot be *less* than *d*, thanks to Constraint BR6_A, discussed later.) Whether we would be able to state Constraint X formally is

FIGURE 12.7
 	
Both current and
historical relvars.
	```S_SINCE { S#, S#_SINCE, STATUS, STATUS_SINCE }```
	``` KEY { S# }```
	
	```SP_SINCE { S#, P#, SINCE }```
	``` KEY { S#, P# }```
	``` FOREIGN KEY { S# } REFERENCES S_SINCE```
	
	```S_DURING { S#, DURING }```
	``` PACKED ON DURING```
	``` KEY { S#, DURING }```
	
	```S_STATUS_DURING { S#, STATUS, DURING }```
	``` PACKED ON DURING```
	``` WHEN UNPACKED ON DURING THEN KEY { S#, DURING }```
	``` KEY { S#, DURING }```
	
	```SP_DURING { S#, P#, DURING }```
	``` PACKED ON DURING```
	``` KEY { S#, P#, DURING }```

FIGURE 12.8

Both current and
historical relvars—
sample values.

S_SINCE

S#	S#_SINCE	STATUS	STATUS_SINCE
S1	*d04*	20	*d06*
S2	*d07*	10	*d07*
S3	*d03*	30	*d03*
S4	*d04*	20	*d08*
S5	*d02*	30	*d02*

SP_SINCE

S#	P#	SINCE
S1	P1	*d04*
S1	P2	*d05*
S1	P3	*d09*
S1	P4	*d05*
S1	P5	*d04*
S1	P6	*d06*
S2	P1	*d08*
S2	P2	*d09*
S3	P2	*d08*
S4	P5	*d05*

S_DURING

S#	DURING
S2	*[d02:d04]*
S6	*[d03:d05]*

SP_DURING

S#	P#	DURING
S2	P1	*[d02:d04]*
S2	P2	*[d03:d03]*
S3	P5	*[d05:d07]*
S4	P2	*[d06:d09]*
S4	P4	*[d04:d08]*
S6	P3	*[d03:d03]*
S6	P3	*[d05:d05]*

S_STATUS_DURING

S#	STATUS	DURING
S1	15	*[d04:d05]*
S2	5	*[d02:d02]*
S2	10	*[d03:d04]*
S4	10	*[d04:d04]*
S4	25	*[d05:d07]*
S6	5	*[d03:d04]*
S6	7	*[d05:d05]*

open to debate, however; note that it would presumably have to include a test of the form "IF $d >$ TODAY()," where TODAY is a niladic built-in operator that returns the date today, and it is not at all clear that we would be allowed, or would want to be allowed, to include such a test within a formal constraint. Why not? Because such a constraint—or the integrity check implied by such a constraint, rather—could succeed on one day and fail on the next, even if the database had not been updated in the interim! (Note that, by contrast, no similar problem arises in connection with a test of the form "IF $d \leq$ TODAY()" [105].)

We now proceed to consider what formal versions of Requirements R1 through R9 might look like for this database.

Requirement R1: If the database shows supplier Sx as being under contract on day d, then it must contain exactly one tuple that shows that fact.

Recall that Requirement R1 has to do with avoiding redundancy—specifically, redundancy within or across relvars S_SINCE and S_DURING, given the database of Figure 12.7. Now, the KEY constraint on S_SINCE guarantees that relvar S_SINCE by itself cannot violate the requirement (see Section 12.3), and the PACKED ON constraint on S_DURING guarantees that relvar S_DURING by itself cannot violate it, either (see Section 12.4). What we need, therefore, is an additional constraint to ensure that the two relvars do not *both* show supplier Sx as being under contract on the same day:

```
CONSTRAINT BR1 IS_EMPTY
   ( ( S_SINCE JOIN S_DURING )
     WHERE S#_SINCE ≤ END ( DURING ) ) ;
```

Without this constraint, relvars S_SINCE and S_DURING might respectively contain, for example, the following tuples at the same time:

S#	S#_SINCE	. . .
S1	d04	. . .

S#	DURING
S1	[d06:d08]

(Both of these tuples show among other things that supplier S1 was under contract on day 7.)

The following point is worth noting. Suppose we introduce a modified version S_SINCE′ of relvar S_SINCE that includes an interval attribute DURING in place of the point attribute S#_SINCE. Suppose further that the current value of S_SINCE′ is identical to that of S_SINCE, except that, wherever S_SINCE has the S#_SINCE value d, S_SINCE′ has the DURING value [d:d99] (where we assume for the sake of the discussion that d99 is "the last day"). Then Constraint BR1 implies the following:

- If we take the projection of relvar S_SINCE′ on S# and DURING and unpack that projection on DURING, and

- if we also unpack relvar S_DURING on DURING, then

- the intersection of those two unpacked results is empty (i.e., no {S#,DURING} value appears in both).

Requirement R2: If the database shows supplier Sx as being under contract on days d and d+1, then it must contain exactly one tuple that shows that fact.

Requirement R2 has to do with avoiding circumlocution within and across relvars S_SINCE and S_DURING. The analysis that follows thus parallels, somewhat, that just given for Requirement R1. First, the KEY constraint on S_SINCE guarantees that relvar S_SINCE by itself cannot violate the requirement, and the PACKED ON constraint on

S_DURING guarantees that relvar S_DURING by itself cannot violate it, either. What we need, therefore, is an additional constraint to ensure that if relvar S_SINCE shows supplier Sx as being under contract since day d, then relvar S_DURING does not show supplier Sx as being under contract on the day immediately preceding day d:

```
CONSTRAINT BR2 IS_EMPTY
  ( ( S_SINCE JOIN S_DURING )
    WHERE PRIOR_DATE ( S#_SINCE ) = END ( DURING ) ) ;
```

Without this constraint, relvars S_SINCE and S_DURING might respectively contain, for example, the following tuples at the same time:

S#	S#_SINCE	...
S1	d04	...

S#	DURING
S1	[d01:d03]

Observing now that the expression following the keyword WHERE in Constraint BR1—see the discussion of Requirement R1 above—could have been stated in the form PRIOR_DATE (S#_SINCE) < END (DURING), we see that Constraints BR1 and BR2 can sensibly be combined into a single formulation, as follows:

```
CONSTRAINT BR1_2 IS_EMPTY
  ( ( S_SINCE JOIN S_DURING )
    WHERE PRIOR_DATE ( S#_SINCE ) ≤ END ( DURING ) ) ;
```

However, there is a small problem here. As explained in Chapter 5, the expression PRIOR_DATE (S#_SINCE) is not defined if S#_SINCE happens to be "the first day," and Constraint BR1_2 as just formulated might thus give rise to run-time errors. Let us therefore invent another operator, IS_PRIOR_T, that takes two arguments of the same point type T, p1 and p2 (in that order), and returns true if p1 is the immediate predecessor of p2 and false otherwise. Then we can restate Constraint BR1_2 as follows:

```
CONSTRAINT BR1_2 IS_EMPTY
  ( ( S_SINCE JOIN S_DURING )
    WHERE END ( DURING ) ≥ S#_SINCE
    OR IS_PRIOR_DATE ( END ( DURING ), S#_SINCE ) ) ;
```

This restatement avoids explicit reference to the predecessor of S#_SINCE, and the run-time errors just mentioned thus cannot occur.

NOTE: For completeness, we should define an analogous IS_NEXT_T operator as well. Of course, IS_NEXT_T(p1,p2) is logically equivalent to IS_PRIOR_T(p2,p1).

Requirement R3: If the database shows supplier S*x* as being under contract on day *d*, then it must also show supplier S*x* as having some status on day *d*.

The relvars that show a given supplier as being under contract on a given day are S_SINCE and S_DURING; the relvars that show a given supplier as having a given status on a given day are S_SINCE again and S_STATUS_DURING. Consider a particular S_SINCE tuple, with S#_SINCE and STATUS_SINCE values *d* and *d'*, respectively. If *d* = *d'*, then that tuple considered in isolation satisfies Requirement R3. However, if *d* < *d'*, then Requirement R3 implies that status information for every point in the interval [*d*:*d'*−1] for the supplier in question must appear in relvar S_STATUS_DURING instead. (Note that we cannot have *d* > *d'*, thanks to Constraint BR6_A, to be discussed later.) Also, of course, Requirement R3 implies that every {S#,DURING} value appearing in the unpacked form of relvar S_DURING must appear in the unpacked form of relvar S_STATUS_DURING as well. Hence:

```
CONSTRAINT BR3
    WITH ( S_SINCE WHERE S#_SINCE < STATUS_SINCE ) AS T1 ,
          ( EXTEND T1
            ADD INTERVAL_DATE ( [ S#_SINCE :
                                        PRIOR_DATE ( STATUS_SINCE ) ] )
            AS DURING ) { S#, DURING } AS T2 ,
          ( T2 UNION S_DURING ) AS T3 ,
            S_STATUS_DURING { S#, DURING } AS T4 :
    USING DURING ◄ T3 ⊆ T4 ► ;
```

Without this constraint, it would be possible for relvar S_SINCE to contain, for example, the following tuple—

S#	S#_SINCE	STATUS	STATUS_SINCE
S1	*d04*	20	*d06*

—while at the same time the unpacked form of relvar S_STATUS_DURING (on DURING) did *not* contain tuples of the form:

S#	STATUS	DURING
S1	......	[*d04*:*d04*]
S1	......	[*d05*:*d05*]

Incidentally, the STATUS value in the tuple for supplier S1 and interval [*d05*:*d05*] here could not be 20, thanks to Constraint BR5 (see later).

NOTE: If we wanted, we could specify the following foreign U_key constraint as part of the definition of relvar S_DURING:

```
USING DURING FOREIGN KEY { S#, DURING }
            REFERENCES S_STATUS_DURING
```

If we did, we could simplify Constraint BR3 slightly by deleting line 7 and replacing the reference in line 9 to T3 by a reference to T2 instead.

Observe now that Constraint BR3 as stated involves a PRIOR_DATE invocation. In contrast with the situation with Constraint BR2, however, that invocation is guaranteed not to fail; that is, its STATUS_SINCE argument is guaranteed not to evaluate to "the first day" (why not?).[3]

Note finally that it is a logical consequence of Requirement R3 that every supplier number appearing in relvar S_DURING also appears in relvar S_STATUS_DURING—an example of an *inclusion dependency* [10]. We mentioned such dependencies in passing in Chapter 4; as noted in that chapter, they can be regarded as a generalization of referential constraints. Some syntactic shorthand for expressing them might be useful in practice.

Requirement R4: If the database shows supplier S*x* as having some status on day *d*, then it must contain exactly one tuple that shows that fact.

The KEY constraint on relvar S_SINCE and the PACKED ON and WHEN/THEN constraints on relvar S_STATUS_DURING are sufficient to guarantee that neither of those relvars can violate this requirement by itself. But we need to add:

```
CONSTRAINT BR4 IS_EMPTY
    ( ( S_SINCE JOIN S_STATUS_DURING { S#, DURING } )
      WHERE STATUS_SINCE ≤ END ( DURING ) ) ;
```

Without this constraint, relvars S_SINCE and S_STATUS_DURING might respectively contain, for example, the following tuples at the same time:

S#	S#_SINCE	STATUS	STATUS_SINCE
S1	*d04*	20	*d05*

S#	STATUS	DURING
S1	20	[*d04:d05*]

---

3. Constraint BR3 as stated also involves a WITH expression that evaluates to a scalar value (actually a truth value); by contrast, all previous examples of WITH expressions in this book have been relation-valued. The constraints discussed under Requirements R6 and R9 later in this section also involve truth-valued WITH expressions. And in Chapter 13, Section 13.4, we will encounter WITH expressions that are tuple-valued, as well as further scalar-valued ones.

Alternatively—what is worse—they might respectively contain, for example, the following tuples at the same time:

S#	S#_SINCE	STATUS	STATUS_SINCE
S1	*d04*	20	*d05*

S#	STATUS	DURING
S1	10	[*d04:d05*]

Now suppose we introduce a modified version S_SINCE´ of relvar S_SINCE that includes an interval attribute DURING in place of the point attribute STATUS_SINCE. Suppose further that the current value of S_SINCE´ is identical to that of S_SINCE, except that, wherever S_SINCE has the STATUS_SINCE value *d*, S_SINCE´ has the DURING value [*d:d99*] (where we assume once again that *d99* is "the last day"). Then Constraint BR4 implies the following:

- If we take the projection of relvar S_SINCE´ on S#, STATUS, and DURING and unpack that projection on DURING, and

- if we also unpack relvar S_STATUS_DURING on DURING, then

- the intersection of those two unpacked results is empty (i.e., no {S#,STATUS,DURING} value appears in both).

Requirement R5: If the database shows supplier S*x* as having the same status on days *d* and *d*+1, then it must contain exactly one tuple that shows that fact.

Again the KEY constraint on S_SINCE and the PACKED ON constraint on S_STATUS_DURING are relevant. In addition, we need:

```
CONSTRAINT BR5 IS_EMPTY
   ( ( S_SINCE JOIN S_STATUS_DURING )
     WHERE PRIOR_DATE ( STATUS_SINCE ) = END ( DURING ) ) ;
```

Or preferably:

```
CONSTRAINT BR5 IS_EMPTY
   ( ( S_SINCE JOIN S_STATUS_DURING )
     WHERE IS_PRIOR_DATE ( END ( DURING ), STATUS_SINCE ) ) ;
```

Without this constraint, relvars S_SINCE and S_STATUS_DURING might respectively contain, for example, the following tuples at the same time:

S#	S#_SINCE	STATUS	STATUS_SINCE
S1	*d04*	20	*d05*

S#	STATUS	DURING
S1	20	*[d04:d04]*

Requirement R6: If the database shows supplier S*x* as having some status on day *d*, then it must also show supplier S*x* as being under contract on day *d*.

Note first that this requirement implies that if the S#_SINCE and STATUS_SINCE values in some S_SINCE tuple are *d* and *d′*, respectively, then we must have $d′ \geq d$. For suppose, contrariwise, that the S_SINCE tuple for supplier S*x* has $d′ < d$. Then Requirement R6 implies among other things that supplier S*x* must have been under contract on day *d*–1, and so a tuple documenting that fact must appear in relvar S_DURING (since it does not appear in relvar S_SINCE). But such a state of affairs would violate Requirement R2. Hence we have:

```
CONSTRAINT BR6_A IS_EMPTY
  ( S_SINCE WHERE STATUS_SINCE < S#_SINCE ) ;
```

This constraint is identical to Constraint CR6 from Section 12.3, except of course for its name. NOTE: We name the constraint "BR6_A" because, as we will see in a moment, we need an additional constraint ("BR6_B") in order to satisfy Requirement R6 fully. We should explain too that we choose to represent Requirement R6 by two separate constraints purely for pedagogical reasons.

Let us now turn to that additional constraint. As noted in Section 12.4, Requirement R6 is effectively the inverse of Requirement R3; as a consequence, a suitable formulation of the constraint needed to take care of the rest of Requirement R6 can be obtained from Constraint BR3 by replacing the "U_⊆" operator in the last line of that constraint by a "U_⊇" operator. However, it obviously makes sense to combine the two constraints by using a "U_=" operator instead:

```
CONSTRAINT BR3_6_B
   WITH ( S_SINCE WHERE S#_SINCE < STATUS_SINCE ) AS T1 ,
        ( EXTEND T1
          ADD INTERVAL_DATE ( [ S#_SINCE :
                                PRIOR_DATE ( STATUS_SINCE ) ] )
          AS DURING ) { S#, DURING } AS T2 ,
        ( T2 UNION S_DURING ) AS T3 ,
          S_STATUS_DURING { S#, DURING } AS T4 :
   USING DURING ◄ T3 = T4 ► ;
```

Without this constraint, it would be possible for relvar S_STATUS_DURING to contain, for example, the following tuple—

S#	...	DURING
S1	...	[d04:d04]

—while at the same time neither relvar S_SINCE nor relvar S_DURING contained a tuple showing that supplier S1 was under contract on day 4.

By the way, it would *not* be correct to specify the following foreign U_key constraint as part of the definition of relvar S_STATUS_DURING (why not?). HINT: Check the sample values in Figure 12.8.

```
USING DURING FOREIGN KEY { S#, DURING }
             REFERENCES S_DURING
```

Note finally that it is a logical consequence of Requirement R6 that every supplier number appearing in relvar S_STATUS_DURING also appears in relvar S_DURING or relvar S_SINCE or both.

Requirement R7: If the database shows supplier Sx as able to supply some specific part Py on day d, then it must contain exactly one tuple that shows that fact.

The KEY constraint on relvar SP_SINCE and the PACKED ON constraint on relvar SP_DURING are sufficient to guarantee that neither of those relvars can violate this requirement by itself. But we need to add:

```
CONSTRAINT BR7 IS_EMPTY
    ( ( SP_SINCE JOIN SP_DURING )
      WHERE SINCE ≤ END ( DURING ) ) ;
```

Without this constraint, relvars SP_SINCE and SP_DURING might respectively contain, for example, the following tuples at the same time:

S#	P#	SINCE
S1	P1	d04

S#	P#	DURING
S1	P1	[d06:d08]

Now suppose we introduce a modified version SP_SINCE′ of relvar SP_SINCE that includes an interval attribute DURING in place of the point attribute SINCE. Suppose further that the current value of SP_SINCE′ is identical to that of SP_SINCE, except that, wherever SP_SINCE has the SINCE value d, SP_SINCE′ has the DURING value [d:d99] (where we assume yet again that d99 is "the last day"). Then Constraint BR7 implies the following:

- If we unpack that relvar SP_SINCE′ on DURING, and

- if we also unpack relvar SP_DURING on DURING, then

- the intersection of those two unpacked results is empty (i.e., no {S#,P#,DURING} value appears in both).

Requirement R8: If the database shows supplier S*x* as able to supply the same part P*y* on days *d* and *d*+1, then it must contain exactly one tuple that shows that fact.

Again the KEY constraint on SP_SINCE and the PACKED ON constraint on SP_DURING are relevant. In addition, we need:

```
CONSTRAINT BR8 IS_EMPTY
   ( ( SP_SINCE JOIN SP_DURING )
     WHERE PRIOR_DATE ( SINCE ) = END ( DURING ) ) ;
```

Or preferably:

```
CONSTRAINT BR8 IS_EMPTY
   ( ( SP_SINCE JOIN SP_DURING )
     WHERE IS_PRIOR_DATE ( END ( DURING ), SINCE ) ) ;
```

Without this constraint, relvars SP_SINCE and SP_DURING might respectively contain, for example, the following tuples at the same time:

S#	P#	SINCE
S1	P1	*d04*

S#	P#	DURING
S1	P1	[*d01:d03*]

Constraints BR7 and BR8 can be combined as follows:

```
CONSTRAINT BR7_8 IS_EMPTY
   ( ( SP_SINCE JOIN SP_DURING )
     WHERE END ( DURING ) ≥ SINCE
     OR IS_PRIOR_DATE ( END ( DURING ), SINCE ) ) ;
```

Requirement R9: If the database shows supplier S*x* as able to supply some part P*y* on day *d*, then it must also show supplier S*x* as being under contract on day *d*.

As in Section 12.3, the foreign key constraint from relvar SP_SINCE to relvar S_SINCE takes care of part of this requirement ("any supplier currently able to supply some part must be currently under contract"), but we also need:

```
CONSTRAINT BR9_A IS_EMPTY
   ( ( S_SINCE JOIN SP_SINCE )
     WHERE S#_SINCE > SINCE ) ;
```

("no supplier currently under contract can supply any part under that contract before that contract began"). In addition, we need:

```
CONSTRAINT BR9_B
    WITH ( EXTEND S_SINCE
            ADD INTERVAL_DATE ( [ S#_SINCE : LAST_DATE ( ) ] )
            AS DURING ) { S#, DURING } AS T1 ,
          ( T1 UNION S_DURING ) AS T2 ,
          SP_DURING { S#, DURING } AS T3 :
    USING DURING ◄ T3 ⊆ T2 ► ;
```

Without this constraint, it would be possible for relvar SP_DURING to contain, for example, the following tuple—

S#	P#	DURING
S1	P1	[*d04:d04*]

—while at the same time neither relvar S_SINCE nor relvar S_DURING contained a tuple showing that supplier S1 was under contract on day 4. Compare and contrast Constraint XFT3 in Chapter 4 (Section 4.3).

By the way, observe that Constraint BR9_B includes an interval selector invocation in which the end time is specified as "the last day"—note the LAST_DATE() invocation—and then effectively goes on to ask for a relation containing such intervals to be unpacked. Naturally we would hope that the implementation does not actually materialize the unpacked relation in question! See Appendix A for further discussion of such matters.

Note finally that it is a logical consequence of Requirement R9 that every supplier number appearing in relvar SP_DURING also appears in relvar S_DURING or relvar S_SINCE or both.

To complete this section, Figure 12.9 shows a revised and completed version of the original database design from Figure 12.7. Observe that we now make use of the U_key shorthand.

FIGURE 12.9

Both current and
historical relvars—
complete design.

```
S_SINCE  { S#, S#_SINCE, STATUS, STATUS_SINCE }
         KEY { S# }

SP_SINCE { S#, P#, SINCE }
         KEY { S#, P# }
         FOREIGN KEY { S# } REFERENCES S_SINCE

S_DURING { S#, DURING }
  USING DURING KEY { S#, DURING }

S_STATUS_DURING { S#, STATUS, DURING }
  USING DURING KEY { S#, DURING }

SP_DURING { S#, P#, DURING }
  USING DURING KEY { S#, P#, DURING }

CONSTRAINT BR1_2 IS_EMPTY
   ( ( S_SINCE JOIN S_DURING )
     WHERE END ( DURING ) ≥ S#_SINCE
     OR IS_PRIOR_DATE ( END ( DURING ), S#_SINCE ) )

CONSTRAINT BR4 IS_EMPTY
   ( ( S_SINCE JOIN S_STATUS_DURING { S#, DURING } )
     WHERE STATUS_SINCE ≤ END ( DURING ) )

CONSTRAINT BR5 IS_EMPTY
   ( ( S_SINCE JOIN S_STATUS_DURING )
     WHERE IS_PRIOR_DATE ( END ( DURING ), STATUS_SINCE ) )

CONSTRAINT BR6_A IS_EMPTY
   ( S_SINCE WHERE STATUS_SINCE < S#_SINCE )

CONSTRAINT BR3_6_B
   WITH ( S_SINCE WHERE S#_SINCE < STATUS_SINCE ) AS T1 ,
        ( EXTEND T1
          ADD INTERVAL_DATE
            ( [ S#_SINCE : PRIOR_DATE ( STATUS_SINCE ) ] )
          AS DURING ) { S#, DURING } AS T2 ,
        ( T2 UNION S_DURING ) AS T3 ,
          S_STATUS_DURING { S#, DURING } AS T4 :
   USING DURING ◄ T3 = T4 ►
```

(continued)

FIGURE 12.9
(Continued)

```
CONSTRAINT BR7_8 IS_EMPTY
   ( ( SP_SINCE JOIN SP_DURING )
     WHERE END ( DURING ) ≥ SINCE
     OR IS_PRIOR_DATE ( END ( DURING ), SINCE ) )

CONSTRAINT BR9_A IS_EMPTY
   ( ( S_SINCE JOIN SP_SINCE )
     WHERE S#_SINCE > SINCE )

CONSTRAINT BR9_B
   WITH ( EXTEND S_SINCE
             ADD INTERVAL_DATE
                ( [ S#_SINCE : LAST_DATE ( ) ] )
             AS DURING ) { S#, DURING } AS T1 ,
          ( T1 UNION S_DURING ) AS T2 ,
          SP_DURING { S#, DURING } AS T3 :
     USING DURING ◄ T3 ⊆ T2 ►
```

12.6 SYNTACTIC SHORTHANDS

From the discussions and examples in Sections 12.3 through 12.5, it certainly seems that the design with both current and historical relvars is the one that involves the most complicated constraints. Nevertheless, we still prefer that design; that is, we believe it is the one that should be used in many situations. In this section, therefore, we investigate ways of making it easier to specify all of the constraints that seem to be needed with that particular design.

We begin by observing that, as is well known, the candidate key and foreign key syntax used in conventional (i.e., nontemporal) relvar definitions is essentially just shorthand for constraints that can be expressed, albeit more longwindedly, using the general "constraint language" portion of any relationally complete language such as **Tutorial D**. However, the shorthands in question are extremely useful: Quite apart from the fact that they save us a considerable amount of writing, they also effectively serve to *raise the level of abstraction,* by allowing us to talk in terms of certain "bundles" of concepts that seem to fit together very naturally. (What is more, they also pave the way for more efficient implementation.) And it is our belief that analogous shorthands can be defined to provide similar benefits in the temporal case, as we now try to show.

Before getting into details, however, we should repeat that we are far more concerned in this book with getting the foundations right than we are with purely syntactic matters. Thus, the following remarks should be seen mainly as "notes toward" the kind of shorthands we believe ought to be feasible in practice. Certainly the concrete syntax needs further work.

Now, it is indeed the case that we can observe some abstract structure in the database of Figure 12.9 that looks as if it would be applicable to temporal databases in general. To be specific, we can make the following observations regarding that database:

1. Each of the current ("since") relvars concerns certain *entities* and specifies certain *properties* of those entities.

2. Within each such current relvar, the entities are identified by a set *K* of candidate key attributes and the properties are specified by other attributes (as usual).[4] Some of those current relvars involve foreign keys that reference other current relvars (again as usual).

3. Within each such current relvar, each property has an associated "since" attribute, and so does the key. Within any given tuple, no "since" attribute has a value less than that of the "since" attribute associated with the key.

4. Given any specific current relvar, each property also has an associated historical ("during") relvar, and so does the key. Each such historical relvar consists of

   - a set of attributes *K* corresponding to the key of the pertinent current relvar
   - attribute(s) corresponding to the pertinent property (except for the historical relvar associated with the key of the current relvar, to which this paragraph does not apply)
   - a "during" attribute

5. Each of those historical relvars is kept packed on its "during" attribute and is subject to a constraint of the form WHEN UNPACKED ON DURING THEN KEY {*K*,DURING}.

6. Each combination of a property (or the key) in a current relvar together with the corresponding historical relvar is subject to certain constraints that are implied by Requirements R1 through R9 from Section 12.2—or by whatever analogs of those requirements apply to whatever temporal database we happen to be dealing with—and the general form of those constraints is as explained in Section 12.5.

We therefore propose a set of syntactic extensions along the following lines.

- First of all, we propose some syntax for specifying that, within a given current relvar, some attribute *B* is the "since" attribute corresponding to some set of attributes *A*. For example (note the text in boldface):

```
VAR S_SINCE RELATION
  { S#            S#,
    S#_SINCE      DATE SINCE_FOR { S# },
    STATUS        INTEGER,
    STATUS_SINCE  DATE SINCE_FOR { STATUS } }
  KEY { S# } ;
```

---

4. We assume for simplicity here that each current relvar has just one candidate key, which we refer to in the rest of the section simply as "the key." Some refinements will be required to our tentative syntax proposals in order to cater for the possibility of current relvars with two or more candidate keys.

```
VAR SP_SINCE RELATION
  { S#          S#,
    P#          P#,
    SINCE DATE SINCE_FOR { S#, P# } }
  KEY { S#, P# }
  FOREIGN KEY { S# } REFERENCES S_SINCE ;
```

Now the system knows that S#_SINCE and STATUS_SINCE are the "since" attributes for {S#} and {STATUS}, respectively, in relvar S_SINCE, and SINCE is the "since" attribute for {S#,P#} in relvar SP_SINCE. It also knows for each of those two relvars which "since" attribute is associated with the key, and in the case of relvar S_SINCE it knows that the constraint

```
IS_EMPTY ( S_SINCE WHERE STATUS_SINCE < S#_SINCE )
```

must be enforced.

■ Next, we propose some syntax for specifying the historical relvar corresponding to a given "since" attribute. For example (again, note the boldface text):

```
VAR S_SINCE RELATION
  { S#           S#,
    S#_SINCE     DATE SINCE_FOR { S# }
                      HISTORY_IN ( S_DURING ),
    STATUS       INTEGER,
    STATUS_SINCE DATE SINCE_FOR { STATUS }
                      HISTORY_IN ( S_STATUS_DURING ) }
  KEY { S# } ;

VAR SP_SINCE RELATION
  { S#    S#,
    P#    P#,
    SINCE DATE SINCE_FOR { S#, P# }
               HISTORY_IN ( SP_DURING ) }
  KEY { S#, P# }
  FOREIGN KEY { S# } REFERENCES S_SINCE ;
```

Now the system knows that relvars called S_DURING, S_STATUS_DURING, and SP_DURING *must* be defined. In fact, those relvar definitions might even be automated (since the system certainly knows what their structure must be), but for explanatory purposes we show them explicitly here:

```
VAR S_DURING RELATION
  { S#     S#,
    DURING INTERVAL_DATE }
  USING DURING KEY { S#, DURING } ;
```

(continued)

```
VAR S_STATUS_DURING RELATION
  { S#       S#,
    STATUS INTEGER,
    DURING INTERVAL_DATE }
  USING DURING KEY { S#, DURING } ;

VAR SP_DURING RELATION
  { S# S#,
    P# P#,
    DURING INTERVAL_DATE }
  USING DURING KEY { S#, P#, DURING } ;
```

Note the use of the "U_key" shorthand in these definitions.

We conjecture that the foregoing specifications taken together should be sufficient for the system to infer Constraints BR1_2, BR4, BR5, BR7_8, BR6_A, BR3_6_B, BR7_8, BR9_A, and BR9_B for itself, therefore avoiding the need for the user to state those constraints explicitly.

Putting all of the foregoing together, we arrive at the (slightly tentative) overall database definition shown in Figure 12.10.

FIGURE 12.10

Both current and historical relvars— shorthand definition (?).

```
VAR S_SINCE RELATION
  { S#             S#,
    S#_SINCE       DATE SINCE_FOR { S# }
                        HISTORY_IN ( S_DURING ),
    STATUS         INTEGER,
    STATUS_SINCE DATE SINCE_FOR { STATUS }
                        HISTORY_IN ( S_STATUS_DURING ) }
  KEY { S# } ;

VAR SP_SINCE RELATION
  { S#      S#,
    P#      P#,
    SINCE DATE SINCE_FOR { S#, P# }
              HISTORY_IN ( SP_DURING ) }
  KEY { S#, P# }
  FOREIGN KEY { S# } REFERENCES S_SINCE ;

VAR S_DURING RELATION
  { S#       S#,
    DURING INTERVAL_DATE }
  USING DURING KEY { S#, DURING } ;
```

(continued)

FIGURE 12.10
(Continued)

```
VAR S_STATUS_DURING RELATION
  { S#      S#,
    STATUS INTEGER,
    DURING INTERVAL_DATE }
  USING DURING KEY { S#, DURING } ;

VAR SP_DURING RELATION
  { S#      S#,
    P#      P#,
    DURING INTERVAL_DATE }
  USING DURING KEY { S#, P#, DURING } ;
```

12.7 CONCLUDING REMARKS

We conclude this chapter with a few miscellaneous observations.

- In conventional databases, relvars are sometimes "dropped" (meaning the relvar in question is deleted, and there is no longer any information regarding the relvar in question in the database catalog). In a temporal database, by contrast, it seems unlikely that a historical relvar would ever be dropped, since the whole point of the database is to maintain historical records.[5] By contrast, a current relvar might indeed be dropped, but it would probably be necessary to move all of the information it contains into appropriate historical relvars first. For obvious reasons, moreover, dropping a current relvar is likely to require a lot of revision to existing constraints.

- Another operation that is sometimes performed in conventional databases is the addition of a new attribute to an existing relvar. In a temporal database, adding a new attribute to a historical relvar seems to make little sense, because—given our recommendations regarding sixth normal form, at any rate—each historical relvar involves the history of just one "property," more or less by definition. By contrast, adding a new attribute to a current relvar might make sense, but the new attribute would probably need an accompanying new "since" attribute, and it would probably need an accompanying new historical relvar as well. New constraints would also be required.

- Finally, we note that constraints in general do change over time (though the kinds of constraints we have been discussing in this chapter are probably less susceptible to change than most). As a consequence, a temporal database might contain data that satisfies some constraint that was in effect when the data was entered

---

5. Perhaps we should say rather that it would seem *unwise* to drop such a relvar. We all know the problem of finding we need something we threw away only yesterday.

into the database but does *not* satisfy some revised version of that constraint that is in effect now. One implication is that constraints themselves might need to include temporal components ("valid times," in fact—see Chapter 3). A further and possibly more serious implication is that the database catalog itself might need to be treated as a temporal database. We do not discuss these possibilities further in this book.

EXERCISES

1. What is a "denseness constraint"?

2. (Repeated from Section 12.2) Requirements R2, R5, and R8 cannot possibly be satisfied, in general, if full vertical decomposition into 6NF has not been performed. Why not?

3. State the nine requirements from Section 12.2 in a form (natural language only) that applies to courses and students instead of suppliers and shipments.

4. Given your answer to Exercise 3, show the corresponding formal constraints for the version of the courses-and-students database discussed in Exercise 6 in Chapter 11.

5. Given your answer to Exercise 4, what SINCE_FOR and HISTORY_IN specifications, if any, would you add to the database definition?

6. The database definition resulting from Exercise 6 in Chapter 11 really needs to be extended still further to allow us to record, in connection with an enrollment, the particular offering to which that enrollment is assigned. State whatever additional natural language requirements you can think of that might arise in connection with such an extension. Also make the corresponding changes to the **Tutorial D** definition of the database.

Chapter

13

DATABASE QUERIES

13.1 INTRODUCTION

In this chapter we consider the (highly nontrivial!) question of what is involved in formulating queries on a temporal database. We base most of our examples and discussions on the various versions of the suppliers-and-shipments database described in Chapter 12; moreover, we assume throughout that the constraints discussed in the last two chapters are in effect, and we make tacit use of that assumption in certain of our query formulations.

Of course, we have seen many examples of queries in this book already, especially in Chapters 6 and 8 (see Sections 6.4 and 8.4, respectively). However, most of those earlier examples were intended primarily to illustrate the functionality of some specific operator; also, they all involved "historical" relvars specifically—or relvars (or relations) with interval attributes, at any rate. In this chapter, by contrast, we concentrate on how we might formulate a variety of arguably more realistic queries on a more comprehensive database. For purposes of future reference, the following list shows the queries we will be considering.

- **Query Q1:** Get the status of supplier S1 on day *dn* (you can assume that supplier S1 is represented in the database).

- **Query Q2:** Get pairs of supplier numbers such that the indicated suppliers were assigned their current status on the same day.

- **Query Q3:** Get supplier numbers for suppliers currently able to supply both part P1 and part P2.

- **Query Q4:** Get supplier numbers for suppliers not currently able to supply both part P1 and part P2.

- **Query Q5:** Get supplier numbers for suppliers currently able to supply some part who have changed their status since they most recently became able to supply some part.

- **Query Q6:** Get intervals during which at least one supplier was under contract.

- **Query Q7:** Suppose the result of Query Q6 is kept as a relvar BUSY. Use relvar BUSY to get intervals during which no supplier was under contract at all.

- **Query Q8:** Get supplier numbers for suppliers currently under contract who also had an earlier contract.

- **Query Q9:** Get S#-PARTS-DURING triples such that the indicated supplier was able to supply the indicated range of parts during the indicated interval.

- **Query Q10:** Suppose the result of Query Q9 is kept as a relvar S_PARTS_DURING. Use relvar S_PARTS_DURING to get S#-P#-DURING triples such that the indicated supplier was able to supply the indicated part during the indicated interval.

- **Query Q11:** Given relvar INFLATION, with attributes ID, DURING, and PERCENTAGE, and both {ID} and {DURING} as candidate keys, get DURING-PERCENTAGE pairs such that the inflation rate for the indicated interval was the indicated percentage.

- **Query Q12:** Suppose the result of Query Q11 is kept as a relvar INFLATION (replacing the previous relvar of that name). Get intervals where the associated percentage is less than 5 percent; for the sake of the example, assume the result is required in packed form.

Incidentally, the point is worth making that certain of these queries—for example, Queries Q6, Q7, Q9, Q11, and Q12—can be handled only rather clumsily (possibly not at all, in some cases) in certain of the other temporal database approaches described in the literature. The reason is that the approaches in question typically violate *The Information Principle* by treating timestamps in general, and interval timestamps in particular, as special in some way, instead of representing them by regular relational attributes [107].

The structure of the chapter is as follows. Following this introductory section, the next two sections show, first, what the sample queries might look like on a database involving current relvars only (Section 13.2), and then what they might look like on a database involving historical relvars only (Section 13.3). Next, Section 13.4 does the same for a database involving both kinds of relvars. Finally, Section 13.5 considers the possibility of providing a collection of predefined *views* or *virtual relvars* in order to simplify the formulation of certain kinds of queries, thereby making the user's life a little easier than it might otherwise be.

13.2 CURRENT RELVARS ONLY

As just indicated, in this section we limit our attention to queries on a version of the database that involves current relvars only. Figure 13.1, a copy of Figure 12.3, shows the database definition in outline (including the pertinent constraints). We remind you that this database cannot represent historical information at all, other than what can be inferred from "since" values; however, it *can* represent future information—certainly implicitly, and possibly explicitly as well. Refer to Figure 12.2 in Chapter 12 (or Endpaper Panel 6) if you want to see some sample values.

FIGURE 13.1

Current relvars only.

```
S_SINCE  { S#, S#_SINCE, STATUS, STATUS_SINCE }
            KEY { S# }

CONSTRAINT CR6 IS_EMPTY
   ( S_SINCE WHERE STATUS_SINCE < S#_SINCE )

SP_SINCE { S#, P#, SINCE }
            KEY { S#, P# }
            FOREIGN KEY { S# } REFERENCES S_SINCE

CONSTRAINT CR9 IS_EMPTY
   ( ( S_SINCE JOIN SP_SINCE ) WHERE SINCE < S#_SINCE )
```

Perhaps we should explain at the outset that some of the query formulations in this section are not very temporal in nature (after all, the database itself is only semitemporal). Part of the point, though, is to pave the way for the discussion of historical and mixed databases in the next two sections. Also, we omit Queries Q11 and Q12 in this section because they are not in the spirit of a "semitemporal database" like that of Figure 13.1.

Query Q1: Get the status of supplier S1 on day *dn* (you can assume that supplier S1 is represented in the database).

As already mentioned, relvars S_SINCE and SP_SINCE are allowed to include explicit information concerning the future (i.e., some "since" value might be greater than the date today). In particular, therefore, relvar S_SINCE might show that some supplier *will be* assigned some status at some future date.

Next, we remind you that if some S_SINCE tuple says supplier S*x* has had or will have status *st* from day *d* onward, we interpret that tuple to mean that supplier S*x* had, has, or will have status *st* on every day from day *d* until "the last day." It follows that Query Q1 can be answered from the database of Figure 13.1 if and only if day *dn* does not precede the STATUS_SINCE date for supplier S1. Assuming this requirement is satisfied, a suitable formulation of the query is straightforward:

```
( S_SINCE WHERE S# = S# ('S1') ) { STATUS }
```

However, a slightly more satisfactory formulation of the query is:

```
( S_SINCE WHERE S# = S# ('S1')
              AND dn ≥ STATUS_SINCE ) { STATUS }
```

If this latter formulation returns an empty result, it will mean that (1) by our assumption, relvar S_SINCE does contain a tuple for supplier S1, but that (2) the STATUS_SINCE date in that tuple is greater than day dn (and so the query cannot be answered, because the information is not in the database).

Query Q2: Get pairs of supplier numbers such that the indicated suppliers were assigned their current status on the same day.

The first point to make here is that the natural language version of this query ought really to be stated in terms of suppliers who were *or will be* assigned their current status on the same day. From this point forward, however, we will mostly ignore such refinements, both in this example and throughout the remainder of this chapter (in our natural language statements, that is, but not, of course, in their formal counterparts).

Observe next that a given supplier has a current status if and only if there exists a (necessarily unique) tuple for that supplier in relvar S_SINCE—and if such a tuple does exist, then the STATUS_SINCE value in that tuple gives the date when that current status was assigned to that supplier. Hence:

```
WITH S_SINCE { S#, STATUS_SINCE } AS T1 ,
     ( T1 RENAME S# AS X# ) AS T2 ,
     ( T1 RENAME S# AS Y# ) AS T3 ,
     ( T2 JOIN T3 ) AS T4 ,
     ( T4 WHERE X# < Y# ) AS T5 :
T5 { X#, Y# }
```

NOTE: Line 5 here requests a restriction of relation T4 to just those tuples where supplier number X# is less than supplier number Y#. We have seen this trick before, in Chapter 6, Section 6.4; the idea is to eliminate pairs of supplier numbers of the form (x,x) and to guarantee that the pairs (x,y) and (y,x) do not both appear. Of course, the operator "<" must be defined for type S# in order for this trick to work.

Query Q3: Get supplier numbers for suppliers currently able to supply both part P1 and part P2.

A formulation of this query is straightforward:

```
WITH ( SP_SINCE WHERE P# = P# ('P1') ) { S# } AS T1 ,
     ( SP_SINCE WHERE P# = P# ('P2') ) { S# } AS T2 :
T1 JOIN T2
```

We could replace the JOIN in the last line here by INTERSECT if we liked.

Query Q4: Get supplier numbers for suppliers not currently able to supply both part P1 and part P2.

Here we have to inspect relvar S_SINCE as well as relvar SP_SINCE, because a supplier who is currently under contract but not currently able to supply any parts at all is certainly one who is not currently able to supply both part P1 and part P2, and such a supplier will be represented in S_SINCE and not in SP_SINCE. Hence:

```
WITH ( SP_SINCE WHERE P# = P# ('P1') ) { S# } AS T1 ,
     ( SP_SINCE WHERE P# = P# ('P2') ) { S# } AS T2 ,
     ( T1 JOIN T2 ) AS T3 :
S_SINCE { S# } MINUS T3 { S# }
```

Query Q5: Get supplier numbers for suppliers currently able to supply some part who have changed their status since they most recently became able to supply some part.

Suppliers who are currently able to supply some part are represented in relvar SP_SINCE, and the date when they most recently became able to supply some part can also be obtained from that relvar. Furthermore, the date when they acquired their current status (i.e., the date of their most recent status change, in effect) is given in relvar S_SINCE. Hence:

```
WITH ( SUMMARIZE SP_SINCE
         PER SP_SINCE { S# }
         ADD MAX ( SINCE ) AS MOST_RECENT_SP_DATE ) AS T1 ,
     ( S_SINCE JOIN T1 ) AS T2 ,
     ( T2 WHERE STATUS_SINCE > MOST_RECENT_SP_DATE ) AS T3 :
T3 { S# }
```

Query Q6: Get intervals during which at least one supplier was under contract.

Given only the semitemporal database of Figure 13.1, the best attempt we can make at answering this query is just to say that if the earliest S#_SINCE date in relvar S_SINCE is d, then at least one supplier is under contract on every day from d to "the last day" (inclusive):

```
RELATION { TUPLE { DURING INTERVAL_DATE
         ( [ MIN ( S_SINCE { S#_SINCE } ) : LAST_DATE ( ) ] ) } }
```

EXPLANATION: The overall expression here is a *relation selector invocation* of the form RELATION {TUPLE {DURING INTERVAL_DATE ([b:e])}}; it returns a relation with one attribute, called DURING, and one tuple. The expression within the outer set of braces is a *tuple* selector invocation; it returns the one tuple in the one-tuple relation, and that tuple has just one component, called DURING. The DURING value in that tuple is specified by means of an *interval* selector invocation of the form INTERVAL_DATE ([b:e]); the b value is obtained by means of an invocation of the aggregate operator MIN, and the e value is obtained by means of an invocation of LAST_DATE.

However, there is a problem with the foregoing formulation. In fact, that formulation will suffice *provided* we can be sure that relvar S_SINCE is nonempty. If it is empty, however, then (as explained in reference [35]) the MIN invocation will return "the last day," and the overall expression will thus yield a relation with one attribute (DURING) and one tuple, containing an interval of the form

```
INTERVAL_DATE ( [ LAST_DATE ( ) : LAST_DATE ( ) ] )
```

The result will thus be incorrect.

It follows that if we cannot assume that relvar S_SINCE is nonempty, a more complicated formulation becomes necessary:

```
WITH ( SUMMARIZE S_SINCE PER S_SINCE { }
         ADD MIN ( S#_SINCE )
         AS EARLIEST ) AS T1 ,
       ( EXTEND T1
         ADD INTERVAL_DATE ( [ EARLIEST : LAST_DATE ( ) ] )
         AS DURING ) AS T2 :
T2 { DURING }
```

Now, if S_SINCE is empty, T1 and T2 are also both empty, and so is the overall result.

Query Q7: Suppose the result of Query Q6 is kept as a relvar BUSY. Use relvar BUSY to get intervals during which no supplier was under contract at all.

If we can assume that relvar BUSY is nonempty, then in fact it will contain exactly one tuple, and the following formulation will suffice:

```
RELATION { TUPLE { DURING INTERVAL_DATE
              ( [ FIRST_DATE ( ) :
                PRE ( DURING FROM ( TUPLE FROM BUSY ) ) ] ) } }
```

EXPLANATION: Again the overall expression here is a relation selector invocation of the form RELATION {TUPLE {DURING INTERVAL_DATE ([b:e])}}; thus, it returns a relation with one attribute, called DURING, and one tuple. The sole DURING value within that relation is specified by means of an interval selector invocation of the form INTERVAL_DATE ([b:e]); the b value is obtained by means of an invocation of FIRST_DATE, and the e value is the date immediately preceding the begin point of the sole DURING value in BUSY. More specifically, that e value is obtained by means of an expression of the form

```
PRE ( DURING FROM ( TUPLE FROM BUSY ) )
```

In general:

- The expression TUPLE FROM *<relation exp>* returns the sole tuple in the one-tuple relation denoted by *<relation exp>* (much as the expression POINT FROM *<interval exp>* returns the sole point in the unit interval denoted by *<interval exp>*).

- The expression *A* FROM *<tuple exp>* returns the value of attribute *A* within the tuple denoted by *<tuple exp>*.

- The expression PRE (*<interval exp>*) returns the point immediately preceding the begin point of the interval denoted by *<interval exp>* (as you will recall from Chapter 6).

This time, however, there are *two* problems with the formulation as shown. In fact, that formulation will suffice provided we can be sure that relvar BUSY is nonempty *and* the sole interval it contains does not have "the beginning of time" as its begin point (it will, of course, have "the end of time" as its end point). Here by contrast is a more complicated formulation that will work correctly in all cases:

```
USING DURING ◄ RELATION { TUPLE { DURING INTERVAL_DATE
                ( [ FIRST_DATE ( ) : LAST_DATE ( ) ] ) } }
            MINUS BUSY ►
```

This expression makes use of a "U_MINUS" operation. Note carefully, however, that we would prefer that the implementation not physically materialize the result of the two UNPACKs implied by that operation!—especially in the case of the left operand, since the unpacked form of that operand contains a tuple for every single time point from the beginning of time to the end of time inclusive. An alternative but ugly formulation that avoids such possible inefficiencies is:

```
CASE
   WHEN IS_EMPTY ( BUSY )
      THEN RELATION { TUPLE { DURING INTERVAL_DATE
                   ( [ FIRST_DATE ( ) : LAST_DATE ( ) ] ) } }
   WHEN IS_EMPTY ( BUSY WHERE BEGIN ( DURING ) >
                                     FIRST_DATE ( ) )
      THEN RELATION { DURING INTERVAL_DATE } { }
   ELSE    RELATION { TUPLE { DURING INTERVAL_DATE
                   ( [ FIRST_DATE ( ) :
                      PRE ( DURING FROM
                             ( TUPLE FROM BUSY ) ) ] ) } }
END CASE
```

Query Q8: Get supplier numbers for suppliers currently under contract who also had an earlier contract.

Given only the semitemporal database of Figure 13.1, this query cannot be answered; in fact, it cannot even be formulated.

Query Q9: Get S#-PARTS-DURING triples such that the indicated supplier was able to supply the indicated range of parts during the indicated interval.

Here we are essentially being asked to construct a relation that looks like relvar S_PARTS_DURING as discussed in Chapter 5, Section 5.4:

```
WITH ( EXTEND SP_SINCE ADD
         ( INTERVAL_P# ( [ P# : P# ] ) AS PARTS ,
           INTERVAL_DATE ( [ SINCE : LAST_DATE ( ) ] )
                                      AS DURING ) )
       AS T :
USING ( PARTS, DURING ) ◄ T { S#, PARTS, DURING } ►
```

Note the use of a "U_projection" here.

Query Q10: Suppose the result of Query Q9 is kept as a relvar S_PARTS_DURING. Use relvar S_PARTS_DURING to get S#-P#-DURING triples such that the indicated supplier was able to supply the indicated part during the indicated interval.

```
WITH ( UNPACK S_PARTS_DURING ON PARTS ) AS T1 ,
     ( EXTEND T1 ADD POINT FROM PARTS AS P# ) AS T2 :
USING DURING ◄ T2 { ALL BUT PARTS } ►
```

Note the use of POINT FROM here to extract the single point from a unit interval (see Chapter 6, Section 6.1).

13.3 HISTORICAL RELVARS ONLY

Now we turn our attention to queries on a version of the database that involves historical relvars only. Figure 13.2, a copy of Figure 12.6, shows the database definition in outline (including the pertinent constraints). The database is fully temporal, but does not separate current and historical information; it can represent information about the future as well as the past, but typically we have to use artificial "end-of-time" values to mark the end of any interval whose true end point is currently unknown. Refer to Figure 12.5 in Chapter 12 (or Endpaper Panel 7) if you want to see some sample values.

FIGURE 13.2

Historical relvars
only.

```
S_DURING { S#, DURING }
    USING DURING KEY { S#, DURING }
    USING DURING FOREIGN KEY { S#, DURING }
                 REFERENCES S_STATUS_DURING

S_STATUS_DURING { S#, STATUS, DURING }
    USING DURING KEY { S#, DURING }
    USING DURING FOREIGN KEY { S#, DURING }
                 REFERENCES S_DURING

SP_DURING { S#, P#, DURING }
    USING DURING KEY { S#, P#, DURING }
    USING DURING FOREIGN KEY { S#, DURING }
                 REFERENCES S_DURING
```

Query Q1: Get the status of supplier S1 on day *dn* (you can assume that supplier S1 is represented in the database).

This query is straightforward:

```
( S_STATUS_DURING WHERE S# = S# ('S1')
                  AND dn ∈ DURING ) { STATUS }
```

Note that this formulation works even if *dn* is a date in the future.

Query Q2: Get pairs of supplier numbers such that the indicated suppliers were assigned some status on the same day.

Observe first that, because the database contains historical relvars only, we have found it necessary to revise the query slightly (previously it referred to *current* status specifically, now it refers just to *some* status). Status assignments are given in relvar S_STATUS_DURING. Here then is a suitable formulation:

```
WITH ( EXTEND S_STATUS_DURING
         ADD BEGIN ( DURING ) AS STB ) { S#, STB } AS T1 ,
       ( T1 RENAME S# AS X# ) AS T2 ,
       ( T1 RENAME S# AS Y# ) AS T3 ,
       ( T2 JOIN T3 ) AS T4 ,
       ( T4 WHERE X# < Y# ) AS T5 :
T5 { X#, Y# }
```

Query Q3: Get supplier numbers for suppliers who were able to supply both part P1 and part P2 at the same time.

Again we have revised the query slightly. Here is a suitable formulation:

```
WITH ( SP_DURING WHERE P# = P# ('P1') ) { S#, DURING } AS T1 ,
     ( SP_DURING WHERE P# = P# ('P2') ) { S#, DURING } AS T2 ,
     ( USING DURING ◄ T1 JOIN T2 ► ) AS T3 :
T3 { S# }
```

Query Q4: Get supplier numbers for suppliers who were never able to supply both part P1 and part P2 at the same time.

Once again we have had to revise the query slightly. Here is a suitable formulation:

```
WITH ( SP_DURING WHERE P# = P# ('P1') ) { S#, DURING } AS T1 ,
     ( SP_DURING WHERE P# = P# ('P2') ) { S#, DURING } AS T2 ,
     ( USING DURING ◄ T1 JOIN T2 ► ) AS T3 :
S_DURING { S# } MINUS T3 { S# }
```

Query Q5: Get supplier numbers for suppliers who, while they were under some specific contract, changed their status since they most recently became able to supply some part under that contract.

Yet again we have had to revise the query; what is more, the revised version is quite complicated! In particular, note the requirement that certain specified events occurred while the contract in question was in effect. This requirement accounts for the restriction operations in lines 3 and 6 below:

```
WITH ( S_STATUS_DURING RENAME DURING AS X ) { S#, X } AS T1 ,
     ( T1 JOIN S_DURING ) AS T2 ,
     ( T2 WHERE X ⊆ DURING ) AS T3 ,
     ( SP_DURING RENAME DURING AS Y ) { S#, Y } AS T4 ,
     ( T4 JOIN T3 ) AS T5 ,
     ( T5 WHERE Y ⊆ DURING ) AS T6 ,
     ( SUMMARIZE T6 PER T6 { S#, DURING } ADD
       ( MAX ( BEGIN ( X ) ) AS BXMAX ,
         MAX ( BEGIN ( Y ) ) AS BYMAX ) ) AS T7 ,
     ( T7 WHERE BXMAX > BYMAX ) AS T8 :
T8 { S# }
```

Query Q6: Get intervals during which at least one supplier was under contract.

```
USING DURING ◄ S_DURING { DURING } ►
```

Query Q7: Suppose the result of Query Q6 is kept as a relvar BUSY. Use relvar BUSY to get intervals during which no supplier was under contract at all.

```
USING DURING ◄ RELATION { TUPLE { DURING INTERVAL_DATE
                 ( [ FIRST_DATE ( ) : LAST_DATE ( ) ] ) } }
           MINUS BUSY ►
```

This formulation is identical to the "best" formulation given for this query in the previous section.

Query Q8: Get supplier numbers for suppliers currently under contract who also had an earlier contract.

```
WITH ( S_DURING WHERE TODAY ( ) ∈ DURING ) { S# } AS T1 ,
      S_DURING { S# } WHERE TODAY ( ) > END ( DURING ) AS T2 :
T1 JOIN T2
```

As in Chapter 12, we are assuming here the availability of a niladic operator called TODAY that returns today's date.

Query Q9: Get S#-PARTS-DURING triples such that the indicated supplier was able to supply the indicated range of parts during the indicated interval.

```
WITH ( EXTEND SP_DURING
         ADD INTERVAL_P# ( [ P# : P# ] ) AS PARTS ) AS T :
USING ( PARTS, DURING ) ◄ T { S#, PARTS, DURING } ►
```

Query Q10: Suppose the result of Query Q9 is kept as a relvar S_PARTS_DURING. Use relvar S_PARTS_DURING to get S#-P#-DURING triples such that the indicated supplier was able to supply the indicated part during the indicated interval.

```
WITH ( UNPACK S_PARTS_DURING ON PARTS ) AS T1 ,
     ( EXTEND T1 ADD POINT FROM PARTS AS P# ) AS T2 :
USING DURING ◄ T2 { ALL BUT PARTS } ►
```

This expression is identical to its counterpart in the previous section.

Query Q11: Given relvar INFLATION, with attributes ID, DURING, and PERCENT-AGE, and both {ID} and {DURING} as candidate keys, get DURING-PERCENTAGE pairs such that the inflation rate for the indicated interval was the indicated percentage.

```
INFLATION { DURING, PERCENTAGE }
```

The point about this example is simply that the result is *not* packed on DURING (see Chapter 11, Section 11.8).

Query Q12: Suppose the result of Query Q11 is kept as a relvar INFLATION (replacing the previous relvar of that name). Get intervals where the associated percentage is less than 5 percent; for the sake of the example, assume the result is required in packed form.

```
PACK ( INFLATION WHERE PERCENTAGE < 5 ) ON DURING
```

13.4 Both Current and Historical Relvars

In this section, we consider queries on a version of the database that involves both current and historical relvars. Figure 13.3, an edited version of Figure 12.7, shows the database definition in outline (including some but not all of the pertinent constraints). This database keeps current information in the "since" relvars and historical information in the "during" relvars. Refer to Figure 12.8 in Chapter 12 (or Endpaper Panel 8) if you want to see some sample values.

Note carefully with respect to this database that, while the "since" relvars have the same meaning as their counterparts in Section 13.2, the "during" relvars do *not* have the same meaning as their counterparts in Section 13.3. To be specific, the "during" relvars in Section 13.3 were allowed to contain information concerning the future and the present as well as the past, but the "during" relvars in this section contain information concerning the past only. (Note, however, that relvars S_STATUS_DURING and SP_DURING might contain *historical* information concerning *current* contracts.) Thus, no END(DURING) value—and *a fortiori* no BEGIN(DURING) value either—is ever greater than the date yesterday.

NOTE: The queries that follow are in fact identical, in their natural language form, to their counterparts from the previous section. Because of the difference in semantics just explained, however, the corresponding precise formulations are sometimes different. Also, we omit Queries Q10, Q11, and Q12, because the precise formulations of those three queries are in fact identical to their counterparts in the previous section.

FIGURE 13.3

Both current and historical relvars.

```
S_SINCE  { S#, S#_SINCE, STATUS, STATUS_SINCE }
         KEY { S# }

SP_SINCE { S#, P#, SINCE }
         KEY { S#, P# }
         FOREIGN KEY { S# } REFERENCES S_SINCE

S_DURING { S#, DURING }
         USING DURING KEY { S#, DURING }

S_STATUS_DURING { S#, STATUS, DURING }
         USING DURING KEY { S#, DURING }

SP_DURING { S#, P#, DURING }
         USING DURING KEY { S#, P#, DURING }
```

Query Q1: Get the status of supplier S1 on day *dn* (you can assume that supplier S1 is represented in the database).

The difficulty here is that we do not know, in general, whether the answer to the query is to be found in relvar S_SINCE or relvar S_STATUS_DURING. Hence:

```
WITH ( S_SINCE WHERE S# = S# ('S1') ) AS T1 ,
     ( EXTEND T1
       ADD INTERVAL_DATE ( [ STATUS_SINCE : LAST_DATE ( ) ] )
       AS DURING ) AS T2 ,
     T2 { STATUS, DURING } AS T3 ,
     ( S_STATUS_DURING WHERE S# = S# ('S1') ) AS T4 ,
     T4 { STATUS, DURING } AS T5 ,
     ( T4 UNION T5 ) AS T6 :
( T6 WHERE dn ∈ DURING ) { STATUS }
```

An alternative formulation, involving what is in effect an explicit test to see which relvar contains the desired information, might look like this:

```
WITH ( TUPLE FROM ( S_SINCE WHERE S# = S# ('S1') ) ) AS t ,
     ( STATUS FROM t ) AS s ,
     ( STATUS_SINCE FROM t ) AS d :
IF dn ≥ d THEN RELATION { TUPLE { STATUS s } }
          ELSE ( S_STATUS_DURING WHERE S# = S# ('S1')
                                  AND dn ∈ DURING ) { STATUS }
END IF
```

Note the tuple- and scalar-valued WITH expressions in this alternative formulation (to be specific, the name *t* in the example denotes a tuple value, and the names *s* and *d* denote scalar values). Note also that the formulation relies (as the previous one did not) on the strong, and in general unwarranted, assumption that there is exactly one tuple for supplier S1 in relvar S_SINCE. The previous formulation is to be preferred.

Query Q2: Get pairs of supplier numbers such that the indicated suppliers were assigned some status on the same day.

The complication here is that relvar S_SINCE might show some supplier S*x* as having been assigned some *current* status on day *d* and relvar S_STATUS_DURING might show some other supplier S*y* as having been assigned some *historical* status on that same day *d*. (Analogous remarks apply to Queries Q3 through Q6 as well, as we will see.) Hence:

```
WITH ( EXTEND S_STATUS_DURING
         ADD BEGIN ( DURING ) AS STATUS_SINCE )
                            { S#, STATUS_SINCE } AS T1 ,
      ( T1 UNION S_SINCE { S#, STATUS_SINCE } ) AS T2 ,
      ( T2 RENAME S# AS X# ) AS T3 ,
      ( T2 RENAME S# AS Y# ) AS T4 ,
      ( T3 JOIN T4 ) AS T5 ,
      ( T5 WHERE X# < Y# ) AS T6 :
T6 { X#, Y# }
```

Query Q3: Get supplier numbers for suppliers who were able to supply both part P1
and part P2 at the same time.

```
WITH ( EXTEND SP_SINCE
         ADD INTERVAL_DATE ( [ SINCE : LAST_DATE ( ) ] )
         AS DURING ) { S#, P#, DURING } AS T1 ,
      ( SP_DURING UNION T1 ) AS T2 ,
      ( T2 WHERE P# = P# ('P1') ) { S#, DURING } AS T3 ,
      ( T2 WHERE P# = P# ('P2') ) { S#, DURING } AS T4 ,
      ( USING DURING ◄ T3 JOIN T4 ► ) AS T5 :
T5 { S# }
```

Query Q4: Get supplier numbers for suppliers who were never able to supply both part
P1 and part P2 at the same time.

```
WITH ( EXTEND SP_SINCE
         ADD INTERVAL_DATE ( [ SINCE : LAST_DATE ( ) ] )
         AS DURING ) { S#, P#, DURING } AS T1 ,
      ( SP_DURING UNION T1 ) AS T2 ,
      ( T2 WHERE P# = P# ('P1') ) { S#, DURING } AS T3 ,
      ( T2 WHERE P# = P# ('P2') ) { S#, DURING } AS T4 ,
      ( USING DURING ◄ T3 JOIN T4 ► ) AS T5 :
S_DURING { S# } MINUS T5 { S# }
```

Query Q5: Get supplier numbers for suppliers who, while they were under some specific contract, changed their status since they most recently became able to supply some
part under that contract.

```
WITH ( EXTEND S_SINCE
         ADD INTERVAL_DATE ( [ S#_SINCE : LAST_DATE ( ) ] )
         AS DURING ) { S#, DURING } AS T1 ,
      ( T1 UNION S_DURING ) AS T2 ,
```

```
        ( EXTEND S_SINCE
          ADD INTERVAL_DATE ( [ STATUS_SINCE : LAST_DATE ( ) ] )
          AS DURING ) { S#, STATUS, DURING } AS T3 ,
        ( T3 UNION S_STATUS_DURING ) AS T4 ,
        ( EXTEND SP_SINCE
          ADD INTERVAL_DATE ( [ SINCE : LAST_DATE ( ) ] )
          AS DURING ) AS T5 ,
        ( T5 UNION SP_DURING ) AS T6 ,
        ( T4 RENAME DURING AS X ) { S#, X } AS T7 ,
        ( T6 RENAME DURING AS Y ) { S#, Y } AS T8 ,
        ( S_DURING JOIN T7 ) AS T9 ,
        ( T9 WHERE X ⊆ DURING ) AS T10 ,
        ( T10 JOIN T8 ) AS T11 ,
        ( T11 WHERE Y ⊆ DURING ) AS T12 ,
        ( SUMMARIZE T12 PER T12 { S#, DURING } ADD
          ( MAX ( BEGIN ( X ) ) AS BXMAX ,
            MAX ( BEGIN ( Y ) ) AS BYMAX ) ) AS T13 ,
        ( T13 WHERE BXMAX > BYMAX ) AS T14 :
   T14 { S# }
```

Query Q6: Get intervals during which at least one supplier was under contract.

```
WITH ( EXTEND S_SINCE
         ADD INTERVAL [ S#_SINCE : LAST_DATE ( ) ]
         AS DURING ) AS T1 ,
       ( T1 { S#, DURING } UNION S_DURING ) AS T2 :
   USING DURING ◄ T2 { DURING } ►
```

Query Q7: Suppose the result of Query Q6 is kept as a relvar BUSY. Use relvar BUSY to get intervals during which no supplier was under contract at all.

```
   USING DURING ◄ RELATION { TUPLE { DURING INTERVAL_DATE
                     ( [ FIRST_DATE ( ) : LAST_DATE ( ) ] ) } }
                 MINUS BUSY ►
```

This expression is identical to its counterpart in the previous section.

Query Q8: Get supplier numbers for suppliers currently under contract who also had an earlier contract.

```
   ( S_SINCE JOIN S_DURING ) { S# }
```

Query Q9: Get S#-PARTS-DURING triples such that the indicated supplier was able to supply the indicated range of parts during the indicated interval.

```
WITH ( EXTEND SP_SINCE ADD
          ( INTERVAL_P# ( [ P# : P# ] ) AS PARTS ,
            INTERVAL_DATE ( [ SINCE : LAST_DATE ( ) ] )
                                        AS DURING ) ) AS T1 ,
      T1 { S#, PARTS, DURING } AS T2 ,
      ( EXTEND SP_DURING
        ADD INTERVAL_P# ( [ P# : P# ] ) AS PARTS ) AS T3 ,
      T3 { S#, PARTS, DURING } AS T4 :
USING ( PARTS, DURING ) ◄ T3 UNION T4 ►
```

13.5 VIRTUAL RELVARS CAN HELP

It is undeniable that several of the query formulations shown in the previous section were fairly complicated: more complicated, in all likelihood, than some users will be prepared to deal with. Yet the database we were discussing in that section was based on the design that we have said repeatedly was the one we preferred! In this section, we explore the possibility of making the user's life a little easier by predefining a suitable collection of *views* for that database—or what, following reference [43], we prefer to call, more formally, not views but *virtual relvars*.

Broadly speaking, the virtual relvars we have in mind have the effect of conceptually undoing the horizontal and vertical decompositions described in Chapter 10. Of course, it is important to understand that the decompositions are indeed only *conceptually* undone; the relvars that result do have the effect of making certain queries easier to state, but they do not actually contravene the design recommendations of Chapter 10. (Indeed, what we are proposing here is a perfectly standard technique. For example, given the original—that is, nontemporal—version of the suppliers-and-shipments database as shown in Figures 1.1 and 1.2 in Chapter 1, we might well want to define the join of suppliers and shipments as a virtual relvar in order to simplify the formulation of certain queries, even though that virtual relvar will not be fully normalized.)

Unfortunately, our running example is a little too simple to illustrate the foregoing ideas properly, so we need to extend that example slightly. Let us therefore bring back *supplier city* information[1] by reinstating attributes CITY and CITY_SINCE in relvar S_SINCE and also reinstating relvar S_CITY_DURING, with its attributes S#, CITY, and DURING:

---

1. We will make no reference to that information in our sample queries, but it helps to make the process of defining the virtual relvars a little more realistic (especially in the case of virtual relvar S″).

```
S_SINCE { S#,     S#_SINCE,
          STATUS, STATUS_SINCE,
          CITY,   CITY_SINCE }
        KEY { S# }

S_CITY_DURING { S#, CITY, DURING }
              KEY { S#, DURING }
```

Providing some sample data values for these relvars is left as an exercise.

Now we can explain exactly the virtual relvars we have in mind. First, we define four virtual relvars S_DURING′, S_STATUS_DURING′, S_CITY_DURING′, and SP_DURING′ that effectively combine current and historical information, thereby undoing the original *horizontal* decompositions:

```
VAR S_DURING' VIRTUAL
    S_DURING UNION
  ( EXTEND S_SINCE
    ADD INTERVAL_DATE ( [ S#_SINCE : LAST_DATE ( ) ] )
    AS DURING ) { S#, DURING } ;

VAR S_STATUS_DURING' VIRTUAL
    S_STATUS_DURING UNION
  ( EXTEND S_SINCE
    ADD INTERVAL_DATE ( [ STATUS_SINCE : LAST_DATE ( ) ] )
    AS DURING ) { S#, STATUS, DURING } ;

VAR S_CITY_DURING' VIRTUAL
    S_CITY_DURING UNION
  ( EXTEND S_SINCE
    ADD INTERVAL_DATE ( [ CITY_SINCE : LAST_DATE ( ) ] )
    AS DURING ) { S#, CITY, DURING } ;

VAR SP_DURING' VIRTUAL
    SP_DURING UNION
  ( EXTEND SP_SINCE
    ADD INTERVAL_DATE ( [ SINCE : LAST_DATE ( ) ] )
    AS DURING ) { S#, P#, DURING } ;
```

NOTE: The **Tutorial D** syntax for defining a virtual relvar was given in Chapter 1, at the end of Section 1.7. Note that there is no need to specify "U_unions" rather than regular unions in the virtual relvar definitions just shown, because in no case will the two UNION operands involve tuples that (1) are identical except for their DURING components and (2) are such that their DURING components meet or overlap.

Next, we define a virtual relvar S″ that effectively combines supplier status and city information, thereby undoing the original *vertical* decomposition:

```
VAR S'' VIRTUAL
    USING DURING ◄ S_STATUS_DURING' JOIN S_CITY_DURING' ► ;
```

There is no need to include S_DURING′ in the join here, because every {S#,DURING} value that appears in S_DURING′ also appears in both S_STATUS_DURING′ and S_CITY_DURING′ and vice versa (why?), and so no information would be added (or lost) if S_DURING′ were included.

For completeness, let us also define a virtual relvar SP″ that effectively does for shipments what S″ does for suppliers:

```
VAR SP'' VIRTUAL
    SP_DURING' ;
```

Since shipments were in fact never vertically decomposed, the virtual relvars SP″ and SP_DURING′ are identical, of course.

Figure 13.4 shows the structure, in outline, of all of these virtual relvars. Note the U_key specifications in particular. As an exercise, you might like to try stating the corresponding predicates (for all of the virtual relvars shown). You might also like to think about any foreign U_key relationships that might exist among the virtual relvars in the figure.

FIGURE 13.4

Structure of the virtual relvars.

```
S_DURING' { S#, DURING }
    USING DURING KEY { S#, DURING }

S_STATUS_DURING' { S#, STATUS, DURING }
    USING DURING KEY { S#, DURING }

S_CITY_DURING' { S#, CITY, DURING }
    USING DURING KEY { S#, DURING }

SP_DURING' { S#, P#, DURING }
    USING DURING KEY { S#, P#, DURING }

S'' { S#, STATUS, CITY, DURING }
    USING DURING KEY { S#, DURING }

SP'' { S#, P#, DURING }
    USING DURING KEY { S#, P#, DURING }
```

We now proceed to reconsider Queries Q1 through Q10 in terms of these virtual relvars (Queries Q11 and Q12 remain unchanged, of course).

Query Q1: Get the status of supplier S1 on day *dn* (you can assume that supplier S1 is represented in the database).

This one is now very easy:

```
( S'' WHERE S# = S# ('S1') AND dn ∈ DURING ) { STATUS }
```

NOTE: We could have specified relvar S_STATUS_DURING′ in place of relvar S″—it would make no difference to the result.

Query Q2: Get pairs of supplier numbers such that the indicated suppliers were assigned some status on the same day.

```
WITH ( EXTEND S_STATUS_DURING'
       ADD BEGIN ( DURING ) AS STB ) { S#, STB } AS T1 ,
     ( T1 RENAME S# AS X# ) AS T2 ,
     ( T1 RENAME S# AS Y# ) AS T3 ,
     ( T2 JOIN T3 ) AS T4 ,
     ( T4 WHERE X# < Y# ) AS T5 :
T5 { X#, Y# }
```

This expression is very similar to the one shown for this query in Section 13.4, except that (1) the reference to relvar S_STATUS_DURING has been replaced by one to relvar S_STATUS_DURING′ instead, and (2) there is now no explicit reference to relvar S_SINCE at all, of course. Observe in particular that there is now no need to give special attention to current information, as we had to do in Section 13.4.

Query Q3: Get supplier numbers for suppliers who were able to supply both part P1 and part P2 at the same time.

```
WITH ( SP'' WHERE P# = P# ('P1') ) { S#, DURING } AS T1 ,
     ( SP'' WHERE P# = P# ('P2') ) { S#, DURING } AS T2 ,
     ( USING DURING ◄ T1 JOIN T2 ► ) AS T3 :
T3 { S# }
```

This expression is considerably simpler than its counterpart in Section 13.4.

Query Q4: Get supplier numbers for suppliers who were never able to supply both part P1 and part P2 at the same time.

```
WITH ( SP'' WHERE P# = P# ('P1') ) { S#, DURING } AS T1 ,
     ( SP'' WHERE P# = P# ('P2') ) { S#, DURING } AS T2 ,
     ( USING DURING ◄ T1 JOIN T2 ► ) AS T3 :
S'' { S# } MINUS T3 { S# }
```

This expression too is quite a bit simpler than its counterpart in Section 13.4.

Query Q5: Get supplier numbers for suppliers who, while they were under some specific contract, changed their status since they most recently became able to supply some part under that contract.

```
WITH ( S'' RENAME DURING AS X ) { S#, X } AS T1 ,
     ( SP'' RENAME DURING AS Y ) { S#, Y } AS T2 ,
     ( S'' JOIN T2 ) AS T3 ,
     ( T3 WHERE X ⊆ DURING ) AS T4 ,
     ( T4 JOIN T2 ) AS T5 ,
     ( T5 WHERE Y ⊆ DURING ) AS T6 ,
     ( SUMMARIZE T6 PER T6 { S#, DURING } ADD
       ( MAX ( BEGIN ( X ) ) AS BXMAX ,
         MAX ( BEGIN ( Y ) ) AS BYMAX ) ) AS T7 ,
     ( T7 WHERE BXMAX > BYMAX ) AS T8 :
T8 { S# }
```

Again this expression is simpler than its counterpart in Section 13.4.

Query Q6: Get intervals during which at least one supplier was under contract.

```
USING DURING ◄ S_DURING'{ DURING } ►
```

NOTE: We could have specified relvar S″ in place of relvar S_DURING′. We could also have used a simple PACK:

```
PACK S''{ DURING } ON DURING
```

Query Q7: Suppose the result of Query Q6 is kept as a relvar BUSY. Use relvar BUSY to get intervals during which no supplier was under contract at all.

The virtual relvars obviously do not help with this query (the formulation remains as it was in Section 13.4).

Query Q8: Get supplier numbers for suppliers currently under contract who also had an earlier contract.

This query is actually *harder* to express using the virtual relvars than it was before! The original formulation from Section 13.4 is preferable.

Query Q9: Get S#-PARTS-DURING triples such that the indicated supplier was able to supply the indicated range of parts during the indicated interval.

```
WITH ( EXTEND SP_DURING'
         ADD INTERVAL_P# ( [ P# : P# ] ) AS PARTS ) AS T :
USING ( PARTS, DURING ) ◄ T { S#, PARTS, DURING } ►
```

Query Q10: Suppose the result of Query Q9 is kept as a relvar S_PARTS_DURING. Use relvar S_PARTS_DURING to get S#-P#-DURING triples such that the indicated supplier was able to supply the indicated part during the indicated interval.

The virtual relvars obviously do not help with this query (the formulation remains as it was in Section 13.4).

A Closing Remark

We close this section, and this chapter, with the observation that it might well be possible to provide the foregoing virtual relvar definitions automatically—much as the *real* relvar definitions discussed in Chapter 12 (Section 12.6) might be provided automatically. We will have more to say regarding this possibility in the next chapter.

EXERCISE

1. Write **Tutorial D** expressions for the following queries on the version of the courses-and-students database discussed in Exercise 6 in Chapter 11:

   a. Get the maximum grade ever achieved by student ST1 on any course.

   b. Get student numbers for students currently enrolled in both course C1 and course C2.

   c. Get student numbers for students not currently enrolled in both course C1 and course C2.

   d. Get intervals during which at least one course was being offered.

   e. Get intervals during which no course was being offered at all.

Chapter

14

DATABASE UPDATES

14.1 INTRODUCTION

In Chapter 13 we examined what we called the nontrivial question of formulating queries against a temporal database. Now we turn our attention to the even more nontrivial question of formulating *updates* against such a database. As usual, we base most of our examples and discussions on the various versions of the suppliers-and-shipments database as described in Chapter 10, and we assume that the integrity constraints discussed in Chapters 11 and 12 are in effect. In contrast to the previous chapter, however, we make no attempt to use the same examples on every version of the database; indeed, it would not really be feasible to do so, for reasons that should become apparent as we proceed through the chapter.

We remind you that we use the generic term *update* to refer to the INSERT, DELETE, and UPDATE operators considered collectively; when we want to refer to the UPDATE operator specifically, we will set it in all uppercase as just shown. We also remind you of a couple of related points from Chapter 1:

- It does not really make sense to talk in terms of INSERTs or DELETEs or UPDATEs on individual tuples—we should really talk in terms of INSERTs or DELETEs or UPDATEs on *sets* of tuples (though the set in question might be of cardinality one, of course, or even zero).

- It also does not really make sense to talk in terms of UPDATEs on an individual tuple, or even on a set of tuples, at all; tuples, like relations, are values, and by definition values cannot be changed. What we really mean when we talk of, for example, performing an UPDATE on tuple *t* is that we are *replacing* tuple *t* (the tuple *value t,* that is) by another tuple (which is, again, a tuple *value*). Analogous remarks apply to phrases such as "updating attribute *A*" within some tuple.

Despite the foregoing, we will continue to talk from time to time in this chapter in terms of INSERTs and DELETEs and UPDATEs on individual tuples, and even in terms of UPDATEs on attributes of tuples—the practice is convenient—but it must be understood that such talk is only shorthand, and (as we said in Chapter 1) rather sloppy shorthand at that.

The structure of the chapter is as follows. Following this brief introduction, the next three sections show, first, what updates might look like on a database involving current relvars only (Section 14.2), and then what they might look like on a database involving historical relvars only (Sections 14.3 and 14.4). Next, Section 14.5 does the same for a database involving both kinds of relvars. Finally, Section 14.6 offers a few closing remarks; in particular, like the final section in the previous chapter, it briefly considers the possibility of providing a collection of predefined virtual relvars, with the aim of simplifying the formulation of certain operations that could otherwise be dauntingly complex.

14.2 CURRENT RELVARS ONLY

In this section we limit our attention to the comparatively simple case of updates on a version of the database that involves the current relvars S_SINCE and SP_SINCE only. Figure 14.1, a copy of Figure 12.2 (equivalently, Endpaper Panel 6), shows some sample values; we will base our examples on those specific values, where it makes any difference. We remind you that this database cannot represent historical information at all, other than what can be inferred from "since" values; however, it can represent future information—certainly implicitly, and possibly explicitly as well. Refer to Figure 12.3 in Chapter 12 if you need to remind yourself of the constraints that apply to this database.

One general remark that is worth making right up front is the following: Given that a database is essentially a collection of propositions—more precisely, propositions that are believed to evaluate to true—a good way to think about update operations in general is to think in terms of adding, removing, and replacing *propositions,* instead of thinking, as we more usually do, in terms of adding, removing, and replacing *tuples.* (This remark applies to the entire chapter, not just to the present section.) This shift in emphasis can be very helpful in understanding what is really going on, especially when we get to later sections of the chapter, where some of the examples are unfortunately quite complicated.

FIGURE 14.1

Current relvars
only—sample
values.

S_SINCE

S#	S#_SINCE	STATUS	STATUS_SINCE
S1	d04	20	d06
S2	d07	10	d07
S3	d03	30	d03
S4	d14	20	d14
S5	d02	30	d02

SP_SINCE

S#	P#	SINCE
S1	P1	d04
S1	P2	d05
S1	P3	d09
S1	P4	d05
S1	P5	d04
S1	P6	d06
S2	P1	d08
S2	P2	d09
S3	P2	d08
S4	P5	d14

Given the foregoing, it is convenient to begin the discussions in this section by once again restating the predicates for relvars S_SINCE and SP_SINCE (in very simplified form):

- S_SINCE: *Supplier Sx has been under contract ever since day dc and has had status st ever since day ds.*

- SP_SINCE: *Supplier Sx has been able to supply part Py ever since day d.*

The propositions we will be discussing in the rest of this section are all instantiations of one or other of these two predicates (in fact, since our examples deal primarily with relvar S_SINCE, they are usually instantiations of the first predicate specifically).

Perhaps we should add that, like the queries in Section 13.2 in the previous chapter (and for the same reason), the updates to be discussed in this particular section are sometimes not very temporal in nature.

Update U1: Add a proposition to show that supplier S9 has just been placed under contract (with effect from today), with status 15.

```
INSERT S_SINCE
    RELATION { TUPLE { S#          S# ('S9') ,
                       S#_SINCE    TODAY ( ) ,
                       STATUS      15 ,
                       STATUS_SINCE TODAY ( ) } } ;
```

EXPLANATION: Recall from Chapter 2 that the **Tutorial D** syntax for INSERT is basically:

```
INSERT R rel-exp ;
```

Here R is a relvar name and *rel-exp* is an expression that yields a relation, *r* say, of the same type as R, and the intent, loosely, is to insert the set of tuples from relation *r* into relvar R. The set of tuples from relation *r* is the *source* and relvar R is the *target*. In the example under discussion, of course, the target is relvar S_SINCE, and the source is a set containing just one tuple—namely, the single tuple contained in the relation returned by the specified relation selector invocation. (As in Chapters 12 and 13, we have assumed the availability of a niladic operator called TODAY that returns today's date.)

We now remind you of another important point: namely, that any given INSERT operation (or DELETE or UPDATE operation) is really shorthand for a certain *relational assignment*. In the case at hand, that assignment might look like this:

```
S_SINCE   :=   S_SINCE
               UNION
               RELATION { TUPLE { S#            S# ('S9') ,
                                  S#_SINCE      TODAY ( ) ,
                                  STATUS        15 ,
                                  STATUS_SINCE  TODAY ( ) } } ;
```

Now (to spell out the obvious), the INSERT in the example can be regarded as adding to the database the proposition "Supplier S9 has been under contract since day *dc* and has had status 15 since day *ds*" (where *dc* and *ds* are both whatever the date happens to be today). But suppose the proposition had specified supplier S1 instead of S9; given the sample values of Figure 14.1, the corresponding INSERT would then have failed on a candidate key (uniqueness constraint) violation. Likewise, if the value of *ds* had been less than *dc* in that proposition, the INSERT would have failed on a violation of Constraint CR6 (see Figure 12.3 in Chapter 12 for a definition of that constraint).

Update U2: Remove the proposition showing that supplier S5 is under contract.

```
DELETE S_SINCE WHERE S# = S# ('S5') ;
```

This DELETE is shorthand for a relational assignment that might look like this:

```
S_SINCE   :=   S_SINCE WHERE NOT ( S# = S# ('S5') ) ;
```

It can be regarded as removing the proposition "Supplier S5 has been under contract since day *dc* and has had status *st* since day *ds*" (where *dc*, *st*, and *ds* are whatever the S#_SINCE, STATUS, and STATUS_SINCE values happen to be for supplier S5). But suppose the proposition had specified supplier S1 instead of S5; then the corresponding DELETE would have failed on a foreign key (referential constraint) violation, because relvar SP_SINCE currently contains some tuples for supplier S1. NOTE: We assume for simplicity here and throughout the chapter that there are no "cascade delete" or similar rules in effect.

Update U3: Replace the proposition showing that supplier S1 was placed under contract on day 4 by one showing that the same supplier was placed under contract on day 3 instead.

```
UPDATE S_SINCE WHERE S# = S# ('S1')
    { S#_SINCE := d03 } ;
```

This UPDATE is shorthand for a relational assignment that might look like this:

```
S_SINCE  :=
   WITH ( S_SINCE WHERE S# = S# ('S1') ) AS T1 ,
        ( EXTEND T1 ADD d03 AS NEW_S#_SINCE ) AS T2 ,
        T2 { ALL BUT S#_SINCE } AS T3 ,
        ( T3 RENAME NEW_S#_SINCE AS S#_SINCE ) AS T4 :
   ( S_SINCE MINUS T1 ) UNION T4 ;
```

Observe that this assignment works correctly even in the special case where relvar S_SINCE contains no tuple at all for supplier S1 (to be specific, it has no effect in that case). Overall, the assignment can be regarded as replacing the proposition "Supplier S1 has been under contract since day 4 and has had status *st* since day *ds*" by the proposition "Supplier S1 has been under contract since day 3 and has had status *st* since day *ds*" (the difference is in the S#_SINCE value). More generally, an UPDATE on relvar S_SINCE involves replacing the proposition "Supplier S*x* has been under contract since day *dc* and has had status *st* since day *ds*" by the proposition "Supplier S*x*′ has been under contract since day *dc*′ and has had status *st*′ since day *ds*′." Of course, the general case can fail on a variety of constraint violations; the details are left as an exercise.

We close this section by remarking that the behavior of relvar SP_SINCE with respect to INSERT, DELETE, and UPDATE operations is not significantly different from that of relvar S_SINCE. The details are left as another exercise.

14.3 Historical Relvars Only (I)

In this section and the next, we consider updates on a version of the database that involves historical relvars only. We split the topic across two sections because we need to discuss two separate concepts under the same overall heading, "U_ updates" and multiple assignment, each of which is important in its own right. We discuss U_ updates in this section and multiple assignment in the next.

The database contains three historical relvars, S_DURING, S_STATUS_DURING, and SP_DURING. Figure 14.2, a copy of Figure 12.5 (equivalently, Endpaper Panel 7), shows some sample values for these relvars; we will base our examples on those specific values, where it makes any difference. The database is fully temporal, but does not separate current and historical information—it can represent information about the future

FIGURE 14.2

Historical relvars
only—sample
values.

S_DURING

S#	DURING
S2	[d02:d04]
S6	[d03:d05]
S7	[d03:d99]

S_STATUS_DURING

S#	STATUS	DURING
S2	5	[d02:d02]
S2	10	[d03:d04]
S6	5	[d03:d04]
S6	7	[d05:d05]
S7	15	[d03:d08]
S7	20	[d09:d99]

SP_DURING

S#	P#	DURING
S2	P1	[d02:d04]
S2	P2	[d03:d03]
S2	P5	[d03:d04]
S6	P3	[d03:d05]
S6	P4	[d04:d04]
S6	P5	[d04:d05]
S7	P1	[d03:d04]
S7	P1	[d06:d07]
S7	P1	[d09:d99]

as well as the past, but typically we have to use artificial "end-of-time" values (*d99* in Figure 14.2) to mark the end of any interval whose true end point is currently unknown. Refer to Figure 12.6 in Chapter 12 if you need to remind yourself of the constraints that apply to this database.

Here are the applicable predicates (in simplified form again):

- S_DURING: *Supplier Sx was under contract throughout interval i.*
- S_STATUS_DURING: *Supplier Sx had status st throughout interval i.*
- SP_DURING: *Supplier Sx was able to supply part Py throughout interval i.*

For simplicity, however, we will consider just relvar SP_DURING in the present section (for the most part); we will consider the other two relvars in the next section.

Update U4: Add the proposition "Supplier S2 was able to supply part P4 on day 2." The following INSERT will suffice:

```
INSERT SP_DURING
    RELATION { TUPLE
            { S# S# ('S2') ,
              P# P# ('P4') ,
              DURING INTERVAL_DATE ( [ d02 : d02 ] ) } } ;
```

But suppose the proposition had specified part P5 instead of P4. Then we cannot *just* insert the corresponding tuple into relvar SP_DURING (even though we are indeed trying to add a proposition to the database, logically speaking), because if we did, that relvar would then contain the following two tuples—

S#	P#	DURING
S2	P5	[d02:d02]

S#	P#	DURING
S2	P5	[d03:d04]

—and thus would no longer be packed on DURING.

In order to address this problem, we introduce a generalized form of INSERT—another shorthand, of course—which we refer to, informally, as U_INSERT. Here is the definition. The statement

```
USING ( ACL ) INSERT R r ;
```

is defined to be shorthand for the relational assignment[1]

```
R  :=  USING ( ACL ) ◀ R UNION r ▶ ;
```

Equivalently:

```
R  :=  PACK
          ( ( UNPACK R ON ( ACL ) )
            UNION
            ( UNPACK r ON ( ACL ) ) )
        ON ( ACL ) ;
```

It follows that U_INSERT can be thought of, loosely, as a regular INSERT of an unpacked version of the source relation into an unpacked version of the target relvar, followed by an appropriate (re)packing on that relvar. The parentheses surrounding the commalist of attribute names in the USING specification in U_INSERT can be omitted if that commalist contains just one attribute name (as usual). Also, of course, if that commalist is empty, then U_INSERT degenerates to a regular INSERT. NOTE: Remarks analogous to those in this paragraph apply to U_DELETE and U_UPDATE as well, of course (see later in this section), and we will not bother to repeat them.

To return to Update U4, the following U_INSERT will suffice regardless of whether the specified part number P*y* is P4 or P5:

---

1. As you can see, U_INSERT is defined in terms of U_UNION, just as regular INSERT is defined in terms of regular UNION. As a consequence, U_INSERT can have the arguably counterintuitive effect of decreasing the cardinality of the target relvar (see the discussion of U_UNION in Chapter 9).

```
USING DURING INSERT SP_DURING
   RELATION { TUPLE
               { S# S# ('S2') ,
                 P# P# ('Py') ,
                 DURING INTERVAL_DATE ( [ d02 : d02 ] ) } } ;
```

There is another point to be made here, however. In the case of a regular INSERT, the INSERT operation will fail if it violates some KEY constraint. In the same kind of way, a U_INSERT operation will fail if it violates some U_key constraint—more precisely, if it violates some WHEN/THEN constraint. (Of course, the same is true of a regular INSERT too.) For example, the following U_INSERT on relvar S_STATUS_DURING will fail in just such a way—

```
USING DURING INSERT S_STATUS_DURING
   RELATION { TUPLE
               { S# S# ('S2') ,
                 STATUS 20 ,
                 DURING INTERVAL_DATE ( [ d03 : d04 ] ) } } ;
```

—because the unpacked form of relvar S_STATUS_DURING (on DURING) already contains a tuple for supplier S2 and DURING = [d03:d04], with status 10. Likewise, the following U_INSERT will also fail for similar (though not identical) reasons:

```
USING DURING INSERT S_STATUS_DURING
   RELATION { TUPLE
               { S# S# ('S2') ,
                 STATUS 5 ,
                 DURING INTERVAL_DATE ( [ d02 : d03 ] ) } } ;
```

Of course, U_INSERTs can violate other kinds of constraints, too. In the particular case of a U_INSERT on relvar SP_DURING, it can fail on a foreign U_key constraint violation. For example, the following U_INSERT will fail in just such a way:

```
USING DURING INSERT SP_DURING
   RELATION { TUPLE
               { S# S# ('S2') ,
                 P# P# ('P4') ,
                 DURING INTERVAL_DATE ( [ d01 : d03 ] ) } } ;
```

(because supplier S2 was not under contract on day 1).

Update U5: Remove the proposition "Supplier S6 was able to supply part P3 from day 3 to day 5" (in other words, after the specified removal has been performed, the database should not show supplier S6 as supplying part P3 on any of days 3, 4, or 5).

Before we consider what is involved in achieving the desired effect here, we should take a moment to think about why we would ever want to remove a proposition from the database, anyway. After all, the database is supposed to contain historical records—so once a given proposition *p* has been included in the database, is not that proposition a historical record that should be kept in that database "forever"?

Well, this discussion takes us straight into the realms of "valid time vs. transaction time," of course (see Chapter 3). The fact that the database did once include proposition *p* is indeed a matter of historical fact, and that fact should indeed be kept "forever," with a transaction-time specification to indicate just when it was that the database did include that proposition. However, proposition *p* itself is *not* a matter of history; if we subsequently discover it is false (perhaps we made a mistake originally and it should never have been included in the database in the first place), then we should definitely remove it.

We will return to such matters and discuss them in depth in the next chapter. For now, let us consider how to achieve the desired effect in the case at hand. In fact, the following DELETE will suffice:

```
DELETE SP_DURING
      WHERE S# = S# ('S6')
      AND   P# = P# ('P3')
      AND   DURING = INTERVAL_DATE ( [ d03 : d05 ] ) ;
```

But suppose the proposition had specified the interval containing just day 4 (instead of the interval from day 3 to day 5). Then the corresponding DELETE statement—

```
DELETE SP_DURING
      WHERE S# = S# ('S6')
      AND   P# = P# ('P3')
      AND   DURING = INTERVAL_DATE ( [ d04 : d04 ] ) ;
```

—will have no effect (it certainly will not delete anything), because there *is* no tuple for supplier S6 and part P3 with DURING = [d04:d04] in relvar SP_DURING! In fact, of course, such a tuple appears only when we *unpack* that relvar on DURING. Clearly, therefore, we need another shorthand, which we refer to, informally, as U_DELETE. Here is the definition: The statement

```
USING ( ACL ) DELETE R WHERE p ;
```

is defined to be shorthand for the relational assignment[2]

```
R   :=   USING ( ACL ) ◄ R WHERE NOT ( p ) ► ;
```

---

2. U_DELETE is thus defined in terms of U_restrict, just as regular DELETE is defined in terms of regular restrict. As a consequence, U_DELETE can have the arguably counterintuitive effect of increasing the cardinality of the target relvar (see the discussion of U_restrict in Chapter 9).

Equivalently:

```
R   :=  PACK
            ( ( UNPACK R ON ( ACL ) ) WHERE NOT ( p ) )
        ON ( ACL ) ;
```

(If *ACL* is empty, then U_DELETE degenerates to a regular DELETE, of course.) Thus, to return to Update U5, the following U_DELETE will suffice regardless of whether the specified interval [*di:dj*] is [*d03:d05*] or [*d04:d04*]:

```
USING DURING DELETE SP_DURING
        WHERE S# = S# ('S6')
        AND   P# = P# ('P3')
        AND   POINT FROM DURING ∈
                        INTERVAL_DATE ( [ di : dj ] ) ;
```

In fact, this U_DELETE will "succeed" even if, for example, *di* is *d02*; an attempt to remove a proposition that does not exist is not usually regarded as an error. (By contrast, in today's systems, an attempt to add one that does usually *is* regarded as an error. We prefer not to legislate on such matters, however, leaving them to be decided on an implementation-by-implementation basis.)

By the way, you might be thinking that removing propositions can never cause a PACKED ON constraint to be violated, and hence that the final PACK step in the U_DELETE expansion is unnecessary. In fact, this conjecture is correct in the specific example just discussed, because the initial unpacking and subsequent repacking are performed on the basis of a single attribute only; however, it is *not* correct (in general) if the unpacking and repacking are performed on the basis of two attributes or more. Consider relvar S_PARTS_DURING from Section 5.4 once again. Suppose that relvar has the following relation as its current value:

S#	PARTS	DURING
S1	[P1:P2]	[*d01:d03*]
S1	[P3:P3]	[*d01:d02*]

Note that this relation is packed on DURING-then-PARTS, as you might care to confirm for yourself. Now consider the following U_DELETE:

```
USING ( PARTS, DURING ) DELETE S_PARTS_DURING
        WHERE DURING = INTERVAL_DATE ( [ d03 : d03 ] ) ;
```

The preliminary UNPACK on (PARTS,DURING) gives:

S#	PARTS	DURING
S1	[P1:P1]	[d01:d01]
S1	[P1:P1]	[d02:d02]
S1	[P1:P1]	[d03:d03]
S1	[P2:P2]	[d01:d01]
S1	[P2:P2]	[d02:d02]
S1	[P2:P2]	[d03:d03]
S1	[P3:P3]	[d01:d01]
S1	[P3:P3]	[d02:d02]

Deleting those tuples with DURING value [d03:d03] gives:

S#	PARTS	DURING
S1	[P1:P1]	[d01:d01]
S1	[P1:P1]	[d02:d02]
S1	[P2:P2]	[d01:d01]
S1	[P2:P2]	[d02:d02]
S1	[P3:P3]	[d01:d01]
S1	[P3:P3]	[d02:d02]

And this relation certainly does violate the constraint PACKED ON (DURING, PARTS) (and the constraint PACKED ON (PARTS, DURING) too, come to that). So it needs to be packed to just:

S#	PARTS	DURING
S1	[P1:P3]	[d01:d02]

Update U6: Replace the proposition "Supplier S2 was able to supply part P5 from day 3 to day 4" by the proposition "Supplier S2 was able to supply part P5 from day 2 to day 4" (the difference is in the interval begin point).

NOTE: The question of why we might ever want to replace a proposition is analogous to the question of why we might ever want to remove one (see the earlier discussion of Update U5). Be that as it may, the following UPDATE will suffice in the particular case at hand:

```
UPDATE SP_DURING
    WHERE  S# = S# ('S2')
    AND    P# = P# ('P5')
    AND    DURING = INTERVAL_DATE ( [ d03 : d04 ] )
  { DURING := INTERVAL_DATE ( [ d02 : d04 ] ) } ;
```

As an aside, we remark that reference [43] would allow the "attribute update" operation (i.e., the assignment) in the last line here to be expressed thus:

```
BEGIN (DURING) := d02
```

This simpler form means, loosely, that the BEGIN point of the DURING interval is to be set to *d02* while the END point is left unchanged. In the same kind of way, the assignment

```
END (DURING) := d07
```

would mean, loosely, that the END point of the interval is to be set to *d07* while the BEGIN point is left unchanged. NOTE: BEGIN (DURING) and END (DURING) are acting in these two assignments as what reference [43] calls *pseudovariables* (see Chapter 1).

Back to the example. Suppose now that the requirement had been to replace the proposition "Supplier S2 was able to supply part P5 on day 3" by the proposition "Supplier S2 was able to supply part P5 on day 2." Then the corresponding UPDATE statement—

```
UPDATE SP_DURING
    WHERE  S# = S# ('S2')
    AND    P# = P# ('P5')
    AND    DURING = INTERVAL_DATE ( [ d03 : d03 ] )
  { DURING := INTERVAL_DATE ( [ d02 : d02 ] ) } ;
```

—will have no effect (it certainly will not update anything), because there *is* no tuple for supplier S2 and part P5 with DURING = [*d03:d03*] in relvar SP_DURING. Once again, of course, we need another shorthand (U_UPDATE). Here is the definition. The statement

```
USING ( ACL ) UPDATE R WHERE p { attribute updates } ;
```

is defined to be shorthand for the relational assignment

```
R  := PACK
         ( ( ( UNPACK R ON ( ACL ) ) WHERE NOT ( p ) )
           UNION
         f ( ( UNPACK R ON ( ACL ) ) WHERE p ) )
      ON ( ACL ) ;
```

where *f* is a function that returns the relation that is the result of applying the specified *attribute updates* to its argument.[3] Of course, if *ACL* is empty, then U_UPDATE degenerates to a regular UPDATE. Thus, to return to Update U6 (revised version), the following U_UPDATE will suffice:

```
USING DURING
UPDATE SP_DURING
       WHERE S# = S# ('S2')
       AND   P# = P# ('P5')
       AND   DURING = INTERVAL_DATE ( [ d03 : d03 ] )
     { DURING := INTERVAL_DATE ( [ d02 : d02 ] ) } ;
```

Like U_INSERTs and U_DELETEs, U_UPDATEs can fail on a variety of constraint violations. The details are left as an exercise.

A Possible Problem (?)

NOTE: You should probably skip this subsection on a first reading.

You might have noticed that the U_DELETE and U_UPDATE operators as described thus far do suffer from a certain limitation, which we now proceed to discuss. Here again is the example we used to introduce the need for U_UPDATE:

Replace the proposition "Supplier S2 was able to supply part P5 on day 3" by the proposition "Supplier S2 was able to supply part P5 on day 2."

Suppose the requirement had been to perform the indicated replacement *only if the interval including day 3 during which the specified supplier S2 was able to supply the specified part P5 was at least seven days long.* (This requirement is plainly somewhat contrived, but it will suffice for our purpose.) Clearly, what we need to do is:

1. Check to see whether the specified interval was indeed at least seven days long.

2. If it was, then update the pertinent tuple appropriately.

Now, we already know that a conventional UPDATE is inadequate for this task. What is more, U_UPDATE is inadequate too! U_UPDATE begins by unpacking the target relvar, conceptually speaking; hence, if we ask for the COUNT of any DURING interval after that unpacking, the result will always be one. What we need is a way to perform the COUNT check *before* the conceptual unpacking is done.

Reference [66] describes an approach to problems like the foregoing that does not involve U_updates, as such, at all. Instead, it relies on a combination of the following:

---

3. Loosely speaking! Tightening up this definition is tedious but essentially straightforward. The details are left as an exercise.

1. A new **PORTION** specification on the regular DELETE and UPDATE statements, which effectively supports the deletion and update of specified tuples (basically those identified by the PORTION specification) in the *unpacked form* of the target relvar.

2. **Automatic repacking** of the target relvar by the system after any "PORTION" DELETE or UPDATE has been performed. In essence, the idea is to extend the semantics of the PACKED ON constraint (see Chapter 11) in such a way as to cause such repacking to be performed automatically after an INSERT or "PORTION" DELETE or UPDATE has been executed. (PORTION can be specified on a DELETE or UPDATE statement only if PACKED ON has been specified in the definition of the corresponding target relvar.) See the brief discussion of the possibility of such automatic "compensating actions" in Chapter 11, Section 11.10.

Our contrived example might look like this in a **Tutorial D** dialect of the proposals of reference [66]:

```
UPDATE SP_DURING
       WHERE S# = S# ('S2')
       AND   P# = P# ('P5')
       AND   d03 ∈ DURING
       AND   COUNT ( DURING ) ≥ 7
       PORTION { DURING = INTERVAL_DATE ( [ d03 : d03 ] ) }
     { DURING := INTERVAL_DATE ( [ d02 : d02 ] ) } ;
```

EXPLANATION: First, relvar SP_DURING is restricted to just those tuples for supplier S2 and part P5 for which the DURING interval includes day 3 and is at least seven days long. The result of that restriction is then unpacked on DURING, thanks to the appearance of DURING = ... in the PORTION specification; the updating assignments are then performed on exactly the tuples of the unpacked form (actually just one tuple, in the example) identified by the PORTION specification;[4] and finally, the necessary repacking is performed.

Note carefully that the UPDATE statement in the foregoing example is a regular UPDATE (except that it includes a PORTION specification), not a U_UPDATE.

By way of a second example, consider this requirement (again somewhat contrived, but never mind): Replace every proposition of the form "Supplier S*x* was able to supply part P8 throughout interval *i*" by one of the form "Supplier S*x* was able to supply part P9 throughout interval *i*"—but only if interval *i* overlaps the interval [*d05:d08*], and then perform the replacement only for that part of interval *i* that overlaps the interval [*d02:d06*]. Here is a possible **Tutorial D** formulation using PORTION:

---

4. This example does not illustrate the point, but in general another packing is required before the updating assignments are done. See the third example in this discussion.

```
UPDATE SP_DURING
      WHERE P# = P# ('P8')
      AND   DURING OVERLAPS INTERVAL_DATE ( [ d05:d08 ] ) )
      PORTION { DURING = INTERVAL_DATE ( [ d02:d06 ] ) }
      { P# := P# ('P9') } ;
```

For a third and final example, suppose relvar S_DURING currently looks like this:

S#	DURING
S1	[d03:d10]
S2	[d02:d05]

Consider the following requirement: Replace the proposition "Supplier S1 was under contract from day 4 to day 8 inclusive" by the proposition "Supplier S2 was under contract from day 6 to day 7 inclusive."[5] Here is a possible formulation using PORTION:

```
UPDATE S_DURING WHERE S# = S# ('S1')
      PORTION { DURING = INTERVAL_DATE ( [ d04:d08 ] ) }
      { S# := S# ( 'S2' ) ,
        DURING := INTERVAL_DATE ( [ d06:d07 ] ) } ;
```

Result:

S#	DURING
S1	[d03:d03]
S1	[d09:d10]
S2	[d02:d07]

As already indicated, however, the PORTION approach does rely on the idea of "compensating actions" (i.e., the automatic repacking). For reasons explained in Chapter 11, Section 11.10 (among others), we prefer not to require the system to support compensating actions (though we do not necessarily prohibit them, of course). Thus, we would prefer to find a way to deal with the kinds of complex updates we have been considering that does not require such actions.

---

5. It might well be argued that this example is not merely contrived but goes beyond the bounds of reasonableness, since *no term* in the new proposition is the same as its counterpart in the old one! ("Term" is being used here in a slightly technical sense.) After all, the idea of updating a tuple in such a way that *every component* is changed is usually looked at a trifle askance, even in nontemporal databases.

One approach would be just to insist that such updates be done by means of explicit relational assignments instead of by means of some shorthand. Here for example is a "pure relational assignment" formulation of the same example:

```
S_DURING   :=
WITH ( RELATION
     { TUPLE { S# S# ('S1'),
                 DURING INTERVAL_DATE ( [ d04:d08 ] ) } } )
     AS T1 ,
     ( RELATION
     { TUPLE { S# S# ('S2'),
                 DURING INTERVAL_DATE ( [ d06:d07 ] ) } } )
     AS T2 ,
     ( USING DURING ◄ S_DURING MINUS T1 ► ) AS T3 :
     ( USING DURING ◄ S_DURING UNION T3 ► ) ;
```

However, if "support for complex updates" turns out to be a major requirement, a better approach (as so often) would be to define a suitable shorthand. For example,[6] we might define the statement

```
UPDATE R WHERE p PORTION { A = a } { B := b } ;
```

to be shorthand for the relational assignment

```
R   :=   WITH ( R WHERE p ) AS T1 ,
              ( UNPACK T1 ON A ) AS T2 ,
              ( T2 WHERE A OVERLAPS a ) AS T3 ,
              ( PACK T3 ON A ) AS T4 ,
              ( EXTEND T4 ADD b AS B' ) AS T5 ,
                T5 { ALL BUT B } AS T6 ,
              ( T6 RENAME B' AS B ) AS T7 ,
              ( USING A ◄ R MINUS T4 ► ) AS T8 :
                USING A ◄ T7 UNION T8 ► ;
```

Here:

- A and B are attributes, and A, at least, is of some interval type.

- a and b are expressions of the appropriate types.

- The PORTION specification can be extended to allow an arbitrary nonempty commalist of entries of the form shown.

---

6. We say "for example" because other approaches, beyond the scope of the present discussion, might be possible.

- The second pair of braces can also include an arbitrary nonempty commalist of entries of the form shown (as in fact we already know).

- The *A*'s in the PORTION specification and the *B*'s in the second pair of braces are not necessarily distinct.

Using this shorthand, the third example (page 281) can be expressed as follows:

```
UPDATE S_DURING WHERE S# = S# ('S1')
       PORTION { DURING = INTERVAL_DATE ( [ d04:d08 ] ) }
    { S# := S# ( 'S2' ) ,
      DURING := INTERVAL_DATE ( [ d06:d07 ] ) } ;
```

As you can see, this formulation is identical to the previous "PORTION" formulation of the same problem. *However, the semantics are different.* The previous formulation required S_DURING to be subject to a PACKED ON constraint, and the necessary repacking was performed as a "compensating action," thanks to the extended semantics of that constraint. The present formulation, by contrast, does not require S_DURING to be subject to a PACKED ON constraint (even though it in fact is); rather, the necessary repacking is performed because it is explicitly requested in the expanded form of the operation.

An analogous "PORTION" form of DELETE could also be defined if desired.

14.4 HISTORICAL RELVARS ONLY (II)

Now we turn to the question of updating the historical relvars S_DURING and S_STATUS_DURING. First we remind you of the design of the relevant portions of the database:

```
S_DURING { S#, DURING }
   USING DURING KEY { S#, DURING }
   USING DURING FOREIGN KEY { S#, DURING }
               REFERENCES S_STATUS_DURING

S_STATUS_DURING { S#, STATUS, DURING }
   USING DURING KEY { S#, DURING }
   USING DURING FOREIGN KEY { S#, DURING }
               REFERENCES S_DURING
```

Note in particular that each of these relvars involves a foreign U_key that references the other: The one in relvar S_STATUS_DURING reflects the fact that any supplier that has some status at some time must be under contract at that time, and the one in relvar S_DURING reflects the fact that any supplier under contract at some time must have some status at that time (recall the discussion of denseness constraints in Chapter 12).

Update U7 *(same as Update U1):* Add the necessary proposition(s) to show that supplier S9 has just been placed under contract (with effect from today), with status 15.

The following code will suffice:

```
INSERT S_DURING RELATION { TUPLE
    { S#      S# ('S9') ,
      DURING INTERVAL_DATE ( [ TODAY ( ) : d99 ] ) } } ,

INSERT S_STATUS_DURING RELATION { TUPLE
    { S#      S# ('S9') ,
      STATUS 15 ,
      DURING INTERVAL_DATE ( [ TODAY ( ) : d99 ] ) } } ;
```

EXPLANATION: Obviously enough, we need two INSERTs here: The target relvars are S_DURING and S_STATUS_DURING, respectively, and the corresponding source expressions are simple relation selector invocations. *Note carefully, however, that the two INSERTs are separated by a comma, not a semicolon, and are thereby bundled into a single statement.* That statement in turn is shorthand for a **multiple assignment**[7] that might look like this (again, note the comma):

```
S_DURING
    := S_DURING UNION RELATION { TUPLE
        { S#      S# ('S9') ,
          DURING INTERVAL_DATE ( [ TODAY ( ) : d99 ] ) } } ,

S_STATUS_DURING
    := S_STATUS_DURING UNION RELATION { TUPLE
        { S#      S# ('S9') ,
          STATUS 15 ,
          DURING INTERVAL_DATE ( [ TODAY ( ) : d99 ] ) } } ;
```

The semantics are as follows:

- First (i.e., before any assignments are done), the source expressions are evaluated.

- Second, the individual assignments are executed in sequence as written.

The net effect is thus that relvars S_DURING and S_STATUS_DURING are updated "simultaneously"—that is, both relvar updates occur as part of the same statement execution. Observe that those relvar updates *must* be part of the same statement execution for at least the following two reasons:

---

7. We mentioned (and illustrated the use of) multiple assignment in passing in Chapter 1 and defined it in Chapter 2, but this is the first time we have really needed to use it.

- First, as already noted, each of the two relvars has a foreign U_key that references the other; thus, if either were updated without the other, a constraint violation would occur.

- Second, we need to guarantee that the two invocations of TODAY both return the same value.

Update U8: Remove the proposition(s) showing that supplier S7 has been under contract. Again a multiple-assignment update is needed:

```
DELETE SP_DURING WHERE S# = S# ('S7') ,

DELETE S_STATUS_DURING WHERE S# = S# ('S7') ,

DELETE S_DURING WHERE S# = S# ('S7') ;
```

(The first comma here could be replaced by a semicolon, but the second could not.) Here is the overall expansion in terms of relational assignment:

```
SP_DURING          :=   SP_DURING
                        WHERE NOT ( S# = S# ('S7') ) ,

S_STATUS_DURING    :=   S_STATUS_DURING
                        WHERE NOT ( S# = S# ('S7') ) ,

S_DURING           :=   S_DURING
                        WHERE NOT ( S# = S# ('S7') ) ;
```

Update U9 *(similar to Update U2, but note the different wording):* Supplier S7's contract has just been terminated. Update the database accordingly.

Update U2 (on a semitemporal database) involved a DELETE operation. Update U9, by contrast (on a fully temporal database), involves UPDATE operations instead:

```
UPDATE S_DURING WHERE S# = S# ('S7')
                AND TODAY ( ) ∈ DURING
    { END ( DURING ) := TODAY ( ) } ,

UPDATE S_STATUS_DURING WHERE S# = S# ('S7')
                       AND TODAY ( ) ∈ DURING
    { END ( DURING ) := TODAY ( ) } ,

UPDATE SP_DURING WHERE S# = S# ('S7')
                 AND TODAY ( ) ∈ DURING
    { END ( DURING ) := TODAY ( ) } ;
```

Note the use of syntax that assigns directly to "END (DURING)" in this example (we explained this syntactic style under the discussion of Update U6, near the end of the previous section). More important, note that the "removal" of certain propositions here is being done by means of UPDATE operations! (The propositions in question all have to do with the notion that supplier S7 is under contract until "the last day.") Indeed, it is often the case in a fully temporal database that there is no simple correspondence between adding or removing or replacing *propositions* and adding or removing or replacing *tuples*. Several examples in the next section will also illustrate this point.

Here for purposes of reference is the expanded form of the first (only) of the three foregoing UPDATE operations:

```
S_DURING  :=
   WITH ( S_DURING WHERE S# = S# ('S7')
                    AND TODAY ( ) ∈ DURING ) AS T1 ,
          ( EXTEND T1
            ADD INTERVAL_DATE ( [ BEGIN ( DURING ) :
                                       TODAY ( ) ] )
            AS NEW_DURING ) AS T2 ,
          T2 { ALL BUT DURING } AS T3 ,
          ( T3 RENAME NEW_DURING AS DURING ) AS T4 :
       ( S_DURING MINUS T1 ) UNION T4 ;
```

We close this section by spelling out the point explicitly that (of course) any of the individual updates in a multiple assignment can be a "U_" update.

14.5 BOTH CURRENT AND HISTORICAL RELVARS

Now we turn to our preferred version of the database, which involves both current and historical relvars. Figure 14.3, a copy of Figure 12.8 (equivalently, Endpaper Panel 8), shows some sample values; we will base our examples on those specific values, where it makes any difference. The database is fully temporal, of course—it keeps current information in the "since" relvars S_SINCE and SP_SINCE and historical information in the "during" relvars S_DURING, S_STATUS_DURING, and SP_DURING. Refer to Figure 12.9 in Chapter 12 if you need to remind yourself of the constraints that apply to this database.

We remind you that the "during" relvars do not contain any information regarding the present or the future; that is, no END(DURING) value is ever greater than the date yesterday. However, the "since" relvars certainly do include implicit information about the future, and they might include explicit future information as well.

FIGURE 14.3

Both current and
historical relvars—
sample values.

S_SINCE

S#	S#_SINCE	STATUS	STATUS_SINCE
S1	d04	20	d06
S2	d07	10	d07
S3	d03	30	d03
S4	d04	20	d08
S5	d02	30	d02

SP_SINCE

S#	P#	SINCE
S1	P1	d04
S1	P2	d05
S1	P3	d09
S1	P4	d05
S1	P5	d04
S1	P6	d06
S2	P1	d08
S2	P2	d09
S3	P2	d08
S4	P5	d05

S_DURING

S#	DURING
S2	[d02:d04]
S6	[d03:d05]

SP_DURING

S#	P#	DURING
S2	P1	[d02:d04]
S2	P2	[d03:d03]
S3	P5	[d05:d07]
S4	P2	[d06:d09]
S4	P4	[d04:d08]
S6	P3	[d03:d03]
S6	P3	[d05:d05]

S_STATUS_DURING

S#	STATUS	DURING
S1	15	[d04:d05]
S2	5	[d02:d02]
S2	10	[d03:d04]
S4	10	[d04:d04]
S4	25	[d05:d07]
S6	5	[d03:d04]
S6	7	[d05:d05]

Here are the applicable predicates (in simplified form once again):

- S_SINCE: *Supplier Sx has been under contract ever since day dc and has had status st ever since day ds.*

- SP_SINCE: *Supplier Sx has been able to supply part Py ever since day d.*

- S_DURING: *Supplier Sx was under contract throughout interval i.*

- S_STATUS_DURING: *Supplier Sx had status st throughout interval i.*

- SP_DURING: *Supplier Sx was able to supply part Py throughout interval i.*

Update U10: Add the proposition "Supplier S4 has been able to supply part P4 since day 10."

The following INSERT will suffice:

```
INSERT SP_SINCE
       RELATION { TUPLE { S#    S# ('S4') ,
                          P#    P# ('P4') ,
                          SINCE d10 } } ;
```

But suppose the proposition had specified day 9 instead of day 10; given the sample values of Figure 14.3, the corresponding INSERT would then have failed on a violation of Constraint BR7_8 (actually on the "BR8" portion of that constraint; see Figure 12.9 in Chapter 12). That constraint, to remind you, is intended to enforce the requirement that if the database shows supplier Sx as able to supply the same part Py on days d and $d+1$, then it must contain exactly one tuple that shows that fact. In the case at hand, if the INSERT were permitted, relvars SP_SINCE and SP_DURING would then respectively contain the following tuples—

S#	P#	SINCE
S4	P4	d09

S#	P#	DURING
S4	P4	[d04:d08]

—and would thereby violate the constraint.

To add that revised proposition, therefore, we need to do the following:

- Delete the tuple for S4 and P4 with DURING = [d04:d08] from relvar SP_DURING.

- Insert a tuple for S4 and P4 with SINCE = d04 into relvar SP_SINCE.

Also, of course, these two updates need to be performed as part of the same statement execution. The following code will thus suffice:

```
DELETE SP_DURING WHERE S# = S# ('S4')
                 AND   P# = P# ('P4')
                 AND   END ( DURING ) = d08 ,

INSERT SP_SINCE
       RELATION { TUPLE { S#    S# ('S4') ,
                          P#    P# ('P4') ,
                          SINCE d04 } } ;
```

Observe now that the code just shown is, of course, specific to a certain specific update and a certain specific set of existing values in the database. Here by contrast is a block of *generic* code that will effectively add the proposition "Supplier S*x* has been able to supply part P*y* since day *d*" to the database, regardless of the specific values of S*x* and P*y* and *d* and regardless of the specific values currently existing in the database:

```
WITH ( SP_DURING WHERE S# = Sx AND P# = Py AND
                       ( IS_PRIOR_DATE ( END ( DURING ) , d ) OR
                         END ( DURING ) ≥ d ) ) AS R1 ;
IF IS_EMPTY ( R1 )
   THEN INSERT SP_SINCE RELATION { TUPLE
                                   { S# Sx, P# Py, SINCE d } } ;
   ELSE
       SP_DURING  :=  SP_DURING MINUS R1 ,
       INSERT SP_SINCE RELATION { TUPLE { S# Sx, P# Py,
          SINCE SINCE FROM ( TUPLE FROM (
       ( SUMMARIZE R1 PER R1 { S#, P# }
          ADD MIN ( BEGIN ( DURING ) ) AS SINCE ) ) ) } } ;
END IF ;
```

Points arising:

- *First and foremost, it is NOT our intent that users should actually have to write code like that just shown.* For example, it might be possible to perform such "generic updates" via appropriate views or virtual relvars (see the final section in this chapter). But our primary concern here is, as always, with fundamental concepts and principles, not so much with details of concrete syntax and the user interface as such.

- The code makes use of a **Tutorial D** feature not explicitly discussed in Chapter 2—namely, the *WITH statement.* The purpose of that statement is to introduce shorthand names for expressions and then to allow those names to be used and reused in subsequent statements. (WITH *expressions,* by contrast, allow such introduced names to be used and reused only within the expression in which those names are actually introduced.)

- The code also makes use of the IS_PRIOR_DATE operator. Just to remind you, IS_PRIOR_DATE takes two arguments *d1* and *d2* of type DATE and returns true if *d1* is the immediate predecessor of *d2* and false otherwise (see the discussion of Requirement R2 in Chapter 12, Section 12.5, if you need to refresh your memory further).

- The code also makes use of TUPLE FROM. Note our reliance in that code on the fact that we know from the context that the relation to which we are applying the TUPLE FROM operator does contain exactly one tuple! (Refer to the discussion of Query Q7 in Chapter 13, Section 13.2, if you need to refresh your memory regarding TUPLE FROM.)

- The code does not bother to check whether a tuple for supplier S*x* and part P*y* already exists in relvar SP_SINCE. If such a tuple does in fact exist, the code will fail on a candidate key constraint violation.

- Similarly, the code also does not bother to check whether a tuple for supplier S*x* exists in relvar S_SINCE. If such a tuple does not in fact exist, the code will fail on a foreign key constraint violation.

- Note that the code works correctly even if the value *d* is not just (as it was in our "day 9" example) the immediate successor of the end point of the most recent interval shown for S*x* and P*y* in SP_DURING but is in fact included within that interval, or even within some earlier interval for that same supplier and part.

- The code could be simplified slightly by omitting the PER specification from the SUMMARIZE invocation; the result of the SUMMARIZE would then involve just the single attribute SINCE instead of the three attributes S#, P#, and SINCE. (See reference [39] for further explanation of this point.)

- Finally, although it is unnecessary in the case at hand, a more general version of the code might need to use a U_MINUS operation instead of a regular MINUS as shown.

Update U11: With immediate effect, supplier S1 is no longer able to supply part P1. Update the database accordingly.

Noting from Figure 14.3 that supplier S1 has been able to supply part P1 since day 4, we see that the following code will suffice:

```
INSERT SP_DURING RELATION
   { TUPLE { S# S# ('S1'), P# P# ('P1'),
             DURING INTERVAL_DATE ( [ d04 : TODAY ( ) ] ) } } ,

DELETE SP_SINCE WHERE S# = S# ('S1') AND P# = P# ('P1') ;
```

Here is code for the general case—that is, generic code to remove the proposition "Supplier S*x* has been able to supply part P*y* since day *d*" from the database:

```
WITH ( SP_SINCE WHERE S# = Sx AND P# = Py ) AS T ;
IF NOT ( IS_EMPTY ( T ) )
THEN
   INSERT SP_DURING RELATION
   { TUPLE { S# Sx, P# Py, DURING INTERVAL_DATE
      ( [ SINCE FROM ( TUPLE FROM T ) : TODAY ( ) ] ) } } ,
   SP_SINCE  :=  SP_SINCE MINUS T ;
END IF ;
```

A more general version of the code might need to use a U_MINUS operation instead of a regular MINUS as shown.

NOTE: To return to Update U11 per se, we were making a tacit assumption that the proposition "Supplier S1 was able to supply part P1 from day 4 to day *d*" (where *d* is today) was in fact true. But suppose we discover that we simply made a mistake originally and the SP_SINCE tuple for S1 and P1 and SINCE = *d04* should never have been included in relvar SP_SINCE in the first place. Then we need to perform an appropriate DELETE on relvar SP_SINCE *without* performing a corresponding INSERT on relvar SP_DURING:

```
DELETE SP_SINCE WHERE S# = S# ('S1') AND P# = P# ('P1') ;
```

Analogous remarks apply to other updates, too: If the reason for the update is simply to correct an earlier mistake, then it might not be appropriate to perform "simultaneous updates" on other relvars. In the rest of this chapter, we will assume such "simultaneous updates" *are* appropriate and necessary—but what is appropriate and necessary in general, of course, will depend on the circumstances at hand.

Update U12: Replace the proposition "Supplier S2 has been able to supply part P1 since day 8" by the proposition "Supplier S2 has been able to supply part P1 since day 7."
The following UPDATE will suffice:

```
UPDATE SP_SINCE WHERE S# = S# ('S2') AND P# = P# ('P1')
     { SINCE := d07 } ;
```

But suppose the new SINCE value should be day 5 instead of day 7; given the sample values of Figure 14.3, the corresponding UPDATE would then have failed on a violation of Constraint BR7_8 (actually on the "BR8" portion of that constraint). For if the UPDATE were permitted, relvars SP_SINCE and SP_DURING would then respectively contain the following tuples—

S#	P#	SINCE
S2	P1	*d05*

S#	P#	DURING
S2	P1	[*d02:d04*]

—and would thereby violate the constraint. Here then is the correct code:

```
DELETE SP_DURING WHERE S# = S# ('S2') AND P# = P# ('P1')
                  AND END ( DURING ) = d04 ,

UPDATE SP_SINCE WHERE S# = S# ('S2') AND P# = P# ('P1')
     { SINCE  :=  d02 } ;
```

More generally, here is the code that will effectively replace the proposition "Supplier S*x* has been able to supply part P*y* since day *d*" by the proposition "Supplier S*x* has been able to supply part P*y* since day *d'*":

```
WITH ( SP_DURING WHERE S# = Sx AND P# = Py AND
                      ( IS_PRIOR_DATE ( END ( DURING ) , d ) OR
                        END ( DURING ) ≥ d ) ) AS R1 ;
IF IS_EMPTY ( R1 )
   THEN UPDATE SP_SINCE WHERE S# = Sx AND P# = Py
            { SINCE := d' } ;
   ELSE
        SP_DURING  :=  SP_DURING MINUS R1 ,
        UPDATE SP_SINCE WHERE S# = Sx AND P# = Py
           { SINCE := SINCE FROM ( TUPLE FROM (
           ( SUMMARIZE R1 PER R1 { S#, P# }
             ADD MIN ( BEGIN ( DURING ) ) AS SINCE ) ) ) } ;
END IF ;
```

As you can see, this code is very similar to the generic "insert" code shown earlier under Update U10, except that the two INSERT operations in that code have been replaced by two UPDATE operations. Note that the code does assume that relvar SP_SINCE already includes a tuple for supplier Sx and part Py.

We conclude this section with the following observations. First, we have addressed attempts to change the SINCE component of an SP_SINCE tuple (loosely speaking), but not attempts to change either the S# or the P# component. We leave it as an exercise to determine that considerations essentially similar to those already discussed apply in these cases too. If you want to try this exercise, we suggest you consider the following examples (expressed as usual in terms of the sample values from Figure 14.3):

1. Replace the P# component of the SP_SINCE tuple for S4 and P5 by P4;

2. Replace the S# component of the SP_SINCE tuple for S1 and P4 by S4.

Second, we have considered updates affecting relvars SP_SINCE and SP_DURING but not ones affecting S_SINCE, S_DURING, and S_STATUS_DURING. However, the behavior of these latter relvars with respect to updates in general is not significantly different from that of relvars SP_SINCE and SP_DURING. The details are left as another exercise.

14.6 VIRTUAL RELVARS CAN HELP

It is clear from the discussions in the foregoing sections that updating a temporal database has the potential to be a seriously complicated matter! Among other things, we have seen that it rarely seems to be possible to talk straightforwardly in terms of adding, removing, or replacing tuples, as we usually (albeit informally) do; rather, it seems to make more sense to talk in terms of adding, removing, or replacing propositions. And we have also seen in particular that if the database involves a mixture of current and historical relvars, then:

- It is often impossible to talk about just one of the three update operators (INSERT, DELETE, and UPDATE) in isolation; frequently, a database update involves, for example, an INSERT on one relvar and a DELETE on another.

- It is also often impossible to talk about updating just current relvars or just historical relvars; frequently, both current and historical relvars need to be updated "simultaneously."

So can we provide some syntactic shorthands to make life a little less daunting for the user in this potentially complex area? We believe the answer to this question is *yes*. By way of example, consider once again the following relvar definitions from Chapter 12 (Section 12.6):

```
VAR S_SINCE RELATION
  { S# S#, ... , STATUS INTEGER,
    STATUS_SINCE DATE SINCE_FOR { STATUS }
                     HISTORY_IN ( S_STATUS_DURING ) }
  KEY { S# } ;

VAR S_STATUS_DURING RELATION
  { S# S#, STATUS INTEGER, DURING INTERVAL_DATE }
  USING DURING KEY { S#, DURING } ;
```

Just to remind you, the SINCE_FOR specification in the definition of attribute STATUS_SINCE for current relvar S_SINCE informs the system that STATUS_SINCE is the "since" attribute for STATUS in that relvar. Likewise, the HISTORY_IN specification in the definition of that same attribute STATUS_SINCE informs the system that relvar S_STATUS_DURING is the corresponding historical relvar. (Also, recall that the definition of that historical relvar can probably be provided automatically.)

We now propose a further syntactic extension—to be specific, an extension to the HISTORY_IN specification of the form illustrated by the following example (note the text in boldface):

```
VAR S_SINCE RELATION
  { S# S#, ... , STATUS INTEGER,
    STATUS_SINCE DATE SINCE_FOR { STATUS }
                     HISTORY_IN ( S_STATUS_DURING )
                     COMBINED_IN ( S_STATUS_DURING' ) }
  KEY { S# } ;
```

The intent of this new specification is to cause the system to provide, automatically, a *virtual relvar definition* of the form

```
VAR S_STATUS_DURING' VIRTUAL
    S_STATUS_DURING UNION
  ( EXTEND S_SINCE
    ADD INTERVAL_DATE ( [ STATUS_SINCE : LAST_DATE ( ) ] )
    AS DURING ) { S#, STATUS, DURING } ;
```

As you will recall from Chapter 13 (Section 13.5), the effect of this definition is to undo the horizontal decomposition of supplier information with respect to status (loosely speaking). In other words, the effect, at least insofar as status information is concerned, is to make the design of Section 14.5 (which involved a mixture of current and historical relvars) look like the design of Sections 14.3 and 14.4 (which involved historical relvars only) instead. As a consequence, users should be able to request the comparatively straightforward kinds of update operations described in Sections 14.3 and 14.4 against such virtual historical relvars, and the system should be able to map those operations into the comparatively complex kinds of operations described in Section 14.5 against the underlying real current and historical relvars. We content ourselves with a single example.

Update U13: Supplier S1's status has just changed to 15. Update the database accordingly.

```
USING DURING UPDATE S_STATUS_DURING'
                WHERE  S# = S# ('S1')
                AND    POINT FROM DURING ∈
                       INTERVAL_DATE ( [ TODAY ( ) : d99 ] )
            { STATUS := 15 } ;
```

Suppose that, prior to the foregoing U_UPDATE, the virtual relvar S_STATUS_DURING′ contained the following "current" tuple (possibly other tuples as well) for supplier S1:

S#	STATUS	DURING
S1	20	[d04:d99]

Suppose too that today is day 10. After the update, then, the relvar will contain the following *two* tuples (possibly others as well) for supplier S1:

S#	STATUS	DURING
S1	15	[d10:d99]
S1	20	[d04:d09]

(More precisely, the underlying real relvars S_SINCE and S_STATUS_DURING will have been updated in such a way as to cause these two tuples to appear in S_STATUS_ DURING´.)

We conjecture that a mechanism along the foregoing lines should be sufficient for the system to be able to conceal from the user much of the complexity described in Section 14.5.

EXERCISES

1. Using the version of the courses-and-students database discussed in Exercise 6 in Chapter 11, give realistic examples (in natural language) of updates that might be required on that database. Be sure to include examples that will require (a) multiple assignment, (b) U_INSERT or U_DELETE or U_UPDATE operations, and (c) "POR-TION" specifications.

2. Given your answer to Exercise 1, write suitable **Tutorial D** statements to perform the specified updates.

3. How might virtual relvars help with Exercise 2?

Chapter

15

STATED TIMES AND LOGGED TIMES

15.1 INTRODUCTION

In this chapter, we take a closer look at the concepts of *valid time* and *transaction time,* which we first encountered in Chapter 3. By way of a quick review, consider the following simple example. Suppose our usual relvar S_DURING currently contains just one tuple for supplier S2, thus:

S#	DURING
S2	[*d02:d04*]

Then we might say, loosely, that the valid time for the proposition "Supplier S2 was under contract" is the interval from day 2 to day 4.

Now suppose further that the foregoing tuple existed in the database from time *t1* to time *t2* (only). Then we might say, again loosely, that the transaction time for the proposition "Supplier S2 was under contract from day 2 to day 4" is the interval from *t1* to *t2.*

Observe, therefore, that:

- Valid times refer to *something we currently believe to be true,* while transaction times refer to *when the database said something was true.* What is more, the two "somethings" in question are, in general, different; that is, they are two different propositions.

- Valid times and transaction times are both, more precisely, *sets* of intervals. In the example, the valid time for the proposition "Supplier S2 was under contract" is the set of intervals {[*d02:d04*]}; and if relvar S_DURING currently shows that supplier S2 was also under contract from day 6 to day 9, then the valid time for the proposition "Supplier S2 was under contract" would be the set of intervals {[*d02:d04*], [*d06:d09*]}. However, when the set of intervals that is some particular valid time or transaction time contains just one interval, we often say, informally, that the valid time or transaction time in question is just that single interval per se.

- Valid times are updatable, but transaction times are not (loosely speaking); in other words, our beliefs about history can change, but history as such cannot.

- Valid times can refer to the past, the present, or the future, but transaction times can refer only to the past and the present. (We cannot possibly say—at least, not sensibly—that *at some future time* the database said something was true.) For similar reasons, transaction times also cannot refer to a time in the past earlier than the time when the pertinent relvar was added to the database.

- All of the "times" we have been dealing with in this book prior to the present chapter have been "valid times" specifically.

All of that being said, we now remind you that there is quite a lot more to say about the valid-time and transaction-time concepts; hence this chapter. NOTE: As the title of the chapter itself suggests, one of the things we want to do is propose some better terms for the concepts, and we will do that in Section 15.4. However, there is a lot of other material that we need to cover first.

One last introductory remark: The transaction-time concept applies to all possible relvars, temporal or otherwise (obviously enough). By contrast, the valid-time concept applies only to temporal relvars, because—by definition—temporal relvars are the only ones that include valid-time attributes. The rest of this chapter explains what we mean when we say that *either* of these two concepts "applies to" some particular relvar!

15.2 A CLOSER LOOK

NOTE: The discussions that follow are, unavoidably, a little complicated (which is why we have left them to this late point in the book). *Caveat lector.*

Consider again the S_DURING tuple from the previous section:

S#	DURING
S2	*[d02:d04]*

Assume as before that:

1. This tuple denotes the proposition—let us call it *p*—"Supplier S2 was under contract from day 2 to day 4."

2. The transaction time for *p* is the interval from *t1* to *t2*.

Observe now, very carefully, that proposition *p* does *not* imply the proposition "Supplier S2 was under contract"! Rather, it implies the proposition "Supplier S2 was under contract *at some time.*" Thus, we might reasonably say that this latter proposition, like the proposition *p* from which it is derived, has transaction time the interval from *t1* to *t2*; however, we certainly cannot say the same for the proposition "Supplier S2 was under contract."

To pursue the point a little further: As a matter of fact, the proposition "Supplier S2 was under contract" is not represented in our database at all, neither explicitly nor implicitly.[1] (Note, therefore, that the valid-time concept typically applies to a proposition *that does not appear in the database.*) While an argument might be made from common sense that the proposition "There exists a time *t* such that supplier S2 was under contract at time *t*" implies the proposition "Supplier S2 was under contract," such an argument is not valid in *logic*. Here is a different example that might make the point more clearly: The proposition "All politicians are corrupt this year" does not imply the proposition "All politicians are corrupt"—not in logic, and possibly not in informal discourse either. (Even if the latter proposition is true, we nevertheless cannot conclude as much from the truth of the proposition "All politicians are corrupt this year" alone.)

---

1. To say that some proposition appears *implicitly* in the database is to say that no tuple representing that proposition appears explicitly, but that such a tuple can be derived in some way from the tuples that do appear explicitly. For example, a tuple representing the proposition "Supplier S2 was under contract on day 3" can be derived from the one representing the proposition "Supplier S2 was under contract from day 2 to day 4."

Back to the original example. Observe now that the statement "The transaction time for proposition *p* is the interval from *t1* to *t2*" is itself a proposition and can therefore be represented as a tuple:

S#	DURING	X_DURING
S2	[d02:d04]	[t1:t2]

(using X_DURING to denote transaction time). This tuple, involving as it does two distinct timestamps, one representing a valid time and the other a transaction time, is an example of what is sometimes referred to in the literature as a **bitemporal** tuple. Note carefully, however, that the valid-time timestamp in that tuple applies to one proposition and the transaction-time timestamp applies to a *different* proposition. As the example suggests, therefore, such a bitemporal tuple can be thought of, a little loosely, as a tuple that shows the transaction time *tt* of the valid time *vt* of some proposition *p*. See Section 15.5 for further discussion.

Now we turn to what is in some respects a simpler example than the ones we have been considering so far. Suppose the database includes the following tuple:

FIGURE	#_OF_SIDES
Triangle	3

The intended interpretation is "Triangles have three sides." Note in particular that, unlike our previous examples, this proposition—let us call it *q*—has no valid-time component at all. Nevertheless, we can certainly think of proposition *q* as having a valid time. To be precise, it is certainly the case that we believe now that *q* is, always was, and always will be true; thus, the valid time for *q* is *always* (i.e., "all of time," or equivalently the interval from the beginning of time to the end of time). And precisely because the valid time is indeed "all of time," there is no point in stating that valid time explicitly in the database. Thus, we can reasonably say that, in general, a proposition that is represented in the database without an explicit valid-time timestamp *implicitly* has a valid-time timestamp of "always."

Here is another example to illustrate the same point. Suppose we want to record the values of various "universal constants"—π, φ, *e*, *c*, and so on—in the database; in other words, we want to record propositions of the form "The value of universal constant *u* is *v*." Then it should be clear that, again, explicit valid-time timestamps make little sense for such propositions.

Observe next that *every* proposition that is recorded in the database has a transaction time, regardless of whether it includes an explicit valid-time timestamp. For example, if the tuple corresponding to proposition *q*—"Triangles have three sides"—is recorded in the database from time *t1* to time *t2* (only), then the transaction time for the proposition "*q* is always true" is the interval from *t1* to *t2*.

Given the foregoing, consider again the following bitemporal tuple (let us call it *bt*):

S#	DURING	X_DURING
S2	[d02:d04]	[t1:t2]

Recall that the corresponding proposition is "The transaction time for proposition *p* is the interval from *t1* to *t2*," where proposition *p* in turn is the proposition "Supplier S2 was under contract from day 2 to day 4."

Suppose now that tuple *bt* itself currently appears in the database (which, as we will see in Section 15.5, it certainly might do). Then the corresponding proposition has a valid time and a transaction time. The valid time is, implicitly, "always" (note that the proposition in question certainly has no explicit valid-time timestamp). What about the transaction time? Well, presumably tuple *bt* was—at least conceptually (again, see Section 15.5)—inserted into the database at some time $t \geq t2$; and if tuple *bt* does indeed, as stated, still *currently* appear in the database, and has done so ever since time *t*, then the transaction time for the proposition corresponding to *bt* is clearly the interval from time *t* to whatever the current time happens to be. (Recall that transaction times cannot refer to the future, so there is no question of saying the transaction time is the interval from *t* to "the end of time.")

With the foregoing examples and discussion to provide the necessary intuitive underpinnings, we can now—at last—offer some precise definitions:

- The **valid time** for a proposition *p* is the set of times *t* such that, according to what the database currently states (which is to say, according to our current beliefs), *p* is, was, or will be true at time *t*. Note that proposition *p* itself probably does not appear in the database, either explicitly or implicitly (though it might).

- The **transaction time** for a proposition *q* is the set of times *t* such that, according to what the database states or stated at time *t*, *q* is, was, or will be true. Note that the proposition *q* must have appeared in the database at some time, either explicitly or implicitly.

In a nutshell:

- Valid times are the times (past and/or present and/or future) when, *according to what we believe right now*, something is, was, or will be true.

- Transaction times are the times (past and/or present) when *the database said* we believed something is, was, or will be true.

Furthermore, we assume that (1) the valid time for any given proposition *p* is represented as a set of intervals, and that set is kept in collapsed form; (2) the transaction time for any given proposition *q* is likewise represented as a set of intervals, and that set is also kept in collapsed form.

15.3 The Database and the Log

Following on from the definitions and explanations of the previous section, we now observe that there is a significant operational difference between the valid-time and transaction-time concepts—a difference that can be characterized informally as follows:

Valid times are kept in the database, while transaction times are kept in the log.

We believe this informal characterization can be a great aid to clear thinking in this potentially confusing area, and we therefore elaborate on it in the present section.

First of all, then, note that a database is really a *variable;* the operation of "updating the database" causes the current value of that variable to be replaced by another value. The values in question are both **database values,** and the variable is a **database variable**. In other words, the crucial distinction between values and variables that we discussed in Chapter 1, both in general terms and in terms of its application to relations in particular, applies to databases as well.[2]

However, there is another way of thinking about the foregoing. To be specific, a database update can be thought of, not so much as *replacing* the current database value by another such, but rather as deriving a "new" database value from the "old" one (thereby making that new value the current value), *at the same time keeping the old value around in the system as well*. The "old" database value is, of course, the one that was current immediately prior to the update.

It follows that the overall database can be thought of as a **sequence** of database values, where each such value is timestamped with the time of the update that produced it, and the complete sequence is ordered chronologically.[3] The most recent database value in the sequence is, of course, the current one—it is the database as it appears "right now," as it were. And the *only* kind of update operation we can apply to the overall database, conceptually speaking, is the one that takes the current database value and derives from it a new value, which then becomes current in turn.

Note next that the overall sequence of database values can usefully be thought of as a **log;** after all, it is effectively an abstraction of the recovery log as implemented in real database systems, and it provides a full historical record of every update that has ever been made to the database. And the most recent log entry—the most recent data-

---

2. In this connection, consider the following (slightly edited) quote from reference [43]: "The first version of this document drew a distinction between database values and database variables, analogous to the distinction between relation values and relation variables. It also introduced the term *dbvar* as shorthand for *database variable*. While we still believe this distinction to be a valid one, we found it had little direct relevance to other aspects of these proposals. We therefore decided, in the interests of familiarity, to revert to more traditional terminology." Now this bad decision has come home to roost! With hindsight, it would have been much better to "bite the bullet" and adopt the more logically correct terms *database value* and *database variable* (or *dbvar*), despite their lack of familiarity.

3. Compare the discussions in Chapter 9, Section 9.8. Note, however, that the sequences discussed in that section were timestamped with valid times, whereas the sequence we are discussing here is timestamped with transaction times.

base value in the chronological sequence—provides a record of our current beliefs.[4] NOTE: In real systems, of course, log entries typically refer to updates at the level of individual tuples (or perhaps individual pages), not at the level of the entire database. This fact does not materially affect the discussion, however. Also, we remark in passing that the well-known concept of *point-in-time recovery* can be seen as a process that makes use of the *real* log, together with a backup copy of the database, to (re)construct one of the database values that make up our *imaginary* log.

By way of illustration, we return to the example from Section 3.3 in Chapter 3, in which a tuple showing supplier S1 as being under contract during some interval was inserted into the database at time *t1* and replaced at time *t2,* and that replacement tuple was then deleted at time *t3.* Let *t2′* and *t3′* be the timestamps of the log entries—that is, the database values—immediately preceding those for times *t2* and *t3,* respectively. Clearly, then, the log entries for times *t1* to *t2′* will include the original tuple; those for times *t2* to *t3′* will include the replacement tuple; and those from time *t3* onward will include no corresponding tuple at all. (We are assuming for the sake of the example that no tuple showing supplier S1 as being under contract appeared in the database either before time *t1* or after time *t3.*) The transaction times for the applicable propositions can thus clearly be obtained from the timestamps associated with the pertinent log entries.

What about the valid times? By now, it should be clear that these do not correspond to log-entry timestamps at all. Indeed, as we saw in Section 15.2, if *p* is a proposition to which the concept of valid time applies, we do not keep *p* (as such) in the database; rather, we keep the corresponding *timestamped extension* of *p* in the database. The timestamps in such timestamped extensions, which denote the applicable valid times, are represented by means of attributes in database relations in the usual way. Hence, valid times—by which we mean, by definition, those times that *we currently believe* to be valid—appear in *the current value* of the database, which always corresponds, again by definition, to the most recent entry in the log.

We now proceed to consider a number of further points that arise in connection with the idea that "the log is the real database." (Some of these points have been touched on or at least hinted at already, but it still seems worthwhile to bring them together and spell them out explicitly here.)

- As noted in Section 15.1, a proposition *p* might have a transaction time that consists of several discrete intervals—from *t1* to *t2,* then from *t3* to *t4,* then from *t5* to *t6,* and so on (where *t1, t2,* and so on, are all distinct). That is, times *t1, t3, t5,* etc., correspond to updates that caused *p* to appear in the database (either implicitly or explicitly), while times *t2, t4, t6,* and so on, correspond to updates that caused *p* to disappear again.

---

4. In other words (loosely): "The database is not the database—the log is the database, and the database is just an optimized access path to the most recent version of the log." The thought expressed by this aphorism is a piece of folklore that has been circulating in the database community for a long time. It appears to have its origin in a paper by Schueler [85].

- Likewise, a proposition *q* might have a valid time that consists of several discrete intervals. Here, however, the intervals concerned are simply values that currently appear in the database. For example, suppose relvar S_DURING contains just the following two tuples for supplier S2:

S#	DURING
S2	[d02:d04]

S#	DURING
S2	[d06:d09]

Then the valid time for the proposition "Supplier S2 was under contract" is the set of intervals {[d02:d04], [d06:d09]}.

- As our examples and definitions have clearly indicated—note in particular the fact that the definitions are asymmetric—if *p* is a proposition to which the valid-time concept applies and *q* is a proposition to which the transaction-time concept applies, then *p* and *q* are typically not the same proposition. Certainly it seems to be hard to find a *nontrivial* proposition that has both a *nontrivial* associated valid time and a *nontrivial* associated transaction time.

- You might be surprised to learn that, in a way, valid times are less interesting than transaction times. Why so? Well, we have seen that valid times are represented by means of attributes of database relations in the usual way. They can thus certainly be queried. Furthermore, we can of course have *relvars* with valid-time attributes too, and valid times can thus be updated as well as queried (loosely speaking); that is, valid times can be changed to reflect changing beliefs. In principle, therefore, valid-time attributes are not significantly different from database attributes of any other kind, at least insofar as their ability to participate in query or update operations is concerned.

  What about transaction times? Well, if transaction times are really based on log-entry timestamps as we have suggested, then it should be clear that (unlike valid times) they are maintained by the system, not by users. Indeed, we pointed out earlier that transaction times are nonupdatable, meaning (of course) that they certainly cannot be updated by users. However, users do need to be able to *query* them. For example, we might want to ask—perhaps for audit purposes— "When did the database say that supplier S2 was under contract on day 3?"

  At least two problems arise immediately from this requirement. First of all, of course, the system does not really maintain the log in the form we have been describing (i.e., as a timestamped sequence of database values); as a consequence, it is highly unlikely that the system will allow us to formulate queries against the database value at some arbitrary past time *t* directly. Second, even if we could formulate such a query, the corresponding timestamp *t* is not itself represented as part of that database value but is, rather, a kind of tag that is associated with that value; as a consequence, we still could not formulate a query—at least, not a *relational* query—that referenced that timestamp directly.

For such a query even to be expressible, therefore, the relevant timestamps, along with the information they timestamp, (1) will have to be made available in standard relational form and (2) will have to be made part of the current database value. (They have to be made part of the *current* database value specifically, because, in a sense, the current database value is the only one that "really exists," and hence the only one that can be directly queried.) Section 15.5 offers some suggestions as to how these two requirements might be satisfied in practice.

- It follows from the foregoing that—despite what we said in this connection earlier—the imaginary log that we have been talking about is best thought of, not as an abstraction of the usual recovery log, but rather as an **audit trail.** After all, its purpose is essentially to serve as a history of update events and to allow questions to be asked later about what was done to the database when, and such questions are certainly questions of an auditing nature and have little to do with recovery.

- We have been talking as if updates take effect on the database at the instant at which they are executed. In practice, of course, such is not the case; rather, updates are applied—conceptually, at least—to the database only if and when the relevant transaction reaches a successful termination. It follows that the transaction-time instant (i.e., the time point) corresponding to a particular update is not exactly the time of the update operation per se but is, rather, the time of the corresponding COMMIT operation at end-of-transaction[5] (implying among other things that several distinct updates might be associated with the same transaction-time instant). This fact might cause certain problems for the implementation. However, it has no effect on the model, and we do not discuss it further in this book.

15.4 Terminology

We have now explained the concepts of *valid time* and *transaction time* at some length. However, we do not much care for those terms, and we would like to come up with some better ones if possible. Such is the purpose of the present section.

First of all, regarding *valid time,* we have to say that we find little need to refer explicitly to the concept at all, precisely because we regard valid times as essentially just regular data. Indeed, you might have noticed that we hardly mentioned the term at all in previous chapters, even though the *concept* underpinned almost all of the discussions

---

5. In fact, it is the time of the COMMIT at the end of the *outermost* transaction, if the transaction in question is nested inside others. (Following reference [43], we do believe it must be possible for transactions to be nested inside others.)

in those chapters.[6] These facts notwithstanding, we would still like to find a term that captures, better than "valid time" does, the essence of what is really going on, so that we do have a good term to use when we find we need to refer to the concept explicitly after all. As for *transaction time,* here we definitely do need to refer to the concept by name from time to time—pun intended—and so we would definitely like to find a better term for it.

It is not worth discussing in detail here all of the various terms we considered and eventually discarded. Suffice it to say that (as the title of this chapter suggests) we finally settled on the terms *stated time* and *logged time* for valid time and transaction time, respectively. Thus:

- The **stated time**—sometimes *currently* stated time, for emphasis—for a proposition p is the set of times t such that, according to what the database currently states (which is to say, according to our current beliefs), p is, was, or will be true at time t.

- The **logged time** for a proposition q is the set of times t such that, according to what the database states or stated at time t, q is, was, or will be true.

Of course, we allow both terms to be used in either the singular or the plural—whichever seems in context to make more sense—in conjunction with any given proposition. Also, it might help to point out explicitly that:

- In the case of logged time, the variable t ranges over the set of all times from the time when the database was created up to the present time.

- In the case of stated time, the variable t ranges over the set of all times appearing explicitly or implicitly as a timestamp in the current database value.

Postscript

By way of a postscript to the foregoing, we briefly consider some definitions from the temporal database literature of the concepts we have been discussing. They (the definitions, that is) are taken from *The Consensus Glossary of Temporal Database Concepts—February 1998 Version* [53]. Italics are as in the original.

- "The *valid time* of a fact is the time when the fact is true in the modeled reality."

---

6. We speculate that it is precisely because so much of the literature espouses a nonrelational approach to temporal data that it needs to (and does) use the term *valid time* so ubiquitously. The approach in question does *not* represent valid times—nor indeed transaction times—by means of attributes in database relations in the usual way; instead, it represents them by means of what might be thought of as "hidden" attributes. As noted in Chapter 3, however, "hidden attributes" are not true relational attributes, "relations" that contain such "attributes" are not true relations, and the overall approach constitutes a clear violation of *The Information Principle.* See reference [107] for further discussion.

- "A database fact is stored in a database at some point in time, and after it is stored, it is current until it is logically deleted. The *transaction time* of a database fact is the time when the fact is current in the database and may be retrieved."

Here is our own gloss on these glossary definitions ... First of all, we observe that the term *fact,* which is mentioned several times, does not itself appear in the glossary; in ordinary English, however, facts are usually taken to be true by definition. (Indeed, a "false fact" is a contradiction in terms, and so, in the definition of valid time, "when the fact is a fact" might perhaps be more apt than "when the fact is true." But then "the fact is a fact" is a tautology.) Also, it is not clear whether any distinction is intended—and if so, what that distinction might be—between *facts* (mentioned in the valid-time definition) and *database facts* (mentioned in the transaction-time definition).

Second, the term *the modeled reality* (also not in the glossary) seems to mean what in such contexts is more usually referred to as "the real world."[7] "Valid time" thus apparently means the time when the "fact" was actually true in the real world, not (as we claimed earlier) the time when it was true *according to our current beliefs.* But if this interpretation is correct, it is not clear why the term is being defined at all. (We can operate only in terms of what we believe to be true, not in terms of any kind of "absolute" truth, and the definition seems to be saying that valid time does have to do with some kind of absolute truth.)

Third, the term *current* seems to be being used in a very strange way. Surely it would be more usual to say that something is "current in the database" if and only if that something was part of the current database value; yet this interpretation is certainly not—it *cannot* be—what is intended in the definition given for *transaction time.*

Fourth, reference [53] elsewhere defines something it calls *transaction-time lifespan:*

- "[The] transaction-time lifespan refers to the time when the database object is current in the database."

Presumably the term *database object* here is meant as a synonym for what was previously called a *database fact* (?). But what about *transaction time* and *transaction-time lifespan?* Are these terms also synonyms? If they are, then the question arises as to why there are two terms; if they are not, then what is the difference between them?

All in all, it seems to us that the definitions in reference [53] simply serve to reinforce our earlier contention that the valid-time and transaction-time concepts need *very* careful explanation, as well as more carefully chosen names. And, of course, the provision of such an explanation and such names has been our aim in this chapter, up to this point. In particular, we feel bound to say that, in our opinion, it is very hard to come up with such an explanation and such names without first facing up to the idea that a database—meaning, specifically, a database *value*—is essentially *a collection of true propositions* (instead of trying to rely on undefined and fuzzy concepts like "database facts" or "database objects").

---

7. Or does it perhaps mean not, as normal English usage would have it, "the reality *that is being* modeled" but, rather, "the *modeled version of* reality"?

15.5 Logged-Time Relvars

We pointed out in Section 15.3 that even though users cannot update logged times, they certainly must be able to query them. We also pointed out that this requirement implies that:

- Logged times must be made available (along with the data they refer to) in standard relational form.

- Moreover, they must be made available as part of the current database value.

In this section, we describe one possible way of achieving these objectives in a user-friendly fashion.

Essentially, what we propose is that if R is a relvar (and is real, not virtual), then the definition of R should be allowed to include a request for the automatic provision and maintenance of an auxiliary relvar—typically though not necessarily a "bitemporal" relvar—that gives the logged-time history for that relvar R (the "logged-time relvar" for relvar R). For example (note the boldface text):

```
VAR S_DURING RELATION
   { S# S#, DURING INTERVAL_DATE }
   .....
   LOGGED_TIMES_IN ( S_DURING_LOG ) ;
```

The effect of this specification is to cause the system to provide a relvar called S_DURING_LOG, with attributes S#, DURING, and (let us agree) X_DURING, and with tuples that together represent the logged times for all of the tuples that have ever appeared, explicitly or implicitly, in relvar S_DURING. (We will explain that "explicitly or implicitly" in just a few moments.) For example, suppose today is day 75. Then Figure 15.1 shows a possible current value for S_DURING, together with a possible corresponding value for S_DURING_LOG. (We have numbered the tuples in relvar S_DURING_LOG for purposes of subsequent reference.)

Figure 15.1

Relvars S_DURING and S_DURING_LOG —sample values.

S_DURING

S#	DURING
S2	[d02:d04]
S6	[d03:d05]

S_DURING_LOG

	S#	DURING	X_DURING
1	S2	[d02:d04]	[d04:d07]
2	S2	[d02:d04]	[d10:d20]
3	S2	[d02:d04]	[d50:d75]
4	S6	[d02:d05]	[d15:d25]
5	S6	[d03:d05]	[d26:d75]
6	S1	[d01:d01]	[d20:d30]
7	S1	[d05:d06]	[d40:d50]

EXPLANATION:

- First of all, relvar S_DURING currently says that supplier S2 was under contract from day 2 to day 4. Tuple *1* of relvar S_DURING_LOG tells us that relvar S_DURING said the same thing at an earlier time, from day 4 to day 7. Tuple *2* of relvar S_DURING_LOG tells us that relvar S_DURING also said the same thing at another earlier time, from day 10 to day 20.

- Tuple *3* of relvar S_DURING_LOG tells us that relvar S_DURING has said the same thing again—that supplier S2 was under contract from day 2 to day 4—from day 50 to the present day (i.e., day 75). Now, in Chapter 10, Section 10.5 (on "the moving point *now*"), we argued that representing "the date today" in the database by an actual value like *d75* was a bad idea. In particular, we pointed out that it implied that all of those *d75*'s would have to be replaced by *d76*'s on the stroke of midnight on day 75. However, those arguments do not apply to the present situation, because:

  - Relvar S_DURING_LOG need not actually exist at all times; it is sufficient for the system to materialize it when it is referenced in some query (and even then it should surely not be necessary to materialize it in its entirety). In other words, a helpful way to think of S_DURING_LOG is as a virtual relvar (i.e., a "view")—but not, like other virtual relvars, one that is defined in terms of other relvars in the database, but rather one that is defined in terms of the system log. Furthermore, of course, the definition of that virtual relvar in terms of the log is provided by the system, not by some human user.

  - Relvar S_DURING_LOG is updatable by the system but not by ordinary users. Thus, the process of replacing all of those *d75*'s by *d76*'s on the stroke of midnight on day 75 is carried out by the system, not by some user (and, of course, that process is probably never *physically* carried out at all).

  - In any case, the proposition "From day 50 to day 75, the database said that supplier S2 was under contract from day 2 to day 4" is true! Certainly we must not use the artificial end-of-time trick in connection with logged times that we do sometimes use in connection with stated times, because (for example) the proposition "From day 50 to *the end of time*, the database said that supplier S2 was under contract from day 2 to day 4" is false. (Recall once again that logged times can never refer to the future.)

- To continue with our explanation of Figure 15.1: Relvar S_DURING currently says that supplier S6 was under contract from day 3 to day 5. By contrast, tuple *4* of relvar S_DURING_LOG tells us that relvar S_DURING said previously (from day 15 to day 25) that supplier S6 was under contract from day 2 to day 5; however, tuple *5* of relvar S_DURING_LOG tells us that ever since day 26, relvar S_DURING has said that supplier S6 was under contract from day 3 to day 5.

- Finally, relvar S_DURING currently has nothing to say about supplier S1 at all. However, tuple *6* of relvar S_DURING_LOG tells us that relvar S_DURING did say from day 20 to day 30 that supplier S1 was under contract, on day 1 only; likewise, tuple 7 tells us that relvar S_DURING said from day 40 to day 50 that supplier S1 was under contract from day 5 to day 6. (We deduce that all information regarding supplier S1 was deleted from relvar S_DURING on day 30 and again on day 50, presumably because it was discovered to be incorrect.)

Let us summarize what we have learned so far. First, let R be a regular relvar, and let R' be the associated logged-time relvar. Also, let R have interval attributes $A1$, $A2$, ..., An, possibly with other attributes as well. Then:

- The heading of R' is the same as that of R, except that it contains an additional interval attribute called X_DURING.

- For every tuple t that has ever appeared in the fully unpacked form of relvar R (see the paragraph immediately following for an explanation of this term), relvar R' effectively contains m distinct tuples for some $m > 0$. Each such tuple consists of t extended with an X_DURING value, such that the transaction time for t (or, rather, for the proposition associated with t) is precisely the set containing just those m X_DURING values. Relvar R' is kept packed on $(A1,A2,...,An,$X_DURING$)$. By the way, observe that the packing of R' *must* be done on attribute X_DURING last, as indicated.

  NOTE: The "fully unpacked form of relvar R" is the result of UNPACK R ON $(A1,A2,...,An)$. When we said earlier that relvar R' gives the logged times for all of the tuples that have ever appeared explicitly *or implicitly* in relvar R, what we meant was all of those tuples that have ever appeared *in that fully unpacked form.*

- Finally, if R satisfies the constraint WHEN UNPACKED ON $(A1,A2,...,An)$ THEN KEY $\{K\}$, then R' satisfies the constraint WHEN UNPACKED ON $(A1,A2,...,An,$X_DURING$)$ THEN KEY $\{K,$X_DURING$\}$.

As a basis for a second example, we turn to our usual current relvar S_SINCE:

```
VAR S_SINCE RELATION
  { S#            S#,
    S#_SINCE      DATE,
    STATUS        INTEGER,
    STATUS_SINCE DATE }
    . . . . .
  LOGGED_TIMES_IN ( S_SINCE_LOG ) ;
```

Figure 15.2 shows some sample values. We leave a detailed examination of that figure to you; however, we draw your attention to the S_SINCE_LOG tuple for supplier S2 in which the S#_SINCE and S_STATUS_SINCE values are both *d07,* while the X_DURING value is [*d06:d75*]. What does this combination of values imply? ANSWER: On day 6 a tuple was inserted into relvar S_SINCE to say that supplier S2 would be placed under contract on day 7—a date in the future, at the time of the INSERT.

FIGURE 15.2

Relvars
S_SINCE and
S_SINCE_LOG—
sample values.

S_SINCE

S#	S#_SINCE	STATUS	STATUS_SINCE
S1	d04	20	d06
S2	d07	10	d07
S3	d03	30	d03
S4	d04	20	d08
S5	d02	30	d02

S_SINCE_LOG

S#	S#_SINCE	STATUS	STATUS_SINCE	X_DURING
S1	d04	15	d04	[d04:d05]
S1	d04	20	d06	[d06:d75]
S2	d02	5	d02	[d01:d02]
S2	d02	10	d03	[d03:d04]
S2	d07	10	d07	[d06:d75]
S3	d03	30	d03	[d03:d75]
S4	d04	10	d04	[d04:d04]
S4	d04	25	d05	[d05:d07]
S4	d04	20	d08	[d08:d75]
S5	d02	30	d02	[d02:d75]
S6	d03	5	d03	[d03:d04]
S6	d03	7	d05	[d05:d05]

15.6 QUERIES INVOLVING LOGGED-TIME RELVARS

Suppose we want to discover whether the database ever showed supplier S6 as being under contract on day 4, and if so when. NOTE: We deliberately start with an example in which—let us assume—we know the supplier in question is not currently under contract. If the supplier was ever under contract at all, therefore, the pertinent stated-time information will appear in the historical relvar S_DURING; such information might or might not still be present in that relvar, but certainly the pertinent logged-time information will still be present in the logged-time relvar S_DURING_LOG. Here then is a suitable formulation of the query:

```
( S_DURING_LOG WHERE S# = S# ('S6')
             AND d04 ∈ DURING ) { X_DURING }
```

Now suppose we do not know whether supplier S6 is currently under contract but (again) we want to discover whether the database ever showed supplier S6 as being under contract on day 4, and if so when. In this case a suitable formulation is slightly more complicated:

```
WITH ( S_SINCE_LOG WHERE S# = S# ('S6')
                     AND d04 ≥ S#_SINCE ) { X_DURING } AS T1 ,
     ( S_DURING_LOG WHERE S# = S# ('S6')
                     AND d04 ∈ DURING ) { X_DURING } AS T2 :
T1 UNION T2
```

By way of a third example, consider the query "On day 4, what did the database say was supplier S6's term of contract?" Note that this query treats logged time as the known value and stated time as the unknown and is thus the inverse of the previous queries, in a sense. A suitable formulation is:

```
WITH ( S_SINCE_LOG WHERE S# = S# ('S6')
                     AND d04 ∈ X_DURING ) { DURING } AS T1 ,
     ( S_DURING_LOG WHERE S# = S# ('S6')
                     AND d04 ∈ X_DURING ) { DURING } AS T2 :
T1 UNION T2
```

We close this section (and the chapter) by noting that, once again, it might be possible to simplify the task of formulating queries—in this case, queries involving logged-time relvars—by providing an appropriate set of predefined virtual relvars, possibly automatically.

EXERCISES

1. Consider Figure 15.2 again. Explain in your own words how to interpret that figure.

2. Are the sample values in Figures 15.1 and 15.2 consistent with each other? Are they consistent with the sample values in Figure 14.3 or Endpaper Panel 8?

3. Instead of having just one logged-time relvar for relvar S_SINCE (as in Section 15.5), might it have made more sense to have separate logged-time relvars for (a) the projection of S_SINCE on {S#,S#_SINCE} and (b) the projection of S_SINCE on {S#,STATUS, STATUS_SINCE}? If so, why?

4. Might it make sense to allow the user to request automatic provision of a logged-time relvar for an *arbitrary* projection (in particular, one not including a key) of an *arbitrary* relvar *R* (in particular, one that includes no interval attributes)? If so, why? What extensions might be needed to **Tutorial D** in order to permit such requests to be specified?

5. Would there be any point in requesting a logged-time relvar for the nullary projection of some relvar *R* (i.e., the projection of *R* on no attributes at all)? If so, why? Again, what extensions (if any) might be needed to **Tutorial D** in order to permit such requests to be specified?

Chapter

16

POINT AND INTERVAL TYPES REVISITED

16.1   INTRODUCTION

It is time to take care of some unfinished business. In Chapter 5 we said that any given interval type involves an underlying *point type*, and a point type is a type that has a *successor function*. Here is the pertinent text from that chapter:

A given type *T* is usable as a point type if all of the following are defined for *T*:

- A *total ordering*, according to which the infix operator ">" (greater than) is defined for every pair of values *v1* and *v2* of type *T*; if *v1* and *v2* are distinct, exactly one of the expressions "*v1 > v2*" and "*v2 > v1*" returns true and the other returns false.

- Niladic *"first"* and *"last"* operators, which return the smallest and the largest value of T, respectively, according to the aforementioned ordering.

- Monadic *"next"* and *"prior"* operators, which return the successor and the predecessor, respectively, of any given value of type T, according to the aforementioned ordering. NOTE: The "next" operator is the successor function, of course.

It turns out, however, that there is much more to be said on the topic of point types (and therefore on the associated topic of interval types as well); hence the present chapter. Unfortunately, however, it also turns out that a great deal of groundwork needs to be laid, and a large number of implications and ramifications need to be explored, before we can really get to the substance of some of the issues. If it seems to be taking a long time for the true significance of the chapter to emerge, therefore, we just have to ask you to be patient; that true significance will—we hope—emerge eventually.

Perhaps we should add that, whereas Sections 16.2 through 16.6 all deal with a single more or less coherent and interrelated set of topics, Sections 16.7 and 16.8 are concerned with matters that might be regarded as somewhat independent of the rest (and of each other). You might therefore want to skip those two sections, at least on a first reading. Nevertheless, we believe the material contained therein does logically belong in the present chapter.

Without further ado, let us begin our detailed discussions.

First of all, you might have noticed that the text from Chapter 5 merely defines a set of conditions that are *sufficient* for a given type T to be usable as a point type. But are they *necessary?* In what follows, we will see (eventually) that the answer to this question is *no*. But first things first. We begin by introducing the important term **ordinal type,** which we use to mean any type that satisfies all of the conditions mentioned in the text from Chapter 5. And, since all of the types, apart from interval types, that we will be dealing with in this chapter—until further notice, at any rate—will be ordinal types in this sense, we will henceforth take the unqualified term "type" to mean an ordinal type specifically, barring explicit statements to the contrary.

Now, in Chapter 5, we made a crucial assumption: To be specific, we assumed that *the successor function for a given point type was unique* (i.e., if T is a point type, then T has *exactly one* successor function). However, we did also point out that this assumption was a very strong one, and we gave the example of a data type, "Gregorian dates," for which we might want to consider two distinct successor functions, "next day" and "next year" (in fact, we might want to consider several successor functions for this type—"next day," "next business day," "next week," "next month," "next year," "next century," and so on). And we promised to come back to this issue later. Now it is time to do so. NOTE: It is worth stating immediately, however, that—as we will eventually discover—our strong assumption of a unique successor function is actually not too wide of the mark after all.

We might as well give the game away right up front … It turns out that the key to the problem we are trying to address is the notion of *type inheritance*. We therefore need to start with a short digression and consider the salient features of that concept first.

16.2 TYPE INHERITANCE

A robust, rigorous, and formal model of type inheritance—which we usually refer to as just *inheritance* for short—is presented in reference [43], and it is that model we will follow here. We mention this point right away because there are many approaches to inheritance described in the literature (and, in some cases, implemented in commercial products and languages), yet we find most if not all of those other approaches to be logically flawed. This is not the place to get into details; please just be aware that the approach to inheritance described here differs in certain important respects from other approaches as described elsewhere in the literature.

The discussion that follows is necessarily only the briefest of brief sketches. For a full description of our inheritance model, see reference [43].

We begin with a simple example. Consider the data type "Gregorian dates" once again. Assume for definiteness that this type is *not* built in (this assumption allows us to illustrate a number of ideas explicitly that might otherwise have to be implicit). We will refer to this type not as DATE but as DDATE, in order to emphasize the fact that it denotes dates on the Gregorian calendar that are accurate to the *day*. Of course, DDATE is an ordinal type; its values are ordered chronologically, and the successor function is basically "next day" (i.e., "add one day"—see below). Here is an appropriate definition:

```
TYPE DDATE
    POSSREP DPRI { DI INTEGER
                   CONSTRAINT DI ≥ 1 AND DI ≤ N } ;
```

EXPLANATION:

- Type DDATE has a *possible representation* called DPRI ("DDATE possible representation as integers") that says that any given DDATE value can possibly be represented by a positive integer called DI.

- The CONSTRAINT portion of the POSSREP specification defines a *type constraint* for type DDATE, constraining values of DI to lie in the range 1 to some large integer N (we leave the actual value of N unspecified here to avoid irrelevancies).

Refer to Chapter 1 if you need to refresh your memory regarding either the concept of possible representations or the concept of type constraints.

Now, we saw in Chapter 1 that any given type requires an associated *equals* operator ("=") and, for each declared possible representation, an associated *selector* operator and a set of associated *THE_* operators (actually just one THE_ operator, in the case at hand). Here are definitions of those operators for type DDATE. NOTE: The implementation code for the "=" operator, at least, can and probably should be provided by the system. We show it explicitly here for pedagogic reasons.

```
OPERATOR DPRI ( DI INTEGER ) RETURNS DDATE ;
   /* code to return the DDATE value represented */
   /* by the given integer DI                    */
END OPERATOR ;

OPERATOR THE_DI ( DD DDATE ) RETURNS INTEGER ;
   /* code to return the integer that represents */
   /* the given DDATE value DD                    */
END OPERATOR ;

OPERATOR "=" ( DD1 DDATE, DD2 DDATE ) RETURNS BOOLEAN ;
   RETURN ( THE_DI ( DD1 ) = THE_DI ( DD2 ) ) ;
END OPERATOR ;
```

The selector operator DPRI allows the user to specify a DDATE value by supplying the appropriate integer. For example, the DPRI invocation

```
DPRI ( 5263 )
```

will return whatever DDATE value (i.e., whatever date in the Gregorian calendar, accurate to the day) happens to be 5,263rd in the overall ordering of such values. However, what is clearly missing is a *user-friendly* way of specifying such DDATE values. So let us extend the type definition to add a second possible representation, as follows:

```
TYPE DDATE
   POSSREP DPRI { DI INTEGER
                  CONSTRAINT DI ≥ 1 AND DI ≤ N }
   POSSREP DPRC { DC CHAR
                  CONSTRAINT ... } ;
```

The CONSTRAINT specification for possible representation DPRC, details of which are omitted here for simplicity, constitutes another type constraint for type DDATE. It consists of a probably rather complicated expression that constrains values of type DDATE to be such that they can possibly be represented by (let us assume) character string values of the form '*yyyy/mm/dd*'—where, of course, *yyyy* is a positive integer in the range 0001 through 9999, *mm* is a positive integer in the range 01 through 12, *dd* is a positive integer in the range 01 through 31, and the overall '*yyyy/mm/dd*' string abides by the usual Gregorian calendar rules.[1] Of course, every value of type DDATE has both a DPRI representation and a DPRC representation, a fact that implies—among other things—that every value of the DPRI possible representation must be representable as a DPRC value and vice versa.

---

1. In practice it would be preferable for type DDATE to be capable of supporting *arbitrary* dates, including in particular dates before 0001/01/01 and after 9999/12/31. We ignore such issues here for simplicity.

We also need a selector and a THE_ operator corresponding to the DPRC possible representation:

```
OPERATOR DPRC ( DC CHAR ) RETURNS DDATE ;
    /* code to return the DDATE value represented */
    /* by the given yyyy/mm/dd string DC         */
END OPERATOR ;

OPERATOR THE_DC ( DD DDATE ) RETURNS CHAR ;
    /* code to return the yyyy/mm/dd string that */
    /* represents the given DDATE value DD       */
END OPERATOR ;
```

Now the user can write, for example, DPRC('2001/01/18') to specify a certain Gregorian date—January 18th, 2001, in the example—and THE_DC(*d*) to obtain the character string representation of a given DDATE value *d*.

NOTE: In practice, we would surely want to define many additional operators in connection with type DDATE: one to return the year corresponding to a given DDATE value, another to return the month, another to return the year and month in the form of a '*yyyy/mm*' string, another to return the day of the week, various arithmetic operators (e.g., to return the date *n* days before or after a specified date), and many others. We omit detailed discussion of such operators here, since they are irrelevant to our main purpose.

To get back to that main purpose, then: We can use type DDATE to illustrate the concept of type inheritance by observing that sometimes we are not interested in dates that are accurate to the day; sometimes accuracy to, for example, the *month* is all that is required (the day within the month is irrelevant). Equivalently, we might say that, for certain purposes, we are interested only in those values of type DDATE that happen to correspond to (let us agree) the first of the month—just as, for example, when we count in tens, we are interested only in those numbers that happen to correspond to the first of each successive sequence of ten integers (0, 10, 20, etc.).

Now, if we are interested only in a subset of the values that make up some type *T*, then *by definition* we are dealing with a **subtype**—let us call it *T′*—of type *T*. In fact, type *T′* is a subtype of *T* if and only if every value of type *T′* is a value of *T*. (Note that it follows immediately from this definition that *T* is a subtype of itself. It also follows that if *T″* is a subtype of *T′* and *T′* is a subtype of *T*, then *T″* is a subtype of *T*.) Also, if there is at least one value of *T* that is *not* a value of *T′*, then *T′* is a **proper** subtype of *T* (thus, although *T* itself is a subtype of *T*, it is not a proper one). And, if and only if *T′* is a subtype of *T*, then *T* is a **supertype** of *T′* (and *T* is a *proper* supertype of *T′* if and only if *T′* is a proper subtype of *T*).

So, to continue with our running example, let us define a type MDATE that is a proper subtype of type DDATE. NOTE: We now begin to stray (but not very far!) into an area of **Tutorial D** that we deliberately did not cover in Chapter 2.

```
TYPE MDATE
   IS DDATE
      CONSTRAINT FIRST_OF_MONTH ( DDATE )
   POSSREP MPRI { MI = THE_DI ( DDATE ) }
   POSSREP MPRC { MC = SUBSTR ( THE_DC ( DDATE ), 1, 7 ) } ;
```

Type MDATE is defined to be a subtype of type DDATE, thanks to the specification IS DDATE; in fact, a DDATE value is an MDATE value if and only if the DDATE value corresponds to the first of the month (we have assumed the existence of an operator called FIRST_OF_MONTH that takes a given DDATE value and returns true if that value does indeed correspond to the first of the month and false otherwise). Like type DDATE, type MDATE has two possible representations, MPRI and MPRC, each of which is derived from the corresponding possible representation for type DDATE. MPRC in particular allows us to think of MDATE values as if they were character strings of the form 'yyyy/mm'. NOTE: In practice, we would probably want to define yet another possible representation for type MDATE, namely "month number," again derived in some way from some possible representation for type DDATE; we omit further consideration of this possibility for simplicity.

Here now are the necessary selector and THE_ operators for type MDATE:

```
OPERATOR MPRI ( MI INTEGER ) RETURNS MDATE ;
   /* code to return the MDATE value represented  */
   /* by the given integer MI (of course, MI must */
   /* correspond to the first of the month)       */
END OPERATOR ;

OPERATOR THE_MI ( MD MDATE ) RETURNS INTEGER ;
   /* code to return the integer that represents */
   /* the given MDATE value MD                   */
END OPERATOR ;

OPERATOR MPRC ( MC CHAR ) RETURNS MDATE ;
   /* code to return the MDATE value represented */
   /* by the given yyyy/mm string MC             */
END OPERATOR ;

OPERATOR THE_MC ( MD MDATE ) RETURNS CHAR ;
   /* code to return the yyyy/mm string that */
   /* represents the given MDATE value MD     */
END OPERATOR ;
```

We have now defined type MDATE as a proper subtype of type DDATE (see the simple **type hierarchy** shown in Figure 16.1). What are the implications of this fact? Probably the most important is the property known as **value substitutability:**

FIGURE 16.1

A simple type
hierarchy.

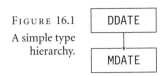

Wherever the system expects a value of type DDATE, we can always substitute a value of type MDATE instead

(because MDATE values *are* DDATE values). In particular, therefore, if *Op* is an operator that applies to DDATE values in general, we can always apply *Op* to an MDATE value specifically.[2] For example, the operators "=", THE_DI, and THE_DC defined above for values of type DDATE all apply to values of type MDATE as well (they are said to be *inherited* by type MDATE from type DDATE). Of course, the converse is not true—operators defined for values of type MDATE do not apply to values of type DDATE (in general), because DDATE values are not MDATE values (again in general).

It follows that, for example, the following code fragment is valid:

```
VAR I INTEGER ;
VAR MDX MDATE ;
VAR DDX DDATE ;

I  :=  THE_DI ( MDX ) ;
IF MDX = DDX THEN ... END IF ;
/* etc., etc., etc. */
```

For simplicity, let us assume for the remainder of this section that the type hierarchy contains types DDATE and MDATE *only*. Given that assumption, let us take a closer look at the two fundamental operations of **assignment** and **equality comparison**. First, assignment. Consider the following example:

```
VAR DDX DDATE ;

DDX  :=  MPRC ('2000/09') ;
```

In the assignment here, the target variable on the left side is declared to be of type DDATE, but the source expression on the right side denotes a value of type MDATE. However, the assignment is valid, thanks to value substitutability. And after the assignment, of course, the variable contains a DDATE value that happens to satisfy the type

---

2. The operator *Op* is thus *polymorphic*. In other words, value substitutability implies polymorphism—*inclusion* polymorphism, to be precise (other kinds exist, as noted in Chapter 6). See reference [43] for a detailed discussion of such issues.

constraint for type MDATE (i.e., it is in fact an MDATE value). We can therefore say that, while (as previously stated) the **declared** type of variable DDX is DDATE, the current **most specific** type—that is, the type of the current value of that variable—is MDATE. (That current value is of type DDATE as well, of course, because MDATE values *are* DDATE values. Thus, a given value has, in general, several types. However, it always has exactly one *most specific* type.)

Now, it is important to understand that the distinction we are discussing here, between declared and current most specific types, applies not just to variables per se but in fact to expressions of arbitrary generality; in other words, *every expression* has both a declared type and a current most specific type. To be more specific, the declared type and current most specific type of an expression X are, precisely, the declared type and current most specific type of the outermost operator involved in X.[3] NOTE: The declared type of an operator is the type named in the RETURNS specification in the definition of the operator in question; the current most specific type is the most specific type of the value returned by the specific invocation in question.

To continue with the example, suppose the following assignment is now executed:

```
DDX  :=  DPRC ('1999/10/17') ;
```

The current most specific type of variable DDX is now DDATE again (because the expression on the right side is of most specific type DDATE).

One more example:

```
DDX  :=  DPRC ('2000/11/01') ;
```

In this case, the DPRC invocation on the right side actually returns a value of type not just DDATE but MDATE (because the value in question satisfies the "first of month" constraint for type MDATE). We refer to this effect as **specialization by constraint,** on the grounds that the result of the DPRC invocation is *further specialized* to type MDATE (precisely because it satisfies the type constraint for type MDATE). And after the assignment, of course, the current most specific type of variable DDX is MDATE, too.

To generalize from the foregoing examples, let V be a variable of declared type T and let T' be a proper subtype of T. Then:

- If the current most specific type of V is T and a value v of most specific type T' is assigned to V, the current most specific type of V becomes T'. This effect is a logical consequence of the phenomenon we call specialization by constraint.

- Conversely, if the current most specific type of V is T' and a value v of most specific type T is assigned to V, the current most specific type of V becomes T. We

---

3. If the expression consists of just a variable name, the "outermost operator" is a *variable reference* operator. In this case, the declared type and most specific type of the expression are just the declared type and most specific type of the variable in question.

refer to this effect as **generalization by constraint,** on the grounds that the current most specific type of V is *further generalized*—it is established as T because the value v satisfies the type constraint for T and not for any proper subtype of T.

As an aside, we remark that it is precisely in this area (i.e., specialization and generalization by constraint as just described) that the inheritance model we advocate departs most obviously from other approaches to inheritance described in the literature.

Be that as it may, you can see from the foregoing examples that it is a rule regarding assignment that the most specific type of the source value can be of any subtype (not necessarily a proper subtype, of course) of the declared type of the target variable. What about equality comparisons? In the absence of subtyping and inheritance, the comparison $v1 = v2$ would require the comparand values $v1$ and $v2$ to be of the same type, T say. With value substitutability, however, we can substitute a value of any subtype of T for $v1$ and a value of any subtype of T for $v2$. It follows that for the comparison $v1 = v2$ to be legitimate, it is sufficient that the most specific types of the comparands have a common supertype. Of course, the comparison will give true if and only if $v1$ and $v2$ are in fact the same value (implying in particular that they are of the same most specific type).

16.3 Point Types Revisited

It should be clear that type DDATE from the previous section meets the requirements of a point type (or, at least, can be made to do so): We can certainly define a total ordering based on a ">" operator for values of the type, and we can certainly define the necessary "first," "last," "next," and "prior" operators as well. In fact, let us invent a new keyword ORDINAL that can be included in a type definition, as here (note the boldface):

```
TYPE DDATE ORDINAL
    POSSREP DPRI { DI INTEGER
                    CONSTRAINT DI ≥ 1 AND DI ≤ N }
    POSSREP DPRC { DC CHAR
                    CONSTRAINT ... } ;
```

We interpret the ORDINAL specification as implying that ">", "first," "last," "next," and "prior" operators[4] *must* be defined for the type (a real language might require the names of those operators to be specified as part of the ORDINAL specification). Here are some appropriate definitions for those operators:

---

4. Possibly IS_PRIOR_T and IS_NEXT_T operators, too (see Chapter 12). Note that these operators, like the "first," "next," etc., operators (to be discussed), do need that "_T" qualifier, for reasons to be explained toward the end of this section.

```
OPERATOR ">" ( DD1 DDATE, DD2 DDATE ) RETURNS BOOLEAN ;
   RETURN ( THE_DI ( DD1 ) > THE_DI ( DD2 ) ) ;
END OPERATOR ;


OPERATOR FIRST_DDATE ( ) RETURNS DDATE ;
   RETURN DPRI ( 1 ) ;
END OPERATOR ;


OPERATOR LAST_DDATE ( ) RETURNS DDATE ;
   RETURN DPRI ( N ) ;
END OPERATOR ;


OPERATOR NEXT_DDATE ( DD DDATE ) RETURNS DDATE ;
   IF DD = LAST_DDATE ( )
      THEN signal error ;
      ELSE RETURN DPRI ( THE_DI ( DD ) + 1 ) ;
   END IF ;
END OPERATOR ;


OPERATOR PRIOR_DDATE ( DD DDATE ) RETURNS DDATE ;
   IF DD = FIRST_DDATE ( )
      THEN signal error ;
      ELSE RETURN DPRI ( THE_DI ( DD ) - 1 ) ;
   END IF ;
END OPERATOR ;
```

NOTE: With respect to the "next" operator here (i.e., NEXT_DDATE), the following simpler definition would in fact have been sufficient:

```
OPERATOR NEXT_DDATE ( DD DDATE ) RETURNS DDATE ;
   RETURN DPRI ( THE_DI ( DD ) + 1 ) ;
END OPERATOR ;
```

In other words, it is not logically necessary to include an explicit test to see whether the argument corresponding to parameter DD happens to be "the last date"; if it is, the DPRI selector invocation will simply fail on a type constraint violation. We included the explicit test merely for reasons of clarity. An analogous remark applies to PRIOR_DDATE, of course.

Back to the main thread of our discussion. Type DDATE now clearly meets the sufficiency requirements for a point type. Note very carefully, however, that the "first," "last," "next," and "prior" operators are named FIRST_*T*, LAST_*T*, NEXT_*T*, and PRIOR_*T*, respectively, where *T* is the name of the type in question (DDATE in the example). Although we followed this naming convention in earlier chapters, we never really discussed it properly, but now we need to do so. First, however, we consider type MDATE in more detail.

We begin by observing that since type MDATE is a proper subtype of type DDATE and DDATE is an ordinal type, we can certainly regard MDATE as an ordinal type as well if we want to (and of course we do want to, because we want to use type MDATE as a point type too). So we need to define associated ">", "first," "last," "next," and "prior" operators for type MDATE. The ">" operator is—in fact, must be (why?)—inherited from type DDATE. So too are the operators NEXT_DDATE and so on; however, those operators are *not* the "next" (etc.) operators we need for type MDATE! For example, given the MDATE value August 1st, 2001, the operator NEXT_DDATE will—by definition—return the date of the next *day* (August 2nd, 2001), not the date of the next *month* (September 1st, 2001). Thus, we need some new operators for type MDATE:

```
OPERATOR FIRST_MDATE ( ) RETURNS MDATE ;
   RETURN MPRI ( op ( 1 ) ) ;
   /* op ( 1 ) computes the integer corresponding */
   /* to the first day of the first month         */
END OPERATOR ;

OPERATOR LAST_MDATE ( ) RETURNS MDATE ;
   RETURN MPRI ( op ( N ) ) ;
   /* op ( N ) computes the integer corresponding */
   /* to the first day of the last month          */
END OPERATOR ;

OPERATOR NEXT_MDATE ( MD MDATE ) RETURNS MDATE ;
   IF MD = LAST_MDATE ( )
      THEN signal error ;
      ELSE RETURN MDATE ( THE_MI ( MD ) + incr ) ;
      /* incr is 28, 29, 30, or 31, as applicable */
   END IF ;
END OPERATOR ;

OPERATOR PRIOR_MDATE ( MD MDATE ) RETURNS MDATE ;
   IF MD = FIRST_MDATE ( )
      THEN signal error ;
      ELSE RETURN MDATE ( THE_MI ( MD ) - decr ) ;
      /* decr is 28, 29, 30, or 31, as applicable */
   END IF ;
END OPERATOR ;
```

We can now see why the "first," "last," "next," and "prior" operators for a given type T are named FIRST_T, LAST_T, NEXT_T, and PRIOR_T, respectively. For example, given the MDATE value August 1st, 2001, the operator NEXT_DDATE will return August 2nd, 2001 (as we already know); the operator NEXT_MDATE, by contrast, will return September 1st, 2001. In other words, NEXT_DDATE and NEXT_MDATE are *different operators*.[5]

We close this section with two further observations:

- We follow reference [43] in using syntax of the form *Op_T* (...), rather than *Op* (..., *T*), because this latter format would raise "type TYPE" issues—that is, what is the type of the operand *T*?—that we prefer to avoid.

- For system-defined point types, at least (and possibly for certain user-defined point types as well), the successor function will be "understood by the system." This fact should make it possible for the system to carry out certain optimizations in implementation.

16.4 Further Examples

We now turn our attention to another set of examples, based on the type NUMERIC (fixed-point decimal numbers), which, to save ourselves some writing, we assume is a built-in type. Recall from Chapter 1 that when we declare a NUMERIC variable, we generally need to specify a *precision* and a *scale factor* for that variable, though for simplicity we did not bother to do so in our examples in that chapter. Here is an example:

```
VAR V NUMERIC(5,2) ;
```

Variable V is of declared type NUMERIC(5,2).[6] Values of that type (and hence of variable V) are decimal numbers with precision five and scale factor two—which is to say those values are precisely as follows:

```
-999.99, -999.98, ..., -000.01, 000.00, 000.01, ..., 999.99
```

---

5. An alternative approach would be to call both the NEXT_DDATE operator and the NEXT_MDATE operator simply "NEXT" and provide two different *implementation versions* of that "NEXT" operator, using the mechanism called overloading [43]. The expression NEXT(*exp*) would then cause the MDATE or DDATE implementation to be invoked according as to whether the type of *exp* was MDATE or just DDATE. (The phrase "the type of *exp*" here could mean either the declared type or the most specific type, depending on factors beyond the scope of this discussion.) However, such a scheme (1) could imply that there would be no way to apply the DDATE version of NEXT to a value of type MDATE, and (2) would violate an important prescription of our inheritance model as described in reference [43], and we therefore reject it.

6. In reference [43], two of the present authors (Date and Darwen) took the position that the type here was simply NUMERIC and the "(5,2)" specification was a constraint on the use of that type in this particular context. We now explicitly disavow that earlier position. (We advocated that position before we had developed our inheritance model; now we realize that inheritance provides a much cleaner and more elegant approach to the problem we were trying to solve at the time.)

In general, the **precision** for a given NUMERIC type specifies the total number of decimal digits,[7] and the **scale factor** specifies the position of the assumed decimal point, within the string of digits denoting any given value of the type in question. A positive scale factor q means the decimal point is assumed to be q decimal places to the left, and a negative scale factor $-q$ means the decimal point is assumed to be q decimal places to the right, of the rightmost decimal digit of such strings of digits. Note, therefore, that the precision and scale factor together serve as an *a priori* constraint on values of the type; in fact, they constitute the applicable type constraint.

We stress the fact that values of type NUMERIC(p,q) must be thought of as being denoted by strings of digits with an *assumed* decimal point. What this means is that if v is such a value, then v can be thought of in terms of a p-digit integer, n say; however, that p-digit integer n must actually be interpreted as denoting the value $v = n * (10^{-q})$. In what follows, we will refer to that multiplier 10^{-q} as the specific **scale** that is defined by the scale factor q (in the foregoing example, the scale is one hundredth).[8] Observe that, by definition, every value of the type is evenly divisible by the scale (i.e., dividing the value in question by the scale never leaves a remainder). We note that the concept of scale can reasonably be applied to the examples of Section 16.3 as well; for type DDATE it is one day, for type MDATE it is one month.

N O T E : From this point forward, we adopt the usual conventions regarding the omission of insignificant leading and trailing zeros in numeric literals. Thus, we might more simply say that the values of type NUMERIC(5,2) are as follows:

```
-999.99, -999.98, ..., -.01, 0, .01, ..., 999.99
```

Figure 16.2 gives several examples of NUMERIC types, with the corresponding scale and a "picture" of a typical value (ignoring the possible prefix minus sign) in each case.

FIGURE 16.2

Examples of NUMERIC types.

Type	Scale	Picture
NUMERIC(4,1)	1/10	xxx.x
NUMERIC(3,1)	1/10	xx.x
NUMERIC(4,2)	1/100	xx.xx
NUMERIC(3,0)	1	xxx.
NUMERIC(3,-2)	100	xxx00.
NUMERIC(3,5)	1/100000	.00xxx

---

7. Actually there is some confusion in the literature over the term *precision*. The definition given here is in accordance with the one given in *The Facts on File Dictionary of Mathematics* (Market House Books Ltd., New York, 1999) and with Java and PL/I usage. Other writers use the term to mean what we prefer to call the *scale factor;* this second interpretation is in accordance with the definition given in *The McGraw-Hill Dictionary of Mathematics* (McGraw-Hill, New York, 1994) and with C++ and sometimes (but not always!) SQL usage.

8. And yes, there is confusion in the literature over the term *scale* too. The definition given here is in accordance (more or less) with that given in *The Facts on File Dictionary of Mathematics*. PL/I, although it agrees with our definition of the term *scale factor,* uses *scale* to refer instead to the distinction between fixed- and floating-point. SQL sometimes (but not always) uses *scale* to mean *scale factor*. Also, *scale* is often used as a synonym for *base* or *radix*.

Points arising:

- Real languages often provide a built-in INTEGER type for the case where the scale factor is 0; that is, another spelling for NUMERIC(p,0) is typically INTEGER(p). Indeed, we have been assuming the existence of such a type in our running example (suppliers and shipments) throughout this book, except that for simplicity we have always omitted the precision p (and we will continue to do so in what follows). NOTE: Although every value of type INTEGER(p) is certainly an integer, it is not the case that every type whose values are all integers is a type of the form INTEGER(p). In fact, every type of the form NUMERIC(p,q) where q is negative also has values that are all integers.

- If the scale factor q is negative, least significant digits of the integer part of the number are missing. Those missing digits are assumed to be zeros. By way of example, values of the type NUMERIC(3,−2) are

  -99900, -99800, ..., -100, 0, 100, ..., 99900

  (all of them numbers—in fact, integers—that are evenly divisible by one hundred, which is the scale).[9]

- If the scale factor q is greater than the precision p, most significant digits of the fractional part of the number are missing. Again, those missing digits are assumed to be zeros. By way of example, values of the type NUMERIC(3,5) are

  -0.00999, -0.00998, ..., -0.00001, 0.0, 0.00001, ..., 0.00999

  (all of them numbers that are evenly divisible by one hundred thousandth, which is the scale).

Now, it is probably obvious to you that any of these NUMERIC types can certainly be used as a point type, and we will examine that possibility in a few moments. However, there is an important issue that needs to be addressed first, as follows:

- Consider the types NUMERIC(3,1) and NUMERIC(4,1). It should be clear that every value of type NUMERIC(3,1) is a value of type NUMERIC(4,1) as well— to be specific, a value of type NUMERIC(4,1) for which the leading digit in the

---

9. Incidentally, we can use this example to illustrate the important difference between a *literal* and a *value* (the concepts are indeed often confused—see, for example, reference [11]). A literal is not a value but is, rather, a symbol that denotes a value. Thus, for example, the symbol 99900 is a literal that might on the face of it be thought of as denoting a value of type NUMERIC(5,0), not NUMERIC(3,−2). However, the value in question happens to satisfy the type constraint for values of type NUMERIC(3,−2), which, as we will see in a moment, is in fact a subtype of NUMERIC(5,0); conceptually, therefore, specialization by constraint comes into play, and the literal thus does indeed denote a value of type NUMERIC(3,−2). Similarly, the literal 5.00 denotes a value of type INTEGER.

integer part happens to be zero. It follows that NUMERIC(3,1) is a proper subtype of NUMERIC(4,1), and so we can (for example) assign a value of the former type to a variable that is declared to be of the latter type.

- Now consider the types NUMERIC(3,1) and NUMERIC(4,2). It should also be clear that every value of type NUMERIC(3,1) is a value of type NUMERIC(4,2) as well—to be specific, a value of type NUMERIC(4,2) for which the trailing digit in the fractional part happens to be zero. It follows that NUMERIC(3,1) is a proper subtype of NUMERIC(4,2) as well.

- Observe now that neither of the types NUMERIC(4,1) and NUMERIC(4,2) is a subtype of the other; for example, 999.9 is a value of the first type that is not a value of the second, while 99.99 is a value of the second type that is not a value of the first. And so we see that type NUMERIC(3,1) has two distinct proper supertypes, neither of which is a subtype of the other. It follows that we are dealing with **multiple** inheritance—that is, a form of inheritance in which a given type can have n proper supertypes ($n > 1$), none of which is a subtype of any other. (By contrast, the form of inheritance discussed in Section 16.2 was, tacitly, what is called **single** inheritance only. Of course, single inheritance is just a degenerate special case of multiple inheritance.)

Thus, we need to digress again for a little while in order to extend the ideas presented for single inheritance in Section 16.2 to deal with the possibility of multiple inheritance.

Multiple Inheritance

Consider NUMERIC types once again. Assume for definiteness and simplicity that the maximum precision the system supports is three—the minimum, of course, is one—and the maximum and minimum scale factors are four and minus four, respectively. Then Figure 16.3 shows the corresponding *type lattice* (a simple type hierarchy will obviously no longer suffice) for the entire range of valid NUMERIC types. NOTE: For simplicity, we abbreviate the type name "NUMERIC(p,q)" throughout the figure to just "(p,q)".

FIGURE 16.3

A simple type lattice.

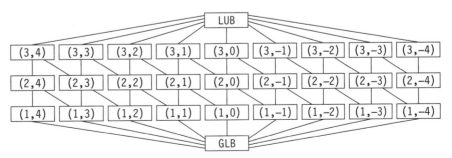

Figure 16.3 should be self-explanatory, except for the two types LUB and GLB shown at the top and bottom of the lattice, respectively, which we now explain. Type LUB ("least upper bound") contains all possible NUMERIC values and is a proper supertype of every other type in the figure.[10] Type GLB ("greatest lower bound"), by contrast, is a type that contains just the single value zero; it is a proper subtype of every other type in the figure.

What extensions are needed to our model of inheritance as sketched in Section 16.2 in order to deal with situations like the one illustrated in Figure 16.3? It turns out that—at least so far as we are concerned in this book—not many extensions are needed at all. In fact, the only one we need consider here is this:

If types *T1* and *T2* overlap (i.e., have at least one value in common), then they must have both

1. a common supertype *T* and
2. a common subtype *T'* such that every value that is of both types *T1* and *T2* is in fact a value of type *T'*.

NOTE: The foregoing statement is both simpler and more complicated than it really needs to be: simpler, because among other things it needs to be generalized to deal with three or more overlapping types; more complicated, because if the right groundwork is laid first, it can be stated much more elegantly and precisely. See reference [43] for further discussion.

Observe now that the foregoing rule is certainly satisfied in Figure 16.3. For example, consider the types NUMERIC(2,1) and NUMERIC(2,0). These two types do overlap—for example, they have the value 9 in common. And (1) they do have a common supertype, namely NUMERIC(3,1);[11] (2) they also have a common subtype, namely NUMERIC(1,0), such that a value is of both the specified types if and only if it is a value of that common subtype.

The foregoing rule regarding overlapping types can be regarded as a rule that type lattices must obey in order to be *well-formed*. And, assuming the type lattice we have to deal with is indeed well-formed in this sense, we can now say that our rule regarding assignment remains unchanged: namely, the most specific type of the source must be some subtype of the declared type of the target. What is more, our rule for equality comparison remains unchanged, too: The most specific types of the comparands must have a common supertype. However, this latter rule now has an extended interpretation. For example, it is possible that a comparison between a NUMERIC(2,1) value and a NUMERIC(2,0) value might give true—but only if the values in question are in fact both of type NUMERIC(1,0) (and both the same value, of course).

---

10. In fact, type LUB is what is called in reference [43] a *dummy type*. It might be used, for example, as the type of a parameter in the definition of some operator (e.g., an "absolute value of" operator) that is meant to apply to all possible numeric values.

11. Of course, NUMERIC(3,1) is not the only common supertype in this example (though it does happen to be the only one apart from type LUB).

NUMERIC Point Types

Now let us get back to the main topic of this chapter. Clearly, all of the various NUMERIC types we have been discussing can be used as point types—they all have a total ordering, and "first," "last," "next," and "prior" operators can be defined for all of them. However, they differ in a certain significant way from the types DDATE and MDATE as discussed in Section 16.2, inasmuch as the definitions of the "first" (etc.) operators are all effectively *implied* by the applicable precision and scale. (More precisely, the precision implies the definitions of the "first" and "last" operators, while the scale implies the definitions of the "next" and "prior" operators.) For example, consider the type NUMERIC(3,1), which consists of the following values (in order):

```
-99.9, -99.8, ..., -0.1, 0, 0.1, ..., 99.9
```

Clearly, the "first" operator here returns –99.9, the "last" operator returns 99.9, the "next" operator is "add one tenth," and the "prior" operator is "subtract one tenth."

We now observe that, in order to be consistent with our earlier remarks regarding operator naming, these operators should by rights be named FIRST_NUMERIC(3,1), LAST_NUMERIC(3,1), NEXT_NUMERIC(3,1), and PRIOR_NUMERIC(3,1), respectively! Setting aside the question of whether such names are even syntactically legal, we would be the first to admit that they are clumsy and ugly. However, as we have said elsewhere in this book (several times, in fact), we are concerned here not so much with matters of concrete syntax, but rather with the question of getting the conceptual foundations right. And conceptually, yes, the "first," "last," "next," and "prior" operators for type NUMERIC(3,1) really are different from the corresponding operators for (e.g.) type NUMERIC(4,2), and they do need different names.[12]

Other Scales

In effect, what the previous subsection was claiming was that to say that a certain NUMERIC type has a certain precision and a certain scale is really just a shorthand way of saying that we have a type that (1) is usable as a point type, (2) has values that are numbers, and (3) has certain specific "first" and "next" (etc.) operators. We now observe, however, that this shorthand—which we might call "the NUMERIC(p,q) shorthand"—*only works if the desired scale is a power of ten.* But other scales are certainly possible, and perhaps desirable. In this subsection, we briefly consider this possibility.

By way of a simple example, suppose we want a point type consisting of *even integers*—which is to say, an ordinal type for which (1) the values are (let us agree) the

---

12. If they need names at all, that is—but they might not. For example, the expression NEXT_NUMERIC (3,1) (*exp*), where *exp* is of declared type NUMERIC(3,1), will clearly return the same result as the expression *exp* + 0.1, and thus the conventional "+" operator might be all we need here. (Even though the declared type of this latter expression will probably be just LUB, the result it returns at run time will certainly be of type NUMERIC(3,1)—and possibly some proper subtype thereof—thanks to specialization by constraint.)

integers –99998, –99996, …, –2, 0, 2, …, 99998, and (2) the "first" (etc.) operators are as suggested by this sequence (i.e., the "first" operator returns –99998, the "next" operator is "add two," and so on). No NUMERIC(p,q) shorthand is capable of expressing these requirements. Instead, therefore, we need to define an explicit subtype, perhaps as follows:

```
TYPE EVEN_INTEGER ORDINAL
    IS INTEGER
        CONSTRAINT MOD ( INTEGER, 2 ) = 0 ... ;
```

MOD here ("modulo") is, let us assume, an operator that takes two integer operands and returns the remainder that results after dividing the first by the second. The reference to the type name "INTEGER" in the CONSTRAINT specification stands for an arbitrary value of type INTEGER (see Chapter 2, Section 2.2, or reference [43] for further explanation).

The "=" and ">" operators for EVEN_INTEGER are inherited from type INTEGER. As for the "first" (etc.) operators, they might be defined as follows:

```
OPERATOR FIRST_EVEN_INTEGER ( ) RETURNS EVEN_INTEGER ;
    RETURN -99998 ;
END OPERATOR ;

OPERATOR LAST_EVEN_INTEGER ( ) RETURNS EVEN_INTEGER ;
    RETURN 99998 ;
END OPERATOR ;

OPERATOR NEXT_EVEN_INTEGER ( I EVEN_INTEGER )
                                RETURNS EVEN_INTEGER ;
    IF I = LAST_EVEN_INTEGER ( )
        THEN signal error ;
        ELSE RETURN I + 2 ;
    END IF ;
END OPERATOR ;

OPERATOR PRIOR_EVEN_INTEGER ( I EVEN_INTEGER )
                                RETURNS EVEN_INTEGER ;
    IF I = FIRST_EVEN_INTEGER ( )
        THEN signal error ;
        ELSE RETURN I - 2 ;
    END IF ;
END OPERATOR ;
```

NOTE: We have taken some liberties in these operator definitions (and we will continue to do likewise in operator definitions throughout the remainder of this chapter). The fact is that, for example, the operand in the RETURN statement in the definition of FIRST_EVEN_INTEGER ought really to be, not just the literal –99998 as shown, but rather an expression of the form TREAT_DOWN_AS_EVEN_INTEGER (–99998). However, detailed discussion of this fact would take us much further from our main topic than we care to go here; thus, we have adopted certain simplifications in order to avoid a detailed discussion of a subject that is not very relevant to our main purpose. For further discussion and explanation, see reference [43].

Analogously, we might define, for example, a point type where the scale is calendar quarters and the "next" operator is "add three months," or a point type where the scale is decades and the "next" operator is "add ten years" (and so on).

16.5 GRANULARITY REVISITED

We now turn our attention to the concept of granularity. Recall from Chapter 3 that the term *granularity* refers, informally, to the "size" of the individual points, or equivalently the size of the gap between adjacent points, for the point type in question. Figure 16.4 lists the various point types we have been considering in this chapter so far and shows the corresponding granularities.

Now, you might have noticed that we did not mention the term *granularity* in previous sections of this chapter at all. One reason for the omission is that in all of the examples discussed in the chapter so far, the granularity is identical to the corresponding scale, as Figure 16.4 clearly shows. For those types, therefore, the concept is simply redundant; it is just another term for a concept for which a better term already exists (not to mention the fact that *scale* is formally defined, while—*pace* references [6] and

FIGURE 16.4

Sample point types and granularities.

Point type	Granularity
DDATE	1 day
MDATE	1 month
NUMERIC(5,2)	1/100
NUMERIC(4,1)	1/10
NUMERIC(3,1)	1/10
NUMERIC(4,2)	1/100
NUMERIC(3,0)	1
NUMERIC(3,-2)	100
NUMERIC(3,5)	1/100000
EVEN_INTEGER	2

[53]—*granularity* seems not to be). However, a more important reason for the omission is that there are some point types for which the concept of granularity simply does not apply. We will give an example in a few moments. First, however, we consider a different example, involving a user-defined type called HEIGHT. Here is the definition:

```
TYPE HEIGHT POSSREP HIPR
    { HI INTEGER CONSTRAINT HI > 0 AND HI ≤ 120 } ;
```

Type HEIGHT is meant to represent person heights; legal HEIGHT values are

```
HIPR ( 1 ), HIPR ( 2 ), ..., HIPR ( 120 )
```

denoting heights in inches (we assume nobody is shorter than one inch or taller than ten feet). Clearly, the granularity is one inch. Or is it? Surely we might equally well say it is two half-inches, or one twelfth of a foot—or even 2.54 centimeters, or 25.4 millimeters, or any of many, many other possibilities. Thus, we see that, in general, granularity requires some associated *unit of measure* (not necessarily unique) in order for it to make sense.

Of course, while there might be many ways (some of which might be more user-friendly than others) to state the granularity in any given situation, those various ways must all be logically equivalent—which is just as well, in fact, since the concept of units of measure has no formal part to play in a type definition. Indeed, reference [43] argues that, as a general rule, types and units should generally not be in any kind of one-to-one correspondence. For example, instead of having one type representing heights in inches and another heights in centimeters, it would be better to have just one HEIGHT type with two distinct possible representations, one for inches and one for centimeters. But now we are beginning to stray too far from our main topic once again … To return to that topic, we now show (as promised) an example of a point type for which the granularity concept does not apply:

```
TYPE RICHTER ORDINAL
    POSSREP RPR { R NUMERIC(3,1)
                    CONSTRAINT R > 0.0 } ;
```

Type RICHTER is meant to represent points on the Richter scale; legal RICHTER values are

```
RPR ( 0.1 ), RPR ( 0.2 ), ..., RPR ( 1.0 ),
RPR ( 1.1 ), RPR ( 1.2 ), ...,
........................., RPR ( 99.9 )  /* help! */
```

The scale is one tenth. As is well known, however, the Richter scale is *nonlinear;* as a consequence, it makes little sense to talk about the concept of granularity in this example—the gaps between one RICHTER value and the next are not of constant size. (Actually, the same could be said for type MDATE, since different months involve different numbers of days.)

What the Richter example demonstrates is that there is an important logical difference between scale and granularity. As already stated, scale is a formal concept; essentially, it is the basis of the definition of the successor function ("next"). Granularity, by contrast, is an informal concept; it helps to explain at an intuitive level what a certain point type is supposed to represent. However, it does tacitly assume that the point type in question involves *evenly spaced values*. In other words, the tacit model underlying the concept of granularity is something like the following:

- We are given a linear axis with certain points marked on it.

- Those marked points (only) are of interest; there are no accessible points "between" adjacent points on the axis. Measurements along the axis are discrete, not continuous (they always correspond to one of the marked points, there are no "half-measures").

- The points are assumed to be evenly spaced. That is, if *p1* and *p2* are any two adjacent points on the axis, then the size *g* of the gap between *p1* and *p2*—which must be measured, be it noted, by going outside the model—is always the same.

- That constant value *g* is the granularity. Furthermore, it corresponds to the scale, in the sense that *g* is what must be "added" to any given point to get to the next.

But the RICHTER example shows that the even-spacing assumption is not always valid. For type RICHTER, scale makes sense, but granularity does not. (More generally, whenever granularity makes sense, then scale does too, but the converse is not true.)

We now consider one last example of a point type in order to show that not only does granularity not always apply, but scale does not always apply either:

```
TYPE PRIME ORDINAL
    IS INTEGER
        CONSTRAINT ... ;
```

Values of type PRIME are—let us agree—prime numbers, starting with two; the CONSTRAINT specification, details of which are omitted for simplicity, consists (presumably) of a reference to some operator that will determine, for any given positive integer *p,* whether *p* is prime.

Now, prime numbers are certainly not evenly spaced, so the concept of granularity does not apply. What is more, there is no obvious scale, either! Certainly there is no positive integer *s* (except, trivially, for the case *s* = 1) such that we can say "values of PRIME are all evenly divisible by *s*." And yet PRIME is clearly usable as a point type— ">" is obviously applicable, and we can define suitable "first" (etc.) operators, thus:

```
OPERATOR FIRST_PRIME ( ) RETURNS PRIME ;
   RETURN 2 ;
END OPERATOR ;

OPERATOR LAST_PRIME ( ) RETURNS PRIME ;
   RETURN N ;
   /* N = the largest representable prime */
END OPERATOR ;

OPERATOR NEXT_PRIME ( P PRIME ) RETURNS PRIME ;
   IF P = LAST_PRIME ( )
      THEN signal error ;
      ELSE RETURN np ( P ) ;
      /* np ( P ) returns the prime immediately following P */
   END IF ;
END OPERATOR ;

OPERATOR PRIOR_PRIME ( P PRIME ) RETURNS PRIME ;
   IF P = FIRST_PRIME ( )
      THEN signal error ;
      ELSE RETURN pp ( P ) ;
      /* pp ( P ) returns the prime immediately preceding P */
   END IF ;
END OPERATOR ;
```

So PRIME is an example of a type that is certainly usable as a point type and yet has no scale[13] (and *a fortiori* no granularity).

To summarize: The concept of granularity (1) is not formally defined, (2) does not always apply, and (3) seems to be identical to the concept of scale when it does apply. Given this state of affairs, it seems a little strange that the concept has received so much attention in the literature: especially since there seems to be a certain amount of confusion surrounding the concept anyway—for example, it is sometimes taken to be the same as *precision* (!). By way of a second example (of apparent confusion), you might like to meditate on the following definition from reference [53]. Italics are as in the original.

- "[The] *timestamp granularity* is the size of each chronon in a timestamp interpretation. For example, if the timestamp granularity is one second, then the duration of each chronon in the timestamp interpretation is one second (and vice-versa) … If the context is clear, the modifier 'timestamp' may be omitted."

NOTE: The concept of "timestamp interpretation" is defined elsewhere in the same document thus:

---

13. Perhaps we might say it does have a scale but the scale in question is *nonuniform*. But the concept of a "nonuniform scale" does not seem very useful.

- "[The] *timestamp interpretation* gives the meaning of each timestamp bit pattern in terms of some time-line clock chronon (or group of chronons)."

16.6 INTERVAL TYPES REVISITED

In Chapter 5 we defined an interval type to be a *generated* type of the form INTERVAL_*T*, where *T* is a point type. And interval types have certain generic operators associated with them: interval selectors, BEGIN and END, PRE and POST, POINT FROM, ∈ and ∋, COUNT, Allen's operators, and (interval) UNION, INTERSECT, and MINUS. In this section, we consider the effect of the ideas discussed in this chapter so far on all of these operators.

We begin by noting that if *T′* is a proper subtype of *T*, then—so long as *T′* contains at least two distinct point values—INTERVAL_*T′* is *not* a subtype of INTERVAL_*T*, because intervals of type INTERVAL_*T′* are not intervals of type INTERVAL_*T*. Indeed, even if intervals *i* and *i′*, of types INTERVAL_*T* and INTERVAL_*T′* respectively, have the same begin and end points *b* and *e*, they are still not the same interval; in particular, they have different sets of contained points. For example, take *T* and *T′* as INTEGER and EVEN_INTEGER, respectively, and consider *i* = [2:6] and *i′* = [2:6]; then *i* contains the integers 2, 3, 4, 5, and 6, while *i′* contains just the even integers 2, 4, and 6.

To pursue the point just a moment longer: Even in the special case where *b* = *e*, in which case intervals *i* and *i′* obviously do have the same set of contained points, they are still not the same interval, precisely because they are of different types. For example, the operator invocations POST(*i*) and POST(*i′*) will give different results, even in this special case (unless *e* happens to be the last value of both types *T* and *T′*, of course, in which case both POST invocations are undefined).

As you can see, then, the type of a given interval cannot in general be inferred from the type of its begin and end points. It follows that—as we already know from earlier chapters—**interval selectors** too need to include that "_*T*" qualifier, just like the "first" and "next" (etc.) operators. Here are two examples:

```
INTERVAL_INTEGER      ( [2:6] )
INTERVAL_EVEN_INTEGER ( [2:6] )
```

The general format—assuming, as usual, closed-closed notation for definiteness—is INTERVAL_*T* ([*b*:*e*]), where *b* and *e* are values of type *T* and *b* ≤ *e*.

A further important observation is as follows. We have just seen that, in general, if *T′* is a proper subtype of *T*, then INTERVAL_*T′* is not a subtype of INTERVAL_*T*. In fact, if *IT* is the interval type INTERVAL_*T*, then there is *no* interval type of the form INTERVAL_*T′*—let us call it *IT′*—that is a proper subtype of *IT*. For suppose, conversely, that such a type *IT′* does in fact exist. Let *i′* = [*b′*:*e′*] be an arbitrary interval of type *IT′*. Then *i′* must be an interval of type *IT* as well. But even if *b′* and *e′* happen to be values of type *T*, *i′* cannot be an interval of type *IT*, because its contained points are determined by the successor function for T', which by definition is distinct from the successor function for T. Contradiction!

NOTE: The remarks in the preceding paragraph are broadly true, but a couple of minor exceptions (or what might be thought of as exceptions, at any rate) should be mentioned:

1. If T' is empty (a possibility noted in Chapter 5), then IT' is certainly a subtype of all possible interval types, and in fact a *proper* subtype of most of them. However, IT' contains no intervals in this case.

2. Perhaps more important, it might be possible to define a type IT' that *is* a proper subtype of IT—for example, IT' might be defined to consist of just those intervals of type IT that happen to be unit intervals—but if T contains at least two points, then such a type IT' could not be defined simply by invoking the type generator INTERVAL, and so it would not be, as stated, a type of the form INTERVAL_T'. To say it again, when we use the term *interval type* in this book, we mean a type that is produced by an invocation of the INTERVAL type generator specifically.

Next, we observe that intervals are of course *values;* therefore, like all values, they carry their type around with them, so to speak [43]. That is, if i is an interval, then i can be thought of as carrying around with it a kind of flag that announces "I am an interval of type INTERVAL_INTEGER" or "I am an interval of type INTERVAL_EVEN_INTEGER" or "I am an interval of type INTERVAL_DDATE" (etc., etc.). From these observations and those of previous paragraphs, therefore, it follows that any given interval carries *exactly one* type with it, and so we can speak unambiguously of *the* type of any given interval. (That type is of course the *most* specific type of the interval in question, but in effect it is the *least* specific type too, and the declared type as well.)

Now consider the operator POST, which, given the interval $i = [b:e]$, returns the immediate successor $e+1$ of the end point e of i. The type of the argument i is known, of course. It follows that the applicable successor function is known as well, and so there is no need for POST to include a _T qualifier. Thus, the following is a valid POST invocation:

```
POST ( INTERVAL_INTEGER ( [2:6] ) )
```

The result, of course, is 7. By contrast, the POST invocation

```
POST ( INTERVAL_EVEN_INTEGER ( [2:6] ) )
```

returns 8, not 7.

It should be clear that remarks analogous to the foregoing apply equally to PRE, BEGIN, END, and indeed to all of the other generic interval operators, because the applicable successor function, when needed, is always known. In other words, the only interval operators that require the _T qualifier are interval selectors. (In fact, of course, interval selectors differ in kind from the other operators mentioned, inasmuch as their operands are points, not intervals. In this respect, they resemble the operators "first," "last," "next," "prior," "is next," and "is prior," all of which take operands that are points, and all of which also need that _T qualifier.)

16.7 CYCLIC POINT TYPES

We come now to another issue that we have deliberately been avoiding prior to this point—the issue of "wraparound" or **cyclic** point types. Examples of such types include "time of day" and "day of week," both with the obvious semantics. Such types share with modular arithmetic the property that the available values can be thought of as points arranged around the circumference of a circle, such that every value has both a successor and a predecessor, but there is no first or last value.

For definiteness, let us concentrate on the weekday example. Here is a possible type definition, together with its associated selector and THE_ operator definitions:

```
TYPE WEEKDAY
   POSSREP WDPRI { WDI INTEGER
                       CONSTRAINT WDI ≥ 0 AND WDI ≤ 6 }
   POSSREP WDPRC { WDC CHAR
                       CONSTRAINT WDC = 'Sun'
                              OR WDC = 'Mon'
                              OR WDC = 'Tue'
                              OR WDC = 'Wed'
                              OR WDC = 'Thu'
                              OR WDC = 'Fri'
                              OR WDC = 'Sat' } ;

OPERATOR WDPRI ( WDI INTEGER ) RETURNS WEEKDAY ;
   /* code to return the WEEKDAY value represented */
   /* by the given integer WDI                     */
END OPERATOR ;

OPERATOR WDPRC ( WDC CHAR ) RETURNS WEEKDAY ;
   RETURN CASE
      WHEN WDC = 'Sun' THEN WDI ( 0 )
      WHEN WDC = 'Mon' THEN WDI ( 1 )
      WHEN WDC = 'Tue' THEN WDI ( 2 )
      WHEN WDC = 'Wed' THEN WDI ( 3 )
      WHEN WDC = 'Thu' THEN WDI ( 4 )
      WHEN WDC = 'Fri' THEN WDI ( 5 )
      WHEN WDC = 'Sat' THEN WDI ( 6 )
   END CASE ;
END OPERATOR ;
```

(continued)

```
OPERATOR THE_WDI ( WD WEEKDAY ) RETURNS INTEGER ;
   /* code to return the integer that represents */
   /* the given WEEKDAY value WD                  */
END OPERATOR ;

OPERATOR THE_WDC ( WD WEEKDAY ) RETURNS CHAR ;
   RETURN CASE
      WHEN THE_WDI ( WD ) = 0 THEN 'Sun'
      WHEN THE_WDI ( WD ) = 1 THEN 'Mon'
      WHEN THE_WDI ( WD ) = 2 THEN 'Tue'
      WHEN THE_WDI ( WD ) = 3 THEN 'Wed'
      WHEN THE_WDI ( WD ) = 4 THEN 'Thu'
      WHEN THE_WDI ( WD ) = 5 THEN 'Fri'
      WHEN THE_WDI ( WD ) = 6 THEN 'Sat'
   END CASE ;
END OPERATOR ;
```

Is WEEKDAY a valid point type? Well, intervals of the form "Wednesday to Friday" or "Friday to Monday" surely do make good intuitive sense. However, WEEKDAY does not fit the definition given in Section 16.1 for an ordinal type, because there is no first value of the type and no last. Of course, it is true that we might assert, somewhat arbitrarily, that (say) Sunday is the first day and Saturday the last, but then we could not deal with intervals like "Friday to Monday." Thus, it seems preferable to say rather that there is an ordering but it is *cyclic*,[14] meaning that (e.g.) Sunday follows immediately after Saturday. How do such considerations affect our point- and interval-type notions?

Referring again to the definition of *ordinal type* from Section 16.1, we see that:

- Type WEEKDAY has no corresponding ">" operator. Of course, it would be possible to define one, in either of two ways:

  - We could define *v1 > v2* to be true if and only if *v1* followed *v2* according to the fixed ordering, say, Saturday > Friday > ... > Monday > Sunday—where Saturday is thus the last day and Sunday the first after all. This definition of ">" does not seem very useful, since among other things it would outlaw intervals like "Friday to Monday."

  - We could define *v1 > v2* to be true if and only if *v1* followed *v2* according to the cyclic ordering. This definition seems even more useless than the previous one, since it implies that ">" would be indistinguishable from "≠" (*v1 > v2* would be true if and only if *v1 ≠ v2* was also true).

---

14. The more usual term in mathematics would be *periodic;* however, the term "periodic" would be likely to lead to confusion in the temporal database context, because the term *period* is often used in that context as a synonym for *interval* (especially in the SQL community).

- As already noted, type WEEKDAY also has no "first" and "last" operators. But it *does* have successor and predecessor functions. Here are the definitions:

```
OPERATOR NEXT_WEEKDAY ( D WEEKDAY ) RETURNS WEEKDAY ;
   RETURN WDPRI ( MOD ( THE_WDI ( D ) + 1, 7 ) ) ;
END OPERATOR ;

OPERATOR PRIOR_WEEKDAY ( D WEEKDAY ) RETURNS WEEKDAY ;
   RETURN WDPRI ( MOD ( THE_WDI ( D ) - 1, 7 ) ) ;
END OPERATOR ;
```

What is more, these functions, unlike their counterparts for types like DDATE, never fail. NOTE: In practice, the literal value 7 appearing in the RETURN statement in the definitions of these operators would better be replaced by an invocation of the COUNT_WEEKDAY operator (to be discussed).

Let us invent some syntax for indicating that a given type is a cyclic type—perhaps as here (note the boldface):

```
TYPE WEEKDAY CYCLIC ... ;
```

We interpret the CYCLIC specification as implying that:

- A niladic "cardinality" operator must be defined, which returns N, the number of values in the type; for type WEEKDAY, of course, N is seven. A real language might require the name of that operator—COUNT_WEEKDAY, say—to be specified as part of the CYCLIC specification.

- Monadic "next" and "prior" operators must also be defined, and they must be isomorphic to "add one" and "subtract one," respectively, in arithmetic modulo N. A real language might require the names of those operators—NEXT_WEEKDAY and PRIOR_WEEKDAY, in our example—to be specified as part of the CYCLIC specification.

Now let us examine the question of whether we can make sense of the idea of an interval type of the form INTERVAL_WEEKDAY. Values of this type, if we can make sense of it, will be intervals of the form [*b:e*], where *b* and *e* are both values of type WEEKDAY. What happens to the associated operators?

First of all, we define the necessary *selector* operator, as follows: The selector invocation INTERVAL_WEEKDAY ([*b:e*]), where *b* and *e* are values of type WEEKDAY, returns the interval consisting of the weekdays *b*, *b*+1, ..., *e*, such that no weekday appears more than once (i.e., no interval is more than one week in length). Here are some examples:

```
INTERVAL_WEEKDAY ( [ WDPRC('Mon') : WDPRC('Fri') ] )
INTERVAL_WEEKDAY ( [ WDPRC('Fri') : WDPRC('Mon') ] )
INTERVAL_WEEKDAY ( [ WDPRC('Wed') : WDPRC('Wed') ] )
INTERVAL_WEEKDAY ( [ WDPRC('Wed') : WDPRC('Tue') ] )
```

The first three of these examples are straightforward: They denote the five-day interval from Monday to Friday, the four-day interval from Friday to Monday, and the unit (one-day) interval consisting of just Wednesday, respectively. The fourth example is a little special, however. On the face of it, of course, it simply denotes the seven-day interval from Wednesday to Tuesday—but that interval is special, in that it includes all possible values of the underlying point type. Various questions arise in connection with such intervals, the most fundamental of which is this: If, for example, [Wed:Tue] and [Fri:Thu]—to adopt an obvious shorthand notation—are two such intervals, are they equal or not? We address this issue as follows:

- First, we define the **origin point** to be that value of the underlying point type that serves as "the zeroth value" (i.e., the value that performs a role analogous to the role of zero in arithmetic modulo N). In the case of WEEKDAY in particular, the origin is the day corresponding to the selector invocation WDPRI(0)—that is, Sunday, according to the way we defined the WEEKDAY type and the WDPRI operator a little while back.

- Next, given a cyclic point type CT, let Org be the corresponding origin point and (again) let N be the number of distinct values of the type. Then we define the *canonical form* of any interval of the form $[Org+k:Org+k+(N-1)]$ (k = 0, 1, ..., $N-1$) to be, precisely, the interval $[Org:Org+N-1]$. For example, if CT = WEEKDAY, then the canonical form for all of the following intervals—

  ```
  [Sun:Sat]
  [Mon:Sun]
  [Tue:Mon]
  [Wed:Tue]
  [Thu:Wed]
  [Fri:Thu]
  [Sat:Fri]
  ```

  —is the interval [Sun:Sat].

- Then we simply define all operators (selector operators in particular) to be such that, if the result of a given invocation of the operator in question is an interval of the form $[Org+k:Org+k+(N-1)]$ for some k, then that result is replaced by the corresponding canonical form $[Org:Org+N-1]$. As a consequence, the fourth of the interval selector invocations shown at the top of this page is defined to return the interval [Sun:Sat].

We turn now to further operators on intervals. BEGIN, END, PRE, POST, and POINT FROM are straightforward—though it might be worth pointing out that if i is the interval resulting from (e.g.) the selector invocation

```
INTERVAL_WEEKDAY ( [ WDPRC('Wed') : WDPRC('Tue') ] )
```

then BEGIN(i) returns Sunday, not Wednesday (!). The expression $d \in i$, where d is of type WEEKDAY and i is of type INTERVAL_WEEKDAY, returns true if and only if d is one of the values in the set {BEGIN(i), BEGIN(i)+1, ..., END(i)}. The expression $i \ni d$ is equivalent to the expression $d \in i$. The expression COUNT(i) returns the cardinality of the set {BEGIN(i), BEGIN(i)+1, ..., END(i)}.

Next we consider Allen's operators. As in Chapter 6, we consider two intervals $i1 = [b1:e1]$ and $i2 = [b2:e2]$ of the same interval type, but now we assume the underlying point type has a cyclic ordering.

Equals (=): This operator is obviously unaffected (that is, $i1 = i2$ is true if and only if $b1 = b2$ and $e1 = e2$ are both true).

Includes ($\supseteq$) and included in ($\subseteq$): These operators do apply, but their definitions need to be stated somewhat differently, as follows. Consider the process of examining the set of points $b1$, $b1+1$, $b1+2$, ..., $e1$ in sequence according to the cyclic ordering. Then $i1 \supseteq i2$ is true if and only if, as we perform this process, we encounter both $b2$ and $e2$ and we do *not* encounter $e2$ before $b2$. In other words, if $i1 \supseteq i2$ is true, then every point p that appears in $i2$ also appears in $i1$; however, the converse is not true.

It follows from this definition that, for example, [Mon:Fri] $\supseteq$ [Tue:Thu] and [Sat:Wed] $\supseteq$ [Sun:Mon] are both true, while [Mon:Fri] $\supseteq$ [Thu:Sat] and [Mon:Fri] $\supseteq$ [Thu:Tue] are both false. Note the last of these examples in particular; as we examine the set of points Mon, Tue, Wed, Thu, Fri, we do encounter both Thu and Tue, but we do so "the wrong way round."

The operators "$\supset$", "$\subseteq$", and "$\subset$" are defined analogously.

BEFORE and AFTER: These operators also apply, but the definitions need to be stated a little differently, as follows: $i1$ BEFORE $i2$ is true if and only if, in the cyclic ordering starting from $b1$, (1) $e1$ is encountered before $b2$, and (2) $e2$ is encountered before $b1$ is encountered a second time. Note that it follows from this definition that $i2$ BEFORE $i1$ is true if and only if $i1$ BEFORE $i2$ is true (!). It also follows that $i1$ BEFORE $i2$ is true if and only if $i1$ and $i2$ are disjoint—that is, there is no point p that appears in both $i1$ and $i2$. Also, $i2$ AFTER $i1$ is true if and only if $i1$ BEFORE $i2$ is true (so in fact the operators BEFORE and AFTER are one and the same). For example, [Tue:Wed] BEFORE [Fri:Sat], [Fri:Sat] BEFORE [Tue:Wed], [Tue:Wed] AFTER [Fri:Sat], and [Fri:Sat] AFTER [Tue:Wed] are all true. By contrast, [Tue:Fri] BEFORE [Wed:Sat] is false.

MEETS: The original definition from Chapter 6 remains unchanged: $i1$ MEETS $i2$ is true if and only if $b2 = e1+1$ is true or $b1 = e2+1$ is true (and $i2$ MEETS $i1$ is true if and only if *i1* MEETS *i2* is true). Note, however, that with ordinal point types, *i1* MEETS *i2* and *i1* OVERLAPS *i2* cannot both be true, but with cyclic point types they can. For example, [Fri:Mon] MEETS [Tue:Sun] and [Fri:Mon] OVERLAPS [Tue:Sun] are both true.

OVERLAPS: The simplest way to define this operator is to say that *i1* OVERLAPS *i2* is true if and only if *i1* and *i2* are not disjoint—that is, there exists at least one point *p* that appears in both *i1* and *i2*. Equivalently, *i1* OVERLAPS *i2* is true if and only if *i1* BEFORE *i2* is false. For example, the following pairs of intervals overlap:

```
[Tue:Thu] and [Wed:Fri]
[Tue:Thu] and [Mon:Wed]
[Tue:Thu] and [Mon:Tue]
[Tue:Thu] and [Mon:Fri]
[Tue:Thu] and [Fri:Wed]
```

The following, by contrast, do not:

```
[Tue:Thu] and [Fri:Sat]
[Tue:Thu] and [Sun:Mon]
[Tue:Thu] and [Fri:Mon]
```

NOTE: Since MEETS and OVERLAPS both apply, it follows that MERGES applies as well.

BEGINS and ENDS: These operators also apply, but once again the definitions need to be stated a little differently, as follows: (1) *i1* BEGINS *i2* is true if and only if *b1* = *b2* and *e1* ∈ *i2* are both true; (2) *i1* ENDS *i2* is true if and only if *e1* = *e2* and *b1* ∈ *i2* are both true.

We turn now to the interval UNION, INTERSECT, and MINUS operators. These operators do apply, but recall that:

- *i1* UNION *i2* is not defined unless *i1* MERGES *i2* is true.

- *i1* INTERSECT *i2* is not defined unless *i1* OVERLAPS *i2* is true.

- *i1* MINUS *i2* is not defined unless *i1* BEGINS *i2*, *i1* ENDS *i2*, *i1* ⊃ *i2*, and *i1* ⊂ *i2* are all false.

In the case of INTERSECT, however, the stated condition is necessary but not sufficient for the operation to be defined. To be specific, *i1* INTERSECT *i2* is defined if and only if:

- *i1* OVERLAPS *i2* is true (as already stated), *and*

- It is not the case that the complement of either operand is included in the other operand without beginning or ending it—where (1) given a cyclic point type, the **complement** of an interval *i* = [*b*:*e*] that is defined over that cyclic point type is the interval [*e*+1:*b*–1], and (2) "beginning" and "ending" refer to the BEGINS and ENDS operators as defined above. NOTE: The effect of this requirement is to ensure that *i1* and *i2* do not overlap "at both ends," as it were; for example, if *i1* = [Mon:Fri] and *i2* = [Thu:Tue], then *i1* INTERSECT *i2* is not defined. We remark in passing that (1) the complement of the complement of *i* is just *i* and (2) the interval [*Org*:*Org*+*N*–1] is its own complement.

Assuming the applicable conditions are met, then:

- *UNION: i1* UNION *i2* is that unique interval *i* such that *p* ∈ *i* is true if and only if at least one of *p* ∈ *i1* and *p* ∈ *i2* is true. NOTE: If *b2* ∈ [*b1*:*e1*+1] and *e2* ∈ [*b1*–1:*e1*] are both true, then *i1* and *i2* together contain every point of the underlying point type, and *i1* UNION *i2* is the interval [*Org*:*Org*+*N*–1]; otherwise, there exists exactly one interval *i* = [*b*:*e*] such that if *p* ∈ *i*, then *p* ∉ *i1* and *p* ∉ *i2* are both true, and *i1* UNION *i2* is the interval [*e*+1:*b*–1].

- *INTERSECT: i1* INTERSECT *i2* is that unique interval *i* such that *p* ∈ *i* is true if and only if *p* ∈ *i1* and *p* ∈ *i2* are both true.

- *MINUS: i1* MINUS *i2* is that unique interval *i* such that *p* ∈ *i* is true if and only if *p* ∈ *i1* and *p* ∉ *i2* are both true.

Some examples of UNION and INTERSECT are given in Figure 16.5 (MINUS is left as an exercise).

FIGURE 16.5

UNION and INTERSECT examples involving intervals defined over a cyclic point type.

i1	*i2*	*i1* UNION *i2*	*i1* INTERSECT *i2*
[Mon:Thu]	[Tue:Fri]	[Mon:Fri]	[Tue:Thu]
[Mon:Fri]	[Tue:Thu]	[Mon:Fri]	[Tue:Thu]
[Thu:Mon]	[Tue:Fri]	[Sun:Sat]	[Thu:Fri]
[Thu:Mon]	[Fri:Tue]	[Thu:Tue]	[Fri:Mon]
[Sat:Sat]	[Sat:Sat]	[Sat:Sat]	[Sat:Sat]

Next we consider EXPAND and COLLAPSE. These operators are straightforward. For example, let *X* be the set of intervals

{ [Tue:Thu], [Wed:Fri], [Sat:Mon] }

Then the expanded form of *X*, *Y* say, is

{ [Tue:Tue], [Wed:Wed], [Thu:Thu], [Fri:Fri],
                  [Sat:Sat], [Sun:Sun], [Mon:Mon] }

And the collapsed form of *X* (or *Y*) is

```
{ [Sun:Sat] }
```

Finally, it follows directly from the foregoing that the PACK and UNPACK operators can be generalized appropriately too. The details are left as an exercise.

Overall, therefore, we conclude that:

1. Cyclic types such as WEEKDAY are indeed valid as point types.

2. Such types behave normally, except that FIRST_*T* and LAST_*T* do not apply and NEXT_*T* and PRIOR_*T* never fail.

3. The corresponding interval types also behave more or less normally, except that certain operators need somewhat revised definitions.

4. The conditions stated in Chapter 5 and Section 16.1 for a type to be usable as a point type are sufficient but not necessary.

16.8 CONTINUOUS POINT TYPES

There is one last issue we need to discuss briefly in this chapter, and that is the possibility of **continuous** point types. All of the point types we have considered in detail in this book so far have been *discrete* or "quantized" types, and we have assumed that intervals are always defined over such types and thus consist of a finite sequence of discrete points. Let us agree to refer to this assumption as *the discreteness assumption*. Then the question is: What happens if we relax, or reject, this assumption? In other words, would it be possible to build an approach to intervals in general (and temporal intervals in particular) that is based on *continuous* point types? After all, time in particular certainly "feels" as if it were continuous, not quantized[15]—so would not such an approach, if it were possible, be more intuitively attractive?

Of course, we are not alone in adopting the discreteness assumption—virtually all of the temporal research literature does the same thing—but we should make it clear that the assumption has not been without its critics, in both industrial and academic circles. That is, there are those who would prefer an approach based on a *continuity* assumption instead. In such an approach, every interval would be perceived as isomorphic to an interval over real numbers, and would therefore involve an infinite set of contained points.[16]

---

15. We are aware that not everyone agrees with this assertion.

16. Unless it happens to be a unit interval and therefore contains exactly one point. But it is not clear that unit intervals even exist under the continuity assumption! Certainly it is impossible to write an interval selector invocation that will return such an interval. The reason is that, under the continuity assumption, the only selector invocation that could return such an interval would have to use the closed-closed style, and the closed-closed style makes little sense under that assumption, as we will see.

However, we have not seen any specific language proposal based on such an approach, and so we confine ourselves here to just a few pertinent comments.

The most obvious and fundamental observation is that the real numbers have no successor function (if n is a real number, there is no "next" real number n'). As an immmediate consequence of this fact, certain of the operators defined earlier in this book for points, intervals, and so forth are no longer available.

- *With regard to points:* The comparison operators ("=", ">", etc.) still work, but the operators NEXT_T, PRIOR_T, IS_NEXT_T, and IS_PRIOR_T make no sense. As for FIRST_T and LAST_T, these operators do still work—in temporal terms they return "the beginning of time" and "the end of time," respectively—but they are subject to a slight anomaly, as we will see in a few moments.

- *With regard to intervals:* First, COUNT clearly no longer applies (continuous intervals contain an *infinite* number of points, in general). Allen's operators do apply, but MEETS in particular requires careful definition; we cannot possibly say (for example) that intervals $[b:n]$ and $[n':e]$ meet, because (again) we can never say that n' is the successor of n. However, if we adopt *closed-open* notation, then we certainly can say that, for example, intervals $[b:n)$ and $[n:e)$ meet. In fact, neither the closed-closed nor the open-open style for writing intervals makes much sense under the continuity assumption, and interval selector operators will have to be limited to one of the other two styles (not both, for reasons that will quickly become clear).

Now we can explain the anomaly that arises in connection with FIRST_T and LAST_T. If we use the open-closed style for interval selectors, then intervals that include "the beginning of time" cannot be expressed. Alternatively, if we use the closed-open style, then intervals that include "the end of time" cannot be expressed. In fact, neither the open-closed nor the closed-open style is a true "possible representation" for the interval type in question, and the same remark applies to the open-open style. What is more, no two of these three styles are equivalent!—each of them can represent some value that the other two cannot. The implications of this state of affairs are unclear.

From this point forward we will assume the closed-open style, for definiteness. Under that assumption, the PRE and END operators are no longer available. Note, however, that the "end point" e of interval $i = [b:e)$ is given by POST(i); however, that "end point" is not actually included in interval i and is thus not truly an end point as such, in the sense in which that term was defined in Chapter 5.

Finally, the EXPAND and UNPACK operators are also no longer available. The loss of UNPACK in particular is a matter for some concern. Although that operator is perhaps not all that useful in its own right, our "U_" relational operators are all defined in terms of it (and so is PACK, if the packing is done on more than one attribute); thus, we would need to revisit all of these operators to see if we could redefine them in such a way as to avoid having to rely on UNPACK. What is more, we would have to verify that those revised operators were all implementable.

We do not feel inclined to investigate these questions any further, however, for the following reasons:

- First, we have seen that certain operators that can be defined when the discreteness assumption is adopted *cannot* be defined when the continuity assumption is adopted instead (except as discussed in the final two paragraphs of this section).

- Second, nobody has yet been able to show us any useful operators that can be defined when the continuity assumption is adopted but not when the discreteness assumption is adopted instead.

It seems, then, that there is nothing to lose, and much to gain, by adopting the discreteness assumption.

There are a couple of final points to be made. First, some computer programmers in particular have expressed concern over the idea that, under the discreteness assumption, the type "floating-point numbers" would not be usable as a point type. In fact, we think it *would* be usable, because the number of *representable* real numbers between any two representable bounds is obviously finite. However, any such point type will inevitably behave in ways that are a little hard to understand; in particular, such types will necessarily involve a lack of uniformity of scale, and hence have a somewhat unusual successor function, much as the point type PRIME did (see the example near the end of Section 16.5).

Second, it has been suggested that it might be possible to make operators that depend on the discreteness assumption work after all, even if we adopt the continuity assumption instead. The idea is that, in effect, the desired scale—equivalently, the desired successor function—could be specified as part of the invocation of the operator in question. For example, let *i* be a continuous interval denoting (say) a certain period of time. We have seen that, for example, the expression COUNT(*i*) makes no sense. However, if we define *j* as the expression—

```
INTERVAL_DDATE ( [ CAST_TO_DDATE ( BEGIN ( i ) ),
                   CAST_TO_DDATE ( POST  ( i ) ) ) )
```

—then the expression COUNT(*j*) clearly does make sense. EXPLANATION: The "cast" invocations effectively convert their argument to a time point that is accurate to the day. The overall interval selector invocation *j* thus (1) effectively converts the continuous interval *i* to a discrete interval whose contained points are accurate to the day, and thereby (2) implicitly specifies the pertinent scale and pertinent successor function.

Our response to the foregoing suggestion is that if the continuity assumption means continuous intervals have to be converted to their discrete counterparts every time we want to apply certain important operators to them, then there seems to be little point in adopting that assumption in the first place. Indeed, if we are correct when we say that adopting that assumption brings with it no useful operators that are unavailable otherwise, then a language based on that assumption would be isomorphic to one based on the discreteness assumption instead, and the entire argument reduces to a mere matter of syntax. However, we note that *not* having to specify the scale and successor function every time we want to perform any of the otherwise undefined operations would surely save a significant amount of writing.

16.9 CONCLUDING REMARKS

In this chapter we have examined (among many other things) the concepts of *point type, interval type, ordering* (both cyclic and acyclic, where acyclic = ordinal is the normal case), *precision, scale, successor function,* and *granularity*. These concepts, though distinct, are very much interwoven; in fact, they are interwoven in rather complicated ways, and it can sometimes be quite difficult to say just where the demarcations lie. What we have tried to do is pin down the distinctions among those concepts as precisely as possible, and thereby shed some light on what often seems, in the literature, to be a very confusing—not to say confused—subject.

EXERCISES

1. Define in your own terms:

    a. Substitutability

    b. Specialization by constraint

    c. Generalization by constraint

2. What do you understand by the term *multiple inheritance?*

3. Let CHAR(*n*) denote a type whose values are character strings of not more than *n* characters. Does CHAR(*n*) make sense as a point type?

4. Give a **Tutorial D** definition for a point type called MONEY (with the obvious semantics; assume for the sake of the exercise that such a type is not built in). Include definitions for all necessary selectors and THE_ operators, also for the successor function and related operators (FIRST_MONEY, IS_PRIOR_MONEY, etc.).

5. Extend your answer to Exercise 4 to incorporate the necessary support for two distinct monetary scales, one expressed in terms of (say) dollars and the other in terms of cents.

6. Define "time of day" as a cyclic point type with a scale of one hour. Show all necessary definitions.

7. Given that *i1* and *i2* denote intervals over the "time of day" point type, fill in the blanks in the following:

i1	*i2*	*i1* UNION *i2*	*i1* INTERSECT *i2*	*i1* MINUS *i2*
[09:17]	[11:21]			
[11:21]	[09:17]			
[08:12]	[12:16]			
[21:07]	[05:11]			
[09:18]	[05:14]			
[05:14]	[05:14]			
[09:15]	[11:14]			
[09:15]	[09:12]			
[09:12]	[09:15]			
[06:18]	[18:06]			

NOTE: We are assuming for simplicity that intervals over the "time of day" point type can be expressed in the form [*xx:yy*], where *xx* and *yy* are two-digit integers in the range 00 through 23 and denote time points accurate to the hour on the 24-hour clock.

8. Summarize in your own words the arguments for and against continuous point types.

APPENDIXES

There are three appendixes:

A. Implementation Considerations

B. Generalizing the EXPAND and COLLAPSE Operators

C. References and Bibliography

Appendix A discusses a variety of transformation laws and algorithms for implementing the various operators (especially PACK and UNPACK) that were described in the body of the book. Appendix B considers the possibility of generalizing the EXPAND and COLLAPSE operators, and hence the UNPACK and PACK operators also, to deal with noninterval data. Appendix C provides an annotated list of bibliographic references.

Appendix

A

IMPLEMENTATION
CONSIDERATIONS

A.1   INTRODUCTION

Our primary aim in this book has been to show how the relational model can be used to address the important problem of temporal data management—or, more generally, how it can be used to address any problem in which the use of interval data is relevant. Essentially, in other words, we have been concerned with getting the underlying *model* right. In this appendix, by contrast, we take a brief (and fairly high-level) look at the corresponding question of *implementation*—though we should say immediately that some of the ideas we will be discussing are still somewhat logical, not physical, in nature, and are thus still model issues in a way. To be specific, we will be considering among other things certain *transformation laws* (which we will refer to as just *transforms* for short) that apply to certain of the relational operators, and those transforms can certainly be regarded as characteristics, or at least logical consequences, of the underlying model. We will also sketch the details of certain implementation algorithms for those operators.

One general point: Of course, we make no claim that what follows is the last word on implementation matters (it would not be the last word even if we were to expand it to include all of our thoughts on the topic). New and better techniques are constantly being invented in this field as in others, and we welcome the possibility of useful innovations on the part of other workers in the area.

A.2 PACK AND UNPACK (I)

In this section we merely list some transforms that apply to the PACK and UNPACK operators specifically (with additional commentary in certain cases). Let r be an arbitrary relation. Then:

1. PACK r ON () $\equiv$ r

2. UNPACK r ON () $\equiv$ r

Next, let r be a relation with an interval attribute A. Then:

3. PACK (PACK r ON A) ON A $\equiv$ PACK r ON A

4. PACK (UNPACK r ON A) ON A $\equiv$ PACK r ON A

5. UNPACK (UNPACK r ON A) ON A $\equiv$ UNPACK r ON A

6. UNPACK (PACK r ON A) ON A $\equiv$ UNPACK r ON A

NOTE: Of course, PACK is defined in terms of a preliminary UNPACK anyway, so it might be objected that Transform 4 above is not very useful; however, see Transform 8 below.

Now let r be a relation with a set of interval attributes $A1, A2, ..., An$, let ACL be a commalist of those interval attribute names in sequence as shown, and let BCL be an arbitrary permutation of ACL. Then:

7. UNPACK r ON (ACL) $\equiv$ UNPACK r ON (BCL)

Note that an analogous transform does *not* apply to PACK, in general.

Next, recall that (as noted a moment ago) PACK r ON (ACL) is defined to require a preliminary UNPACK r ON (ACL):

PACK r ON (ACL) $\equiv$
PACK (... (PACK (PACK r' ON $A1$) ON $A2$) ...) ON An

where r' is

UNPACK r ON ($A1, A2, ..., An$)

However, there is in fact no need to do the preliminary UNPACK on *A1*. In other words, the following is a valid transform:

```
8. PACK r ON ( ACL )  ≡
     PACK ( ... ( PACK ( PACK r'' ON A1 ) ON A2 ) ... ) ON An
```

where *r″* is

```
UNPACK r ON ( A2, ..., An )
```

As an important special case of Transform 8, we can ignore the implicit initial UNPACK when packing on just a single attribute (as in fact we already know from Chapter 8).

Now let *r* be a relation with an interval attribute *A*, and let *B* be all of the attributes of *r* apart from *A*. Let *r1, r2, ..., rk* be a partitioning of *r* on *B*—that is, a grouping of the tuples of *r* into distinct sets (*partitions*) such that (1) all *B* values in a given partition are the same and (2) *B* values in different partitions are different. Then:

```
 9. PACK r ON A   ≡   ( PACK r1 ON A ) UNION
                      ( PACK r2 ON A ) UNION
                      .........        UNION
                      ( PACK rk ON A )

10. UNPACK r ON A ≡   ( UNPACK r1 ON A ) UNION
                      ( UNPACK r2 ON A ) UNION
                      ..........         UNION
                      ( UNPACK rk ON A )
```

We will make use of Transform 9 in particular in our discussion of the SPLIT operator in the next section.

We close this section by observing that

- if *r* is a relation with an interval attribute *A* and *B* is all of the attributes of *r* apart from *A* (as for Transforms 9 and 10), and

- if *r* is represented in storage by a stored file *f* such that there is a one-to-one correspondence between the tuples of *r* and the stored records of *f*, and

- if *f* is physically sorted in *A*-within-*B* order (more precisely, on BEGIN(*A*)-within-*B* order),

then both PACK *r* ON *A* and UNPACK *r* ON *A* can be implemented in a single pass over *f*. The PACK case in particular is important, and we therefore offer some further comments in connection with it.

Suppose we are indeed processing the stored file *f* in *A*-within-*B* order. Consider a particular *B* value *b*; by definition, all stored records having *B* = *b* will be physically grouped together. Therefore, when we are processing that particular group of stored records, as soon as we encounter one whose A value neither meets nor overlaps the A value from the immediately preceding record, we can emit an output record (and similarly when we reach the end of the entire group). The PACK implementation can thus be **pipelined**; that is, the result can be computed "one tuple at a time," as it were (more correctly, one record at a time), and there is no need for the invoker to wait for the entire result to be materialized before carrying out further work.

The foregoing observations are pertinent to many of the implementation algorithms to be discussed in the sections to follow. In particular, those observations imply that whenever such an algorithm talks about inserting a tuple into some result that is being built up gradually, it might be possible for the implementation simply to return the tuple in question—or the record, rather—directly to the invoker; the overall result (usually representing some relation in some unpacked form) might never need to be physically materialized in its entirety.

In addition, if f is indeed sorted on B as suggested, then that fact permits an obvious and efficient implementation for the operation of partitioning r on B. This point is worth making explicitly because several of the algorithms to be discussed in the sections to follow make use of such partitioning.

A.3 PACK AND UNPACK (II)

The various U_ operators to be discussed in Sections A.5 through A.7 are all defined in terms of PACK and UNPACK. A good implementation of these operators is thus highly desirable! In this section, we take a closer look at this issue.

PACK

We focus our attention first on PACK. The fundamental problem with PACK from an implementation perspective is that it is defined in terms of a preliminary series of implicit *UNPACKs*, and UNPACKs have the potential to be extremely expensive in execution (in terms of both space and time). Following reference [69], therefore, we now proceed to show how

- certain of those implicit UNPACKs can be "optimized away" entirely, and

- others can be replaced internally by a more efficient operator called SPLIT.

It is convenient to begin by introducing an operator that we will call PACK– ("pack minus"). Informally, PACK– is the same as the regular PACK, except that it does not require the preliminary unpacking on all specified attributes that the regular PACK does require. (In our implementation algorithms, therefore, we will take care to use PACK– in place of PACK only when we know it is safe to do so—in particular, when we know the input relation is appropriately unpacked already.) Here first is the definition of PACK– when the packing is to be done on just a single attribute:

```
PACK- r ON A  ≡  WITH ( r GROUP { A } AS X ) AS T1 ,
                      ( EXTEND T1 ADD COLLAPSE ( X ) AS Y )
                                            { ALL BUT X } AS T2 :
                 T2 UNGROUP Y
```

This definition is identical to the one we first gave for the regular PACK operator in Chapter 8 (near the end of Section 8.2), where we were concerned with packing on the basis of a single attribute only. It follows that PACK– is identical to PACK if the packing is to be done on the basis of a single attribute.

Next, we define PACK– on *n* attributes *A1, A2, ..., An* (in that order) thus:

```
PACK- r ON ( A1, A2, ... An )  ≡
PACK- ( ... ( PACK- ( PACK- r ON A1 ) ON A2 ) ... ) ON An
```

Here is an example. Consider Figure A.1, which shows a possible value for relvar S_PARTS_DURING (a relvar with two interval attributes, PARTS and DURING[1]). We have labeled the tuples in the figure for purposes of subsequent reference. Observe that the relation as shown does involve certain redundancies; for example, tuples *x3* and *x4* both tell us among other things that supplier S1 was able to supply part P06 on day *d08*.

FIGURE A.1
Relvar S_PARTS_
DURING
—sample value.

S_PARTS_DURING		S#	PARTS	DURING
	x1	S1	[P01:P02]	[d01:d04]
	x2	S1	[P04:P09]	[d01:d04]
	x3	S1	[P06:P10]	[d03:d08]
	x4	S1	[P01:P08]	[d07:d10]
	x5	S2	[P15:P20]	[d01:d10]
	x6	S3	[P01:P05]	[d10:d15]
	x7	S3	[P01:P05]	[d16:d20]
	x8	S3	[P05:P10]	[d25:d30]

Now, we can eliminate those redundancies—also any circumlocutions that might be present—by replacing the current value of relvar S_PARTS_DURING by the result of evaluating the following expression (which uses PACK, not PACK–, please note):

```
PACK S_PARTS_DURING ON ( PARTS, DURING )
```

The result is shown in Figure A.2.

---

1. Most of the discussions in this appendix are expressed in terms of packing and unpacking on exactly two attributes, for definiteness. However, those discussions all extend gracefully to apply to the *n*-attribute case for arbitrary *n* [71]; in particular, they apply to the important common case *n* = 1, a case that is much easier to deal with in practice, as we will see.

FIGURE A.2

Packing the relation
of Figure A.1 on
(PARTS,
DURING).

	S#	PARTS	DURING
y1	S1	[P01:P02]	[d01:d04]
y2	S1	[P04:P09]	[d01:d02]
y3	S1	[P04:P10]	[d03:d04]
y4	S1	[P06:P10]	[d05:d06]
y5	S1	[P01:P10]	[d07:d08]
y6	S1	[P01:P08]	[d09:d10]
y7	S2	[P15:P20]	[d01:d10]
y8	S3	[P01:P05]	[d10:d20]
y9	S3	[P05:P10]	[d25:d30]

Next we observe that the foregoing PACK expression is, of course, logically equivalent to this longer one:

```
PACK
    ( UNPACK S_PARTS_DURING ON ( DURING, PARTS ) )
ON ( PARTS, DURING )
```

(We have deliberately specified the attributes in the sequence DURING-then-PARTS for the UNPACK and PARTS-then-DURING for the PACK, for reasons that will become clear in just a moment. Of course, the sequence makes no difference anyway in the case of UNPACK.)

We now note that the argument to PACK in the foregoing longer expression is guaranteed to be appropriately unpacked, and we can therefore safely replace that PACK by PACK– instead, thus:

```
PACK-
    ( UNPACK S_PARTS_DURING ON ( DURING, PARTS ) )
ON ( PARTS, DURING )
```

This expression in turn is logically equivalent to:

```
WITH ( UNPACK S_PARTS_DURING ON DURING ) AS T1 ,
     ( UNPACK T1 ON PARTS ) AS T2 ,
     ( PACK- T2 ON PARTS ) AS T3 :
PACK- T3 ON DURING
```

However, the middle two steps here can obviously be combined into one, thanks to the identity

```
PACK- ( UNPACK T1 ON PARTS ) ON PARTS  ≡  PACK- T1 ON PARTS
```

(This identity is clearly valid, because (1) PACK– is identical to PACK if the operation is performed on the basis of a single attribute, and (2) we know from Section A.2 that the identity that results if we replace PACK– by PACK on both sides is valid.) It follows that the overall expression can be simplified to just

```
WITH ( UNPACK S_PARTS_DURING ON DURING ) AS T1 ,
     ( PACK- T1 ON PARTS ) AS T3 :
PACK- T3 ON DURING
```

So we have succeeded in optimizing away one of the UNPACKs, and the operation is thus more efficient than it was before.

Can we get rid of the other UNPACK as well? Well, we have already indicated that the answer to this question is *yes*, but the details are a little more complicated than they were for the first UNPACK. Basically, the idea is to avoid unpacking "all the way," as it were (i.e., unpacking all the way down to unit intervals); instead, we "unpack" (or *split*, rather) only as far as is truly necessary—which is to say, down to certain *maximal nonoverlapping subintervals*. The effect is to produce a result with fewer tuples than a full UNPACK would produce, in general; however, that result is still such as to allow us "to focus on the information content at an atomic level, without having to worry about the many ways in which that information might be bundled into clumps" (as we put it in Chapter 7).

By way of an example, consider tuple *x3* from Figure A.1:

	S#	PARTS	DURING
x3	S1	[P06:P10]	[*d03*:*d08*]

This tuple can be split into the following three tuples (note the tuple labels):

	S#	PARTS	DURING
x31	S1	[P06:P10]	[*d03*:*d04*]

	S#	PARTS	DURING
x32	S1	[P06:P10]	[*d05*:*d06*]

	S#	PARTS	DURING
x33	S1	[P06:P10]	[*d07*:*d08*]

Of course, tuples *x31* through *x33* together represent the same information as the original tuple *x3* did.

Why exactly would we want to split tuple *x3* in the way just shown? In order to answer this question, consider first the relation—let us call it relation X—that is the restriction of the relation shown in Figure A.1 to just the tuples for supplier S1:

	S#	PARTS	DURING
x1	S1	[P01:P02]	[*d01:d04*]
x2	S1	[P04:P09]	[*d01:d04*]
x3	S1	[P06:P10]	[*d03:d08*]
x4	S1	[P01:P08]	[*d07:d10*]

Note that the tuple to be split, tuple *x3*, has DURING value $i = [d03:d08]$. Intuitively speaking, then, we split tuple *x3* the way we did because:

- Interval *i* consists of the six points *d03*, *d04*, *d05*, *d06*, *d07*, and *d08*.

- Of these six, the four points *d03*, *d04*, *d07*, and *d08* (only) are boundary points—either begin or end points—for the DURING value in at least one tuple in X.

- Those boundary points divide interval *i* into precisely the subintervals [*d03:d04*], [*d05:d06*], and [*d07:d08*].

- Hence the indicated split.

Here then is our general algorithm for splitting all of the tuples in some given relation. NOTE: We will state and illustrate the algorithm initially with reference to the simple relation X just shown, containing just the tuples for supplier S1 (i.e., tuples *x1* through *x4*) from Figure A.1; then we will extend the algorithm to deal with an arbitrary relation, using the relation shown in Figure A.1 as the basis for an extended example.

Step 1: Create an ordered list L consisting of all points p such that p is equal to either b or $e+1$ for some DURING value [*b:e*] in X. (In other words, b is BEGIN(DURING) and $e+1$ is POST(DURING) for the DURING value in question.) In our example, L is the list

    d01, d03, d05, d07, d09, d11

Step 2: Let x be some tuple in X. Create an ordered list Lx consisting of all points p from L such that $b \le p \le e+1$, where [*b:e*] is the DURING value in x. For example, in the case of tuple *x3*, Lx is the list

    d03, d05, d07, d09

Step 3: For every consecutive pair of points (b,e) appearing in Lx, produce a tuple obtained from tuple x by replacing the DURING value in x by the interval [*b:e*–1]. For tuple *x3*, this step yields the three tuples *x31* through *x33* shown earlier. We say that tuple *x3* has been *split with respect to the points in L*.

If we now repeat Steps 2 and 3 for every tuple in X and make a relation containing all and only the tuples thus produced, we obtain the relation Y shown in Figure A.3. For the purposes of this appendix, we will express this fact by saying that Y is obtained by evaluating the expression

```
SPLIT X ON DURING VIA L
```

In other words, we will pretend for the purposes of this appendix that we have an operator called SPLIT available to us whose syntax is SPLIT *R* ON *A* VIA *L*, where *R* is either a *<relvar name>* or an *<introduced name>*, *A* is the name of an interval attribute, and *L* is the name of a list of values of the point type underlying the interval type of that attribute *A*.

	S#	PARTS	DURING
x11	S1	[P01:P02]	[*d01:d02*]
x12	S1	[P01:P02]	[*d03:d04*]
x21	S1	[P04:P09]	[*d01:d02*]
x22	S1	[P04:P09]	[*d03:d04*]
x31	S1	[P06:P10]	[*d03:d04*]
x32	S1	[P06:P10]	[*d05:d06*]
x33	S1	[P06:P10]	[*d07:d08*]
x41	S1	[P01:P08]	[*d07:d08*]
x42	S1	[P01:P08]	[*d09:d10*]

FIGURE A.3 Relation Y = SPLIT X ON DURING VIA L.

And now the expression

```
PACK- Y ON ( PARTS, DURING )
```

gives us all of the tuples to be found for supplier S1 in the result of packing S_PARTS_DURING on (PARTS, DURING)—in other words, tuples *y1* through *y6* as shown in Figure A.2—*without performing any UNPACKs, as such, at all.*

As an aside, we remark that our algorithm does have the slightly unfortunate effect of first splitting tuple *x1* into tuples *x11* and *x12* and then recombining those two tuples to obtain tuple *x1* again—or tuple *y1*, rather, as it is labeled in Figure A.2. It would be possible to enhance the algorithm in such a way as to avoid such unnecessary splitting and recombining, but care would be needed to ensure that the enhancement did in fact decrease the overall execution time and not increase it. We omit further discussion of this possibility here.

Just to complete our discussion of SPLIT: Clearly, in order to split every tuple in the original S_PARTS_DURING relation, we need to partition that relation on attribute S# (in our example, we obtain three partitions, one each for supplier S1, supplier S2, and supplier S3), and repeat Steps 1 through 3 with each partition in turn taking on the role of X.

Having now explained SPLIT, we can present *an efficient five-step algorithm* for implementing PACK (PACK, not PACK–) in terms of SPLIT on a relation *r* with two interval attributes *A1* and *A2*. Let *B* be all of the attributes of *r* apart from *A1* and *A2*. Then:

Step 1: Initialize *result* to empty.

Step 2: Partition *r* on *B*. Let the resulting partitions be *r1, r2, ..., rk*.

Step 3: For each *ri* (*i* = 1, 2, ..., *k*), do Steps 4 and 5.

Step 4: Create an ordered list L consisting of all points *p* such that *p* is equal to either BEGIN(*A2*) or POST(*A2*) for some *A2* value in *ri*.

Step 5: Execute the following:

```
WITH ( SPLIT ri ON A2 VIA L ) AS T1 ,
     ( PACK- T1 ON A1 ) AS T2 ,
     ( PACK- T2 ON A2 ) AS T3 :
result  :=  result UNION T3 ;
```

We observe that, in comparison with an implementation involving explicit UNPACKS, the foregoing algorithm (1) is considerably faster and (2) requires substantially less space, because it is applied to each partition of the original relation separately. Additional implementation techniques, such as the use of suitable indexes (on the final result as well as on the original relation and intermediate results), can be used to improve execution time still further. Details of such additional techniques are beyond the scope of this appendix, however. (The foregoing remarks apply equally, *mutatis mutandis,* to the algorithms we will be presenting in later sections for U_UNION, U_MINUS, and so on. We will not repeat them in those later sections, letting this one paragraph do duty for all.)

We close this discussion by observing that the implementation algorithm for PACK becomes *much* simpler in the important special case in which the packing is done on the basis of just a single attribute, because in that case no splitting or unpacking is needed at all. That is, if *r* is a relation with an interval attribute *A* and *B* is all of the attributes of *r* apart from *A,* then we can implement PACK *r* ON *A* by simply implementing PACK– *r* ON *A*. And if *r* is represented in storage by a stored file *f* such that there is a one-to-one correspondence between the tuples of *r* and the stored records of *f,* then an efficient way to implement PACK– *r* ON *A* is to sort *f* into *A*-within-*B* order and then perform the packing in a single pass over *f*.

UNPACK

Now we turn to UNPACK. Again, let *r* be a relation with two interval attributes *A1* and *A2,* and let *B* be all of the attributes of *r* apart from *A1* and *A2*. We consider the expression

```
UNPACK r ON ( A1, A2 )
```

The first thing we do is PACK (yes, pack) r on (A1,A2), using the efficient implementation for PACK as described above. Let r′ be the result of this step. Then we execute the following (pseudocode):

```
initialize result to empty ;
do for each tuple t ∈ r′ ;
   do for each p1 ∈ (A1 FROM t) ;
      do for each p2 ∈ (A2 FROM t) ;
         insert tuple { A1 [p1:p1], A2 [p2:p2], B (B FROM t) }
         into result ;
      end do ;
   end do ;
end do ;
```

Of course, we are assuming here that materialization of the unpacked form of r on (A1,A2) is actually required. In practice, it is to be hoped that various transforms can be used to "optimize away" the need for such materialization, in which case it will be sufficient to perform just the preliminary PACK step. In other words, it might not be necessary to produce the unpacked form at all, if (as will usually be the case) the result of the original UNPACK is to be passed as an argument to some operator Op and the desired overall result can be obtained by applying Op (or some other operator Op′) directly to r′ instead. In particular, it should *never* be necessary to materialize the result of unpacking a relation on the basis of just one attribute, except in the unlikely case in which the user explicitly requests such a materialization.

A.4 A GRAPHICAL REPRESENTATION

Certain of the ideas discussed in the previous section lend themselves to a graphical or geometric representation, and some readers might find such a representation helpful. Consider once again the relation X from Section A.3, containing just the tuples *x1* through *x4* (the ones for supplier S1) from Figure A.1:

	S#	PARTS	DURING
x1	S1	[P01:P02]	[d01:d04]
x2	S1	[P04:P09]	[d01:d04]
x3	S1	[P06:P10]	[d03:d08]
x4	S1	[P01:P08]	[d07:d10]

Figure A.4 shows a graphical representation of the PARTS and DURING components of the four tuples in this relation. The redundancy or overlap among those tuples is very obvious from that figure.

Figure A.5 shows a graphical representation for the corresponding "packed tuples" *y1* through *y6* from Figure A.2. Here it is obvious that the overlaps have disappeared. In like manner, figures analogous to Figures A.4 and A.5 for supplier S3 would show that (1) tuples *x6* and *x7* (see Figure A.1) correspond to *adjacent*—not overlapping—rectangles and that (2) packing those two tuples yields tuple *y8* (see Figure A.2), corresponding to a single combined rectangle. (*Adjacent* here means, more precisely, that the right edge of the *x6* rectangle and the left edge of the *x7* rectangle exactly coincide.)

Now recall the following expression which, given the relation of Figure A.1 as input, yields the relation of Figure A.2 as output:

```
WITH ( UNPACK S_PARTS_DURING ON DURING ) AS T1 ,
     ( UNPACK T1 ON PARTS ) AS T2 ,
     ( PACK- T2 ON PARTS ) AS T3 :
PACK- T3 ON DURING
```

Figures A.6, A.7, and A.8 show graphical representations of T1, T2, and T3, respectively (tuples for supplier S1 only in every case). As for the result of the overall expression, we have already seen the graphical representation for that (for supplier S1, at least) in Figure A.5.

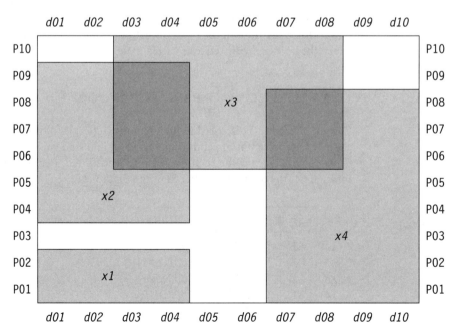

FIGURE A.4

Graphical representation of tuples *x1* through *x4*.

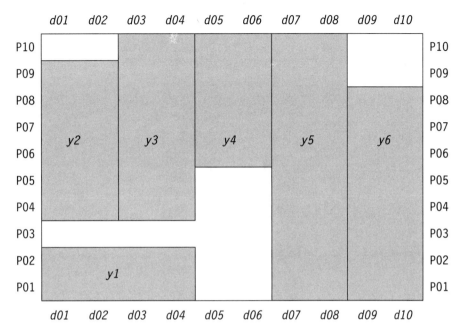

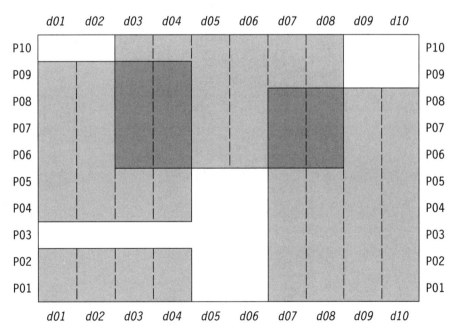

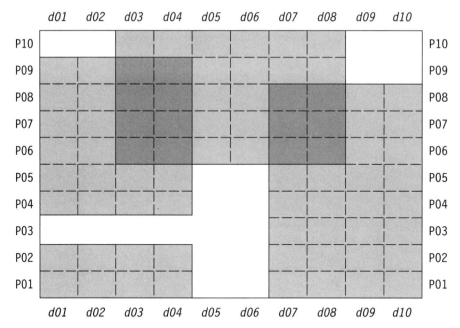

FIGURE A.7

Result of the second UNPACK (on PARTS).

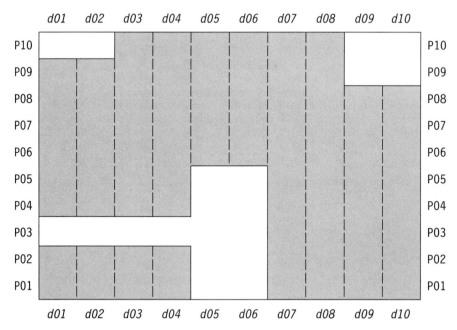

FIGURE A.8

Result of the first PACK– (on PARTS).

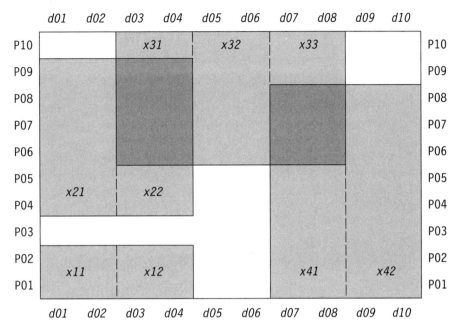

Finally, if once again X is the relation containing tuples *x1* through *x4* only and L is the list *d01, d03, d05, d07, d09, d11,* then Figure A.9 is a graphical representation of the result of the expression

```
SPLIT X ON DURING VIA L
```

(see Figure A.3).

A.5 OTHER RELATIONAL OPERATORS

Now we turn our attention to the generalized or "U_" versions of the traditional relational operators (union, join, restrict, and so on). All of these operators are defined to do a preliminary UNPACK on their relation operand(s). As always, however, we want to avoid actually having to perform those UNPACKs if we possibly can. Fortunately, there are several transforms and algorithms available to help us in this connection, which we now proceed to describe.

U_UNION

We begin by noting that UNPACK distributes over UNION (regular UNION, that is, not the general U_UNION). In other words, if *r1* and *r2* are relations of the same type, then

```
UNPACK ( r1 UNION r2 ) ON ( ACL )  ≡  ( UNPACK r1 ON ( ACL ) )
                                       UNION
                                       ( UNPACK r2 ON ( ACL ) )
```

Hence, the expression

```
USING ( ACL ) ◀ r1 UNION r2 ▶

≡  PACK
       ( ( UNPACK r1 ON ( ACL ) )
           UNION
         ( UNPACK r2 ON ( ACL ) ) )
   ON ( ACL )

≡  PACK
       ( UNPACK ( r1 UNION r2 ) ON ( ACL ) )
   ON ( ACL )

≡  PACK ( r1 UNION r2 ) ON ( ACL )
```

Thus, we can implement the original U_union by applying the five-step PACK algorithm described in Section A.3 directly to the regular union of r1 and r2. Note in particular, therefore, that no unpacking is required.

We can improve matters still further—in particular, we can avoid actually materializing the union of r1 and r2—by means of the following algorithm (a modified version of the PACK algorithm from Section A.3). Let r1 and r2 each have interval attributes A1 and A2 and let B be all of the attributes apart from A1 and A2 in each. Then:

Step 1: Initialize *result* to empty.

Step 2: Let r be the result of r1 UNION r2.[2] Partition r on B into $z1, z2, \ldots, zk$. (We refer to the partitions as $z1, z2$, etc., instead of $r1, r2$, etc., simply to avoid confusion with the original relations r1 and r2.)

Step 3: For each zi ($i = 1, 2, \ldots, k$), do Steps 4 and 5.

Step 4: Create an ordered list L consisting of all points p such that p is equal to either BEGIN(A2) or POST(A2) for some A2 value in zi.

Step 5: Execute the following:

```
WITH ( SPLIT zi ON A2 VIA L ) AS T1 ,
     ( PACK- T1 ON A1 ) AS T2 ,
     ( PACK- T2 ON A2 ) AS T3 :
result  :=  result UNION T3 ;
```

---

2. We repeat that there is no need for r to be physically materialized, as we will see after Step 5.

NOTE: Although Steps 2 and 3 both refer to relation *r* (the union of *r1* and *r2*), there is no need for *r* to be physically materialized; instead, the implementation can simply perform a search on *r1* and *r2* to locate all of the tuples that belong to any given partition *zi* (indeed, Steps 4 and 5 effectively do just that). In this connection, we remind you that sorting can be useful in the implementation of partitioning.

Further improvements are also possible. In particular, Step 5 can sometimes be simplified to just

```
result  :=  result UNION zi ;
```

For example, suppose relations *r1* and *r2* are as shown in Figure A.10 (note that they are both restrictions of the relation shown in Figure A.1), and consider, for example, tuple *x5*. Since that tuple has an S# value that appears in *r1* and not in *r2*, it can be inserted directly into the result without any need for the SPLIT and the two PACK– operations. In appropriate circumstances, it should be possible to insert entire sets (involving any number of tuples) directly into the result in this manner.

FIGURE A.10
Relations *r1* and *r2*.

r1	S#	PARTS	DURING
x1	S1	[P01:P02]	[d01:d04]
x2	S1	[P04:P09]	[d01:d04]
x4	S1	[P01:P08]	[d07:d10]
x5	S2	[P15:P20]	[d01:d10]
x6	S3	[P01:P05]	[d10:d15]

r2	S#	PARTS	DURING
x3	S1	[P06:P10]	[d03:d08]
x7	S3	[P01:P05]	[d16:d20]
x8	S3	[P05:P10]	[d25:d30]

This brings us to the end of our discussion of U_UNION. We have considered this operator in some detail in order to give an idea as to the range of implementation and optimization possibilities that might be available in general. In our discussions of the other operators, we will not usually try to be so comprehensive.

U_MINUS

Consider the expression

```
USING ( A1, A2 ) ◄ r1 MINUS r2 ►
```

where *r1* and *r2* are as for U_UNION above. Here is the implementation algorithm:

Step 1: Initialize *result* to empty.

Step 2: Partition *r1* on B into *r11, r12, ..., r1h*. Partition *r2* on B into *r21, r22, ...,* *r2k*.

Step 3: For each *r1i* (*i* = 1, 2, ..., *h*) and each *r2j* (*j* = 1, 2, ..., *k*) such that the B values in *r1i* and *r2j* are equal, do Steps 4 and 5.

Step 4: Create an ordered list L1 consisting of all points *p1* such that *p1* is either BEGIN(*A1*) or POST(*A1*) for some *A1* value in *r1i* UNION *r2j*. Also, create an ordered list L2 consisting of all points *p2* such that *p2* is either BEGIN(*A2*) or POST(*A2*) for some *A2* value in *r1i* UNION *r2j*.

Step 5: Execute the following:

```
WITH ( SPLIT r1i ON A1 VIA L1 ) AS T1 ,
     ( SPLIT T1  ON A2 VIA L2 ) AS T2 ,
     ( SPLIT r2j ON A1 VIA L1 ) AS T3 ,
     ( SPLIT T3  ON A2 VIA L2 ) AS T4 ,
     ( T2 MINUS T4 ) AS T5 ,
     ( PACK- T5 ON A1 ) AS T6 ,
     ( PACK- T6 ON A2 ) AS T7 :
  result  :=  result UNION T7 ;
```

U_INTERSECT

U_INTERSECT is a special case of U_JOIN, *q.v.,* and the same techniques apply.

U_JOIN

We observe first that (as we saw in Exercise 5 in Chapter 9) U_JOIN can be defined without explicit reference to UNPACK. Here is that definition (we assume for simplicity that the packing and unpacking is to be done on the basis of a single attribute *A*):

```
USING A ◀ r1 JOIN r2 ▶

≡ WITH ( r1 RENAME A AS X ) AS T1 ,
       ( r2 RENAME A AS Y ) AS T2 ,
       ( T1 JOIN T2 ) AS T3 ,
       ( T3 WHERE X OVERLAPS Y ) AS T4 ,
       ( EXTEND T4 ADD ( X INTERSECT Y ) AS A ) AS T5 ,
       T5 { ALL BUT X, Y } AS T6 :
    PACK T6 ON A
```

(Note that the INTERSECT operator invoked in the EXTEND step here is the *interval* INTERSECT, not the relational one.)

We exploit the ideas underlying the foregoing definition in the following algorithm for implementing the expression

```
USING ( A1, A2 ) ◀ r1 JOIN r2 ▶
```

We assume that

- *r1* has attributes *A*, *B*, *A1*, and *A2*;

- *r2* has attributes *A*, *C*, *A1*, and *A2*; and

- *A1* and *A2* are interval attributes.

Step 1: Initialize *result* to empty.

Step 2: Execute the following (pseudocode):

```
let a be an A value that appears both in some tuple ∈ r1
                                 and in some tuple ∈ r2 ;
do for each such a ;
   do for each tuple t1 ∈ r1 with A = a ;
      do for each tuple t2 ∈ r2 with A = a ;
         if (A1 FROM t1) OVERLAPS (A1 FROM t2) AND
            (A2 FROM t1) OVERLAPS (A2 FROM t2)
            then insert tuple
               { A a, B (B FROM t1), C (C FROM t2),
                 A1 ((A1 FROM t1) INTERSECT (A1 FROM t2)),
                 A2 ((A2 FROM t1) INTERSECT (A2 FROM t2)) }
               into result ;
         end if ;
      end do ;
   end do ;
end do ;
```

Step 3: Using the PACK algorithm from Section A.3, execute the following:

```
result  :=  PACK result ON ( A1, A2 ) ;
```

NOTE: If the U_JOIN is performed on the basis of just a single attribute *A* and the input relations *r1* and *r2* are already packed on *A*, then Step 3 here is unnecessary.

U_restrict

The expression

```
USING ( ACL ) ◀ r WHERE p ▶
```

is defined to be equivalent to

```
PACK ( ( UNPACK r ON ( ACL ) ) WHERE p ) ON ( ACL )
```

In the special case where *p* mentions no attribute in *ACL*, this latter expression can be simplified to just

```
PACK ( r WHERE p ) ON ( ACL )
```

The implementation algorithm for this simple case is immediate:

```
WITH ( r WHERE p ) AS T1 :
PACK T1 ON ( ACL )
```

Furthermore, if relation *r* is already packed on *ACL*, the PACK step is unnecessary.

More generally (and more usually), *p* will include some mention of at least one attribute from *ACL*. For simplicity and definiteness, we use a specific example in order to illustrate the corresponding implementation algorithm. Let relation *r* have attributes *A1, A2,* and *B*, where *A1* and *A2* are both interval attributes and *B* is of type INTEGER, and consider the U_restriction

```
USING ( A1, A2 ) ◀ r WHERE A1 = A2 AND B > 5 ▶
```

Step 1: Initialize *result* to empty.

Step 2: Execute the following (pseudocode):

```
do for each tuple t ∈ r ;
    if (B FROM t) > 5
        then
        do for each p1 ∈ (A1 FROM t) ;
            do for each p2 ∈ (A2 FROM t) ;
                if p1 = p2
                    then insert tuple
                        { A1 [p1:p1], A2 [p2:p2], B (B FROM t) }
                            into result ;
                end if ;
            end do ;
        end do ;
    end if ;
end do ;
```

Step 3: *result* := PACK *result* ON (A1, A2) ;

Points arising:

1. The purpose of the early IF test on the noninterval attribute B in Step 2, line 2, is simply to save execution time by avoiding the need to examine the interval attributes $A1$ and $A2$, if possible.

2. In this example, the *interval* comparison $A1 = A2$ is implemented in terms of the *point* comparison $(p1$ FROM $A1) = (p2$ FROM $A2)$. Clearly, the precise implementation of any given restriction condition will depend on the specific interval operators involved in that condition. For example, the condition $A1$ MERGES $A2$ will have to be implemented by means of an expression that looks something like the following:

```
( ( p1 FROM A1 ) = ( p2 FROM A2 ) ) OR
( NEXT_T ( p1 FROM A1 ) = ( p2 FROM A2 ) ) OR
( ( p1 FROM A1 ) = NEXT_T ( p2 FROM A2 ) )
```

(where T is the point type underlying the interval type of attributes $A1$ and $A2$). In general, therefore, we need to find the specific point expression that corresponds to, and can be used to implement, any given interval expression. We omit further details here, except to note that this approach does mean we can always avoid the need to perform the implicit initial UNPACK.

U_project

The expression

```
USING ( ACL ) ◀ r { BCL } ▶
```

is defined to be equivalent to

```
PACK ( ( UNPACK r ON ( ACL ) ) { BCL } ) ON ( ACL )
```

However, there is in fact no need to perform the initial UNPACK shown in this definition. In other words, the latter expression can be further simplified to just

```
PACK r { BCL } ON ( ACL )
```

The implementation algorithm is immediate:

```
WITH r { BCL } AS T1 :
PACK T1 ON ( ACL )
```

U_EXTEND

The expression

```
USING ( ACL ) ◄ EXTEND r ADD exp AS B ►
```

is defined to be equivalent to

```
PACK
    ( EXTEND ( UNPACK r ON ( ACL ) ) ADD exp AS B )
ON ( ACL )
```

In the special case where *exp* mentions no attribute in *ACL*, this expression can be simplified to just

```
PACK ( EXTEND r ADD exp AS B ) ON ( ACL )
```

The implementation algorithm for this simple case is immediate:

```
WITH ( EXTEND r ADD exp AS B ) AS T1 :
PACK T1 ON ( ACL )
```

Furthermore, if relation *r* is already packed on *ACL,* the PACK step is unnecessary.

More generally (and more usually), *exp* will include some mention of at least one attribute from *ACL.* For simplicity and definiteness, we use a specific example in order to illustrate the corresponding implementation algorithm. Let relation *r* have interval attributes *A1* and *A2* and let *B* be all of the attributes of *r* apart from *A1* and *A2,* and consider the U_extension

```
USING ( A1, A2 ) ◄ EXTEND r ADD ( A1 = A2 ) AS BOOL ►
```

Step 1: Initialize *result* to empty.

Step 2: Execute the following (pseudocode):

```
do for each tuple t ∈ r ;
    do for each p1 ∈ (A1 FROM t) ;
        do for each p2 ∈ (A2 FROM t) ;
            insert tuple
                { A1 [p1:p1], A2 [p2:p2], B (B FROM t),
                  BOOL (p1 = p2) }
            into result ;
        end do ;
    end do ;
end do ;
```

Step 3: `result := PACK result ON ( A1, A2 ) ;`

Comments analogous to those for the general case of U_restrict apply here also.

U_SUMMARIZE

The expression

```
USING ( ACL ) ◄ SUMMARIZE r1 PER r2 ADD summary AS B ►
```

is defined to be equivalent to

```
PACK
    ( SUMMARIZE ( UNPACK r1 ON ( ACL ) )
      PER ( UNPACK r2 ON ( ACL' ) )
      ADD summary AS B ) )
ON ( ACL' )
```

where *ACL′* is identical to *ACL,* except that any attribute of *ACL* not appearing in *r2* is omitted.

In the special case where *ACL′* is empty, this expression can be simplified to just

```
SUMMARIZE ( UNPACK r1 ON ( ACL ) ) PER r2 ADD summary AS B
```

The implementation algorithm for this simple case is essentially straighforward; in particular, an obvious trick can be used to avoid the need for unpacking. Here is an example. Suppose relvar S_STATUS_DURING currently looks like this:

	S#	STATUS	DURING
x1	S1	20	[*d01:d05*]
x2	S1	30	[*d06:d08*]
x3	S1	10	[*d09:d10*]

Consider the U_SUMMARIZE

```
USING DURING ◄ SUMMARIZE S_STATUS_DURING
               PER S_STATUS_DURING { S# }
               ADD SUM ( STATUS ) AS SS ►
```

We process the tuples one at a time, say in the order *x1, x2, x3,* and compute SS as a running total, thus:

- After processing tuple *x1*, the value of SS is 100, computed as 20 ∗ 5—20 being the STATUS value in tuple *x1* and 5 being the number of points in the corresponding DURING interval (and hence the number of tuples that would be derived from tuple *x1* if we were actually to do the UNPACK).

- Next, after processing tuple *x2*, the value of SS becomes $100 + 30 * 3 = 190$.

- Finally, after processing tuple *x3*, the value of SS becomes $190 + 10 * 2 = 210$.

The overall result is thus:

S#	SS
S1	210

Other kinds of *summary* can be treated analogously: In all cases, the implementation can avoid actually unpacking by performing a "smart" summarization instead of a "naïve" one (in the example, the smart summarization involves multiplication, whereas the naïve one would have involved repeated addition). The details are left as an exercise.

We now turn to the more general and more usual case in which *r2* does include at least one attribute from *ACL'* (implying that *ACL'* is nonempty). For simplicity and definiteness, we use a specific example in order to illustrate the corresponding implementation algorithm. Let relation *r1* have interval attributes *A1* and *A2*, let relation *r2* have interval attribute *A1* but not *A2*, and let *B* be all of the attributes of *r2* apart from *A1*. Consider the expression

```
USING ( A1, A2 ) ◀ SUMMARIZE r1 PER r2 ADD SUM ( X ) AS SUMX ▶
```

(where *X* is some numeric attribute of *r1*).

Step 1: *result* := WITH (USING A1
                  ◀ r2 MINUS r1 { A1, B } ▶) AS T1 :
        EXTEND T1 ADD 0 AS SUMX ;

This step produces result tuples for tuples of *r2* with no counterpart in *r1*. Note in particular that 0 is the *identity* for SUM (i.e., 0 is the unique value of *y* that satisfies the equations $x + y = x$ and $y + x = x$ for all possible numbers *x*) and is thus the value to return when summing no *X* values at all [43]. NOTE: We did not mention the fact earlier, but a step analogous to Step 1 is also needed, in general, in the special case where *ACL'* is empty.

Step 2: Prepare to scan the tuples of *r1* in the sequence "END(*A1*) DESC within BEGIN(*A1*) within *B*" (where DESC means descending sequence).

Step 3: Use the first tuple *t1* of *r1* to initialize *accums*. Here *accums* is an ordered list of tuple variables, one for each point $p1 \in (A1$ FROM $t1)$. Each such variable has attributes {*A1,B,*SUMX} and is initialized as follows: *A1* is set to [*p1:p1*]; *B* is set to (*B* FROM *t1*); SUMX is set to 0.

Step 4: Execute the following (pseudocode):

```
do for each tuple t ∈ r1 ;
    if t{B} ≠ TUPLE FROM (accums{B})            /* see Note 1 */
        then
            do ;
                insert accums into result ;      /* see Note 2 */
                use t to initialize accums ;     /* see Step 3 */
            end do ;                             /* above       */
        else
            if BEGIN(A1 FROM t) >
                BEGIN(A1 FROM first accums tuple)
                then
                    revamp accums ;              /* see Note 3 */
            end if ;
    end if ;
    do for each p1 ∈ (A1 FROM t) ;
        do for each p2 ∈ (A2 FROM t) ;           /* see Note 4 */
            update tuple variables in accums ;   /* see Note 5 */
        end do ;
    end do ;
end do ;
```

Step 5: Insert *accums* into *result* ;   /* see Note 2 */

Step 6: `result := PACK result ON ( A1 ) ;`

NOTES:

1. Observe that all *accums* tuples have the same *B* value, so projecting them over *B* gives a result containing just one tuple. (We are pretending here for simplicity that it makes sense to apply projection to a list of tuples!)

2. Actually this insertion is conditional; we have to cater for the arguably perverse case in which the result of unpacking *r2* on *A1* is a proper subset of the result of unpacking *r1*{*A1,B*} on *A1*. Let *at* be an *accums* tuple that is being considered for insertion. Then *at* is actually inserted if and only if *r2* includes a tuple *bt* such that *bt*{*B*} = *at*{*B*} and (*A1* FROM *bt*) $\supseteq$ (*A1* FROM *at*). Obviously it would be more efficient not to create such unwanted tuples in the first place, but we have not attempted to include such considerations in our pseudocode above.

3. "Revamping *accums*" entails

- inserting those *accums* tuples with BEGIN(*A1*) < BEGIN(*A1* FROM *t*) into *result*;
- removing the corresponding tuple variables from *accums*;
- keeping those *accums* tuple variables with BEGIN(*A1*) ≤ END(*A1* FROM *t*);
- adding new *accums* tuple variables for the remaining points in *A1* FROM *t*.

Observe that an implementation could save both space and time by effectively keeping the set of *accums* variables packed at all times on *A1*. "Revamping *accums*" would then involve a process akin to that involved in the SPLIT operation described earlier in this appendix.

4. This inner loop can be avoided by applying the kind of "smart" summarizing described under the simple special case earlier.

5. In general, each *accums* tuple variable is updated as determined by the *summary* expressions. In the particular case under consideration ("ADD SUM(*X*) AS SUMX"), for each *accums* tuple variable, the result of evaluating SUMX + (*X*) is used to replace the value of SUMX in that variable.

U_GROUP

It is easiest to explain the implementation of U_GROUP in terms of a concrete example. Suppose the current value of relvar SP_DURING is as follows:

S#	P#	DURING
S1	P1	[*d01:d05*]
S1	P2	[*d03:d08*]
S1	P3	[*d04:d10*]

Consider the expression

```
USING DURING ◄ SP_DURING GROUP { P# } AS P#_REL ►
```

This expression is defined to be equivalent to

```
PACK
    ( UNPACK SP_DURING ON DURING ) GROUP { P# } AS P#_REL )
ON DURING
```

Here then is the implementation algorithm:

Step 1: Initialize *result* to empty.

Step 2: Partition SP_DURING on S#. In the example, this step yields a single partition, for supplier S1.

Step 3: For each resulting partition *p,* do Steps 4 through 6.

Step 4: Split the tuples in *p.* For the single partition in the example (for supplier S1), this step yields:

S#	P#	DURING
S1	P1	[d01:d02]
S1	P1	[d03:d03]
S1	P1	[d04:d05]
S1	P2	[d03:d03]
S1	P2	[d04:d05]
S1	P2	[d06:d08]
S1	P3	[d04:d05]
S1	P3	[d06:d08]
S1	P3	[d09:d10]

Step 5: Apply the specified grouping, to yield *px,* say. In the example, this step yields:

S#	P#_REL	DURING
S1	p#r1	[d01:d02]
S1	p#r2	[d03:d03]
S1	p#r3	[d04:d05]
S1	p#r4	[d06:d08]
S1	p#r5	[d09:d10]

where the relation values *p#r1, p#r2, p#r3, p#r4,* and *p#r5* are as follows:

p#r1	*p#r2*	*p#r3*	*p#r4*	*p#r5*
P#	**P#**	**P#**	**P#**	**P#**
P1	P1	P1	P2	P3
	P2	P2	P3	
		P3		

Step 6: `result := result UNION ( PACK px ON DURING ) ;`

U_UNGROUP

The implementation algorithm for U_UNGROUP is very similar to that for U_GROUP, except that no splitting is needed in Step 4 and (of course) UNGROUP is used instead of GROUP in Step 5. We omit the details here.

A.6 RELATIONAL COMPARISONS

For simplicity we limit our attention here to "U_=" only (the other U_ comparisons are analogous). The expression

```
USING ( ACL ) ◀ r1 = r2 ▶
```

is defined to be equivalent to

```
( UNPACK r1 ON ( ACL ) ) = ( UNPACK r2 ON ( ACL ) )
```

Here is the implementation algorithm:

```
WITH ( PACK r1 ON ( ACL ) ) AS T1 ,
     ( PACK r2 ON ( ACL ) ) AS T2 :
T1 = T2
```

NOTE: The two PACKs here are correct—they are not typographical errors for UNPACK.

A.7 UPDATE OPERATORS

We assume throughout this section that the relvar R to be updated has heading $\{A,B,A1,A2\}$ and key $\{A,A1,A2\}$, where $A1$ and $A2$ are interval attributes and B is all of the attributes of R apart from A, $A1$, and $A2$. We further assume that R is subject to the constraints

```
PACKED ON ( A1, A2 )
```

and

```
WHEN UNPACKED ON ( A1, A2 ) THEN KEY { A, A1, A2 }
```

In other words, *R* is subject to the U_key constraint USING (*A1,A2*) KEY {*A,A1,A2*}.

Intuitively, the basic point with respect to all three of U_INSERT, U_DELETE, and U_UPDATE is that it is not necessary to unpack (or split, rather) and subsequently repack *all* of the tuples that are involved in the operation—it is sufficient to split and repack just those tuples that are *relevant,* as we will see.

U_INSERT

Let the set of tuples to be inserted into *R* constitute (the body of) relation *r.*

Step 1: If *r* contains two distinct tuples *t1* and *t2* such that

```
( ( A FROM t1 ) = ( A FROM t2 ) ) AND
( ( A1 FROM t1 ) OVERLAPS ( A1 FROM t2 ) ) AND
( ( A2 FROM t1 ) OVERLAPS ( A2 FROM t2 ) )
```

then signal error: *WHEN/THEN constraint violation.* NOTE: Of course, U_INSERTs, U_DELETEs, and U_UPDATEs can all fail on a variety of constraint violations. We do not show the code to deal with such errors in general, but we do mention WHEN/THEN constraints in particular (in connection with U_INSERT only) because of their fundamental nature—also because they are conceptually easy to deal with.

Step 2: If *r* and *R* contain two distinct tuples *t1* and *t2,* respectively, such that the condition specified in Step 1 is satisfied, then signal error: *WHEN/THEN constraint violation* (see Step 1).

Step 3: Partition *r* on {*A,B*}. For each resulting partition *pr,* do Steps 4 through 6.

Step 4: Let *t1* be a tuple of *R* such that there exists some tuple *t2* in *pr* such that

```
( ( A FROM t1 ) = ( A FROM t2 ) ) AND
( ( B FROM t1 ) = ( B FROM t2 ) ) AND
( ( A1 FROM t1 ) MEETS ( A1 FROM t2 ) OR
  ( A2 FROM t1 ) MEETS ( A2 FROM t2 ) )
```

Let *r1* be the set of all such tuples *t1.*

Step 5: Delete all tuples of *r1* from *R.*

Step 6: Let *r2* be the result of USING (*A1,A2*) ◄ *r1* UNION *pr* ►. Insert all tuples of *r2* into *R.* Note that no key uniqueness checking will be needed in this step.

U_DELETE

We deliberately do not consider the completely general case here, but limit ourselves to U_DELETEs of the "almost completely general" form[3]

```
WITH ( R WHERE p ) AS R' :
USING ( A1, A2 ) DELETE R' WHERE A1 OVERLAPS a1
                                AND   A2 OVERLAPS a2 ;
```

Step 1: Let *r1* be the set of all tuples *t1* of *R* satisfying

```
( p ) AND
( ( A1 FROM t1 ) OVERLAPS a1 ) AND
( ( A2 FROM t1 ) OVERLAPS a2 )
```

Step 2: Let tuple *t1* of *r1* be as follows:

```
TUPLE { A a, B b, A1 i1, A2 i2 }
```

Let *r2* be the set of all tuples *t2* of the form

```
TUPLE { A a, B b, A1 (i1 INTERSECT a1), A2 (i2 INTERSECT a2) }
```

Step 3: Let *r3* be the result of

```
USING ( A1, A2 ) ◄ r1 MINUS r2 ►
```

Step 4: Delete all tuples of *r1* from *R*.

Step 5: Use the algorithm for U_INSERT to insert the tuples of *r3* into *R*.

U_UPDATE

We deliberately do not consider the completely general case here, but limit ourselves to U_UPDATEs of the "almost completely general" form

```
WITH ( R WHERE p ) AS R' :
USING ( A1, A2 ) UPDATE R' WHERE A1 OVERLAPS a1
                                AND   A2 OVERLAPS a2
                     { attribute updates } ;
```

---

3. You might notice that we are using WITH here not just, as elsewhere in the book, to introduce a name for the result that is produced by evaluating some expression, but rather to introduce a name for *that very expression itself*. It might help to think of that introduced name as the name—*R´* in the case at hand—of a *virtual relvar* that happens to be defined "inline" as part of the statement that then immediately goes on to use it. NOTE: It should be said that this trick does raise certain further issues of semantics and language design; however, the issues in question are not germane to the major topic at hand and are beyond the scope of this book. In any case, we could if desired reformulate the U_DELETE under discussion in such a way as to avoid the use of WITH, using relational assignment, though such a reformulation would probably be more cumbersome.

The following algorithm is very similar to that for U_DELETE.

Step 1: Let *r1* be the set of all tuples *t1* of *R* satisfying

```
( p ) AND
( ( A1 FROM t1 ) OVERLAPS a1 ) AND
( ( A2 FROM t1 ) OVERLAPS a2 )
```

Step 2: Let tuple *t1* of *r1* be as follows:

```
TUPLE { A a, B b, A1 i1, A2 i2 }
```

Let *r2* be the set of all tuples *t2* of the form

```
TUPLE { A a, B b, A1 (i1 INTERSECT a1), A2 (i2 INTERSECT a2) }
```

Step 3: Let *r3* be the result of

```
USING ( A1, A2 ) ◀ r1 MINUS r2 ▶
```

Step 4: Let *r2*´ be that relation that results from applying the specified *attribute updates* to *r2*.

Step 5: Delete all tuples of *r1* from *R*.

Step 6: Use the algorithm for U_INSERT to insert the tuples of *r3* into *R*.

Step 7: Use the algorithm for U_INSERT to insert the tuples of *r2*´ into *R*.

A.8 A FINAL REMARK

The UNPACK operator is a crucial conceptual component of our approach to the management of interval data in general and temporal data in particular. But UNPACK has been much criticized in the literature on the grounds that it necessarily entails poor performance. We hope the discussions in this appendix will help to lay such criticisms to rest. To say it again, UNPACK is a crucial *conceptual* component of our approach— but it is only a conceptual component. We do not want unpackings per se ever to be physically performed if we can possibly avoid them; and in this appendix we have shown how they can be avoided.

B

GENERALIZING THE EXPAND AND COLLAPSE OPERATORS

B.1 INTRODUCTION

In Chapter 7 we introduced the operators EXPAND and COLLAPSE, and we considered their effect on sets of intervals specifically. As we mentioned in that chapter, however, there is no reason why we should not generalize the operators to work on other kinds of sets, and indeed there might be good reasons for doing so. In this appendix, we briefly investigate this possibility.

NOTE: As explained in Chapter 7, Section 7.5, we ought really to be talking about *unary relations* rather than general sets. For simplicity, however, we will stay with general sets until we get to the final section of the appendix (Section B.6).

B.2 SETS OF RELATIONS

Let X be a set of *relations,* all of the same relation type RT (say). Then we define EXPAND(X) and COLLAPSE(X) as follows:

■ EXPAND(X) returns a set Y of relations of that same type RT, such that each relation in Y is of cardinality one, and a relation containing tuple t appears in Y if and only if a relation containing tuple *t* appears in *X*. Note in particular, therefore, that if *X* is empty, then *Y* is empty also. (What happens if *X* contains just one relation and that relation is empty?)

- COLLAPSE(*X*) returns a set *Y* containing exactly one relation of that same type *RT*, namely, the union of all of the relations in *X*. Note in particular, therefore, that if *X* is empty, then *Y* contains just the empty relation of type *RT*, and if *X* contains just one relation *r*, then *Y* also contains just that one relation *r*. (Refer to Chapter 1 if you need to refresh your memory regarding unions involving just one relation and unions involving no relations at all.)

Figure B.1 shows (1) a sample set of relations and (2) the corresponding expanded and collapsed forms of that set.

FIGURE B.1

Expanding and collapsing sets of relations (example).

Given set of relations:

S#
S2

S#
S2
S4

S#
S1
S2
S4

S#
S1
S3
S4

S#
S1
S2
S3

S#
S2
S3

Expanded form:

S#
S1

S#
S2

S#
S3

S#
S4

Collapsed form:

S#
S1
S2
S3
S4

B.3 SETS OF SETS

In similar manner we can define EXPAND and COLLAPSE for sets of *sets*. Let *ST* be some set type. (The term *set type* has not been defined or used previously in this book, but its meaning is surely obvious. Analogous remarks apply to the term *bag type* in the next section.) Let *X* be a set of sets, all of type *ST*. Then:

- EXPAND(X) returns a set Y of sets of that same type ST, such that each set in Y is of cardinality one, and a set containing the value v appears in Y if and only if a set containing the value v appears in X. If X is empty, Y is empty also. (What happens if X contains just one set and that set is empty?)

- COLLAPSE(X) returns a set Y containing exactly one set of that same type ST, namely the union of all of the sets in X. If X is empty, Y contains just the empty set of type ST; and if X contains just one set s, then Y also contains just that one set s.

Figure B.2 gives an example.

FIGURE B.2

Expanding and collapsing sets of sets—example.

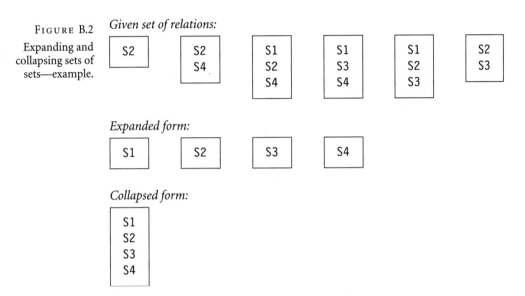

Given set of relations:

| S2 | | S2 S4 | | S1 S2 S4 | | S1 S3 S4 | | S1 S2 S3 | | S2 S3 |

Expanded form:

| S1 | | S2 | | S3 | | S4 |

Collapsed form:

| S1 S2 S3 S4 |

B.4 SETS OF BAGS

We can also, albeit somewhat less satisfactorily, define EXPAND and COLLAPSE for sets of *bags*, where a bag (also known as a *multiset*) is an unordered collection of values, like a set, but unlike a set is allowed to contain duplicates. Let X be a set of bags—not a bag of sets, please note, and certainly not a bag of bags!—all of the same type BT (say). Then:

- EXPAND(X) returns a set Y of bags of that same type BT, such that each bag in Y is of cardinality one, and a bag containing the value v appears in Y if and only if a bag containing the value v appears in X. *Note carefully that each bag in Y is in fact a set, and furthermore that (by definition, since Y is a set) no bag appears in Y more than once.*

- COLLAPSE(X) returns a set Y containing exactly one bag of that same type BT, namely, the union of all of the bags in X.

At this point, however, we run into a problem. If A and B are bags, there are three interpretations that might be given to the expression "the union of A and B"—that is, there are three union operators that can apply to bags:

- The first is the regular set union operator, which returns a result—in fact, a set—in which the value v appears exactly once if and only if it appears at least once in either A or B. In SQL terms, this is the regular UNION operator (more or less).

- The second is what might be called the "union+" operator, which returns a result—a bag—in which the value v appears exactly n times if and only if it appears exactly a times in A and exactly b times in B and n = a+b. In SQL terms, this is the UNION ALL operator (again, more or less).

- The third is the so-called bag union operator, which returns a result—again a bag—in which the value v appears exactly n times if and only if it appears exactly a times in A and exactly b times in B and n = MAX(a,b). SQL does not directly support this operator.

Thus, the question arises: Which union operator is the one to be used in the definition of "bag COLLAPSE"?

- If it is a regular set union, then the result will contain no duplicates. In a sense, therefore, information—specifically, "degree of duplication" information—represented by the original set of bags will be lost (in general).

- On the other hand, if that union operator is not the regular set union but one of the other two unions instead, then one unfortunate consequence is that the expressions COLLAPSE(X) and COLLAPSE(EXPAND(X)) will produce different results (again in general).

In order to illustrate these points, let us suppose that set X contains just two bags, one containing just one occurrence of the supplier number S1 and nothing else, and the other containing just two occurrences of the supplier number S1 and nothing else. Then:

- EXPAND(X) returns a set containing just one bag (actually a set) containing just one occurrence of S1.

- COLLAPSE(EXPAND(X)) thus also returns a set containing just one bag (actually a set) containing just one occurrence of S1—and we get this same result no matter which union operator we use in the definition of COLLAPSE.

- However, COLLAPSE(X) returns three different results, depending on which kind of union we use:

  - *(Regular set union)* COLLAPSE(X) returns the same result as COLLAPSE (EXPAND(X)): namely, a set containing just one bag containing just one occurrence of S1. (But therefore the "degree of duplication" information—the fact that S1 appeared once in one bag and twice in the other in the original set of bags X—has been lost. Of course, the same observation applies to EXPAND(X) also in this example.)

  - *(Union+)* COLLAPSE(X) returns a set containing just one bag containing three occurrences of S1. This result is different from the result of COLLAPSE (EXPAND(X)).

  - *(Bag union)* COLLAPSE(X) returns a set containing just one bag containing two occurrences of S1. This result is also different from the result of COLLAPSE (EXPAND(X)).

From the foregoing analysis, it follows that, while we certainly can define EXPAND and COLLAPSE operators for sets of bags if we want to, on the whole it looks as if it might not be a good idea to do so. Moreover, analogous remarks apply to sets of lists and sets of arrays and, more generally, to sets involving *any* kind of "collection," if individual collections of the kind in question can include distinct elements with the same value.

B.5 OTHER KINDS OF SETS

What about sets of values that are not collections—for example, a set of integers or a set of tuples? Without going into details, suffice it to say that we have investigated this question, and it is our current feeling that EXPAND(X) and COLLAPSE(X) should both be simply defined to return their input in such cases.

B.6 EFFECT ON PACK AND UNPACK

Since the PACK and UNPACK operators are defined in terms of COLLAPSE and EXPAND, it follows that these operators too can be generalized if desired. In this section, we consider just one example of this possibility; to be specific, we show what is involved in packing a relation on an attribute that is *relation*-valued. Figure B.3 shows such a relation; let us call it r. Note the redundancy in relation r—for example, note that it shows supplier S2 paired with part P2 twice. Note too that it shows supplier S3 paired with no parts at all.

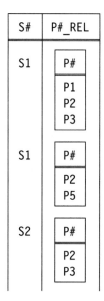

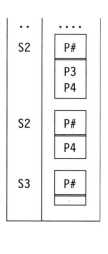

From the definition of the PACK operator in Chapter 8, we have the following as the expansion for the expression PACK *r* ON P#_REL:

```
WITH ( r GROUP { P#_REL } AS X ) AS R1 ,
      ( EXTEND R1 ADD COLLAPSE ( X ) AS Y )
                          { ALL BUT X } AS R2 :
R2 UNGROUP Y
```

We consider this expansion one step at a time. First, we evaluate the expression

```
r GROUP { P#_REL } AS X
```

The result is shown in Figure B.4. Observe that not only does that result—which we have labeled R1—include an attribute, X, that is relation-valued (such is always the case in the result of a GROUP operation), but the relations that are values of that attribute have a single attribute, P#_REL, that is relation-valued in turn.

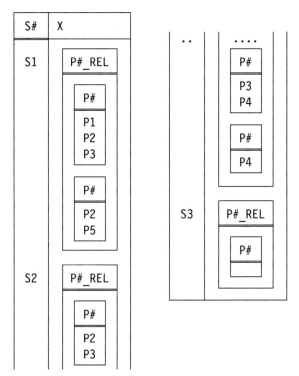

FIGURE B.4

R1 = *r* GROUP {P#_REL} AS X.

Next, we evaluate the expression

```
( EXTEND R1 ADD COLLAPSE ( X ) AS Y ) { ALL BUT X }
```

The result, R2, is shown in Figure B.5.

FIGURE B.5
R2 = (EXTEND R1 ADD COLLAPSE (X) AS Y) {ALL BUT X}.

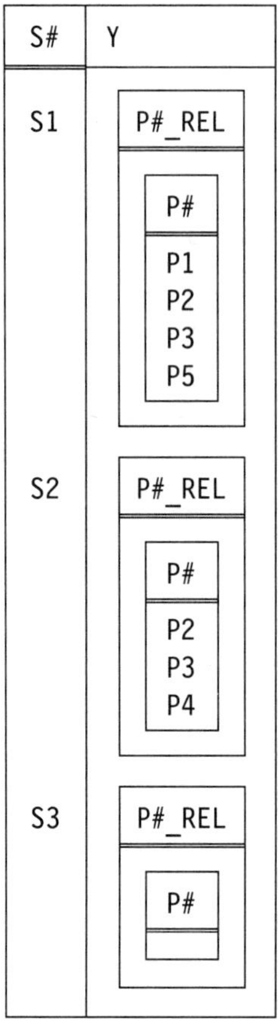

S#	Y
S1	P#_REL: P# { P1, P2, P3, P5 }
S2	P#_REL: P# { P2, P3, P4 }
S3	P#_REL: P# { }

FIGURE B.6
Overall result of PACK r ON P#_REL.

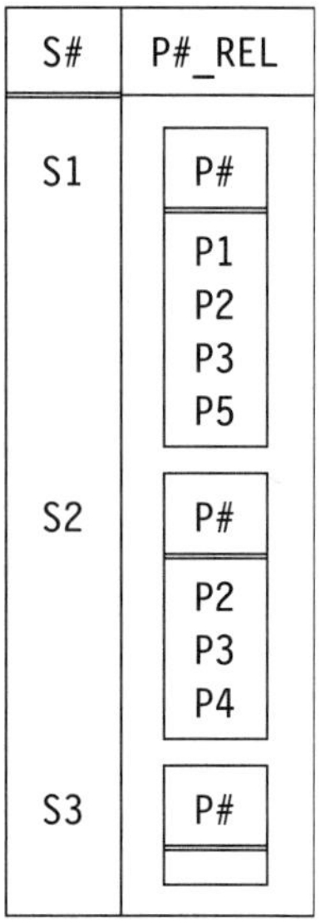

S#	P#_REL
S1	P# { P1, P2, P3, P5 }
S2	P# { P2, P3, P4 }
S3	P# { }

Finally, we evaluate the expression

```
R2 UNGROUP Y
```

The result is shown in Figure B.6. Note that the net effect is to eliminate all of the redundancies in the original relation r. The parallels with packing a relation on an interval-valued attribute should be obvious.

Appendix

C

REFERENCES AND BIBLIOGRAPHY

This appendix provides a consolidated, and mostly annotated, list of references for the entire book. If a given reference is *not* annotated, it means the reference in question is discussed—or at least mentioned, along with some indication as to its content—at some appropriate earlier point in the book.

1. Ilsoo Ahn and Richard T. Snodgrass: "Partitioned Storage Structures for Temporal Databases," *Information Systems 13,* No. 4 (1988).

    The partitioning referred to in the title of this paper is akin to our idea of *horizontal decomposition* (see Chapter 10). As that title suggests, however, the emphasis in the paper is more on the use of such decomposition as a physical, not a logical, design technique. (To quote reference [93]: "Temporal partitioning is ... in the domain of physical design.")

2. James F. Allen: "Maintaining Knowledge about Temporal Intervals," *CACM 16,* No. 11 (November 1983).

    The source of Allen's operators (see Chapter 6). For purposes of reference, we repeat here the list of operators from Chapter 6 and show Allen's original names for them (in italics where they differ from ours). Note that some of our operators have no direct counterparts in Allen's paper.

Operator	Allen's equivalent
=	=
⊃	
⊇	
⊂	
⊆	*DURING*
BEFORE	BEFORE
AFTER	AFTER
MEETS	MEETS
OVERLAPS	OVERLAPS
MERGES	
BEGINS	*STARTS*
ENDS	*FINISHES*

3. Khaled K. Al-Taha, Richard T. Snodgrass, and Michael D. Soo: "Bibliography on Spatiotemporal Databases," *ACM SIGMOD Record 22,* No. 1 (March 1993).

    Here is a very slightly reworded quote from the preamble to this bibliography: "Only recently have issues concerning the simultaneous support of both space and time in databases been considered. While this new area of research was presaged by Thrift's observation in 1977 that time could be considered to be an additional dimension in a two- or three-dimensional space [Thrift 1977], little was done until Nikos Lorentzos's and Gail Langran's doctoral dissertations [Langran 1989A, Lorentzos 1988]." (To elaborate: Reference [Thrift 1977] is N. Thrift: "An Introduction to Time Geography," in *Concepts in Modern Geography 13,* Geo-Abstracts Ltd., London, UK (1977); reference [Langran 1989A] is G. Langran: "Time in Geographic Information Systems," Ph.D. Dissertation, University of Washington (1989); reference [Lorentzos 1988] is our reference [57].) It is particularly interesting to see that the authors of this bibliography [3] are here on record as agreeing that "time is just another dimension"—a position we agree with, though we do not actually use the term *dimension* in this context.

4. Gad Ariav: "A Temporally Oriented Data Model," *ACM TODS 11,* No. 4 (December 1986).

    The approach described in this paper differs from just about every other in the literature (with the possible exception of reference [17]); in effect, it timestamps entire relations, instead of individual attributes—more precisely, attribute *values*—or tuples (see the annotation to reference [18]). An algebra and an SQL extension are defined. However, the algebra is incomplete—only three operators are defined—and the author states explicitly that further work is needed.

5. J. Ben-Zvi: "The Time Relational Model," Ph.D. Dissertation, Computer Science Department, University of California at Los Angeles (1982).

    Ben-Zvi was one of the earliest workers in the temporal database field. A useful brief summary of his ideas and contributions can be found in a short paper by Gadia [50].

6. Claudio Bettini, Curtis E. Dyreson, William S. Evans, Richard T. Snodgrass, and X. Sean Wang: "A Glossary of Time Granularity Concepts," in reference [46].

    This paper is an attempt to inject some rigor into the granularity issue. It is intended as a formal extension to reference [53].

7. Michael H. Böhlen: "Temporal Database System Implementations," *ACM SIGMOD Record 24,* No. 4 (December 1995).

    A survey of thirteen implemented systems, with a high-level analysis of system features supported (or not, as the case may be). The following observations regarding the systems examined are worthy of note: "Transaction time support is negligible ... The focus is on queries. Updates, rules, and integrity constraints are neglected ... Temporal database design has barely found its way into products."

8. Michael H. Böhlen, Christian S. Jensen, and Richard T. Snodgrass: "Temporal Statement Modifiers," *ACM TODS 25,* No. 4 (December 2000).

    Among other things, this paper defines ATSQL, an SQL-based temporal language that is similar in spirit to TSQL2 [89–90].

9. Michael H. Böhlen, Richard T. Snodgrass, and Michael D. Soo: "Coalescing in Temporal Databases," *Proc. 22nd Int. Conf. on Very Large Data Bases,* Mumbai (Bombay), India (September 1996).

    The operation of *coalescing* is analogous, more or less, to our PACK operation. This paper presents a set of algebraic transformation rules for expressions involving such coalescing and investigates approaches to the implementation of such expressions.

    As an aside, we remark that the PACK operator and the related UNPACK operator are known by a variety of names in the literature.[1] Reference [83] calls them CONTRACT and EXPAND, respectively. References [28] and [39] call them COALESCE and UNFOLD. PACK has also been called COMPRESS [79]. And reference [60] (among several others by Lorentzos and various coauthors) defines a pair of operators called FOLD and UNFOLD, but those operators are not quite the same as PACK and UNPACK; loosely, FOLD "packs" a set of *points* into a set of intervals, and UNFOLD "unpacks" a set of intervals into a set of points (the same paper uses NORMALIZE— originally spelled NORMALISE—for what we call PACK). Finally, at least one paper [80] uses PACK and UNPACK to mean something quite different: namely, operators that are akin, somewhat, to the relational GROUP and UNGROUP operators.

10. Marco A. Casanova, Ronald Fagin, and Christos H. Papadimitriou: "Inclusion Dependencies and Their Interaction with Functional Dependencies," *Proc. 1st ACM SIGACT-SIGMOD Symposium on Principles of Database Systems,* Los Angeles, CA (March 1982).

    The origin of the concept of inclusion dependencies (INDs). As noted in Chapter 4, INDs can be regarded as a generalization of referential constraints; this paper provides a sound and complete set of inference rules for INDs.

11. R. G. G. Cattell and Douglas K. Barry (eds.): *The Object Data Standard: ODMG 3.0.* San Francisco, CA: Morgan Kaufmann (2000).

12. James Clifford: "A Model for Historical Databases," *Proc. Workshop on Logical Bases for Data Bases,* Toulouse, France (December 1982).

    See the next reference, also the annotation to reference [18].

13. James Clifford and Albert Croker: "The Historical Relational Data Model (HRDM) Revisited," in reference [95].

    Revises and extends the proposals of reference [12].

14. James Clifford, Albert Croker, and Alexander Tuzhilin: "On Completeness of Historical Relational Query Languages," *ACM TODS 19,* No. 1 (March 1994).

    A quote: "In this paper we define *temporally grouped* and *temporally ungrouped* historical data models and propose two notions of *historical relational completeness,* analogous to Codd's notion of relational completeness, one for each type of model" (italics as in the original). The paper additionally considers to what extent various approaches

---

1. Actually this remark is not quite accurate, because most of the literature defines the operators, whatever they might be called, in terms of "relations" with "hidden attributes" (see Chapter 3, Section 3.1). By contrast, our PACK and UNPACK operators are defined strictly in terms of relations in which, by definition, all attributes have explicit names and can—and in fact must—be referenced by those names.

satisfy the proposed completeness criteria. The approaches in question are HRDM [13], Gadia's approach [49], TQuel [88], and Lorentzos's approach [58].

15. J. Clifford and A. Rao: "A Simple General Structure for Temporal Domains," in reference [82].

Proposes a formalism for defining a variety of (1) temporal point types, (2) associated interval types, and (3) operators on values of those types.

16. J. Clifford and A. Tuzhilin (eds.): *Recent Advances in Temporal Databases (Proc. Int. Workshop on Temporal Databases,* Zurich, Switzerland, September 17–18, 1995). New York: Springer-Verlag (1995).

17. James Clifford and David S. Warren: "Formal Semantics for Time in Databases," *ACM TODS 8,* No. 2 (June 1983).

Describes an approach based on the idea that any given relvar (our term) can be thought of as a sequence of timestamped relations; the timestamps in question correspond to logged-time instants (not intervals) as discussed in Chapter 15. The major contribution of the paper is a formal definition of the approach in terms of *intensional logic.*

18. James Clifford and Abdullah Uz Tansel: "On an Algebra for Historical Relational Databases: Two Views," *Proc. ACM SIGMOD Int. Conf. on Management of Data,* Austin, TX (May 1985).

In the first part of this paper, Clifford proposes an algebra for dealing with "temporal relations" in which attribute values can be relations and the tuples within those inner relations can be timestamped with stated-time *instants.* In the second part, Tansel proposes another algebra in which the timestamps are *intervals* rather than instants (see also references [94] and [96]). NOTE: Timestamping tuples within values of relation-valued attributes is known, loosely, as "timestamping attributes"; it is contrasted with "timestamping tuples," which refers to the idea of timestamping tuples in the *containing* instead of the *contained* relation, an idea that seems to have originated in reference [12]. The approach advocated in the present book is somewhat akin to "timestamping tuples," except that the "timestamps" in question are actually part of the tuples in question; in other words, they are represented by means of relational attributes in the usual way. (Also, of course, a given tuple can include any number of such timestamps.)

19. James Clifford, Curtis Dyreson, Tomás Isakowitz, Christian S. Jensen, and Richard T. Snodgrass: "On the Semantics of 'Now' in Databases," *ACM TODS 22,* No. 2 (June 1997).

Argues in favor of allowing database tuples to include the variable referred to in Chapter 10 as "the NOW marker" (and several other similar variables as well). To quote: "This article ... provides a formal basis for defining the semantics of databases with variables ... [It] demonstrates that existing variables, such as *now* and *until changed,* are indispensable in databases. It also ... introduces new *now-relative* and *now-relative indeterminate* [variables]." Note that "variables" here does not refer to our *relation* variables (relational databases always include variables of that kind, of course); rather, it refers to "the NOW marker" and similar constructs.

20. E. F. Codd: "Derivability, Redundancy, and Consistency of Relations Stored in Large Data Banks," IBM Research Report RJ599 (August 19, 1969).
   Codd's very first published paper on the relational model.

21. E. F. Codd: "A Relational Model of Data for Large Shared Data Banks," *CACM 13*, No. 6 (June 1970). Republished in "Milestones of Research," *CACM 26*, No. 1 (January 1982).
   A revised and extended version of reference [20].

22. E. F. Codd: "Relational Completeness of Data Base Sublanguages," in Randall Rustin (ed.), *Data Base Systems: Courant Computer Science Symposia 6*. Englewood Cliffs, NJ: Prentice-Hall (1972).

23. E. F. Codd and C. J. Date: "Much Ado about Nothing," in C. J. Date, *Relational Database Writings 1991–1994*. Reading, MA: Addison-Wesley (1995).
   Codd is probably the best-known advocate of nulls and many-valued logics as a basis for dealing with missing information. This article contains the text of a debate between Codd and Date on the subject.

24. Hugh Darwen: "Into the Unknown," in C. J. Date, *Relational Database Writings 1985–1989*. Reading, MA: Addison-Wesley (1990).

25. Hugh Darwen: "The Nullologist in Relationland," in C. J. Date and Hugh Darwen, *Relational Database Writings 1989–1991*. Reading, MA: Addison-Wesley (1992).

26. Hugh Darwen: "What a Database *Really* Is: Predicates and Propositions," in C. J. Date, Hugh Darwen, and David McGoveran, *Relational Database Writings 1994–1997*. Reading, MA: Addison-Wesley (1998).

27. Hugh Darwen: "Valid Time and Transaction Time Proposals: Language Design Aspects," in reference [46].
   Among other things, this paper advocates the language design principle known as **syntactic substitution:** "A language definition should start with a few judiciously chosen primitive operators … Subsequent development is, where possible, [done] by defining new operators in terms of … previously defined [ones]. Most importantly, syntactic substitution does not refer to an imprecise principle such as might be expressed as 'A is something like, possibly very like, B,' where A is some proposed new syntax and B is some expression using previously defined operators. If A is close in meaning to B but cannot be specified by true syntactic substitution, then we have a situation that is disagreeable and probably unacceptable, in stark contrast to true syntactic substitution, which can be very agreeable and acceptable indeed."

28. Hugh Darwen and C. J. Date: "Temporal Database Systems," in M. Pratini and O. Diaz (eds.), *Advanced Databases: Technology and Design*. Norwood, MA: Artech House Books (2000).
   This article is a lightly edited version of Chapter 22 of reference [39].

29. Hugh Darwen, Mike Sykes, et al.: "Concerns about the TSQL2 Approach to Temporal Databases," Kansas City, MO (May 1996); *ftp://sqlstandards.org/SC32/WG3/Meetings/MCI_1996_05_KansasCity_USA/mci071.ps*.

A precursor to reference [30], criticizing among other things the notion of *temporal upward compatibility* (advocated in reference [91], also in reference [8]). Briefly, temporal upward compatibility means it should be possible to convert an existing nontemporal database into a temporal one by just "adding temporal support," and then have existing nontemporal applications run unchanged against the now temporal database. See reference [107] for further discussion. NOTE: Although the term *temporal upward compatibility* is not used in the body of the present book, the requirement it represents is addressed by the proposals for *horizontal decomposition* discussed in Chapter 10.

30. Hugh Darwen, Mike Sykes, et al.: "On Proposals for Valid-Time and Transaction-Time Support," Madrid, Spain (January 1997); *ftp://sqlstandards.org/SC32/WG3/Meetings/ MAD_1997_01_Madrid_ESP/mad146.ps.*

   A response to reference [91].

31. C. J. Date: "NOT Is Not "Not"! (Notes on Three-Valued Logic and Related Matters)," in *Relational Database Writings 1985–1989*. Reading, MA: Addison-Wesley (1990).

32. C. J. Date: "EXISTS Is Not "Exists"! (Some Logical Flaws in SQL)," in *Relational Database Writings 1985–1989*. Reading, MA: Addison-Wesley (1990).

33. C. J. Date: "Three-Valued Logic and the Real World," in C. J. Date and Hugh Darwen, *Relational Database Writings 1989–1991*. Reading, MA: Addison-Wesley (1992).

34. C. J. Date: "Oh No Not Nulls Again," in C. J. Date and Hugh Darwen, *Relational Database Writings 1989–1991*. Reading, MA: Addison-Wesley (1992).

35. C. J. Date: "Empty Bags and Identity Crises," in *Relational Database Writings 1991–1994*. Reading, MA: Addison-Wesley (1995).

36. C. J. Date: "The Primacy of Primary Keys: An Investigation," in *Relational Database Writings 1991-1994*. Reading, MA: Addison-Wesley (1995).

37. C. J. Date: "The Final Normal Form!" (in two parts), *Database Programming & Design 11*, No. 1 (January 1998) and No. 2 (February 1998).

   The "final" normal form of this article's title is 5NF, not 6NF (!). See Chapter 10.

38. C. J. Date: "Encapsulation Is a Red Herring," *Database Programming & Design 12*, No. 9 (September 1998).

39. C. J. Date: *An Introduction to Database Systems* (7th edition). Reading, MA: Addison-Wesley (2000).

   Parts II and III of the present book consist of a hugely revised and expanded version of Chapter 22 from this reference. Unfortunately, that chapter contains a large number of errors!—but the overall approach is still more or less as described in the present book.

40. C. J. Date: *The Database Relational Model: A Retrospective Review and Analysis.* Reading, MA: Addison-Wesley (2001).

   A short critical assessment (150 pages) of Codd's original pioneering papers on the relational model, including references [20–22] in particular.

41. C. J. Date: "Constraints and Predicates: A Brief Tutorial" (in three parts), published on the Web sites *www.dbdebunk.com* (May 2001) and *www.BRCommunity.com* (May–September 2001).

42. C. J. Date and Hugh Darwen: *A Guide to the SQL Standard* (4th edition). Reading, MA: Addison-Wesley (1997).

    A comprehensive tutorial on SQL:1992, including coverage of the Call-Level Interface and Persistent Stored Modules features, SQL/CLI and SQL/PSM (which were added in 1995 and 1996, respectively), and a preliminary look at SQL:1999 (previously known as SQL3).

43. C. J. Date and Hugh Darwen: *Foundation for Future Database Systems: The Third Manifesto* (2nd edition). Reading, MA: Addison-Wesley (2000).

44. Christina Davies, Brian Lazell, Martin Hughes, and Leslie Cooper: "Time Is Just Another Attribute—Or at Least Another Dimension," in reference [16].

    To quote: "[The] flexibility and simplicity of the relational model are too valuable to be jettisoned without good reason … [A] much stronger case must be made against the unextended relational model before it is rejected or modified for temporal applications." The paper presents three case studies and identifies some limitations of TSQL2 [89–90]. It also argues that if SQL is to be extended, then the extensions in question should not be limited to temporal intervals only.

45. Barry Devlin: *Data Warehouse from Architecture to Implementation*. Reading, MA: Addison-Wesley (1997).

46. Opher Etzion, Sushil Jajodia, and Suryanaryan Sripada (eds.): *Temporal Databases: Research and Practice*. New York: Springer-Verlag (1998).

    This book is an anthology giving "the state of the temporal database art" as of about 1997. It is divided into four major parts, as follows:

    1. Temporal Database Infrastructure
    2. Temporal Query Languages
    3. Advanced Applications of Temporal Databases
    4. General Reference

    Several of the references listed in this appendix—in particular reference [27]—are included in this book.

47. Ronald Fagin: "Normal Forms and Relational Database Operators," *Proc. 1979 ACM SIGMOD Int. Conf. on Management of Data*, Boston, MA (May–June 1979).

    This paper, which is the one that introduced projection/join normal form (also known as 5NF), is the definitive reference on classical normalization theory.

48. Shashi K. Gadia and Jay H. Vaishnav: "A Query Language for a Homogeneous Temporal Database," *Proc. 4th ACM SIGACT-SIGMOD Symposium on Principles of Database Systems*, Portland, OR (March 1985).

    Sketches a language for dealing with "temporal relations" in which, as in reference [18], attribute values can be relations and tuples within those inner relations can be timestamped (see also reference [49]). The timestamps are sets of intervals in collapsed form (to use the terminology of Chapter 7), and they represent stated times, not logged times. The term *homogeneous* in the paper's title refers to the restriction that—as the paper puts it—"the temporal domain within a tuple does not vary from one attribute to another … [As a consequence,] there are several weaknesses in the model. For example, … information about persons, their parents and dates of birth [cannot be represented in the same relation]."

49. Shashi K. Gadia: "A Homogeneous Relational Model and Query Languages for Temporal Databases," *ACM TODS 13,* No. 4 (December 1988).

     A more formal and comprehensive treatment of the model underlying the proposals of reference [48].

50. Shashi K. Gadia: "Ben-Zvi's Pioneering Work in Relational Temporal Databases," in reference [95].

51. Patrick Hall, John Owlett, and Stephen Todd: "Relations and Entities," in G. M. Nijssen (ed.), *Modelling in Data Base Management Systems.* Amsterdam: North-Holland (1976).

52. International Organization for Standardization (ISO): *Database Language SQL,* Document ISO/IEC 9075:1999. Also available as American National Standards Institute (ANSI) Document ANSI NCITS.135-1999.

     The formal definition of the official SQL standard. Note, however, that the original monolithic document has since been replaced (or is at least in the process of being replaced) by an open-ended series of separate "parts" (ISO 9075-1, -2, etc.), under the general title *Information Technology—Database Languages—SQL.* At the time of writing, the following parts have been defined:

     Part 1: Framework (SQL/Framework)

     Part 2: Foundation (SQL/Foundation)

     Part 3: Call-Level Interface (SQL/CLI)

     Part 4: Persistent Stored Modules (SQL/PSM)

     Part 5: Host Language Bindings (SQL/Bindings)

     Part 6: *There is no Part 6*

     Part 7: *See below*

     Part 8: *There is no Part 8*

     Part 9: Management of External Data (SQL/MED)

     Part 10: Object Language Bindings (SQL/OLB)

     It is intended that Part 7, if and when it is defined, will become "SQL/Temporal." NOTE: The next edition of the standard is expected in 2003, at which time the following revisions are expected:

     ■ The material from Part 5 will be folded into Part 2 and Part 5 will be dropped.

     ■ The material from Part 2 defining the standard database catalog (the "Information Schema") will be moved to a new Part 11, "SQL Schemata."

- A new Part 13, "Java Routines and Types (SQL/JRT)," will standardize further integration of Java with SQL.

- A new Part 14, "XML-Related Specifications (SQL/XML)," will standardize features supporting the inclusion of XML documents in SQL databases.

53. Christian S. Jensen and Curtis E. Dyreson (eds.): "The Consensus Glossary of Temporal Database Concepts—February 1998 Version," in reference [46].

This article follows on from, and subsumes, two earlier glossaries that appeared in *ACM SIGMOD Record 21,* No. 3 (September 1992) and *ACM SIGMOD Record 23,* No. 1 (March 1994), respectively. We applaud and strongly agree with the article's opening remarks: "A technical language is an important infrastructural component of any scientific community. To be effective, such a language should be well-defined, intuitive, and agreed-upon." The authors then go on to give not just their own preferred terms and definitions as such, but also discussions of alternative terms, justifications for their choices, and so on.

NOTE: Some concepts in our book appear to have no counterpart in this glossary. Here are some examples:

- Point types
- Ordinal types
- Cyclic types
- Successor functions (NEXT_*T*), etc.
- Interval types and the interval type generator
- BEGIN, END, PRE, POST, and POINT FROM
- Allen's operators
- Interval UNION, INTERSECT, and MINUS
- EXPAND and COLLAPSE
- UNPACK
- Equivalence (for sets of intervals)
- "The moving point *now*"

54. Christian S. Jensen, Richard T. Snodgrass, and Michael D. Soo: "Extending Existing Dependency Theory to Temporal Databases," *IEEE Transactions on Knowledge and Data Engineering 8,* No. 4 (August 1996).

This paper is one of many that define "temporal" versions of familiar relational concepts: specifically (in the case at hand), temporal functional dependencies, temporal primary keys, and temporal normal forms. The definitions in question all rely on an assumption that timestamps are not represented by regular relational attributes (where a regular relational attribute is, by definition, an attribute that has an explicit name and can—and in fact must—be referenced by that name).

55. S. Jones and P. J. Mason: "Handling the Time Dimension in a Data Base," *Proc. Int. Conf. on Data Bases, Aberdeen, Scotland* (July 1980). London, UK: Heyden & Son, Ltd. (1980).
One of the very earliest proposals (possibly *the* earliest).

56. Mark Levene and George G. Loizou: *A Guided Tour of Relational Databases and Beyond.* London, UK: Springer-Verlag (1999).

Includes one chapter (Chapter 7) on temporal matters. Section 4 of that chapter ("A Historical Relational Algebra") describes Lorentzos's work [58,60].

57. Nikos A. Lorentzos: "A Formal Extension of the Relational Model for the Representation and Manipulation of Generic Intervals," Ph.D. Dissertation, Birkbeck College, University of London, England (August 1988).

The approach to temporal data described and advocated in the present book has its foundations in Lorentzos's original research as reported in his Ph.D. dissertation (as well as in numerous subsequent publications by Lorentzos and other researchers; see, for example, references [58], [60], and [66]). So far as the present authors are aware, that dissertation was (1) the first to propose the interval abstraction as such, (2) the first, or one of the first, to propose a truly *relational* approach to the problem, and (3) the first to propose the idea that temporal support should be at least partly just a special case of support for intervals in general. (We note in passing that reference [78] effectively supports these claims.)

Given the truth of the foregoing, we need to add a remark regarding the dissertation title. The term "extension" in that title refers primarily to the introduction of

- a generic interval data type (or rather, as we would now say, an interval *type generator*), along with
- a variety of new operators that can be applied to relations with attributes of some interval type, as well as—this is important, because it means the relational closure property [22] is preserved—to relations without such attributes.

As explained in Chapter 3, however, the question of which types and type generators are supported is orthogonal to the question of support for the relational model as such. And support for "new operators" is part of (and is implied by) support for "new types." In other words, the two "extensions" above can certainly be regarded as an extension to *something*, but they are not an extension to the relational model. It is this fact that enables us to claim, legitimately, that our approach to temporal database issues is a truly *relational* one and involves no changes or extensions to the classical relational model.

Remarks analogous to the foregoing apply equally to the titles of several other references in this appendix—for example, references [60] and [64]—and we will not bother to repeat them every time.

58. Nikos A. Lorentzos and R. G. Johnson: "TRA: A Model for a Temporal Relational Algebra," in reference [82].

This paper and reference [59], which overlap somewhat, were the first to discuss the FOLD and UNFOLD operators (see the annotation to reference [9]). NOTE: Despite the reference in the paper's title to "a temporal relational algebra," the authors are careful to state explicitly that they are not proposing any "new elementary relational algebra operations." In other words, their "temporal relational algebra" is just the classical relational algebra, enhanced with certain useful shorthands (as in the present book).

59. Nikos A. Lorentzos and R. G. Johnson, "Extending the Relational Algebra to Manipulate Temporal Data," *Information Systems 3*, No. 3 (1988).

    See the annotation to reference [58].

60. Nikos A. Lorentzos: "The Interval-Extended Relational Model and Its Application to Valid-Time Databases," in reference [95].

61. Nikos A. Lorentzos: "DBMS Support for Time and Totally Ordered Compound Data Types," *Information Systems 17*, No. 5 (September 1992).

    In the body of this book, we have described the nature of interval types at considerable length, but we have said comparatively little about the nature of the point types in terms of which those interval types are defined (except for a few remarks in Chapter 16). This paper and the next [62] address this latter issue. In essence, they propose a new type generator that would allow users to define temporal point types that almost certainly will not be available as built-in types. An example might be time points measured in terms of week and day numbers (e.g., "week 5, day 2"). Another might be time points measured using a cesium-based atomic clock, in which the time unit is 1/9,192,631,770th of a second (such a point type is needed in certain scientific applications). Nontemporal point types (e.g., weights measured in stones, pounds, and ounces) can also be defined by means of the proposed type generator. NOTE: Alternative proposals for dealing with such matters—in particular, with the question of units and granularity—can be found in Section 16.5 of the present book, also in reference [43].

62. Nikos A. Lorentzos: "DBMS Support for Nonmetric Measurement Systems," *IEEE Transactions on Knowledge and Data Engineering 6*, No. 6 (December 1994).

    See the annotation to reference [61].

63. Nikos A. Lorentzos and Hugh Darwen: "Extension to SQL2 Binary Operations for Temporal Data" (invited paper), *Proc. 3rd HERMIS Conf.*, Athens, Greece (September 26–28, 1996).

    This paper extends the work described in reference [66]. It proposes the addition of analogs of certain of our "U_" operators to "SQL2" (i.e., the SQL:1992 standard); to be specific, it discusses what we would now call U_JOIN, U_UNION, U_INTERSECT, and U_MINUS, and gives examples in each case.

64. Nikos A. Lorentzos and R. G. Johnson, "An Extension of the Relational Model to Support Generic Intervals," in Joachim W. Schmidt, Stefano Ceri, and Michel Missikoff (eds.), *Extending Database Technology*. New York: Springer-Verlag (1988).

    The first paper to show that temporal data management is actually a special case of a more general problem: namely, that of supporting a "generic interval type" (what we would now call an interval type generator), together with operators to deal with relations that include interval data.

65. Nikos A. Lorentzos and Vassiliki J. Kollias: "The Handling of Depth and Time Intervals in Soil Information Systems," *Comp. Geosci. 15*, 3 (1989).

    Defines a set of operators for dealing with data related to (1) changes in the composition of soil with depth and (2) the way those changes themselves change with time.

(We include this reference here primarily as a concrete example of an application area in which at least some of the pertinent intervals are nontemporal ones specifically.)

66. Nikos A. Lorentzos and Yannis G. Mitsopoulos: "IXSQL: An Interval Extension to SQL," *Proc. Int. Workshop on an Infrastructure for Temporal Databases,* Arlington, TX (June 14–16, 1993).

    An informal presentation of the ideas discussed more formally in reference [69].

67. Nikos A. Lorentzos and Yannis Manolopoulos: "Efficient Management of 2-Dimensional Interval Relations," *Proc. 5th DEXA Int. Conf.,* Athens, Greece (September 1994), in D. Karagiannis (ed.), *Lecture Notes in Computer Science 856.* New York: Springer-Verlag (1994).

    The source of the SPLIT operator described in Appendix A of the present book (in fact, Appendix A is heavily based on ideas first presented in this paper). NOTE: The term "2-dimensional interval relation" in the title of the paper refers to relations with two distinct interval attributes, not to relations with a single attribute whose values are themselves two-dimensional intervals.

68. Nikos A. Lorentzos and Yannis Manolopoulos: "Functional Requirements for Historical and Interval Extensions to the Relational Model," *Data and Knowledge Engineering 17* (1995).

    Identifies a number of criteria that support for interval (and therefore temporal) data should satisfy. Two broad approaches to the problem are described, *nonnested* and *nested*. The authors show that all of the approaches intended for temporal data in particular can in fact be used for interval data in general. They then proceed to evaluate all known approaches in terms of the criteria identified in the paper.

69. Nikos A. Lorentzos and Yannis G. Mitsopoulos: "SQL Extension for Interval Data," *IEEE Transactions on Knowledge and Data Engineering 9,* No. 3 (May–June 1997).

    Describes IXSQL, "an *Interval Extension to SQL* for the management of interval data" (see also reference [66]).

70. Nikos A. Lorentzos, Alexandra Poulovassilis, and Carol Small: "Implementation of Update Operators for Interval Relations," *BCS Comp. J. 37,* No. 3 (1994).

    Describes optimized implementation algorithms for operations on relations with two or more interval attributes.

71. Nikos A. Lorentzos, Alexandra Poulovassilis, and Carol Small: "Manipulation Operations for an Interval-Extended Relational Model," *Data and Knowledge Engineering 17* (1995).

    This paper is a more formal version of reference [70]. Complexity and simulation results are included.

72. Nikos A. Lorentzos, Nektaria Tryfona, and Jose R. Rios Viqueira: "Relational Algebra for Spatial Data Management," *Proc. Int. Workshop on Integrated Spatial Databases: Digital Images and GIS,* Portland, ME (June 14–16, 1999).

This paper defines spatial data types in terms of *spatial quanta*. It shows that FOLD and UNFOLD (predecessors of PACK and UNPACK) can be used to manage spatial data, and therefore spatiotemporal data also (see reference [3]).

73. V. Lum et al.: "Designing DBMS Support for the Temporal Dimension," *Proc. ACM SIGMOD Int. Conf. on Management of Data,* Boston, MA (June 1984).

This paper recognizes the need for supporting both logged times and stated times, but proposes that only logged times be given special treatment by the system—stated times are to be dealt with by means of regular attributes (see the annotation to reference [54]). The paper gives numerous reasons why an implementation that does not give special internal treatment to logged times will not perform well. Special storage structures and access methods are proposed to address such problems.

74. N. G. Martin, S. B. Navathe, and R. Ahmed: "Dealing with Temporal Schema Anomalies in History Databases," *Proc. 13th Int. Conf. on Very Large Data Bases,* Brighton, England (September 1987).

To quote from the abstract: "Because history databases do not discard data, they cannot discard outdated database schemas. Thus, in any proposal for a practical history database system, some method must be provided for accessing data [described by] outdated, yet historically valid, schemas." See Section 12.7 of the present book.

75. David McGoveran: "Nothing from Nothing" (in four parts), in C. J. Date, Hugh Darwen, and David McGoveran, *Relational Database Writings 1994–1997.* Reading, MA: Addison-Wesley (1998).

Part I of this four-part paper explains the crucial role of logic in database systems. Part II shows why that logic must be two-valued logic (2VL) specifically, and why attempts to use three-valued logic (3VL) are misguided. Part III examines the problems that 3VL is supposed to solve. Finally, Part IV describes a set of pragmatic solutions to those problems—including in particular some recommended database design approaches—that do not involve 3VL.

76. E. McKenzie and R. Snodgrass: "Supporting Valid Time: An Historical Algebra," Tech. Report TR87-008, Dept. of Computer Science, University of North Carolina, Chapel Hill, NC (1987).

Defines an algebra for the management of valid time (called stated time in the present book). A *historical relation* must have at least one valid-time attribute (though apparently not a regular attribute—see the annotation to reference [54]); values of such an attribute are *sets of time instants* (e.g., {d01,d02,d03,d04,d08,d09,d10}). Tuples that are identical except possibly for their valid-time component are said to be *value-equivalent*; relations are not allowed to contain distinct but value-equivalent tuples. The existing operators of the relational algebra are adjusted in such a way as to enforce this requirement. New operators are also defined.

77. Edwin McKenzie and Richard Snodgrass: "Extending the Relational Algebra to Support Transaction Time," *Proc. ACM SIGMOD Int. Conf. on Management of Data,* San Francisco, CA (May 1987).

This paper provides a formalization of the concept of transaction time (called logged time in the present book) in terms of denotational semantics. The fundamental observation is that, as explained in Chapter 15, a database is really a *variable;* an update causes one value of that variable to be replaced by another, and the complete set of such values over time can be thought of as a chronologically ordered sequence. (Actually, the paper talks in terms of individual relations rather than the database as a whole, but the foregoing remarks are still applicable, *mutatis mutandis.*) The paper proposes extending the relational algebra to include an update operator called *rollback* (note that the relational algebra as originally defined, and as described in Chapter 1, consists of read-only operators exclusively).

NOTE: In the introduction, the paper says that in "Codd's relational algebra ... the relations ... model the current reality as is currently best known." We believe we have shown in the present book how "Codd's relational algebra" can be used to deal with all kinds of temporal data, not just current but past and future as well.

78. L. Edwin McKenzie, Jr. and Richard T. Snodgrass: "Evaluation of Relational Algebras Incorporating the Time Dimension in Databases," *ACM Comp. Surv. 23,* No. 4 (December 1991).

To quote from the abstract: "In this paper we survey extensions of the relational algebra [to support queries on temporal databases] ... We identify 26 criteria that provide an objective basis for evaluating temporal algebras ... Twelve time-oriented algebras are summarized and then evaluated against the criteria." NOTE: Another approach to evaluating alternative temporal proposals can be found in reference [68].

79. Shamkant B. Navathe and Rafi Ahmed: "Temporal Extensions to the Relational Model and SQL," in reference [95].

Proposes a scheme in which intervals are represented by distinct "begin" and "end" attributes (i.e., the interval [*b:e*] is represented by distinct attributes with values *b* and *e,* respectively). As for the relational operators, *project* remains unchanged. *Restrict* is extended to support interval comparisons such as OVERLAPS (expressed in the SQL extension by means of a new WHEN clause). Four distinct *joins* are defined, two giving a result with one pair of begin/end attributes and two giving a result with two such pairs. Finally, four new *restrict*-like operators are defined that involve only the begin and end attributes.

80. G. Özsoyoglu, Z. M. Özsoyoglu, and V. Matos: "Extending Relational Algebra and Relational Calculus with Set-Valued Attributes and Aggregate Functions," *ACM TODS 12,* No. 4 (December 1987).

81. Raymond Reiter: "Towards a Logical Reconstruction of Relational Database Theory," in Michael L. Brodie, John Mylopoulos, and Joachim W. Schmidt (eds.), *On Conceptual Modelling: Perspectives from Artificial Intelligence, Databases, and Programming Languages.* New York: Springer-Verlag (1984).

82. C. Rolland, F. Bodart, and M. Leonard (eds.): *Temporal Aspects in Information Systems.* Amsterdam: North-Holland (1988).

83. N. L. Sarda: "Algebra and Query Language for a Historical Data Model," *BCS Comp. J. 33,* No. 1 (February 1990).

This paper and the next [84] both appeared shortly after reference [58] (which they do resemble, somewhat). The present paper defines a "temporal relational algebra" consisting of Codd's original operators plus two more whose functionality resembles that of FOLD and UNFOLD as defined in reference [58]. Reference [84] applies the ideas of the present paper [83] to SQL specifically.

84. N. L. Sarda: "Extension to SQL for Historical Databases," *IEEE Transactions on Knowledge and Data Engineering 2,* No. 2 (February 1990).

See the annotation to reference [83].

85. B.-M. Schueler: "Update Reconsidered," in G. M. Nijssen (ed.), *Architecture and Models in Data Base Management Systems.* Amsterdam: North-Holland (1977).

The source of the important idea that "the log is the real database" (see Chapter 15). Schueler argues forcefully that destructive overwriting operations—in other words, UPDATE and DELETE operations as conventionally understood—should be outlawed. Instead, every item in the database should be thought of as a chronologically ordered stack: The top entry in the stack represents the current value of the item, and previous values are represented by entries lower down (an INSERT or UPDATE thus places a new entry on the top of the stack and pushes all existing entries one place down). Each entry is timestamped, and all entries are accessible at all times. Schueler claims that such a scheme would dramatically simplify the structure of the system in such areas as recovery, auditability, locking, archiving, understandability, and usability—not to mention the purely temporal issues that are the primary focus of the present book—and hence reduce system costs and improve system functionality in a variety of important ways.

86. Arie Shoshani and Kyoji Kawagoe: "Temporal Data Management," *Proc. 12th Int. Conf. on Very Large Data Bases,* Kyoto, Japan (August 1986).

Sketches another nonrelational "temporal data model." The model in question was motivated by research into scientific and statistical databases, which typically contain sets of measurements, results of experiments, and so on. The basic data object is the *time sequence,* which is a time-ordered sequence of *<time:value>* pairs for some given *surrogate* (where the surrogate in question denotes some entity). For example, the time sequence <1999:130>, <2000:138>, <2001:142> might represent the weight of some person on three consecutive birthdays.

87. Richard Snodgrass and Ilsoo Ahn: "A Taxonomy of Time in Databases," *Proc. ACM SIGMOD Int. Conf. on Management of Data,* Austin, TX (May 1985).

The source of the terms *transaction time, valid time,* and *user-defined time.* N O T E : Transaction time and valid time are discussed at length in the present book (see Section 3.3 and Chapter 15), but user-defined time is not. The term *user-defined time* is used by reference [87] (among others) to refer to temporal values and attributes that are "not interpreted by the DBMS"; examples are date of birth, date of last salary increase, and time of arrival. Note that in the approach to temporal databases advocated in the present book, transaction times and valid times are also—like all other values and attributes— "not interpreted by the DBMS."

88. Richard Snodgrass: "The Temporal Query Language TQuel," *ACM TODS 12,* No. 2 (June 1987). See also Richard Snodgrass: "An Overview of TQuel," in reference [95].

TQuel was a version of the Ingres language QUEL, extended to support temporal data. This paper describes the TQuel language and a prototype implementation.

89. R. T. Snodgrass et al.: "TSQL2 Language Specification," *ACM SIGMOD Record 23,* No. 1 (March 1994).

90. Richard T. Snodgrass (ed.): *The TSQL2 Temporal Query Language.* Norwell, MA: Kluwer Academic Publishers (1995).

This book is the definitive reference on the TSQL2 language as of 1995. The following quote (from a Kluwer brochure) gives a sense of the book's scope: "A consensus effort of eighteen temporal database experts has resulted in a new temporal database query language, TSQL2, which is upwardly compatible with the international standard [SQL:1992]. TSQL2 provides comprehensive support for temporal applications. No other temporal query language covers as much ground. TSQL2 was designed to be compatible with existing database design and implementation methodologies. The complete specification of the language is included. TSQL2 is also an effective platform for teaching temporal database concepts, eliminating the need to constantly switch between incompatible language proposals." See also reference [89].

91. Richard T. Snodgrass, Michael H. Böhlen, Christian S. Jensen, and Andreas Steiner: "Adding Valid Time to SQL/Temporal" and "Adding Transaction Time to SQL/Temporal," Madrid, Spain (January 1997); *ftp://sqlstandards.org/SC32/WG3/Meetings/MAD_1997_01_Madrid_ESP/mad146.ps.*

These two papers together constitute a TSQL2-based proposal for "SQL/Temporal" [52]. They were originally submitted to the January 1997 meeting of the ISO committee JTC1/SC21/WG3 Database Languages rapporteur group, but subsequently withdrawn.

92. Richard T. Snodgrass, Michael H. Böhlen, Christian S. Jensen, and Andreas Steiner: "Transitioning Temporal Support in TSQL2 to SQL3," in reference [46].

See reference [91], also reference [107].

93. Richard T. Snodgrass: *Developing Time-Oriented Database Applications in SQL.* San Francisco, CA: Morgan Kaufmann (2000).

This book uses the ideas of TSQL2 [89–90] as a basis for explaining in generic terms how to implement "time-oriented" applications and databases in SQL:1992 (in other words, using SQL DBMSs that have no built-in temporal support, other than the usual SQL:1992 "datetime" types [42,52] or something analogous). It also includes product-specific information and suggestions for several different commercially available (but, at the time of writing, nontemporal) products: Microsoft Access and SQL Server, IBM DB2 Universal Database, Oracle8 Server, Sybase SQLServer, and UniSQL.

94. Abdullah U. Tansel: "Adding Time Dimension to Relational Model and Extending Relational Algebra," *Information Systems 11,* No. 4 (1986).

This paper can be seen as a more formal version of material from reference [18]. See also reference [97].

95. Abdullah Uz Tansel, James Clifford, Shashi Gadia, Sushil Jajodia, Arie Segev, and Richard Snodgrass (eds.): *Temporal Databases: Theory, Design, and Implementation.* Redwood City, CA: Benjamin/Cummings (1993).

This book is a collection of papers. It is divided into four parts, as follows:

1. Extensions to the Relational Data Model
2. Other Data Models
3. Implementation
4. General Language and Other Issues in Temporal Databases

Several of the references listed in this appendix are included in this book.

96. A. U. Tansel and L. Garnett: "Nested Historical Relations," *Proc. ACM SIGMOD Int. Conf. on Management of Data,* Portland, OR (June 1989).

See the annotation to references [18] and [97].

97. Abdullah Uz Tansel and Erkan Tin: "Expressive Power of Temporal Relational Query Languages and Temporal Completeness," in reference [46].

The idea of trying to define some notion of "temporal completeness" seems like a worthy objective (in this connection, see also references [14] and [99]). This paper proposes that a temporal query language (1) should be *relationally* complete [22] and (2) should also support interval selectors and the "point ∈ interval" operator (to use the terminology of the present book). The paper evaluates a number of proposed approaches with respect to these criteria.

98. David Toman: "Point-Based Temporal Extensions of SQL and Their Efficient Implementation," in reference [46].

As the title suggests, this paper proposes an extension to SQL based on time points instead of intervals. Some interesting questions are raised concerning implementation. Answers to those questions could be relevant to interval-based languages too, because the unit intervals resulting from UNPACK are "almost" points, in a sense.

99. Alexander Tuzhilin and James Clifford: "A Temporal Relational Algebra as a Basis for Temporal Relational Completeness," *Proc. 16th Int. Conf. on Very Large Data Bases,* Brisbane, Australia (August 1990).

To quote from the abstract: "We define a temporal algebra that is applicable to *any* temporal relational data model ... We show that this algebra has the expressive power of a safe temporal calculus ... We propose [this] temporal algebra ... and the equivalent temporal calculus as ... alternative [bases for defining] temporal relational completeness."

100. J. W. van Roessel: "Conceptual Folding and Unfolding of Spatial Data for Spatial Queries," in V. B. Robinson and H. Tom (eds.), *Toward SQL Database Extensions for Geographic Information Systems.* National Institute of Standards and Technology Report NISTIR 5258, Gaithersburg, MD (1993).

This reference uses Lorentzos's FOLD and UNFOLD operators (predecessors of PACK and UNPACK) as the basis for defining an approach to dealing with spatial data. See also reference [101].

101. J. W. van Roessel: "An Integrated Point-Attribute Model for Four Types of Areal GIS Features," *Proc. 6th Int. Symp. on Spatial Data Handling,* Edinburgh, UK (September 5–9, 1994).

102. Costas Vassilakis: "Design and Optimized Implementation of a System for the Management of Historical Data," Department of Informatics, University of Athens, Greece (October 1995).

    Describes some follow-up research based on Lorentzos's FOLD and UNFOLD operators [57, 58].

103. Costas Vassilakis, Nikos Lorentzos, and Panagiotis Georgiadis: "Implementation of Transaction and Concurrency Control Support in a Temporal DBMS," *Information Systems 23,* No. 5 (1998).

    Identifies transaction management problems (and describes solutions) in a temporal DBMS implemented as a separate software layer on top of a conventional DBMS. For example, an operator such as PACK, if implemented in such a separate layer, might map to a sequence of several operations—possibly including operations to write intermediate results into the database—at the level of the underlying DBMS.

104. Yu Wu, Sushil Jajodia, and X. Sean Wang: "Temporal Database Bibliography Update," in reference [46].

    This is the most recent in a cumulative series. Earlier contributions are as follows (in reverse chronological sequence):

    - Vassilis J. Tsotras and Anil Kumar: "Temporal Database Bibliography Update," *ACM SIGMOD Record 25,* No. 1 (March 1996).
    - Nick Kline: "An Update of the Temporal Database Bibliography," *ACM SIGMOD Record 22,* No. 4 (December 1993).
    - Michael D. Soo: "Bibliography on Temporal Databases," *ACM SIGMOD Record 20,* No. 1 (March 1991).
    - Robert B. Stam and Richard T. Snodgrass: "A Bibliography on Temporal Databases," *Data Engineering Bulletin 11,* No. 4 (December 1988).
    - Edwin McKenzie: "Bibliography: Temporal Databases," *ACM SIGMOD Record 15,* No. 4 (December 1986).
    - A. Bolour, T. L. Anderson, L. J. Dekeyser, and Harry K. T. Wong: "The Role of Time in Information Processing: A Survey," *ACM SIGMOD Record 12,* No. 3 (April 1982).

    See also reference [3].

105. Fred Zemke: "Determinism Cleanup and One Enhancement," Helsinki, Finland (October 2000); *ftp://sqlstandards.org/SC32/WG3/Meetings/HEL_2000_10_Helsinki_FIN/hel043r1.pdf.*

106. Y. Zhang: "Multi-Temporal Database Management with a Visual Query Interface," Ph.D. Dissertation, Department of Computer and Systems Services, Royal Institute of Technology and Stockholm University, Sweden (October 1997).

Zhang's dissertation is based on Lorentzos's FOLD and UNFOLD operators [57, 58].

107. Hugh Darwen and C. J. Date: "An Overview and Analysis of Proposals Based on the TSQL2 Approach" (to appear; tentative title). A preliminary draft is available on the website *www.thethirdmanifesto.com*.

Of previously published proposals for dealing with the temporal database problem, TSQL2 is probably the best known [89, 90], and several other proposals (including in particular those of reference [91]) have been based on it. This paper provides an overview and critical analysis of such proposals, comparing and contrasting them with the approach espoused in the present book.

Index

during relvar. *See* historical relvar
Dyreson, Curtis E., 392, 394, 399

E

eliminating redundancy. *See* redundancy
END, 84
    pseudovariable, 278
ENDS, 93
    cyclic point type, 342
equality, 7
    cyclic point type, 341
    interval, 91
    with inheritance, 321
equivalence
    n-ary relations, 133, 156
    sets of intervals, 100
    unary relations, 107
Etzion, Opher, 397
Evans, William S., 392
even integers (point type), 329–331
EXPAND, 103, 104
    cyclic point type, 343
    generalizing, 383–387
    nullary relation, 107
    unary relation, 106
expanded form, 101
expression, 6
EXTEND, 27
external predicate, 15

F

Fagin, Ronald, 393, 397
false circumlocution, 200
FD. *See* functional dependency
fifth normal form. *See* 5NF
FIRST_*T,* 90
    See also _*T* qualifier
first normal form. *See* 1NF
first (operator), 82
foreign key, 20
    generalized. *See* foreign U_key

foreign U_key, 223
FROM tuple. *See* attribute
"fully packed," 138
functional dependency, 20–21
future, 59
    current relvar, 169
    historical relvar, 169, 179
    See also prediction

G

Gadia, Shashi K., 397, 398, 407
Garnett, L., 407
G by C. *See* generalization by constraint
generalization by constraint, 321
generalized relational operators. *See*
    U_MINUS; *U_operators*
    intuitive interpretation, 156–158
    regular operators a special case, 158–159
Georgiadis, Panagiotis, 408
granularity, 62, 331–335
    intervals, 142
granule, 62
Gregorian calendar, 68
GROUP, 30–32

H

Hall, Patrick A. V., 398
heading, 11
hidden attributes, 55, 306
historical relvar, 169
historical relvars only
    constraints, 220–226
    queries, 252–255
    updates, 271–286
HISTORY_IN, 241
horizontal decomposition, 182
Hughes, Martin, 397

I

identity
    additive, 374
    equality. *See* equality
    projection, 67, 120
immediate checking. *See* constraints
implementation, 351–381
    vs. model. *See* model *vs.* implementation
implicit proposition. *See* proposition
implicit valid time. *See* valid time
includes
    cyclic point type, 341
    interval, 91
    properly, 41, 91
    relation, 41
inclusion dependency, 73, 232, 393
inclusion polymorphism. *See* polymorphism
IND. *See* inclusion dependency
Information Principle, The, 35
inheritance. *See* type inheritance
    multiple, 327–328
    single, 327
INSERT, 17, 269–270
instantiation. *See* predicate
integrity checking. *See* constraints
integrity constraint. *See* constraints
intended interpretation, 15
internal predicate, 15
interpretation. *See* intended interpretation
INTERSECT
    cyclic point type, 342–343
    interval, 94
    relation, 24–25, 27
    special case of join, 26, 45
interval, 77–98
    applications, 80–81
    closed, 77
    definition, 84
    one-dimensional, 81
    open, 77
    SQL, 77
INTERVAL_*T* selector, 90, 335
    See also _*T* qualifier

INTERVAL_*T* type, 90, 337
    See also _*T* qualifier
interval type. *See* INTERVAL type generator
    no subtypes, 335
INTERVAL type generator, 83
irreducibility (candidate key). *See* candidate
    key
irreducible component (vertical
    decomposition), 173
IS_EMPTY, 22, 48
IS_NEXT_*T,* 230
IS_PRIOR_DATE, 289
IS_PRIOR_*T,* 230
is a member of. *See* belongs to
[is] in. *See* belongs to
[is] included in
    cyclic point type, 341
    interval, 91
    properly, 41, 91
    relation, 41
Isakowitz, Tomás, 394
ISO, 398–399

J

Jajodia, Sushil, 397, 407, 408
Jensen, Christian S., 392, 394, 399, 406
Johnson, R. G., 400, 401
JOIN, 26–27
join dependency, 174
    generalized, 175
    implied by candidate keys, 175
    trivial, 175, 176
Jones, S., 399

K–L

Kawagoe, Kyoji, 405
key. *See* candidate key; foreign key;
    primary key
Kline, Nick, 408
Kollias, Vassiliki J., 401, 408
Kumar, Anil, 408

ABOUT THE AUTHORS

C.J. Date is an independent author, lecturer, researcher, and consultant specializing in relational database systems. He was one of the first persons anywhere to recognize the fundamental importance of Codd's pioneering work on the relational model. He was also involved in technical planning for the IBM products SQL/DS and DB2 at the IBM Santa Teresa Laboratory in San Jose, California. He is best known for his books, especially, *An Introduction to Database Systems* (7th edition, 2000), the standard text in the field, which has sold well over 650,000 copies worldwide and (with Hugh Darwen) *Foundation for Future Database Systems: The Third Manifesto* (2nd edition, 2000). Mr. Date enjoys a reputation that is second to none for his ability to explain complex technical material in a clear and understandable fashion.

Hugh Darwen has been involved in software development since 1967 as an employee of IBM United Kingdom Ltd. He has been active in the relational database arena since 1978, and was one of the chief architects and developers of an IBM product called Business System 12, a product that faithfully embraced the principles of the relational model. His writings to date include his notable contributions to C. J. Date's *Relational Database Writings* series (1990, 1992, 1998) and *A Guide to the SQL Standard* (4th edition, 1997). He is also the coauthor with C.J. Date of *Foundation for Future Database Systems: The Third Manifesto* (2nd edition, 2000). He has been an active participant in the development of SQL international standards since 1988. In his spare time he is a tutor and consultant in connection with the Open University's database courses in the United Kingdom.

Nikos A. Lorentzos received his first degree in Mathematics (Athens University, 1975), a Master's degree (Computer Science, Queens College, CUNY, 1981), and a Ph.D. (Computer Science, Birkbeck College, London University, 1988). As part of his research, he formalized a temporal relational algebra and IXSQL, an SQL extension for interval data. He has been involved in many projects funded by the European Union. He was the director of ORES (ESPRIT III) in which a temporal DBMS and an SQL extension, amongst others, were developed. In CHOROCHRONOS (Training and Mobility

Research) he formalized spatial quanta and applied his research results on temporal databases to the management of spatial and spatio-temporal data. References to his work, with positive comments, have appeared in journals and books. His research has stimulated subsequent work at various universities and organizations. He has acted as evaluator of programs submitted for funding to the European Union and as an examiner of Ph.D. dissertations in universities of the European Union. He serves as a reviewer for international journals and conferences. Today he is an associate professor at the Agricultural University of Athens, Informatics Laboratory. His major research interests are temporal, interval, and spatial databases, and image processing.

Requirement R1: If the database shows supplier Sx as being under contract on day d, then it must contain exactly one tuple that shows that fact.

Requirement R2: If the database shows supplier Sx as being under contract on days d and d+1, then it must contain exactly one tuple that shows that fact.

Requirement R3: If the database shows supplier Sx as being under contract on day d, then it must also show supplier Sx as having some status on day d.

Requirement R4: If the database shows supplier Sx as having some status on day d, then it must contain exactly one tuple that shows that fact.

Requirement R5: If the database shows supplier Sx as having the same status on days d and d+1, then it must contain exactly one tuple that shows that fact.

Requirement R6: If the database shows supplier Sx as having some status on day d, then it must also show supplier Sx as being under contract on day d.

Requirement R7: If the database shows supplier Sx as able to supply some specific part Py on day d, then it must contain exactly one tuple that shows that fact.

Requirement R8: If the database shows supplier Sx as able to supply the same part Py on days d and d+1, then it must contain exactly one tuple that shows that fact.

Requirement R9: If the database shows supplier Sx as able to supply some part Py on day d, then it must also show supplier Sx as being under contract on day d.

ENDPAPER
PANEL 6
Current relvars
only—sample
values (Figures
12.2 and 14.1).

S_SINCE

S#	S#_SINCE	STATUS	STATUS_SINCE
S1	d04	20	d06
S2	d07	10	d07
S3	d03	30	d03
S4	d14	20	d14
S5	d02	30	d02

SP_SINCE

S#	P#	SINCE
S1	P1	d04
S1	P2	d05
S1	P3	d09
S1	P4	d05
S1	P5	d04
S1	P6	d06
S2	P1	d08
S2	P2	d09
S3	P2	d08
S4	P5	d14